THE STAR TREK® BOOK

THE
STAR TREK
BOOK

For DK

SENIOR EDITORS
Tori Kosara, Laura Palosuo, Cefn Ridout

SENIOR DESIGNER
Nathan Martin

EDITORS
Kathryn Hill, Esther Ripley,
Sarah Tomley

DESIGNERS
Sam Bartlett, Marcel Carry, Gary Hyde

ILLUSTRATOR
Nathan Martin

PRE-PRODUCTION PRODUCER
Marc Staples

SENIOR PRODUCER
Alex Bell

MANAGING EDITOR
Paula Regan

DESIGN MANAGER
Guy Harvey

PUBLISHER
Julie Ferris

ART DIRECTOR
Lisa Lanzarini

PUBLISHING DIRECTOR
Simon Beecroft

DK would like to thank
Beth Davies and Hannah Dolan
for editorial assistance, Alex Beeden
for proofreading the book, and
Helen Peters for creating the index.

For CBS

VICE PRESIDENT OF
PRODUCT DEVELOPMENT
John Van Citters

PRODUCT DEVELOPMENT MANAGER
Marian Cordry

With special thanks to Paula Block.

First American Edition, 2016
Published in the United States by
DK Publishing
345 Hudson Street
New York, New York 10014

Page design copyright © 2016
Dorling Kindersley Limited, DK,
a Division of Penguin Random House LLC

16 17 18 19 10 9 8 7 6 5 4 3 2 1

001—280587—June/2016

Published in Great Britain by
Dorling Kindersley Limited.

A catalog record for this book is available
from the Library of Congress.

ISBN: 978-1-4654-5098-2

DK books are available at special
discounts when purchased in bulk for
sales promotions, premiums, fund-raising,
or educational use. For details, contact:
DK Publishing Special Markets,
345 Hudson Street,
New York, New York, 10014
SpecialSales@dk.com.

Printed and bound in China.

A WORLD OF IDEAS:
SEE ALL THERE IS TO KNOW

www.dk.com

CONTRIBUTORS

PAUL RUDITIS, LEAD AUTHOR

Paul Ruditis has written companion books for popular TV shows such as *The Walking Dead*, *Buffy the Vampire Slayer*, *Charmed*, *Battlestar Galactica*, and *The West Wing*. His work on the *Star Trek* publishing program includes *Star Trek: The Visual Dictionary* and the humorous holiday picture book *A Very Klingon Khristmas*. His diverse résumé also includes original young adult novels, comic books, and novelty books.

SANDFORD GALDEN-STONE, AUTHOR

Sandford Galden-Stone ("Sandy") is a freelance writer based in Los Angeles, specializing in sci-fi and fantasy genres. Sandy was lead content producer for the official *Star Trek* website, working at Paramount Pictures alongside the productions of *Star Trek: Voyager* and *Star Trek: Enterprise*. He has also contributed to special features of *Star Trek* DVDs, *Star Trek*: The Experience, and *Star Trek* magazines.

SIMON HUGO, CONSULTANT EDITOR

Simon Hugo is a former senior editor of the official *Star Trek Magazine* and other film and TV tie-in titles including *Star Wars Insider* and *Torchwood: The Official Magazine*. He has written for *Doctor Who Adventures* and *Doctor Who Monster Invasion*, and most recently authored *Marvel's Spider-Man: Adventures of the Web-Slinger*, published by DK.

CONTENTS

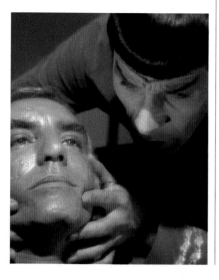

FEDERATION ALLIES AND ENEMIES

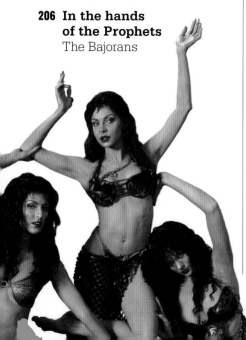

INTRODU

CTION

When the casual television viewer thinks of *Star Trek*, it might bring to mind the much-loved, pointy-eared alien with the stoic demeanor known as Spock. Or a well-known phrase—many people have uttered "Beam me up, Scotty," without really knowing what it means or the fact that the phrase has never actually been used on screen, either in the movies or TV series. Like Superman, Mickey Mouse, or a more modern hero, Harry Potter, *Star Trek* is known and loved around the world, and even people who have never seen it on screen have some basic familiarity with its setting and characters.

The *Star Trek* movies and TV series span over 50 years, and have built a vast fictional realm unlike any other. The filming of the initial pilot episode took place in 1964, and although that episode never aired in its original form during the series' first run, it inspired over 700 hours of TV episodes and movies, adding to a library that continues to expand today. During that time, the writers of *Star Trek* have created a fully developed universe filled with alien species, novel languages, and a rich history with several timelines.

To some, the complexities of this universe are intimately familiar. The true fans know the series and movies in minute detail, having examined the motivations and repercussions of the characters' actions across their many screen appearances. Others may find it daunting, and may be wondering how to even begin to get a taste of *Star Trek*'s rich storytelling. *The Star Trek Book* offers an easy but comprehensive way of entering this dense and fascinating universe.

Cowboys in space

Gene Roddenberry created *Star Trek* in 1964, pitching it to network executives as "*Wagon Train* to the stars," referring to a popular Western series on US television in the late 1950s and early 60s. The initial pilot for *Star Trek* was called "The Cage," and it introduced the core concept: in the 23rd century, a crew onboard a spaceship known as the *Starship Enterprise* were exploring space. NBC network executives liked the overall concept but asked for many changes—particularly in the casting—and made an unusual request for a second pilot.

That second pilot, called "Where No Man Has Gone Before," sold

It isn't all over—everything has not been invented; the human adventure is just beginning.
Gene Roddenberry

NBC on the series, but neither pilot would serve as the public's introduction to *Star Trek*. A further episode, called "The Man Trap," would do that. This premiered at 8:30 pm on Thursday, September 8, 1966, two years after the original pilot had been filmed. The show had won a timeslot, but it fell to second place the following week and throughout the season, though it still posted respectable ratings compared to other series launched that year.

The challenge of the science-fiction series was that its special effects, and alien costumes and

makeup required a considerably higher budget than the typical TV show. *Star Trek* struggled in the ratings through its second season but rumors of its cancellation led to an intense letter-writing campaign from fans. The high-production budget ultimately led to the series' cancellation at the end of a third season, but—luckily for fans—this turned out to be just the beginning of the *Star Trek* story.

Strangely, *Star Trek*'s audience actually grew after cancellation, bolstered by repeat airings in syndication. Burgeoning fan interest led to a kind of resurrection for the show in 1973, when Gene Roddenberry introduced a new cartoon series starring most of the cast in what became known as *Star Trek: The Animated Series*, or simply *TAS*.

Star Trek: The movie

It was a few more years before the studio that owned *Star Trek* at the time, Paramount Pictures, decided to give the fans what they had really been asking for: A new, live-action TV series. But while the studio was grappling with the financial challenges of producing the show, George Lucas's *Star Wars*

was released in cinemas. It was a massive success, and this inspired Paramount to take a new direction. *Star Trek: The Motion Picture* premiered in 1979, acting as a sequel film to the TV series. More movies followed, starring the familiar crew, and they enjoyed various levels of financial and critical success. Then, in 1987, less than a decade after the first movie, *Star Trek* returned to television with a new crew on board spaceship *U.S.S. Enterprise NCC-1701-D* in *Star Trek: The Next Generation*.

A new generation

Set a century later than the first series, the new series was to break syndication ratings records. It ran for more than twice as many years as the original *Star Trek*. While most fans embraced the series as a new entry in what was becoming a franchise, there was also a clash with those who remained loyal to the original cast. This debate in the fandom spilled over to pop culture, where parodies played up the inherent differences between the two supposedly divergent fandoms, although it was likely just a few vocal detractors. The growing popularity of *Star Trek: The Next*

Generation, or *TNG* as it became known, eventually united the fans and inspired future sequel series.

Star Trek: Deep Space Nine (*DSN* or *DS9*), *Star Trek: Voyager* (*VOY*), and *Star Trek: Enterprise* (*ENT*) were series titles of those produced from 1992–2005. Each enjoyed their own levels of success and used dramatically different storytelling techniques. *Deep Space Nine* took a darker view of »

The *Starship Enterprise* had no destination. It just was out there, visiting multiple places. That may have been a first. To transform your idea of 'space is a way for me to get from A to B,' to 'space is a limitless frontier to explore.'
Neil deGrasse Tyson

the future than Roddenberry's original vision, showing the horrors of war and how even those living in a near-utopian society can make questionable decisions. *Voyager* took the final frontier a step further: It sent a starship crew into deep space to embrace the theme of exploration that had inspired the original. *Enterprise* then took a step back, providing viewers with a closer look at the founding of the United Federation of Planets—the interstellar government that lies at the heart of the *Star Trek* universe.

For much of its life, *Star Trek* was known simply by that name, but with the birth of the additional series, the first in the line began to be referred to as "Star Trek: The Original Series (TOS)."

Star Trek experienced a recent resurgence with the rebooted film franchise under the leadership of director J.J. Abrams. By replacing the show's history with an alternative timeline, which became known as the Kelvin Timeline (see box below), Abrams reintroduced the original crew of the *Enterprise* to new audiences. Accordingly, these characters were now played by different actors. This allowed the franchise to explore original and familiar stories while satisfying both new and long-time *Star Trek* fans.

An iconic show

At some point during the 50 years it has been in existence, *Star Trek* became a pop culture phenomenon, inspiring catchphrases, parodies, and even real-world scientific discoveries. A new generation of explorers grew up with the series, inspired by what they saw on screen. These boys and girls went on to fill roles at NASA and space agencies around the world. They became astronauts, inventors, and even storytellers who helped expand the *Star Trek* universe decades later.

Star Trek gadgets proved to be inspirational too. Some of the technology introduced on *Star Trek* would come to pass in the real world: The series' communicators inspired cell phones, and tricorders evolved as advanced diagnostic equipment. PADDs became iPads. These real-world devices then backtracked into the series as *Star Trek* expanded into a fully immersive franchise. Cell phones were designed to look like communicators, and iPad apps were created in the familiar display

Kelvin Timeline

When producers began to think about ways to reboot the *Star Trek* franchise in 2009, they were faced with a choice: They could either set the new movie within the established timeline, or scrap everything and start from scratch. They decided to do both, by taking characters from the 24th century and sending them back to the 23rd, starting a new timeline that played out differently from the 40-odd years of existing franchise history.

The movie explains how a Romulan mining vessel called the *Narada* altered history. This ship accidentally time traveled from the year 2387 back to the year 2233, where it attacked a Starfleet ship called the *U.S.S. Kelvin* (where a baby to be called James T. Kirk was being born). These events caused the future to play out differently, so the events on this timeline are noted in this book as being in the "Kelvin Timeline."

> Perhaps one of the primary features of *Star Trek* that made it different from other shows was, it believed that humans are improving—they will vastly improve in the 23rd century.
> **Gene Roddenberry**

design of computers on the *Enterprise*-D. Fans could not only dress as their favorite characters in costume replicas, but also embrace the technology of *Star Trek* in their everyday lives. The franchise grew to include novels, comic books, video games, toys, T-shirts, and a wide variety of products.

How to explore this book

The pages that follow provide an in-depth look at the fictional universe of *Star Trek* through a history that begins with the dawn of the universe and continues into the 24th century and beyond. The major alien species are introduced, along with key players, their ships, and the technology that powers them. Through a series of articles, infographics, spotlighted information, and quotes, the reader will gain a deeper understanding of the complex *Star Trek* universe.

Captain's logs at the start of each section provide facts and obscure information that offer an entertaining insight into the worlds and characters. Timelines place events in historical perspective and help explain some of the more challenging aspects of linear time in a universe where time travel is possible. Topic boxes highlight some of the more notable facets of the *Star Trek* universe. Quotes, peppered throughout, sample some of the many voices that have been heard over the 700 hours (and growing) of entertainment that *Star Trek* has provided over five decades.

The Star Trek Book is presented as though in-universe, primarily from a 24th-century perspective. Aspects introduced in the film series that launched in 2009 are integrated where appropriate, and these are noted as existing in the Kelvin Timeline. Of course this in-universe perspective has to cheat from time to time, to include events that no one in the United Federation of Planets could know about. The challenge of multiple timelines is that sometimes significant events are completely forgotten when the timeline is reset. Moments like the resurrection of the *Enterprise*-C in "Yesterday's Enterprise" or *Voyager's* destruction during their own personal "Year of Hell" are included even though, logically, no one in the *Star Trek* universe should remember that these events ever happened.

The Star Trek Book is designed as an entertaining overview of the franchise that has existed for over 50 years. It is by no means a complete examination of the series, which can only be fully enjoyed in its original form through the many episodes and movies. However, the book offers an important and useful package of information for those who are coming to *Star Trek* for the first time. For long-term fans it serves as an entertaining reminder of exactly why *Star Trek* has endured for such a long period of time and why it will no doubt prosper for years to come. ■

SPACE, THE FINA FRONTIE

L

R

This is the story of humankind's journey from warlike, inward-looking tribespeople to united citizens of the universe. It is the story of how four very different species found similarities and shared values across the stars, forging an alliance that grew to encompass new worlds and new civilizations—and even ventured into other realities beyond their own.

THE KNOWN UNIVERSE

ALPHA, BETA, GAMMA, AND DELTA QUADRANTS

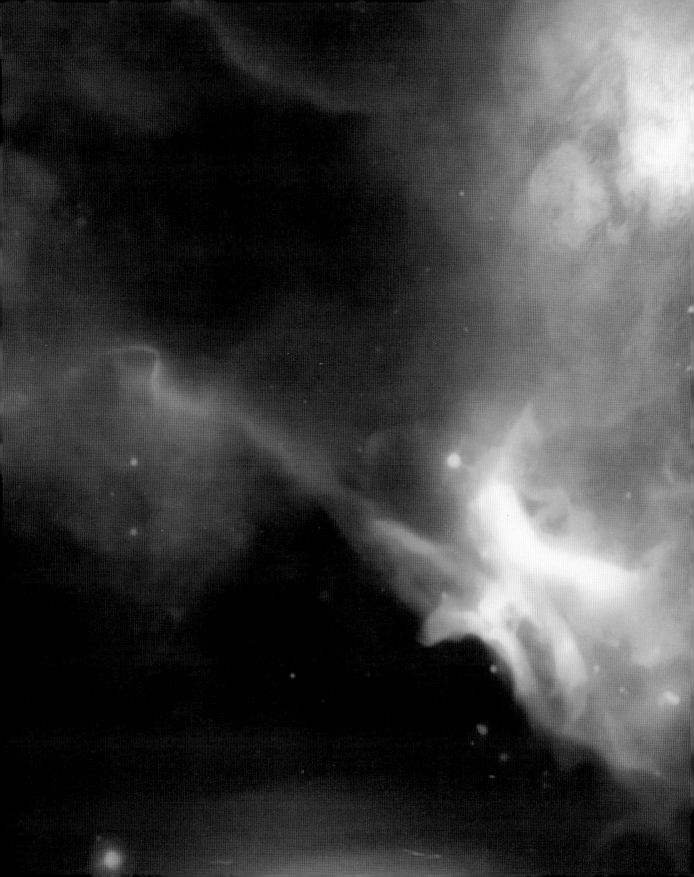

The "Big Bang" creates the known universe; the crew of *U.S.S. Voyager* bears witness to the birth from a Q Continuum "hiding place."

Earth and other Class-M planets form.

The building blocks of life come into existence on Earth when a group of amino acids combine to form the first proteins.

A mammalian species on Earth develops intelligence and eventually evolves into what is today known as Human.

c. 13.8BN B.C.   c. 4.5BN B.C.   c. 3.5BN B.C.   c. 1M B.C.

c. 13.2BN B.C.   c. 4BN B.C.   c. 20M B.C.   c. 600K B.C.

The Milky Way Galaxy forms.

A highly advanced humanoid species visits this side of the Milky Way Galaxy and seeds planets with genetic material similar to their own, setting a course for the development of future humanoid life.

An intelligent saurian species known as the Voth evolves on Earth, develops spaceflight, and eventually emigrates to the Delta Quadrant.

Sargon's people colonize the Galaxy, possibly influencing or initiating intelligent life on Vulcan.

It began with a bang. In just a fraction of a second, the universe burst from a high-density state, smaller than an atom, to comparatively infinite space, billions of light years in diameter. Stars formed, planets coalesced, and chemical reactions on the infant worlds triggered the very first stirrings of life. Over billions of years, countless unique plant and animal species evolved independently on planets across the universe. Some became highly intelligent and even self-aware, and they began to fashion tools, build societies, and wonder what

Space is disease and danger wrapped in darkness and silence.
Dr. Leonard "Bones" McCoy

might exist beyond the confines of the world they knew. As these lifeforms developed, so did their capability to explore beyond their own planets, and species that had previously existed in isolation came to realize they were not alone.

The Milky Way Galaxy is the part of the universe that most known species call home. This largely navigable area of space consists of four quadrants: Alpha, Beta, Gamma, and Delta. These regions radiate out from the galactic core and spread out over an area more than 100,000 light years in diameter. Each quadrant is

A species in the Delta Quadrant adds cybernetic elements to humanoid lifeforms, creating a being eventually known as the Borg.

After near self-destruction, the Vulcan people learn to embrace a new philosophy of logic and pacifism.

On the planet Qo'noS, Kahless the Unforgettable establishes the Klingon Empire.

The United Federation of Planets is eventually formed, spanning portions of the Alpha and Beta Quadrants, as it grows in size and influence for at least nine centuries.

c. 200k B.C.   c. 300 A.D.   c. 900 A.D.   2161 A.D.

c. 10k B.C.   c. 400 A.D.   2063 A.D.   2369 A.D.

A species of shapeshifters in the Gamma Quadrant establish the Dominion in response to persecution suffered from "solids."

A dissident faction on Vulcan, rejecting the new pacifism, leaves the planet and settles on Romulus and Remus, forming the Romulan Star Empire.

Humans develop warp-capable spaceflight and quickly become an influential factor in interstellar affairs.

A stable wormhole is discovered near Bajor providing a permanent bridge between the Alpha and Gamma Quadrants of the Galaxy.

---

inhabited by its own unique array of sentient species, many capable of building vessels that travel through space at warp speeds. This type of faster-than-light travel is essential for species that seek to interact with others across the vast reaches of space and form a larger interstellar community beyond their own solar systems. Such species may be very different from one another, but most also share some common ground—whether it is in aspects of their physical form, their philosophical outlook, or simply the unifying impulse to find out who else is out there.

In the 22nd century and reaching into the 24th and beyond, Humans from Earth sought out like-minded civilizations across the Alpha and Beta Quadrants, eventually forming a United Federation of Planets, with the shared mission to explore the universe. Hundreds of species make up the Federation in the 24th century, while many more—such as the Klingons and the Ferengi—coexist alongside it, enjoying largely peaceful relations. However, other forces in this part of the Galaxy, such as the Romulans and, for a time, the Cardassians, are more antagonistic toward the Federation.

In the latter half of the 24th century, Federation ships set out to explore the Gamma and Delta Quadrants, using discoveries that enabled them to traverse enormous distances in moments. Breakthroughs like these opened up the Galaxy and introduced the Federation to new allies and enemies. The map of the Galaxy continues to spread beneath the flag of the Federation's exploratory arm, Starfleet. The limits of knowledge expand, like space itself, to accommodate new worlds and new civilizations, as Starfleet boldly goes where no one has gone before. ■

CAPTAIN'S LOG

NAME
The Milky Way Galaxy

AGE
13+ billion years

DIAMETER
100,000+ light-years

MASS
875 billion solar masses

BRIEFING
Humans derived the name "Milky Way" from the vivid off-white band of stars in Earth's night sky, which seem to light a path across the cosmos

The Milky Way is a spiral-shaped galaxy comprised of an estimated 100 billion stars. The Galaxy's four quadrants contain thousands of sectors, both inhabited and uninhabited. Sector designations within each quadrant are mostly used as coordinates for navigation, and are named with regard to their position relative to key locations within the United Federation of Planets (UFP). The Milky Way is one of approximately 200 billion galaxies in the known universe, and it has not yet been fully explored by the Federation.

The Alpha Quadrant

From the perspective of the UFP, the central section of the known universe is located in the Alpha Quadrant. The Sol system (and its primary inhabited planet, Earth) is designated as Sector 001 for navigational purposes. Sector 002 is adjacent and includes Alpha Centauri—the star closest to Sol at a distance of approximately 4.3 light-years. The Alpha Centauri system was the first area of the Galaxy to be explored by Humans beyond their own solar system.

Many UFP worlds are located in the Alpha Quadrant, though member planets and affiliated worlds are also found deep into the Beta Quadrant. Beyond the planets of the Sol system, notable Federation Alpha Quadrant worlds include Betazed, Bajor, Denobula, Trill, and Tellar. Unaffiliated planets of the Alpha Quadrant include Ferenginar and Talos IV. Visiting the latter planet is strictly forbidden to Federation personnel under Starfleet General Order 7, because of the potential danger posed by the native population of telepaths. Other planets in the quadrant that have traditionally opposed the Federation are Cardassia Prime, Tholia, and Breen, though the first two worlds would establish diplomatic relations with the UFP by the late 24th century.

The Alpha Quadrant is also home to various spatial anomalies with rare and unique properties. The most significant of these is a stable wormhole located near the planet Bajor, which serves as a near-instantaneous passageway to the distant Gamma Quadrant. In 2369, after it was determined that the wormhole was stable, the Federation and the Bajorans moved the space station Deep Space 9 nearer to the Alpha Quadrant-side opening, to monitor the phenomenon and allow passage through it.

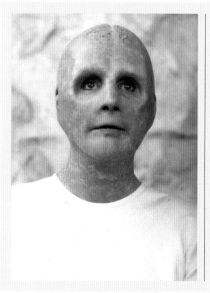

The Progenitors

As Humans have explored the Galaxy, seeking out new life and new civilizations, they have found many sentient species with the same anatomical structure as their own, including two arms, two legs, and a face with two eyes above a nose and a mouth. While shared environmental challenges offer an evolutionary explanation, the question remains as to why these similarities were quite so common.

An answer emerged in the 24th century. A purposefully engineered genetic puzzle was found embedded in the DNA of humanoid species from several different worlds. When pieced together, the puzzle revealed a holographic message from the progenitors of these species. The first civilization to evolve in their part of the Galaxy, some four billion years ago, they traveled the stars but found no species that resembled theirs. So they seeded the primordial oceans of various planets to direct the evolution of intelligent species toward a physical form similar to their own. They encoded the hidden message in the hope of being remembered by their eventual descendants.

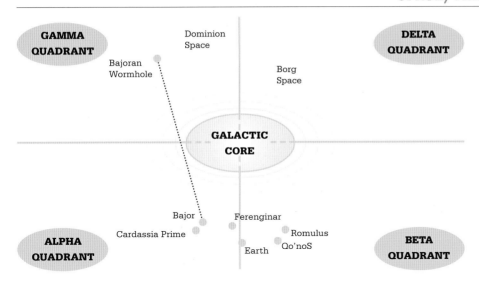

GAMMA QUADRANT

Dominion Space

Bajoran Wormhole

Borg Space

DELTA QUADRANT

GALACTIC CORE

Bajor

Ferenginar

Cardassia Prime

Romulus

Qo'noS

Earth

ALPHA QUADRANT

BETA QUADRANT

Milky Way Galaxy
The United Federation of Planets is located in the Alpha and Beta Quadrants, while the Bajoran Wormhole and an alien Caretaker have opened up the Gamma and Delta Quadrants to exploration.

The Beta Quadrant

Though the UFP is primarily considered an interstellar political power of the Alpha Quadrant, it also lays claim to a large region of the Beta Quadrant, with the Sol system situated along the theoretical dividing line between the two quadrants. Some consider the Beta Quadrant to be an even more politically important region of the Galaxy, as it contains some of the most significant civilizations in the known universe.

Two of the founding planets of the UFP, Vulcan and Andoria, are located in the Beta Quadrant. Without these two civilizations, the UFP would never have been created, despite the governments of both worlds being initially resistant to the notion of any form of planetary coalition. Other UFP planets in this quadrant include Benzar, Bolarus, and the pleasure planet Risa, which is a popular vacation spot for species from across the Alpha and Beta Quadrants. Much of the original mission of *Enterprise* NX-01—the first starship from Earth capable of deep space travel—took place in the Beta Quadrant.

The two other notable powers in this quadrant are the Klingon Empire and the Romulan Star Empire. The UFP has been forced to contend with both of these superpowers for much of its history, and it was the Earth-Romulan war of the 22nd century that led to the

Early allies The sight of the *Enterprise* NX-01 in orbit around the planet Vulcan was a sign of United Earth's expanding role in the Galaxy.

foundation of the Federation. After the conflict, a neutral zone of space was established to act as a buffer between the Federation and the Romulans, and remains in place in the late 24th century. For a time, there was a similar neutral zone between the Federation and the Klingon Empire, but the relationship between these two powers improved considerably with the signing of the Khitomer Accords in 2293, which brought about a new era »

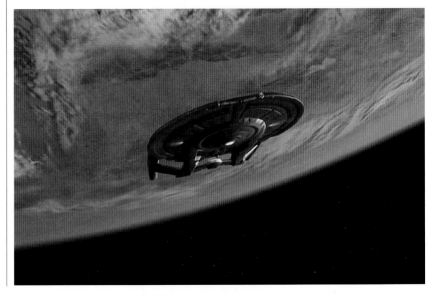

Let's see what's out there.
Jean-Luc Picard

of peace between the previously hostile blocs.

The Beta Quadrant is also home to the Xindi, an alliance of related species that attacked Earth in the 2150s. The Xindi's planet, Xindus, was in the dangerous Delphic Expanse, where numerous spatial anomalies and surrounding clouds of thermobaric gas pose a threat to starship navigation. It was

Friendship 1 Sending a goodwill greeting out to the universe, United Earth's *Friendship 1* carried plans for a communications array that would teach distant aliens how to contact Humans.

destroyed during a planet-wide civil war during the first half of the 21st century. Another Beta Quadrant species that has proved hostile to Humans and the UFP is the lizard-like race, the Gorn Hegemony.

The Gamma Quadrant
The UFP first explored the Gamma Quadrant via the Quadros-1 probe in the 22nd century. More than 200 years later, access to the quadrant by crewed vessels became possible with the discovery of the stable Bajoran wormhole.

This subspace tunnel between two distant points has a terminus in the Idran system of the Gamma Quadrant, 70,000 light-years from Federation space. Ships at either end of the tunnel can now travel this vast distance in moments, opening up trading and cultural relations between the far sides of the Galaxy. As a result, the nearby space station Deep Space 9 immediately becomes the most active and strategically important outpost in the entire UFP.

Much of the Gamma Quadrant remains unexplored, though the UFP has encountered an array of

species from within the quadrant. The Dominion is the chief political faction of the region and, like the Federation, includes several species. But this is where the similarities end; the bioengineered species of the Dominion (primarily the Vorta and the Jem'Hadar) toil under the oppressive leadership of shape-shifting beings known as the Founders. This xenophobic race waged war on the UFP in 2373, bringing devastation to many planets in the Alpha Quadrant.

The Delta Quadrant
The distance between the Delta Quadrant and Federation space, combined with the challenges of navigating the galactic core, made missions into the quadrant logistically difficult. It would take at least 30 years for the average Starfleet vessel to reach the outer edge of the quadrant. As such, few resources were given over to exploring the region beyond the *Friendship 1* probe launched by the United Earth Space Probe Agency in 2067. That all changed in 2371, when alien technology transported the *U.S.S. Voyager*

Planetary classes

Starfleet uses single-letter names to classify the different types of planets explored by its starships. These classifications are based on factors such as mass, atmosphere, surface conditions, and the planet's ability to support organic life.

Class-M planets are Earth-like—rocky worlds with plant and animal life sustained by oxygen-nitrogen atmospheres. Most life as we know it evolved on and inhabits Class-M planets. Besides Earth, examples include Vulcan, Risa, and Bajor.

Class-L planets have oxygen-argon atmospheres and plant life, but no native animals. Humans can survive on these worlds for short periods of time.

Class-K planets can sustain microbial life, but are only inhabited by complex lifeforms that rely on life-support systems and pressure domes.

Class-H covers a range of desert worlds; Class-J planets are gas giants such as Jupiter and Saturn; Class-D are moons or small planets with little or no atmosphere; and Class-Y is used to denote worlds with harsh or toxic conditions, which are also nicknamed "Demon" planets.

and another ship 70,000 light-years away from Sector 001. As part of their long journey back to the Alpha Quadrant, the crews of the two ships united aboard *Voyager* to explore the region in detail.

The *Voyager* crew made first contact with diverse species in the Delta Quadrant and charted the region in their search for a speedier route home. Members of two species, a Talaxian and an Ocampa, even joined the ship's crew.

Even before *Voyager*'s journey, the Delta Quadrant was known to the UFP as the heart of Borg space. Thousands of star systems in the region had been assimilated into this collective of cybernetic beings, depriving their inhabitants of any individual will or emotion. Though the UFP had some prior knowledge of the Borg, it did not become fully aware of the threat they posed until the *U.S.S. Enterprise*-D was briefly flung into the Delta Quadrant by the omnipotent being known as Q.

The Delta Quadrant is dotted with gaseous anomalies that make traversing the area a challenge. The Nekrit Expanse,

covering thousands of light-years at the periphery of Borg space, constantly changes shape, making it impossible to map. There is also a Mutara-class nebula that emits subnucleonic radiation harmful to Humans. When *Voyager* crossed the nebula, the majority of its crew was placed in stasis pods while the Emergency Medical Hologram and the one Borg crew member took control of the ship for its month-long journey across 110 light-years.

Two barriers

The galactic barrier forms the perimeter of the Milky Way, while the largely unexplored galactic core sits at the center of the four quadrants. Both of these areas contain energy fields that affect starship systems, and are nearly impossible to navigate as a result.

The galactic barrier boasts neurogenic properties that affect the minds of humanoid beings, in some cases causing spikes in extra-sensory perception (ESP) and bestowing psychokinetic abilities. In 2065, the barrier's effects on the crew of the *S.S. Valiant* led to the

ship's total destruction. The *U.S.S. Enterprise* NCC-1701, commanded by James Kirk, later encountered the barrier when the crew recovered a recorder-marker launched from the *Valiant* some 200 years earlier. The *Enterprise*'s proximity to the barrier altered the mental faculties of Lieutenant Commander Gary Mitchell and Dr. Elizabeth Dehner, giving them incredible capabilities including telepathy and telekinesis, but ultimately caused their deaths.

Years later, Kirk's crew aboard the *Enterprise*-A encountered the Great Barrier that surrounds the galactic core. This wall of energy is a spherical field approximately 15,000 light-years in diameter, and emits high levels of radiation and gravimetric flux that make it very difficult to navigate. Under the control of the outcast Vulcan prophet Sybok, the *Enterprise*-A became the first known vessel to penetrate the barrier. Sybok hoped to discover God. Instead, he and the crew found a barren planet and a malevolent being that wanted to escape from its prison within the barrier. ■

A DREAM THAT BECAME A REALITY...
THE UNITED FEDERATION OF PLANETS

Under one flag The standard of the United Federation of Planets depicts the UFP seal of a starfield enclosed by a laurel wreath, commemorating the successful union of member worlds.

CAPTAIN'S LOG

FOUNDED
2161

FOUNDING MEMBERS
Humans, Vulcans, Andorians, Tellarites

MEMBER PLANETS
150+ (as of 2373)

HEAD OF GOVERNMENT
President of the UFP

CAPITAL
United Earth, Alpha Quadrant Sector 001

EXPLORATORY AND PEACEKEEPING BRANCH
Starfleet

The United Federation of Planets is unique in the Galaxy. The 150-plus worlds of its joint government were not brought together under one banner by conquering and empire building. They were unified in peaceful cooperation, forging mutually beneficial relationships that emphasized scientific and cultural growth through shared discovery and development. Such an approach could hardly be more different from the aggression and posturing of the Klingon Empire, the isolationism and stealth of the Romulan Star Empire, and the all-conquering assimilations of the Borg collective.

Straddling the Alpha and Beta Quadrants, this interstellar federal republic comprises the most diverse collection of species ever united under one democratic central government. The people of every world in the Federation have a voice in crafting its laws through a legislative council, which is overseen by a single president, based on Earth. Individuals from numerous UFP planets and species ranging from Human to Grazerite have served in the office of the president, and all are recognized as equal members of the government.

The reason why the seat of Federation government is located on Earth—out of many possible UFP worlds—is linked to the role Humans played in uniting the Federation in its early days. Before humanity took its first steps into deep space exploration, the main political powers of the Alpha and Beta Quadrants—Vulcan, Andoria, and Tellar Prime—had decidedly strained relationships. However, the loose coalition between these three worlds and Earth grew into something far more enduring with a single, centralized government. The UFP is still expanding in the 24th century, with almost 2,000 protectorates and affiliated worlds.

Pacifist beliefs

There are many examples of the peaceful outreach of the Federation. One such instance occurred in 2267 during negotiations between Captain Kirk of the *U.S.S. Enterprise* and the Halkans. The Federation

They were humanitarians and statesmen, and they had a dream; a dream that became a reality and spread throughout the stars.
James T. Kirk

sought the right to mine dilithium crystals on the Halkans' planet. The substance, used to power warp drive in starships, was of great value to the Federation, but the intensely pacifistic Halkans refused to grant permission out of fear that the crystals could one day be used for evil purposes. Where a more violent society could easily have overpowered the Halkans and taken the dilithium, Captain Kirk used his diplomatic skills to convince the Halkans of the UFP's commitment to peace.

Historically, not every member of the Federation has subscribed to this pacifistic approach to life. In the year 2293, a group of Starfleet officers attempted to derail a peace conference between the UFP and the Klingon Empire. Some 80 years later, during the Dominion War, a high-ranking Starfleet cabal sought

Historic handshake The four founding species of the Federation (from left to right): Tellarite, Human, Vulcan, and Andorian.

to forcibly relocate the people of a planet with rejuvenating properties that could help the war effort.

However, the most damaging threat to the philosophy of the UFP followed the Temporal Incursion of 2233. This attack by a time-traveling Romulan from 2387 created an alternative reality where Vulcan—one of the founding worlds of the UFP—was destroyed, and led to Starfleet's secretive Section 31 investigating more aggressive forms of defense. The resulting conspiracy almost destroyed Starfleet and its mission of peaceful exploration, and only the intervention of the *Enterprise* was enough to avert catastrophe. »

Yet in spite of (perhaps, in part, because of) the ongoing challenges to the fundamental beliefs that underpin the Federation, the union has remained strong.

History of conflict

The many different threads that had to combine for the UFP to form are difficult to quantify. On Earth, three global conflicts occurred before the citizens of the planet came together under a single unified government. Its new leaders were still working to unite the world's population when Zefram Cochrane developed Earth's first warp-capable spaceship in 2063. His test flight attracted the attention of a Vulcan survey team in the vicinity, and led to first contact between the two species, both of which would go on to become founding members of the UFP.

It would take a century of strained cooperation between Humans and Vulcans before the groundbreaking voyage of Earth's first deep-space-capable starship—*Enterprise* NX-01—opened up relations with more races in the Galaxy. During the decade-long mission of *Enterprise*, Captain Jonathan Archer and his crew made first contact with numerous species, establishing dialogs with major political powers including the Andorians and the Tellarites. In fact, Archer and his crew went to great lengths to unite these species with each other, not least during the Babel Crisis of 2154.

Today the planet Babel often serves as a neutral meeting point for Federation trade negotiations and resolving interplanetary disputes. This precedent was set before the founding of the UFP with a trade conference between the Andorians and the Tellarites. After a Romulan attack on ships traveling to the meeting, war was narrowly averted thanks to the intervention of the *Enterprise* crew. Several months later in January 2155, the Andorians and Tellarites met with Humans, Vulcans, and like-minded species in San Francisco on Earth to begin discussion about the formation of a Coalition of Planets.

> The Galaxy's a big place, with thousands of species. Not all of them have the same values we have.
> **Jonathan Archer**

The following year, Romulans attacked Earth, and members of the new Coalition rallied to support the planet in what would come to be known as the Earth-Romulan War. The conflict culminated in 2160 with the Battle of Cheron, in which Earth and its Coalition allies struck a decisive blow against the Romulans. With the war over, the four main allies (Humans, Vulcans, Andorians, and Tellarites) along with the government of the Earth

The Federation Charter

Signed in 2161, the Charter of the United Federation of Planets is the founding document of the interplanetary alliance formed in that year by Andoria, Earth, Tellar, and Vulcan. It lays out the principles and values upon which the Federation would be based, and remains in effect more than two centuries later.

The charter begins: "We the lifeforms of the United Federation of Planets," and establishes that the purpose of the alliance is to "save succeeding generations from the scourge of war," and to "reaffirm faith in the fundamental rights of sentient beings" as well as "the dignity and worth of all lifeforms." It goes on to encourage justice, equal rights, and social progress among its member planets.

Signed in San Francisco by dignitaries of the era including Captain Jonathan Archer of the *Enterprise* NX-01, the charter also sets out certain conditions for achieving membership, such as a unified world government and the rejection of caste-based discrimination. It also forbids any interference in the internal affairs of a sovereign power.

United Federation of Planets Timeline

2063
Vulcans make first contact with Humans.

2161
Charter of the United Federation of Planets ratified in San Francisco, Earth.

2311
Tomed Incident leads to Treaty of Algeron with Romulan Star Empire.

2370
Demilitarized Zone formed with Cardassians; controversial truce leads to rise of rebellious faction called the Maquis.

2060   2380

2155
"Coalition of Planets" formed among handful of planetary allies to benefit trade and mutual security.

2293
Khitomer Accords establish long-lasting détente with the Klingon Empire.

2365
First encounter with Borg collective, becoming a persistent threat.

2375
Dominion War, bloodiest and costliest conflict in Federation history, is won.

---

colony on Alpha Centauri went on to sign the Federation Constitution on October 11, 2161.

Threats to the Federation

Throughout its history, the UFP has been threatened by enemies within its own ranks and from all four quadrants of the Galaxy. The Klingon Empire poses an ongoing threat throughout the first century of the Federation's existence, with relations between the superpowers taking a long time to recover from their unfortunate first contact. It is not until 2293, when an environmental disaster threatens to destroy the Empire, that the two governments come together in peace, paving the way for the Federation to aid its former enemy.

Tensions between the UFP and the Romulan Star Empire continue long after the Earth-Romulan War of the 22nd century. Encounters between the two galactic powers remain tense, particularly along the Neutral Zone established by the Treaty of Algeron, but never again escalate into all-out war. However, the two factions do come close to open hostilities in 2379, when the Empire is seized in a coup by the Romulans' slave caste, the Remans. The Remans install their cloned leader, Shinzon, as the head of the Romulan Senate, enabling him to attack the Federation under the guise of peace negotiations. The crew of the *Enterprise*-E eventually thwart Shinzon's plan, but only at significant personal cost.

Chief among the threats to the Federation from beyond the Alpha and Beta Quadrants is the Borg, the cybernetically enhanced species originating in the Delta Quadrant. In the second half of the 24th century, two Borg incursions into Federation territory result in a devastating loss of Starfleet ships and UFP citizens, who are either killed or assimilated into the Borg collective. On both occasions the Borg are repelled, but it is only

Federation enemies The Cardassians and Dominion formed an alliance to take over the major political powers of the Alpha and Beta Quadrants.

when the *U.S.S. Voyager* attacks the primary Borg Unicomplex in the Delta Quadrant—destroying one of its transwarp hubs—that the Federation is able to deal the collective a lasting blow.

A more drawn-out conflict is initiated in 2373 by the Gamma Quadrant superpower known as the Dominion. Ruled by a species of shape-shifters, the Dominion is able to augment its firepower by imitating key Federation personnel, manipulating its enemy from within, and fomenting distrust between allies. To avoid falling under Dominion rule, the planets of the UFP, the Klingon Empire, and even the Romulan Star Empire form an uneasy alliance, finally defeating the Dominion with a combination of united strength, diplomacy, and even forms of biological warfare.

By the end of the 24th century, in the wake of Borg attacks and the Dominion War, the Federation is bloodied but unbowed. Perhaps more importantly in times of danger rather than of calm, the UFP continues to invite applications for membership. It welcomes all worlds with united governments and warp capability, so long as its inhabitants are dedicated to peace, and agree to abide by the rule of law. ∎

A DANGEROUS, SAVAGE, CHILD RACE
UNITED EARTH

CAPTAIN'S LOG

NAME
Earth

CLASSIFICATION
Class-M planet

LOCATION
Sol system, Alpha Quadrant Sector 001

MOON
Luna

POLITICAL AFFILIATION
United Federation of Planets (Founding Member in 2161)

BRIEFING
Primarily known as Earth, the planet also goes by the names Terra, Sol III, and (less frequently) Gaia

The Human race has been motivated by its desire to explore since before the dawn of its civilization. Humans have an innate desire to grow and to discover more about what lies beyond their borders—though this drive has not always been acted upon in the most noble ways. Early mariners in search of better trade routes also discovered new lands to conquer, explorers funded their journeys by plundering the riches of less technologically advanced

Extended explorer The United Earth starship *Enterprise* NX-01 was the first Earth vessel capable of travel at warp 5, making it suitable for extended deep space missions.

people, and armies took control of distant lands and subjugated their inhabitants to claim their resources as their own. Over the course of many centuries, empires rose and fell through a combination of wars, natural disasters, and the use of destructive technologies.

Yet while it is true that Human history is filled with examples of terrible violence, these have often been paired with incredible leaps in understanding. It was in the 20th century, at the height of a cold war between rival planetary superpowers, that Humans first ventured into space, taking their initial small steps into a greater universe. That desire to explore has not abated in the following four centuries, but Humans gradually learned to reject violence and evolved into one of the Galaxy's most benevolent species.

The Class-M planet

Earth is the third planet from the sun in the Sol system. It has an oxygen/nitrogen atmosphere and is mostly covered by water. The climate ranges from tropical to arctic, in contrast to worlds such as Vulcan and Andoria, which have far more uniform conditions across their entire surface.

Earth is home to millions of diverse species, which Humans have dominated for tens of thousands of years. As a result,

Humans have been responsible for the extinction of many animal species, through destruction of habitat, and hunting for food and sport. One example, the humpback whale, had been the subject of a study by an unidentified alien species before it was hunted to extinction by Humans in the 21st century. When a probe belonging to that alien species was unable to make contact with the whales in the 23rd century, its volatile reaction threatened to destroy all land-life on Earth. It fell to the former command crew of the *U.S.S. Enterprise* NCC-1701 to absolve Humanity's past failings by repopulating the species using time travel.

Humanity shares a common ancestry with the Voth, a sentient saurian species found far from Earth in the Delta Quadrant. According to one Voth scientist, their species abandoned Earth some time before Humans evolved. The two species share 47 genetic markers, but this information was suppressed by the Voth Ministry of Elders, as it undermined the belief that the Voth had evolved in the Delta Quadrant.

> We don't know what to do about Humans. Of all the species we've made contact with, yours is the only one we can't define. You have the arrogance of Andorians, the stubborn pride of Tellarites. One moment you're as driven by your emotions as Klingons, and the next you confound us by suddenly embracing logic.
> **Soval**

The new kid on the block

Many species consider Humans to be one of the Galaxy's younger civilizations. Of the main Alpha and Beta Quadrant political blocs, United Earth was one of the last to expand its reach into deep space. »

Zefram Cochrane and the *Phoenix*

One of the most significant turning points in Human history was Zefram Cochrane's flight of the *Phoenix* in 2063. Naming it after the mythological bird that "arose from the ashes," Cochrane built his faster-than-light spacecraft—Earth's first—in the aftermath of the planet's third world war, repurposing the titanium casing of a deactivated nuclear missile for its hull.

During its first experimental flight, the warp signature of the *Phoenix* attracted the attention of a Vulcan survey ship that was passing nearby, prompting the

Vulcans to land on Earth and meet the pilot. This enshrined April 5 as "First Contact Day," on Earth, and thrust Humanity irrevocably into the spotlight of the interstellar community.

Posterity hails Cochrane as an altruist, but his motivations for building the *Phoenix* were thoroughly pragmatic: he just wanted to make enough money so he could retire to an island. In fact, he retired to a colony in the Alpha Centauri system, and disappeared on a solo flight into deep space, aged 87, where he presumably died.

Whale song Admiral James Kirk and his crew traveled back in time to the 20th century to return humpback whales to their own era, where the species was, by then, extinct.

This was in no small part due to the efforts of the Vulcans, who covertly slowed Humanity's technological development after making first contact with the species. In the 24th century, an alien from the mysterious, powerful Q Continuum symbolically put all of Humanity on trial, declaring that the species lacked the ability to cope with the true complexities of the Galaxy. Contrary to Q's expectations, this comparatively short-lived and fragile species has made incredible progress during the 300 years since its discovery of warp drive.

By the end of the 21st century, Humans had eliminated warfare between nation-states and leaders on their planet. After World War Three, every nation joined together in peace to form a single United Earth government. This new unity became the driving force behind the Human race's development as a spacefaring species, with colonies on the Earth's moon, on Mars, in

the Alpha Centauri star system, and eventually on numerous other worlds throughout the Galaxy.

A history of war

The seeds of Earth's third world war were born out of an earlier conflict. In the late 20th century, scientists began to engineer a race of genetically augmented Humans with enhanced physical and mental capabilities. Their intention was to usher in a new era of peace and reason, but the opposite occurred. The so-called "Augments" rebelled

against their creators and set out to seize control of Earth. A series of brutal "Eugenics Wars" followed, pitting genetic "supermen" against non-enhanced Humans. The Augments were eventually defeated, though one of their most powerful leaders, Khan Noonien Singh, escaped the planet with a group of his followers.

Genetic manipulation was still a cause of conflict in the first half of the 21st century, when terrorists led by Colonel Phillip Green began a crusade intended to wipe out all "impure" Humans. This purge soon spiraled into Earth's third and final global war, during which 37 million people died and entire cities were wiped off the face of the planet. In 2053, the fighting ended when representatives from governments around the world gathered in San Francisco to agree to a cease-fire that led directly to the formation of a single, united world government.

Direct hit to the bridge Starfleet Headquarters and the Golden Gate Bridge in San Francisco smolder after a Breen attack in 2375. The structural damage was repaired within a year.

Sol system Humans have expanded their presence in the Sol system with space stations and colonies on or orbiting above their planetary neighbors.

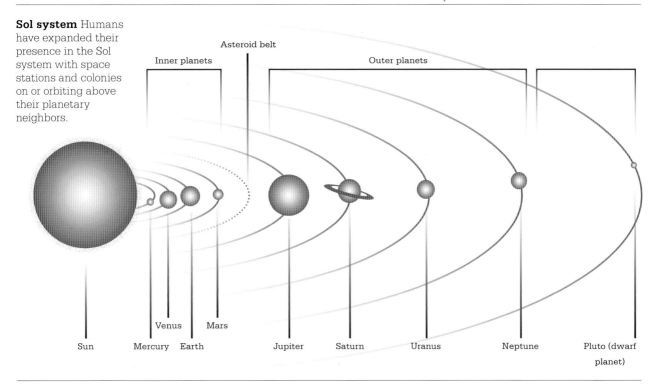

Asteroid belt

Inner planets

Outer planets

Venus   Mars

Sun   Mercury   Earth   Jupiter   Saturn   Uranus   Neptune   Pluto (dwarf planet)

Earth... A thousand years ago it had character: Crusades, Spanish Inquisition, Watergate. Now it's just mind-numbingly dull.
Q

Citizens of the universe

After Humanity's initial warp flight and first contact with the Vulcans, Earth's strategic importance began to grow, and increased significantly when it was established as capital of the Federation in 2161. Since that time, the planet has come under assault from numerous species including the Romulans, the Xindi, the Dominion-Breen alliance, and the Borg. It has survived each of these attacks through a combination of its standing planetary defenses and the intervention of Starfleet, which has deployed its own ships as well as rallying its allies and even non-allied and occasionally hostile worlds with a vested interest in the planet's survival.

Despite its tortured past, Earth in the 24th century is considered a prime example of everything the United Federation of Planets stands for. Poverty and famine have been eliminated through technology and social growth, which has allowed all inhabitants to share in its resources without wastefully depleting them. The planet's economy is no longer based on individuals' wealth and possessions; instead Humans seek knowledge and experience over material assets. Medicine has advanced to a level where disease is largely eradicated, and the average Human lifespan has almost doubled since the late 20th century.

Of course, not everything is perfect in this seemingly utopian society. Personal prejudices still existed well into the 23rd century, with some Humans desperate to destroy the fragile peace between the Federation and Klingons due to their deeply held biases. When the shape-shifting Founders were suspected of infiltrating Earth in the 24th century, Humans tried to justify their repressive and paranoid behavior. But it is recognition of these failings that make Humans strive to be better, engendering humility over a sense of superiority seen in some species. As explorers, they continue to visit far regions of the Galaxy, on missions that reveal how much they still have to learn. ∎
See also: The United Federation of Planets, Starfleet, *Enterprise* NX-01

INFINITE DIVERSITY IN INFINITE COMBINATIONS
THE VULCANS

CAPTAIN'S LOG

NAME
Vulcan

CLASSIFICATION
Class-M planet

LOCATION
Vulcan system (40 Eridani), Beta Quadrant Sector 005

MOON
None

POLITICAL AFFILIATION
United Federation of Planets (Founding Member in 2161)

BRIEFING
The planet has also been referred to as Vulcanis, and its people Vulcanians, though both terms have largely fallen out of use

Vulcan is an arid planet, and its people were once as fiery as the sun that beats down on its deserts. In their volatile past, Vulcans regularly waged war among themselves, threatening the very future of their world. Their lives were filled with debauchery honoring their many gods, in celebrations such as the Rumarie—a festival of libidinous pleasures. Some of these rites lasted well into Vulcan's modern age, but most were lost when its people turned away from highly charged emotional states in an era known as the Time of Awakening.

Life begins again The Vulcan sun rises over Mount Seleya, silhouetting the temple that is one of the planet's most sacred locations.

Led by the Vulcan philosopher Surak more than 2,000 years before the founding of the Federation, the Time of Awakening centered on an ideology of pure logic and espoused its use in controlling emotion. His followers spread a message of reason and pacifism throughout the world, but were not always met with a warm reception. Conflict between the old and new ways led to nuclear war, which

> The demands on a Vulcan's character are extraordinarily difficult. Do not mistake composure for ease.
> **Tuvok**

devastated parts of the planet. Peace was only achieved when the most violent sects of the old religion left Vulcan in search of a new home. Those who stayed behind embraced Surak's teachings, while those who left eventually became known as Romulans.

An era of logic

With the most warlike having left their society, the remaining Vulcans focused on mental discipline and logic to purge their own violent emotions. This took many centuries to achieve, but eventually most Vulcans exhibited such a degree of self-control that other species questioned whether they had emotions at all. In truth, Vulcan passions remain strong, but are well hidden beneath a stoic and unflappable resolve.

The central tenet of Vulcan philosophy is "Infinite Diversity in Infinite Combinations," which refers to the incalculable variety of everything in the universe, always combining anew to initiate growth and progress. It is represented by the IDIC symbol, which combines a triangle superimposed upon a circle, and is referred to in the Vulcan language as *Kol-Ut-Shan*.

Rites and rituals

There are many rituals in modern Vulcan society, but chief among them is the *kolinahr*, an intensive two-to-five year study period that includes techniques to purge all emotion and allow the individual to achieve the ideal of pure logic. *Kolinahr* masters instruct others and are among the most highly regarded people in their society.

Despite this extreme emotional control, mating urges still cause Vulcans to revert to a primal state. Every seventh year, adult Vulcans experience *Pon farr*—a drive that overrides their intellect and can be deadly if not sated. In the distant past, Vulcans would kill to win a mate, but by the 22nd century, this had evolved into a system of telepathic bonding in childhood to assign a future mate and, when rendered necessary by the presence of a rival, ritual combat. If combat or consummation are not available to a Vulcan undergoing *Pon farr*, the only other way to quell the feverish mating drive is through intense meditation. »

Blood fever Vulcans rarely speak of *Pon farr*, the ancient mating urge that every member of their race experiences in seven-year intervals.

Surak of Vulcan

A brilliant scientist and the father of modern Vulcan thought, Surak lived in the 4th century. He died of radiation poisoning after exposure to atomic weapons in Vulcan's Time of Awakening, but his philosophy eventually brought peace to all of Vulcan.

Just before his death Surak's *katra,* or living spirit, was placed inside an ark, where it remained until 2137. It was discovered by the Vulcan, Syrran, who took Surak's *katra* into his own mind and subsequently founded a movement to honor his teachings.

Prior to Syrran's death, he placed Surak's *katra* into the mind of Captain Jonathan Archer, the Human captain of *Enterprise* NX-01, who began to have visions of Surak's era. Compelled to undertake a quest on Vulcan, Archer discovered the *Kir'Shara*, an artifact housing the ancient wisdom of Surak in holographic form. Archer's discovery transformed Vulcan society. New interest in Surak's teachings was reflected in a change of government and a more open accord with Earth.

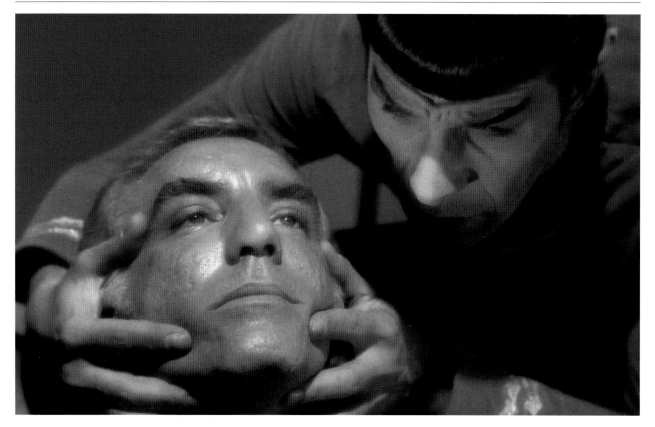

Melder and Gelder Spock performs mind-meld on the Human, Dr. Simon Van Gelder, in order to learn the truth about strange events on the Tantalus Penal Colony in 2266.

Vulcans' telepathic abilities include the mind-meld, which allows its practitioner access to the unspoken thoughts and memories of another being. The technique requires the melder to touch their subject—usually by placing a hand on their face—and may be assisted by a ritual chant. It is not without risk to both parties, and does not work on all species. A mind-meld can also plant suggestions in a subject's mind and, when a Vulcan is near death, can transfer their *katra,* or "living spirit," into the mind of another. This allows everything the person has experienced in life to live on after their body dies.

The planet Vulcan

The Vulcan homeworld is located in a trinary star system and shares its orbit with a sister planet called T'Khut. Unlike Earth, with its variety of climate zones, Vulcan is mostly covered by desert with temperatures higher than the average on Earth. It also has a thinner atmosphere and a higher

Live long
and prosper.
Vulcan salutation

gravity, which means that Vulcans are generally physically stronger than their Human counterparts.

One of the harshest areas of the planet is the canyon known as Vulcan's Forge, where Surak is thought to have made a pilgrimage, and where his followers continued to follow his path during the 22nd century. It is a dangerous environment, as the extreme heat is compounded by violent electrical sandstorms and geomagnetic instability that affect the operation of most forms of technology.

Located at the far end of Vulcan's Forge, Mount Seleya is a sacred site, and the place where Surak is believed to have died. Some of the most significant Vulcan rites are performed in a temple on the mountain, including the *fal-tor-pan,* or "refusion," between a Vulcan's *katra* and their lifeless body.

Building alliances

Vulcans have been exploring in space for more than 2,000 years, but they did not develop the warp technology needed for deep-space travel until the middle of the 20th century. Around this time, a party of Vulcans crash-landed on Earth, an event unrecognized in Human history as the Vulcans, who preferred to limit their relations to other warp-capable species, did not reveal themselves as extraterrestrials. One of their first recorded Vulcan contacts was with the Andorians, in a neighboring system. This led to a border dispute that lasted for approximately 200 years. Relations with another interstellar power, the Tellarites, are more cordial in spite of that species' reputation for belligerence.

The Vulcans' most notable galactic relationship began in 2063.

The three-person crew of the Vulcan survey ship *T'Plana-Hath* was exploring the Sol system at the time of Zefram Cochrane's test flight in the warp-capable *Phoenix*. This was not unusual, as the Vulcan High Command had been quietly observing Humans for decades. When the survey ship identified the warp trail from the *Phoenix*, the Vulcan team landed at Cochrane's launch site on Earth and made official first contact with Humans. This led to cooperation, a coalition, and ultimately to the founding of the Federation.

However, the path to interstellar alliances is not always an easy one. The relationship Vulcans fostered with Humanity was marginally better than the one it shared with the Andorians, but initially the Vulcans did not trust the people of Earth to deal with

> The needs of the many outweigh the needs of the few, or the one.
> **Vulcan philosophy**

the challenges that lay beyond their own borders. Under the guise of helping Humans prepare for deep-space travel, the Vulcans instead slowed Earth's progress wherever possible. The Vulcan ambassador, Soval, even tried to delay the launch of the first Earth starship, *Enterprise* NX-01 in 2151, but was thwarted when a Klingon vessel crash-landed on the Earth, and the *Enterprise* crew volunteered to return an injured Vulcan to his home planet.

Soval then insisted that a Vulcan should be included among *Enterprise*'s mostly Human crew, in the form of Subcommander T'Pol. This compromise went a long way to strengthen relations between the two worlds. T'Pol became a vital part of the ship's crew, and witnessed first-hand the ingenuity and resolve of her emotionally uninhibited shipmates. Over the centuries, Humans and Vulcans have become two of the closest allies in the Federation. Many Vulcans continue to serve in Starfleet, while others, such as Ambassador Sarek, have gone on to have families with their Human partners. ■

See also: The United Federation of Planets, The Temporal Incursion of 2233, T'Pol, Spock, Tuvok

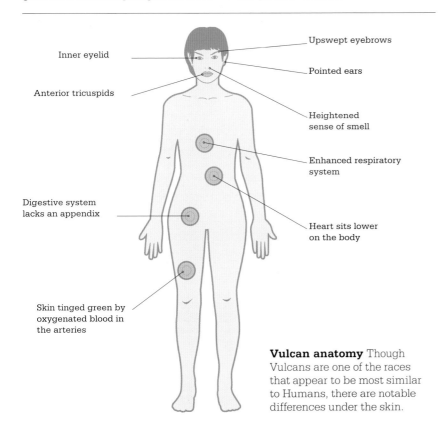

Inner eyelid

Anterior tricuspids

Digestive system lacks an appendix

Skin tinged green by oxygenated blood in the arteries

Upswept eyebrows

Pointed ears

Heightened sense of smell

Enhanced respiratory system

Heart sits lower on the body

Vulcan anatomy Though Vulcans are one of the races that appear to be most similar to Humans, there are notable differences under the skin.

BREAKING THE ICE
THE ANDORIAN EMPIRE

CAPTAIN'S LOG

NAME
Andoria

CLASSIFICATION
Class-M moon

LOCATION
Andorian system (Procyon), Beta Quadrant Sector 006

POLITICAL AFFILIATION
United Federation of Planets (Founding Member in 2161)

BRIEFING
Andoria is the name of both the inhabited moon and the capital city of the Andorian people

A people forged in ice, the Andorians have long favored a militaristic approach to the universe. By their own admission, they consider themselves to be a violent species, and their motivation to reach out to the stars was not to befriend other lifeforms, but to search for a more hospitable home than the

ice moon Andoria. The Andorians live beneath the surface of this moon in subterranean cities built in vast, linked caverns and heated by geothermal activity.

Legendary combat skills
Andorians are a proud species, with many traditions linked to their code of honor and their history of ice mining. One example is the *Ushaan*—an honor duel fought with traditional ice mining tools. Physical defense training begins in childhood to develop legendary combat skills. Members of the Andorian Imperial Guard are some of the most highly regarded members of society, and a remnant of those who die in service—say a vial of blood—is brought to the Wall to preserve the individual's memory.

Yet Andorians are not only fighters—they are artists as well.

Frozen assets Andoria is not a planet, but an icy moon in orbit of a ringed gas giant. Its cities and culture are hidden beneath its frozen surface.

They are noted throughout the Alpha and Beta Quadrants for their artistic talent, and in the 24th century, the Andorian Academy was regarded as one of the top art schools in the Federation.

Extreme physiology
Andorians' most notable physical traits are their blue skin, their silvery white hair, and the pair of antennae on their heads. These antennae function independently

The Vulcans say that the desert teaches men the meaning of endurance, but it's the ice that forges real strength.
Shran

The Aenar

Andorians share their homeworld with the related subspecies, the Aenar. Physically similar to their Andorian cousins, the Aenar lack skin or hair pigmentation, giving them a pale appearance. They make their homes beneath the ground in Andoria's Northern Wastes—an especially cold area of the ice moon that is so isolated their existence was considered mythical until the 22nd century.

Since then, though the Aenar have established communication with the Andorians, it is still rare for them to interact with their blue-skinned relations, much less outsiders.

Though all Aenar are blind, they are able to navigate their world using their antennae and advanced telepathic skills. The Aenar communicate with each other almost exclusively using telepathy, and while they can exchange thoughts with other species in this way, they do not do so without permission.

of one another and assist with balance. Therefore, the loss of an antenna can temporarily disable an Andorian, though it will grow back within nine months. It is the indignity of the loss that inflicts greater pain to a proud Andorian.

The blood of an Andorian is a deeper blue than their skin. Due to the extreme climate of their frozen world, Andorian bodies are highly adept at adjusting to the harshest conditions, and they are just as able to cope with extreme heat as extreme cold.

Interstellar relations

Like Humans, when Andorians began to explore the stars, they encountered the Vulcans in a neighboring system. The Vulcan response to the Andorians' entry into space was just as oppressive as their early dealings with Humans, and

the relationship soon became strained. This became typical of Andorian encounters with their interstellar neighbors; early interactions with the Tellarites were even less cordial.

Contact with Humans also began poorly, but relations quickly improved, thanks largely to the bond formed between Thy'lek Shran, an Andorian commander, and Jonathan Archer, the Human captain of *Enterprise* NX-01. Archer and his crew not only uncovered a Vulcan surveillance post spying on the Andorians, but also helped Shran to improve relations with the Tellarites. When the retired Shran needed help with a personal matter in 2161, Archer brought *Enterprise* to his aid at great cost to his own crew, further cementing the bond between the men and their respective species. ■

See also: Tellarites, *Enterprise* NX-01

Duel purpose

Andorian Commander Thy'lek Shran, wearing a gauntlet and wielding the *ushaan-tor* blade, is ready to be tethered to his opponent in an Ushaan duel of honor.

ADDING INSULT TO DIPLOMACY

TELLARITES

CAPTAIN'S LOG

NAME
Tellar Prime

CLASSIFICATION
Class-M planet

LOCATION
Tellar system (61 Cygni System), Alpha Quadrant Sector 007

POLITICAL AFFILIATION
United Federation of Planets (Founding Member in 2161)

BRIEFING
Canines are considered a delicacy on Tellar Prime

Short of stature, but long-winded in conversation, the Tellarites have been referred to as natural politicians. With their predisposition to argue, Tellarites will always open conversation with a complaint or—failing to find fault with anything specific—go straight for a direct insult. It is not meant to be offensive. It is just their nature. Arguing is a sport on Tellar Prime.

Tellarites are shorter than the average humanoid, and have deep-set eyes with dark pupils, broad snouts, and hands with hooflike qualities. Males mostly wear full beards and often have long, bushy hair. The Tellarite diet consists largely of fruits and vegetables,

but they are not exclusively vegetarian and include doglike mammals as part of their cuisine.

Early interstellar relations

In spite of the Tellarite propensity toward stubborn and sometimes extremely emotional behavior, the stoical Vulcans found them to be among the more agreeable species to deal with prior to the founding of the Federation. Tellarites even traded successfully with the Orions, despite that species' reputation as untrustworthy business partners.

Conversely, however, Tellarites and Andorians had an adversarial

Journey to Babel From left to right: Naarg and another assistant attend the Tellarite ambassador Gral, on their way to the first Babel conference in 2154.

Archer and the bounty hunter

The first face-to-face encounter between Humans and Tellarites was far removed from diplomatic protocols: it was an abduction.

By the 22nd century, Humans knew about Tellarites from the Vulcans—and their reputation for being difficult preceded them. But when a Tellarite called Skalaar approached *Enterprise* NX-01, he was more than difficult, he was desperate. His freighter had been seized by the Klingons and he was determined to trade them the *Enterprise* captain, Jonathan Archer, to get it back.

Skalaar kidnapped Archer, but by the time he reached his Klingon contacts, his ship had been stripped bare, and he was shortchanged on the reward he had expected. Following a crisis of conscience, Skalaar helped Archer plan his escape from the Klingons. This change of heart started the largely amicable relationship that still endures between the two species.

relationship for decades after their first contact. Relations deteriorated into all-out combat on at least one occasion, when a Tellarite vessel forcibly drove an Andorian Empire ship back into its own territory. Tensions between the two species came to a head in 2154 en route to a conference on the neutral planet Babel, when Romulan operatives attempted to drive a deeper wedge between the two governments.

In what became known as the Babel Crisis, the crew of *Enterprise* NX-01 responded to a distress call while carrying Tellarite diplomats through Andorian space to Babel. A Tellarite freighter had seemingly attacked a pair of Andorian ships, destroying one with the Andorian ambassador on board. Later, when *Enterprise* appeared to come under fire from an Andorian ship, it was determined that it was, in fact, the same vessel that had previously posed as a Tellarite freighter.

The *Enterprise* followed the mystery craft and identified it as a Romulan ship equipped with holographic emitters that allowed it to mimic other ships. With the Romulan plot to destabilize the Babel Conference revealed, the *Enterprise* crew worked with

the Tellarites and the Andorians to combat their shared enemy. This cooperation was the exact opposite of what the Romulans had intended, and helped to pave the way for a Coalition of Planets.

As one of the closest galactic neighbors to Earth, Tellar Prime subsequently became a vital ally of Humanity during the Earth-Romulan War. This show of unity helped strengthen a loose Coalition into the more formally codified United Federation of Planets.

United in Federation

The Babel Crisis was not the only time that Tellarites were targeted in a plot to sow discord. A century

> Tellarites do not argue for a reason, they simply argue.
> **Sarek**

Babel talk Vulcan ambassador Sarek, Captain Kirk, and Tellarite ambassador Gav converse on board the *Enterprise* NCC-1701, on the way to Babel in 2268.

later, Tellarite ambassador Gav was assassinated on board the *Enterprise* NCC-1701—en route to another Babel conference with various other dignitaries. When it was discovered that the killer had employed a Vulcan execution technique, suspicion fell upon the Vulcan ambassador, Sarek (also the father of the ship's first officer, Spock). However, the *Enterprise* crew was able to unmask the true assassin as an Orion operative disguised as an Andorian. A new Babel Crisis was averted, and the ship continued to the conference. ∎
See also: The Andorian Empire, *Enterprise* NX-01

OUR DIFFERENCES COMBINE TO CREATE MEANING AND BEAUTY

WORLDS OF THE FEDERATION

CAPTAIN'S LOG

NAME
Denobula, Alpha Centauri, Betazed, Trill, Risa, et al.

CLASSIFICATION
Inhabited planets

LOCATION
Alpha and Beta Quadrants

POLITICAL AFFILIATION
United Federation of Planets

BRIEFING
Alpha Centauri is the name of a star system rather than a planet, but is used colloquially to refer to settlements in the system

On January 19, 2155 representatives from the worlds that would become the four founding members of the Federation—Andoria, Earth, Tellar Prime, and Vulcan—gathered with a handful of other Alpha and Beta Quadrant species for discussions on the formation of a Coalition of Planets. The participants hoped that this would benefit trade and interstellar relations, while also providing support to any member that faced aggressive action from outside the alliance.

Other planets attending the conference included Denobula, Rigel, and Coridan. Though none of these was a superpower in the region, each world brought its own unique qualifications to make for a stronger alliance. The opening Coalition meeting took place in San Francisco on Earth and was almost derailed by a terrorist plot initiated by xenophobic Humans opposed to interspecies relations. However, the crew of *Enterprise* NX-01 thwarted the terrorists' plans and the Coalition formed successfully, evolving into the United Federation of Planets (UFP) six years later.

Coalition members
Central to the early success of the Coalition was Denobula, a Class-M planet in the Denobula Triaxa system of the Alpha

From ear to ear Denobulans such as Dr. Phlox can express pleasure through unusually wide smiles, and respond to threats by inflating their facial features.

Two people aren't
even enough for a
Denobulan marriage.
A proper one, anyway.
Phlox

Dazzling diplomat Ambassador Lwaxana Troi—daughter of the Fifth House, holder of the Sacred Chalice of Rixx, heir to the Holy Rings of Betazed.

Quadrant, on the other side of the Tellar System from Earth. In the 22nd century, the planet was home to approximately 12 billion individuals, all crowded on one single landmass—the world's only continent. Denobulan society of the era encouraged polygamous relationships, and it was common for a Denobulan to have multiple spouses, making their immediate families quite large compared to those of most other species.

Prior to the formation of the Coalition, Denobula participated in an interspecies medical exchange program set up by the Vulcans to cultivate wider medical knowledge of other humanoid species. As part of this program, the Denobulan Dr. Phlox was assigned to Earth, and then to *Enterprise* NX-01 after he successfully treated the very first Klingon ever to be seen on Earth.

Phlox's work on *Enterprise* was most likely a motivating factor in his species joining the Coalition. But when the Earth-Romulan War broke out in 2156, Denobula chose to remain neutral after a Romulan sneak attack resulted in several million casualties. As a result, the species did not initially join the Federation along with its fellow Coalition members.

Other planets in the original Coalition were also slow to join the Federation. Coridan, for example, was still not a member more than a century later, when the topic of its admission was discussed at the Babel Conference of 2268.

Founding the Federation

Though Andoria, Earth, Tellar Prime, and Vulcan are formally credited with the foundation of the UFP, there is also another part of the Galaxy that contributed to the historic union. Located in Sector 002, the Alpha Centauri system is home to more than one inhabited planet—and to some of the very first interstellar Human colonists. Alpha Centauri was also named as a founding member of the UFP in 2161, and went on to thrive as a seat of culture and learning— as well as being noted as the final home of the pioneering warp drive engineer Zefram Cochrane.

From these beginnings, the Federation established its policy of exploration and diplomacy, so that, by the mid-24th century, it boasted more than 150 member worlds and at least 2,000 trustee colonies.

The tools of diplomacy

While each Federation world has an equal voice in government, some species choose to be more actively involved than others. Betazed, for example, is one of many planets »

> For a joined Trill, nothing
> is more important than
> to protect the life of the
> symbiont. Nothing.
> **Julian Bashir**

to host Federation events such as
the biennial Trade Agreements
Conference, and which proudly
sends its most vocal ambassadors
out into the universe. Betazoids are
a telepathic race, which can have
obvious benefits for diplomatic
negotiations, though most of their
people refrain from invading the
thoughts of other species without
permission. Betazoid telepathic
skills develop in adolescence and
are present in almost all members

of the population. Betazoids can
often be blunt in their opinions
and value honesty above all else.
This is a natural extension of their
society being filled with openly
accessible thoughts.

For most of its history, Betazed
has been a peaceful world, safely
removed from most interplanetary
conflicts. That changed in 2374,
when it was occupied during the
Dominion War. The planet was
a valuable strategic location, due
to its proximity to some of the
most powerful Federation worlds.
It fell to Dominion forces within
ten hours of attack. Starfleet made
repeated attempts to liberate the
planet, but the occupying forces
remained until the end of the war.

Two become one

The Federation planet Trill is home
to two very different species that
not only coexist, but join together
in a symbiotic relationship. One of
the two species is humanoid and
acts as the host for the other, which
is an intelligent, sluglike species.
When the chosen host is at least
20 years of age, the symbiont is
implanted into his or her abdomen,

Forced separation Joined Trill Jadzia
Dax is forcibly separated in a procedure
that threatens the life of the humanoid
Jadzia and the Dax symbiont.

and once the bodies are joined,
they become fully dependent on
one another within 93 hours. The
result is a Trill with a new, blended
personality and all the memories

Becoming a Federation member

Planets with a united democratic
world government, which share
the values of the UFP and meet
certain other criteria, are allowed
to petition for membership of the
galactic organization.

Applicant worlds are subject
to an in-depth review of their
cultures to determine their
suitability, and must welcome a
Federation delegation on their soil.
If the society under review is
involved in a protracted conflict or
dispute with another world, they
must allow the UFP to attempt to
facilitate a resolution or treaty.

The length of time it takes
for a planet to be admitted to
the UFP varies, but it usually
takes several years and much
negotiation. Once a petition
is approved, it is recognized as
a great success for both sides,
and a formal signing ceremony
is arranged. But admission is
only the beginning. The new
member's defense forces must
be absorbed into Starfleet, it
must select representatives for
the Federation Council, and a
plethora of other organizational
details must be addressed.

Planets of the Federation

The worlds that make up the United Federation of Planets are spread across the Alpha and Beta Quadrants with new civilizations frequently petitioning for membership and expanding its borders.

Neural

Izar

FIRST FEDERATION

Delta

FERENGI ALLIANCE

Bolarus

ROMULAN STAR EMPIRE

Benzar

Denebular Triaxa

Tellar

Alpha Centauri

Earth

Andoria

TZENKETHI COALITION

Vulcan

BADLANDS

Bajor

Coridan

CARDASSIAN UNION

Risa

Betazed

Ba'ku

The horga'hn is the Risian symbol of sexuality. To own one is to call forth its powers. To display it is to announce you are seeking jamaharon.
Joval

relation to the number of potential hosts, becoming joined is seen as a great honor in Trill society, and there is a rigorous selection process to find the best host candidates.

A planet for pleasure

The so-called "Pleasure Planet" of Risa is a popular vacation spot for many members of the Federation. The Risians use a weather control network and seismic regulators to maintain an idyllic environment, in contrast to the driving rain and violent earthquakes that previously affected their world. The planet is proud of its open attitudes toward relationships of all sorts, and natives are not shy about expressing sexual desire, inviting visitors to enjoy all that their world—and its people—have to offer.

Betazed, Trill, and Risa are just three planets with prominent roles to play in Federation society. Some of the most fascinating species in the Galaxy are UFP members—and Starfleet's mission to seek out new civilizations is central to expanding that diverse community, for the benefit of members old and new. ■

that the symbiont may have gained from life with its previous hosts. Through this process, symbionts can live for centuries in different hosts; some Trill have lived male and female lives, and some may have witnessed the entire history of the Federation. But as joined Trill are encouraged to pursue new lives

in each body, they are barred from continuing romantic relationships from one host to the next.

Prior to joining, symbionts live and breed in The Caves of Mak'ala on Trill, where they are cared for by unjoined humanoid Trill known as the Guardians. Owing in part to the small number of symbionts in

A CAPTAIN'S MOST SOLEMN OATH
THE PRIME DIRECTIVE

CAPTAIN'S LOG

NAME
Starfleet General Order Number One, or the Prime Directive

WORDING
No starship may interfere with the normal development of any alien life or society

BRIEFING
The Prime Directive has 47 sub-orders in 2375

The guiding principle of the United Federation of Planets is embodied in the Prime Directive of its Starfleet. Codified as General Order Number One, this set of rules demands that Starfleet ships and their personnel must not interfere in the affairs of non-UFP worlds, placing self-determination above the interests of Starfleet and the Federation. It exemplifies the fundamental purpose of the UFP as a benign union of distinct and different cultures, rather than a conquering, homogenizing force. The importance of the Prime Directive is so great that Starfleet officers are expected to give up their lives and their ships rather than violate its principles.

Chief among the orders of the full directive is the ban on making contact with worlds that have yet to achieve warp drive technology. Such cultures may be observed for study by UFP representatives, but communication must be avoided—with specific regard to revealing anything about other civilizations or advanced technology. It is also forbidden for Starfleet to share any foreknowledge of natural disasters, or to take sides in conflicts within (or between) non-warp societies.

First contact protocols

Some first-contact scenarios have had frankly disastrous outcomes. On a preliminary First Contact mission to the planet Malcor III, *Enterprise* Commander Riker tried to pass himself off as a native Malcorian. But following an injury, he was disclosed as an alien, creating mass panic. Incidents like this are rare. The Federation has laid down precise procedures for establishing relationships with previously isolated societies. When a planet is close to developing warp drive technology (and thus interstellar travel), highly trained UFP observation teams are sent to live incognito among its people for several years. If it is determined that the population would react positively to visitors from other worlds, first contact with members of the scientific community is arranged, followed by world leaders. If first contact results in the Federation being asked to leave and never return, the UFP team honor the request.

Lessons learned

The Prime Directive is not as old as the Federation itself, but the need for a code of conduct predates it—with the precise nature of what it would include discussed on board *Enterprise* NX-01 a full decade before the founding of the UFP in 2161. Seven years later, one of the most significant demonstrations of the need for strict rules took place when the *U.S.S. Horizon* made first contact with Sigma Iotia II, a world in the early stages of its industrial era. On leaving the planet, one of the crew members accidentally left behind a book from Earth, setting the planet's development on a whole new course. During the next 100 years, the Iotians built their whole society around the book—a study of Earth gangsters in the 1920s—and when the *Enterprise* NCC-1701 visited Sigma Iotia II in 2268, the planet resembled nothing so much as prohibition-era, 20th-century Chicago. With the damage done and no way to undo it, Captain James Kirk had no choice but to engage the Iotians on their own terms. He convinced them that the Federation was the "mob" to side with, in the hope that its peaceful influence would guide the planet down a more ethical path.

Challenges posed

Ever since the Prime Directive was established, the challenges presented by Starfleet's mission of exploration have, at times, come into conflict with the letter of the law. But it has continued to serve as a central doctrine, and potential breaches of the order are usually long-debated beforehand, and subject to investigation afterwards. In his first four years as captain of the *U.S.S. Enterprise* NCC-1701-D, Captain Jean-Luc Picard had cause to violate the directive nine times, supplying full reports to Starfleet after the fact. Yet, when the crew of the *Enterprise*-E found evidence of a plot within Starfleet to forcibly relocate a species called the Ba'ku, Captain Picard risked his career to defend the directive, and the Ba'ku's right to determine their own fate, which it enshrined.

In the parallel reality created by the Temporal Incursion of 2233, Captain Kirk was also responsible for a breach of the Prime Directive, leading to his temporary removal as captain of the *Enterprise*. Faced with revealing the ship to the pre-industrial people of Nibiru or losing Commander Spock to an explosion in a volcano, Kirk chose the former. But, having saved his first officer, he exposed the Nibirans to technology several thousand years in advance of their own, potentially affecting the development of their society.

The only instance in which the Prime Directive is superseded is when a Starfleet ship detects the devastatingly powerful "Omega molecule." Known only to officers with the rank of captain or higher, the "Omega Directive" authorizes Starfleet to destroy the molecule by any means, and was implemented by Captain Kathryn Janeway on board the *U.S.S. Voyager* in 2374. ◼

> The Prime Directive is not just a set of rules; it is a philosophy— and a very correct one.
> **Jean-Luc Picard**

READY TO MAKE SOME HISTORY
TIME TRAVEL

CAPTAIN'S LOG

NAME
Temporal mechanics

DESCRIPTION
The science of time travel and related phenomena

NOTABLE EXPONENTS
Jonathan Archer, James Kirk, Kathryn Janeway

BRIEFING
The Department of Temporal Investigations monitors time travel within the Federation

For Humanity, the concept of traveling through time moved beyond theory in 2151, when the crew of *Enterprise* NX-01 learned of a temporal cold war being waged in their own era by time travelers from the future. One member of *Enterprise*'s crew revealed himself as a "temporal agent" native to the 31st century, and later sent other crew members back to Earth in the years 2004 and 1944 in order to rectify changes to the established historical record.

Although travel through time did not become commonplace as a result of these encounters, there were enough subsequent incidents involving Starfleet officers for the organization to establish its own Temporal Prime Directive, which was being followed in principle as early as the 23rd century.

The Temporal Prime Directive states that Starfleet is forbidden to change or interfere with historical events, and should seek to protect time from interference by others. Starfleet officers that do travel to the past or future are also subject to restrictions when discussing their experiences.

The slingshot effect

Most of the time travel in Starfleet history has occurred accidentally, either as the result of an anomaly in the space-time continuum, or by some method of alien interference. On the rare occasions when time travel is deliberately undertaken, one of the more common methods used is the light-speed breakaway factor, known colloquially as "the slingshot effect."

The slingshot effect requires a ship traveling at high warp speed to interact with the strong gravity of a large celestial body such as

Someone once told me that time is a predator that stalks us all our lives. But I rather believe time is a companion who goes with us on the journey and reminds us to cherish every moment.
Jean-Luc Picard

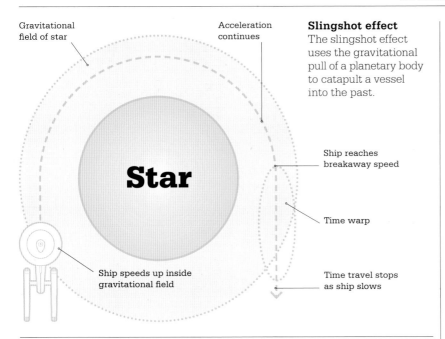

Gravitational field of star

Acceleration continues

Slingshot effect
The slingshot effect uses the gravitational pull of a planetary body to catapult a vessel into the past.

Ship reaches breakaway speed

Star

Time warp

Ship speeds up inside gravitational field

Time travel stops as ship slows

---

a star. The gravitational pull allows the ship to accelerate beyond normal warp speeds to a point where the vessel begins to move backwards through time, while also breaking away from the star's pull. However, the maneuver is considered very dangerous, owing to the precise calculations involved, and the risk of being pulled into the star.

The crew of the *U.S.S. Enterprise* NCC-1701 discovered the slingshot effect by accident in 2267, when the ship encountered the gravitational pull of an uncharted black star. This sent the ship hurtling through time and space to Earth in the year 1969. Observed by Earth's United States Air Force of the era, the crew had to retrieve filmed footage of their ship, before using Earth's sun to recreate the effect that would return them to their own time. One year later, the *Enterprise* was purposely sent back to the 20th century using the slingshot method to carry out historical research.

The most significant use of the slingshot technique did not occur until 2286, however. By this time, the *Enterprise* NCC-1701 had been destroyed, and its senior staff were in possession of a small Klingon ship that they were using to return to Earth. As they neared the planet, they found it was under attack by an alien probe that was attempting to communicate with extinct humpback whales. Admiral James Kirk and his crew used the Klingon vessel to slingshot around Earth's sun and travel back to 1986 to acquire two whales that could communicate with the probe. In bringing them to the future, they saved Earth from destruction. However, their actions did impact egregiously on history. While finding a way to store the whales, Commander Montgomery Scott "invented" the as-yet undiscovered alloy transparent aluminum. »

The Temporal Cold War

As technological advances made time travel increasingly common for many species beyond the 24th century, regulations were put in place to prevent damage to the timeline and even the destruction of time itself. By the 28th century, a "Temporal Accord" stated that time travel should only be used for scientific research.

However, time travel presented a powerful weapon, and factions intent on molding history for their own benefit used time travel not for science but to destabilize their rivals in their relative infancy.

Federation agents from the 31st century went to great lengths to oppose these factions and undo their violations, which included interfering in the 22nd century to incite civil war in the Klingon Empire, and traveling to Earth in the 1940s to alter the path of the planet's second world war.

Fought in secret, the conflict was known as the "Temporal Cold War" and nearly escalated to all-out physical warfare. This was averted by 22nd-century captain, Jonathan Archer, and the crew of *Enterprise* NX-01.

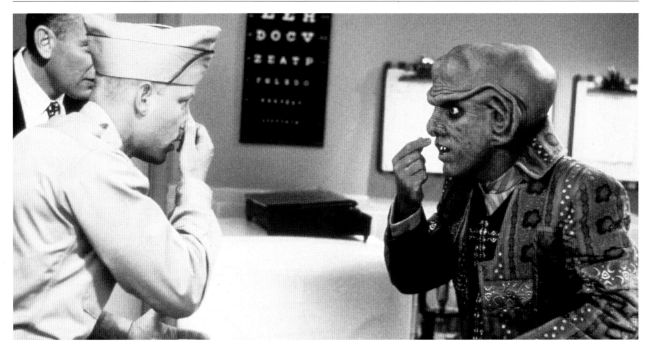

In addition, Dr. Leonard McCoy used 23rd-century medicine to cure a woman with kidney disease, and Dr. Gillian Taylor, a 20th-century native, disappeared from her own time and chose to relocate to the future to watch over "her" whales.

Technical malfunctions

Federation technology is capable of triggering time travel by other means, too, though not always

intentionally. In 2266, a cold restart of the warp engines of the *Enterprise* NCC-1701 caused a controlled matter/antimatter implosion that sent the ship 72 hours back in time.

Over a century later, a Ferengi shuttle traveling to Earth was sent back to the year 1947 owing to a reaction between the ship's cargo and plasma that had been vented from its warp core. When the ship crashed in the United States of America on 20th-century Earth, the three Ferengi on board—Rom, Quark, and Nog—made unofficial first contact with Humanity. Details of the incident were suppressed by the United States government, but it became known in Earth history as "The Roswell Incident"—named for the location in New Mexico where the Ferengi landed.

La Barre, France c. 2395 Jean-Luc Picard at his family vineyard in a possible future he visited while under the influence of Q.

New Mexico, old Earth 24th-century Ferengi, Quark, is held by authorities on 20th-century Earth after his ship crash-lands in Roswell, New Mexico.

External interference

Entities and devices from other planets and dimensions have also been responsible for sending Federation members on journeys through time with varying degrees of seriousness. Members of the Q Continuum have no problem using their vast powers to effect temporal journeys without technology, most notably the Q that took an interest in the crews of the *U.S.S. Enterprise*-D and the *U.S.S. Voyager*. His whims have sent Starfleet crews back to the dawn of the universe and into the distant future. He transported the *Enterprise*-D captain, Jean-Luc Picard, back in time to relive a few days as his 22-year-old self, newly graduated from Starfleet Academy, and also forward in time to experience his potential future as a forgetful old man.

> Time travel! Ever since my first day as a Starfleet captain I swore I'd never get caught in one of these god-forsaken paradoxes: the future is the past, the past is the future. It all gives me a headache.
> **Kathryn Janeway**

Advanced alien technology has also provided a route into the past for Starfleet crews. The atavachron machine on the planet Sarpeidon worked in conjunction with a time portal to send the inhabitants of that doomed world back to an earlier period in its history, while the mysterious and ancient Guardian of Forever was built by an unknown species for travel across time, space, and dimensions.

The Orb of Time is one of the sacred relics of Bajor, created by non-corporeal beings that live within the Bajoran wormhole. It was responsible for two trips into the past for members of the Deep Space 9 crew—the most notable of which saw the senior staff stop another time traveler from killing Captain James Kirk on board the *U.S.S. Enterprise* NCC-1701.

Two temporal vortexes created by alien technology were also the cause of trips into Earth's past for

No tribble at all A 24th-century assassin journeyed back in time to kill Captain Kirk by planting a bomb in the most unlikely of places: inside a tribble.

Captain Picard's *Enterprise* crew. The first was a passageway that was established between the planet Devidia II and 19th-century Earth, which allowed a pair of Devidians to harvest neural energy from dying Humans during an outbreak of cholera. The crew of the *Enterprise*-D used the portal to find out how the severed head of their android officer, Lieutenant Commander Data, had been found among 19th-century artifacts on Earth— an example of "predestination paradox" whereby earlier events are made possible only by later actions carried out with foreknowledge.

Five years later, a much larger temporal rift resulted in the entire *Enterprise*-E being transported back to Earth in 2063, along with the Borg sphere that had created the vortex in order to change Earth's history. Before going back in time, the *Enterprise* crew caught a frightening glimpse of a changed timeline in which the Borg had conquered Earth. But by following the sphere into the temporal distortion, they were

ultimately able to defeat the Borg and keep the history of Humanity on its proper path.

Future technology

More than 200 years after Captain Archer and his crew were caught up in the events of the Temporal Cold War, future technology once again sent a Starfleet crew into the past. In 2373, the 29th-century timeship *Aeon* tried to destroy the *U.S.S. Voyager* to avert a future catastrophe. Instead, both *Voyager* and the *Aeon* were thrown back in time to Earth in the 1990s. There, the timeship's technology fell into the hands of a 20th-century Human who harnessed its secrets for his own financial gain. In 2375, the *Voyager* crew encountered another 29th-century timeship, *Relativity*, on a mission to prevent *Voyager* being sabotaged by future technology. On this occasion, it turned out that the saboteur was in fact a future version of the *Relativity*'s captain himself, who was suffering from temporal psychosis as a result of his eventful time-traveling career. ∎
See also: Guardian of Forever

THE FUTURE BEGINS AGAIN

THE TEMPORAL INCURSION OF 2233

CAPTAIN'S LOG

NAME
Nero

SPECIES
Romulan

OCCUPATION
24th-century mining ship captain, 23rd-century terrorist

BRIEFING
Nero lost his wife and unborn child in the destruction of Romulus in 2387

In 2387, the ongoing tensions between the Romulans and the Federation, which plagued the galactic superpowers for centuries, were rendered meaningless when a supernova destroyed the Romulan homeworld, Romulus. This event became a flashpoint that altered events in the universe across time, starting at a pivotal point more than 150 years earlier.

In the run-up to the disaster, the Romulans and the Federation put aside their differences and worked together on a plan to save the planet. Federation ambassador Spock would pilot a ship carrying highly volatile "red matter" and use it to create a black hole that would contain the energy from the nova. But Spock arrived too late. Though he was able to detonate some of the red matter and save the wider region, he was not in time to stop the destruction of Romulus.

Man out of time The Romulan mining ship captain Nero was sent back in time to the year 2233 by a black hole created by Ambassador Spock in 2387.

As the black hole took effect, Spock's ship was attacked by the Romulan mining vessel *Narada*. Its captain, a Romulan called Nero, blamed Spock for the loss of his homeworld and his family. Both ships were pulled into the black hole, sending them to different points in the past. The *Narada*

his assault on the *Kelvin*, making use of his own ship's more advanced capabilities. With Robau gone and the *Kelvin* badly outgunned, the ship's first officer, Commander George Kirk, assumed command and had no choice but to give the order to abandon ship. In his few moments as captain of the *Kelvin*, he set the starship on a collision course with the *Narada*, sacrificing his own life to give his crew time to evacuate in shuttles »

While the essence of our culture has been saved in the elders who now reside upon this ship, I estimate no more than 10,000 have survived. I am now a member of an endangered species.
Spock

Mine craft Nero's 24th-century mining vessel, the *Narada*, was more powerful than the most advanced Starfleet ships in the early 2200s.

emerged in the year 2233, leading to an encounter that would alter the course of history.

Destruction of the Kelvin

The *U.S.S. Kelvin* NCC-0514 under the command of Captain Richard

Robau was observing the sudden appearance of the black hole in 2233 when the *Narada* emerged. At first, the Romulan crew was unaware that their ship had traveled through time. Nero attacked the Federation ship, demanding to know the location of Ambassador Spock. When the truth became clear, Nero expressed his rage by killing Captain Robau and redoubling

The *Jellyfish*

The fastest ship in the Vulcan fleet, the *Jellyfish* was used by Ambassador Spock in his attempt to contain the supernova that threatened Romulus and the area surrounding it. Commissioned by the Vulcan Science Academy in 2387, the ship's unique rotating tail section is evocative of the sea creature from which it takes its name. However, the interior of the ship resembles the IDIC—the symbol representing the Vulcan philosophy of Infinite Diversity in Infinite Combinations. When viewed from the cockpit area, the triangular pilot's chair and a circular viewscreen converge in the same way as the geometric shapes of the Vulcan icon.

The ship was outfitted with a containment unit designed to safely suspend highly volatile "red matter." This allowed for extraction in single droplets, which could then be delivered into an exploding star to induce a singularity (or black hole). The ship was destroyed by Spock's younger self from an alternative timeline in a collision with the Romulan mining ship, *Narada*.

Temporal Incursion timeline

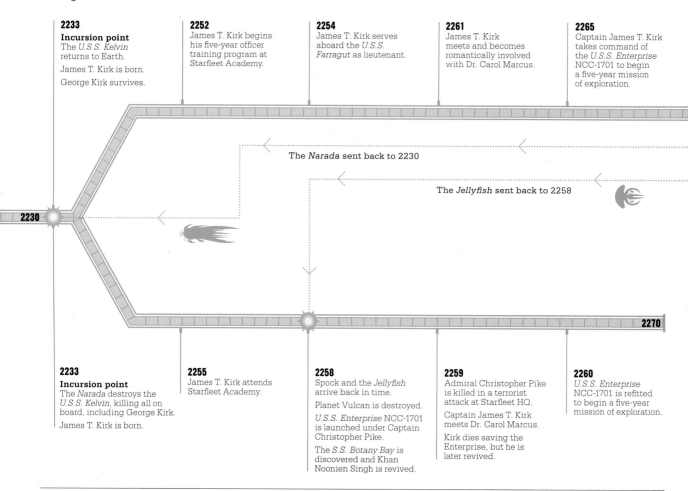

2233
Incursion point
The *U.S.S. Kelvin* returns to Earth.
James T. Kirk is born.
George Kirk survives.

2252
James T. Kirk begins his five-year officer training program at Starfleet Academy.

2254
James T. Kirk serves aboard the *U.S.S. Farragut* as lieutenant.

2261
James T. Kirk meets and becomes romantically involved with Dr. Carol Marcus.

2265
Captain James T. Kirk takes command of the *U.S.S. Enterprise* NCC-1701 to begin a five-year mission of exploration.

The *Narada* sent back to 2230

The *Jellyfish* sent back to 2258

2230

2270

2233
Incursion point
The *Narada* destroys the *U.S.S. Kelvin*, killing all on board, including George Kirk.
James T. Kirk is born.

2255
James T. Kirk attends Starfleet Academy.

2258
Spock and the *Jellyfish* arrive back in time.
Planet Vulcan is destroyed.
U.S.S. Enterprise NCC-1701 is launched under Captain Christopher Pike.
The *S.S. Botany Bay* is discovered and Khan Noonien Singh is revived.

2259
Admiral Christopher Pike is killed in a terrorist attack at Starfleet HQ.
Captain James T. Kirk meets Dr. Carol Marcus.
Kirk dies saving the Enterprise, but he is later revived.

2260
U.S.S. Enterprise NCC-1701 is refitted to begin a five-year mission of exploration.

---

and escape pods. Among the 800 people saved by the actions of Captain George Kirk were his wife, Winona Kirk, and their newborn son, James Tiberius Kirk.

Immediate fallout
Following the destruction of the *Kelvin*, Nero and the *Narada* were captured and imprisoned by the Klingons. In the intervening years, the ongoing development of Starfleet and the Federation were shaped by the repercussions of the unprovoked attack. With the knowledge that such a technologically advanced ship existed, Starfleet adjusted

Whatever our lives might have been, if the time continuum was disrupted, our destinies have changed.
Spock

its training methods, and cadets studied the destruction of the *U.S.S. Kelvin*, with particular reference to George Kirk's noble sacrifice. With the Galaxy now considered an even more dangerous place, some voices within the Federation called for Starfleet to review its policy of peaceful exploration.

The *Narada* incident also saw changes to personal histories that had played out differently before Nero went back in time. The death of officers such as George Kirk caused a ripple effect that spread across the following decades. However, as people in this new

2266
Fleet Captain Christopher Pike is permanently incapacitated by severe radiation exposure.

2267
The *S.S. Botany Bay* is discovered. Khan Noonien Singh is revived.

2285
Spock dies saving the *Enterprise* from destruction wrought by Khan, but he is later revived.

2368
Now a Federation Ambassador, Spock begins working toward Vulcan-Romulan reunification.

2387
Spock pledges to save Romulus from a supernova, but fails to do so in time. Nero in the *Narada* confronts Spock in the *Jellyfish*; both ships are pulled into a singularity and thrust back in time at different rates.

2400

Double take Ambassador Spock from the future meets the younger Commander Spock from the alternative timeline.

Spock's ship and the *Narada*'s own mining gear to create a new black hole, this time deep within Vulcan. Spock was forced to watch the end of his own world, just as Nero had seen Romulus destroyed.

Seven starships set course for Vulcan with orders to investigate the seismic activity and evacuate the planet if necessary. Of these, six were destroyed by the *Narada*, with only the *U.S.S. Enterprise* saved by a piloting error that delayed its arrival at the scene. In the revised timeline, this was the first voyage of the *Enterprise* NCC-1701—under Captain Christopher Pike—and among those on board were the son of George Kirk and this timeline's own, younger version of Spock.

Billions of people were killed in the destruction of Vulcan, including Spock's Human mother, Amanda. The *Enterprise* was able to rescue around 10,000 survivors, but the Vulcan species— that had thrived well beyond the 23rd century in the unaltered timeline—was suddenly an endangered diaspora. »

timeline were unaware of how their lives differed in the other reality, even the most significant changes were not recognized. One such difference was that the Orions—a species wholly at odds with the Federation prior to Nero's incursion in time—now had representatives serving in Starfleet. However, the most dramatic effect of the temporal incursion didn't occur until 2258.

The death of Vulcan
Twenty-five years after the *Narada* arrived in the 23rd century, Spock's ship emerged in the same location. Nero and his crew were waiting for him, ready to enact a plan that had been forming for decades. Seizing Spock's ship, Nero abandoned the ambassador on a planet in sight of his homeworld, Vulcan. He then used a quantity of red matter from

> You're assuming that Nero knows how events unfold. The contrary. Nero's very presence has altered the flow of history, beginning with the attack on the *U.S.S. Kelvin*, culminating in the events of today, thereby creating an entire new chain of incidents that cannot be anticipated by either party.
> **Spock**

With Captain Pike held captive on board the *Narada* and acting captain Spock emotionally affected by his personal loss, James T. Kirk took temporary command of the *Enterprise*. In an encounter with the older Spock, Kirk learned that Nero had changed history, and that he would be the captain of the *Enterprise* in the unaltered timeline, as well as a close friend of his first officer, Spock. Armed with this knowledge, Kirk worked closely with the younger Spock for the first time to devise a plan to defeat Nero. Young Spock gained access to the red matter on board Nero's ship (realizing in the process that it had previously been in the possession of a future version of himself) and used it to destroy both Nero and the *Narada*.

With Nero defeated, elements of the new timeline became more closely aligned with the unaltered reality than they had been for many years. Kirk and Spock served on the *U.S.S. Enterprise* as captain and first officer, and counted Dr. Leonard McCoy, Lieutenant Commander Montgomery Scott, Lieutenants Nyota Uhura and Hikaru Sulu, and Ensign Chekov among their crew. But much remained very different, with an incognito Elder Spock working to establish New Vulcan.

Fragile cargo A highly unstable substance, a single drop of red matter can create a black hole capable of absorbing the energy of a supernova.

Khan and Section 31

With the deliberate destruction of an entire inhabited planet, opinions hardened about reasonable means of defense in the Federation, and Section 31—a secretive, officially non-existent adjunct of Starfleet—became almost solely focused on acquiring a defensive edge by any means necessary. When Section 31

Bridging reality The altered timeline still resulted in the same core crew eventually serving together on the bridge of the *U.S.S. Enterprise* NCC-1701.

Black hole sun Nero altered Spock's beneficial plan to save the universe by creating a black hole within a supernova and turned it into a devastating attack on worlds.

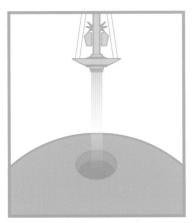

Step 1:
Use the *Narada*'s drill to dig to the planet's core.

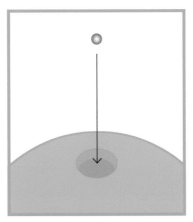

Step 2:
Drop a small amount of red matter into the core.

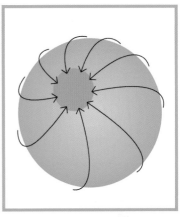

Step 3:
Form a black hole to destroy the planet.

A Khan for all ages In the new timeline, Khan took the alias John Harrison, but revealed his real name and true nature to Kirk and Spock.

operatives located an Earth sleeper ship launched into space at the end of the 20th century, they found the crew in stasis. These were some of the genetically augmented Humans that had wreaked havoc in Earth's Eugenics Wars—and among them was Khan Noonien Singh, a genius and a megalomaniacal dictator.

In the unaltered timeline, it was the *Enterprise* that found Khan and his people, reviving them and then exiling them within the Ceti Alpha system to make a new home on an uninhabited planet after they tried to take over the *Enterprise*.

In the new timeline, Section 31 revived only Khan, and used his fellow Augments as leverage to coerce him into utilizing his amoral brilliance to develop new weapons for Starfleet. Khan cooperated in the design of a new warship, but also pursued his own agenda. He failed in an attempt to free the other Augments and went to war with Section 31. In the unaltered reality, events played out very differently, with Captain Kirk having a brush with death while saving his ship from Khan. ■

See also: *U.S.S. Enterprise* NCC-1701, James T. Kirk, Spock, The Romulan Star Empire

PARALLEL LIVES
ALTERNATIVE REALITIES

The term "alternative reality" refers to naturally occurring or constructed universes that exist alongside one's own reality, but exhibit differences from it. Such differences may be as dramatic as a shift in the political structure of an entire quadrant, or as seemingly insignificant as a change in the life of one individual.

According to quantum theory, an infinite number of alternative realities exist, playing out every possible outcome of every possible event. Separate from the quantum multiverse, further realities may be generated by time travel incidents, anomalies in space-time, and the influence of powerful otherworldy beings. While rare, these are the most likely ways for an individual to experience life in a parallel world—though that individual may not be aware that any change has occurred. The following are just a few examples of alternative realities that have been recorded over the centuries.

The end of world Alternate realities have depicted the destruction of Earth, Vulcan, and the very universe as we know it.

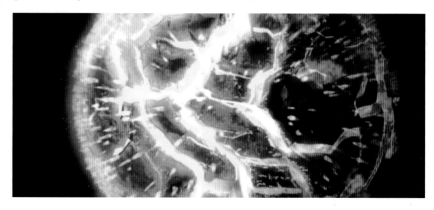

Time shift The *U.S.S. Enterprise* NCC-1701-C forged a bleak new reality when its travel through a temporal rift avoided its intended destruction in 2344.

Alternative timelines

Starting in the year 2153, the crew of *Enterprise* NX-01 experienced a 12-year period of time that was later rewritten, allowing their lives to follow different paths. At the start

You can pulp a story, but you cannot destroy an idea. Don't you understand? That's ancient knowledge. You cannot destroy an idea! That future... I created it! And it's real!
Benjamin Sisko

of this period, Captain Jonathan Archer was infected by subspace parasites that existed outside the realm of normal space-time. While he was incapacitated, *Enterprise* was unable to stop a Xindi attack that destroyed Earth and killed many of the crew. Unable to form new long-term memories, Archer lived the next 12 years learning afresh each day that his world no longer existed, and that the Xindi were wiping out the few surviving humans. At the same time that Dr. Phlox devised a method to cure Archer using the warp core of the badly damaged *Enterprise*, the ship came under attack from the Xindi. Understanding that Phlox's cure would destroy the parasites in the past as well as the present, Archer used the warp core to kill himself and the parasites before the ship could be destroyed. The resulting subspace implosion cured Archer at the point of infection, rendering him fit to command *Enterprise* in 2153. This set time on a new path, leaving Archer and his crew with no memory of the alternative reality.

In 2366, an alternative reality was created when the *Enterprise* NCC-1701-C, under the command of Captain Rachel Garrett, emerged from a temporal rift, avoiding its recorded destruction in its own era more than 20 years earlier. In the new reality created by this event, the Federation was at war with the Klingon Empire, and the *U.S.S. Enterprise* NCC-1701-D, commanded by Captain Jean-Luc Picard, was a warship. Some of its usual crew were missing, though the late Lieutenant Natasha Yar was still alive and at her post. The only person on either *Enterprise* aware of the changes was the *Enterprise*-D's El-Aurian bartender, Guinan, who convinced Picard that a dramatic shift had taken place. Picard and his crew realized that if the *Enterprise*-C returned to its own time period, it could defend a Klingon outpost from Romulan attack, and potentially avert 20 years of war— but Captain Garrett and the crew of her badly damaged ship knew that by going back they would be doomed to die in the battle. »

A year in hell Captain Janeway destroyed the *Starship Voyager* to put an end to a year of hell, resetting the timeline as if it never happened.

If that ship is destroyed, all of history might be restored. And this is one year I'd like to forget.
Kathryn Janeway

Despite this, the *Enterprise*-C crew selflessly agreed to return, as did Lieutenant Yar—who had now learned of her death in the original timeline. Upon the *Enterprise*-C's departure, the alternative reality ceased to exist, with Guinan the only person on the *Enterprise*-D to have truly experienced the events of the temporal rift—events that had now been wiped from history. However, an anomaly of the time rift meant that Tasha Yar continued to exist on board the *Enterprise*-C and even have a child in the now fully restored timeline.

Time was intentionally used as a reality-altering weapon by the Krenim of the Delta Quadrant. This species used a temporal shockwave to remove objects—or even entire species—from space and time. The effect created a reality in which the target had never existed, with only those aboard the Krenim temporal weapon ship retaining any memory of it. One use of the weapon by its inventor, Annorax, unexpectedly led to the destruction of the Krenim themselves—including Annorax's own family. He spent the next 200 years trying to restore the timeline with further shockwaves, each one of which created new realities and erased or altered billions of lives.

In 2374, the crew of *Voyager* found a way to protect themselves from Annorax's temporal weapon, but their run-ins with the Krenim were still devastating. Over the course of a year, many of the crew were killed or badly injured, and Captain Kathryn Janeway was eventually faced with no choice but to sacrifice *Voyager* to destroy the Krenim temporal weapon ship. This erased Annorax's invention from existence and restored all his victims to their proper place in space and time. It also had the effect of canceling out a year of terrible losses for *Voyager*'s crew.

Doors between realities

Over the centuries, Starfleet crews have found entrances to universes and planes of existence where life does not function as we know it. On one such occasion, Captain James Kirk's *Enterprise* NCC-1701 found itself at the heart of an anomaly that affected the entire known universe. A man called Lazarus had emerged from a "rip in space" that linked the universe of matter to a parallel one made from antimatter. By traveling between the two realities, Lazarus threatened both, but he was driven insane by the knowledge that he had a counterpart in the other

Worf's Quantum Flux

A sobering demonstration of the nature of "reality" occurred in 2370 when Lieutenant Worf of the *Enterprise*-D inadvertently flew a shuttlecraft through a quantum fissure where many alternative universes intersected. The ship's engines ruptured the barriers between realities and sent Worf into a state of quantum flux. This caused him to experience life in parallel universes, shifting from some with only minor differences from his original reality to others that were radically changed.

As the *Enterprise* crew in one of these universes tried to find the reality from which Worf originated, an energy surge caused thousands of different *Enterprises* to appear in that quantum universe—including one from a Federation that had been devastated by the Borg.

The fissure was eventually sealed by an inverse warp field created by Worf's shuttlecraft, which sent him and the various *Enterprises* back to their own quantum realities.

universe, whom he was determined to kill at any cost. Captain Kirk was able to meet this other Lazarus, a sane and reasonable man, who assisted the *Enterprise* by sealing himself and his deranged duplicate inside a neutral "corridor" between the two universes. His actions saved both realities, but also condemned him to an eternity locked in an endless struggle with himself.

Twenty-six years later in 2293, Captain Kirk encountered another portal to an alternative reality, in the form of a vast ribbon of energy known as the nexus. Aboard the *Enterprise* NCC-1701-B as a guest of honor during its maiden voyage, Kirk was drawn inside the nexus while saving the new ship from the anomaly's gravimetric pull. For the next 78 years, Kirk was believed to be dead, but he survived within the ribbon, where time did not pass. When Captain Picard also entered the nexus in 2371, he found Kirk, who had not aged a day. Both men experienced the nexus as an idyllic manifestation of the things they most wished for in life, but they chose to leave it behind to combat Soran, a scientist intent on destroying an

inhabited star system to fulfill his personal desire to return to his own fantasy life within the nexus.

Constructed realms
In some instances, an alternative reality is a contained phenomenon that affects only a specific target, while the "normal" universe exists unseen around it. In 2367, Dr. Beverly Crusher began to notice that people were vanishing from the *Enterprise*-D, but that no one else on board acknowledged the change. In fact, it was Dr. Crusher that had disappeared, becoming trapped inside a shrinking pocket universe inadvertently created on board the ship by her son, Wesley.

A year later on the same ship, Captain Picard lived out a lifetime as a citizen of the planet Kataan, following contact by a probe from that long-extinct civilization. The experience lasted decades in his mind, and he came to accept it as reality, but it took less than half an hour in the physical realm.

Captain Benjamin Sisko also experienced non-corporeal realities in his dealings with the wormhole beings known as the Prophets while in command of Deep Space 9 (DS9).

Musical memories Captain Picard plays a Ressikan flute, a treasured memento of another life lived on another world.

On one occasion, he found himself on an imagined Earth in the 1950s, believing himself to be a science-fiction writer called Benny Russell, who had invented DS9 as a story. In other "visions", he communicated with the Prophets through fragmented re-creations of moments from his own life. After the end of the Dominion War, Sisko left normal space-time to join the Prophets on their non-linear plane of existence. ■

See also: James T. Kirk, Jean-Luc Picard, Miles O'Brien, Jake Sisko

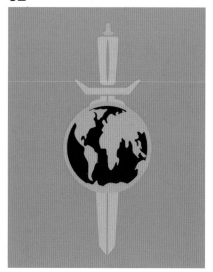

THROUGH THE LOOKING GLASS
THE MIRROR UNIVERSE

CAPTAIN'S LOG

NAME
The mirror universe

CLASSIFICATION
Alternative reality

POLITICAL AFFILIATIONS
Terran Empire, Klingon-Cardassian Alliance

NOTABLE FIGURES
Hoshi Sato (self-proclaimed Empress of the Terran Empire), Spock (reformer), Kira Nerys (Intendant of Bajor), Benjamin Sisko (resistance leader), Worf (Klingon Regent)

BRIEFING
Captains in the Terran Empire Starfleet often assumed command of their ships by mutiny and by murdering other officers

There is one alternative universe that has been visited many times by Starfleet officers from the prime reality, and which continues to exist in parallel with it. In many ways, it could be referred to as a "mirror universe," because it has much in common with the reality of the Federation, but for all its familiar faces, it is scarred by a much darker history and a much less hopeful outlook.

Starfleet became aware of this mirror universe in 2267 when the *Enterprise* NCC-1701 experienced a transporter malfunction while beaming up a landing party during an ion storm. This caused Captain Kirk, Dr. McCoy, Uhura, and Scott to swap places with their mirror counterparts on a near duplicate of the *Enterprise* in a mirror universe. Here, the crew wore different uniforms and expressed markedly different attitudes, while serving under the flag of the Terran Empire—an Earth-based regime that ruled other worlds by force.

The Terran Empire had existed for centuries, and shaped events such as Earth's first contact with Vulcans. In the mirror universe, as in the original reality, this followed

Friend and foe Intendent Kira Nerys of the parallel universe was obsessed with power. Her role in the Klingon-Cardassian Alliance shifted along with her loyalties.

It started me thinking how each of us might have turned out, had history been just a little different.
Miles O'Brien

Zefram Cochrane's first warp flight. But in the mirror version of events, Cochrane and his fellow Terrans killed the Vulcans and raided their ship for its technology, instead of establishing peaceful relations.

Kirk and his officers were able to return to their own universe, but their trip had a profound effect on the other reality. Its version of the *Enterprise*'s science officer, Spock, heeded Kirk's argument that the violence of the Terran Empire was not sustainable, and he rose within the Empire promoting a message of peace. His work reformed the Empire, but also made it an easier target for attack. It was eventually overthrown by an alliance between

Changing its Spocks Logic transcends universes as First Officer Spock on the *I.S.S. Enterprise* relied on reason and good intentions to unwittingly destroy an empire.

the Klingons and the Cardassians that rose up to rule in its place.

The next recorded visit to this other universe from the Federation took place in 2370, when Dr. Julian Bashir from Deep Space 9 crossed over, along with Major Kira Nerys. After a malfunction in the warp drive of their runabout while navigating the Bajoran wormhole, their trip took them to Terok Nor—a version of DS9 where Terrans were enslaved by allied Bajorans and Cardassians. In this reality, Kira's counterpart was in charge of Terok Nor, while a few other familiar faces from DS9 tried their best to establish a Terran resistance.

This visit inspired advances in technology that allowed for more frequent crossings between the two universes. Over the following years, several DS9 crew members interacted with the mirror reality as the Terran resistance grew. In

time, Terrans took control of Terok Nor, and captured Worf, the Regent of the Klingon-Cardassian Alliance. By 2375, the Ferengi had even tried to trade with the other reality, raising the possibility of a more integrated future for both realities. ■

The Tholian Rift

Most crossovers between the universes occur on a stable timeline, consistent for both sides. However, one intense rupture between the two did not follow this parallel path.

In 2155, when the mirror universe Tholians detonated a tricobalt warhead inside the gravity well of a dead star, it caused a rift between the two universes. They sent a signal into the rift and waited for a response from the other side.

The ship that responded was the Federation starship *Defiant* from 113 years in the Tholians' future. Its crew was driven mad by its interphasic shift, and the ship was seized by the Tholians. The Terran Empire learned about the futuristic ship and launched an assault to acquire it. They succeeded, but the ship's advanced technology quickly changed the balance of power in their empire.

STARFL

EET

Exploring and expanding the final
frontier for more than 200 years,
Starfleet is the Galaxy's greatest
outreach program—extending the hand
of friendship to each new civilization it
encounters. Its officers seek knowledge
not power, and its starships and space
stations are beacons of peace and hope
in an often dangerous universe. Above
all, it embodies a spirit of enterprise.

TO BOLDLY GO WHERE NO ONE HAS GONE BEFORE

STARFLEET

Zefram Cochrane's flight of the *Phoenix* inaugurates Humanity as a warp-capable species.

2063

The Warp Five Complex is established in Montana to develop a warp engine capable of taking humanity "where no man has gone before."

2119

Starfleet's NX Program breaks warp 2 barrier, and soon after, warp 2.5.

2143

Construction begins on *Enterprise* NX-01, a starship intended to be capable of warp 5 speed.

2149

c. 2067

The United Earth Space Probe Agency (UESPA) is formed, and launches its first deep-space unmanned probe, *Friendship 1*.

c. 2135

United Earth Starfleet is chartered as a separate entity from UESPA to develop and operate high-warp vessels.

2144

NX Program breaks warp 3.

2151

Enterprise NX-01 launched on its first mission under command of Jonathan Archer, with a maximum theoretical speed of warp 4.5.

With its powerful armada of starships and naval rank structure, Starfleet could be mistaken for a primarily military organization. In fact, it has adopted the commitment to new technology and self-discipline that characterized Earth's martial past and directed those qualities toward a new end: peaceful, methodical exploration. The unknown factors facing each mission mean that Starfleet ships must stand ready to defend themselves, however, and with no standing army, it is logical that the Federation sees this highly mobile, widely spread fleet as its first line of defense in the event of attack. This means that Starfleet personnel must be as well versed in combat as they are in science and diplomacy.

First and foremost, however, Starfleet officers are explorers and as a result they provide the first glimpse of the Federation for those civilizations that have yet to join the wider galactic community. It takes years of training to serve in the Federation's fleet, and Starfleet Academy on Earth accepts only the best and brightest candidates from member worlds. As well as learning leadership skills and

> The first duty of every Starfleet officer is to the truth... It is the guiding principle on which Starfleet is based.
> **Jean-Luc Picard**

Enterprise NX-01 fulfills earlier hopes and becomes the first Earth vessel to reach warp 5. First clash between Earth and Romulan vessels occurs.

Enterprise returns from Delphic Expanse. *Columbia* NX-02 launched under command of Captain Erika Hernandez.

Starfleet re-chartered under the new United Federation of Planets; Starfleet Academy established.

Development of *Galaxy*-class starship begins at Utopia Planitia Fleet Yards.

2152   **2154**   **2161**   **c. 2350**

2153   **2155**   **c. 2245**   **2364**

NX-01 dispatched on joint mission with Military Assault Command Operations (MACO) to Delphic Expanse, after Xindi attack on Earth.

Earth-Romulan War; United Earth Starfleet emerges victorious with help from interstellar allies.

Federation Starfleet commissions 12 *Constitution*-class starships for five-year tours of duty, including the flagship *U.S.S. Enterprise* NCC-1701.

Starfleet launches its flagship *Galaxy*-class starship, the *U.S.S. Enterprise* NCC-1701-D under command of Captain Jean-Luc Picard.

various forms of critical thinking, many Starfleet cadets also become experts in specialist fields such as medicine and engineering. Every one is taught to be an ambassador for the Federation, and to greet new challenges—and new species—with open arms, not weapons blazing.

As the Federation's most diverse and versatile organization, Starfleet is also responsible for a wide range of diplomatic and humanitarian duties alongside its exploratory and defensive roles. As escorts, Starfleet ships confer a level of authority to dignitaries and ambassadors from member worlds, and show respect and serious intent to guests from outside the Federation. Even when there are no diplomatic officials in attendance, every Starfleet officer on board a Federation ship must be a diplomat of sorts, too.

In its humanitarian mission, Starfleet stands ready to render aid to any species that asks for help, whether on board a ship in distress or on a planet hit by disaster. The Prime Directive precludes giving assistance to species in the early stages of development, however, and the Federation cannot be seen to take sides in a conflict between non-member worlds.

Starfleet's vast complement of starships and smaller vessels is mostly deployed around the Alpha and Beta Quadrants of the Milky Way Galaxy, where considerable expanses of space have still to be explored. By the close of the 24th century, however, the organization had made significant inroads to the Delta and Gamma Quadrants.

Yet no matter the coordinates, space remains the final frontier—and Starfleet its boldest explorers. Its mission continues to expand the Federation's knowledge—and its membership—under a flag of peace and cooperation. ■

The deep-space exploratory, diplomatic, and defensive agency Starfleet predates the United Federation of Planets. It was developed on Earth alongside the NX Project to develop the first warp 5-capable starship. The result was *Enterprise* NX-01, launched in 2151 with Captain Jonathan Archer in command. Its mission was to explore the Galaxy and to establish contact with unfamiliar species. When the Federation was founded in 2161, it was thanks in large part to the efforts of *Enterprise* and her crew, and so Starfleet was chosen as the Federation's primary agency for reaching out to the universe.

As part of the new Federation, Starfleet opened up its ranks to all member species. Individuals from every corner of the Alpha and Beta Quadrants were accepted into the organization over time—although some member worlds were slower to enlist than others. Despite being one of the founding species of the Federation, it was more than 100 years before the first Vulcan, Spock, applied to join Starfleet Academy.

Rules and regulations

Starfleet's operational brief is laid out in its charter (separate from the Federation Charter) and expanded in its extensive list of regulations

Starfleet Academy The academy offered a four-year training program for Starfleet personnel. Admission was through an entrance exam.

and General Orders. That its rules and guidelines are so numerous is in part due to the sheer breadth of foreseeable scenarios that a ship in deep space might encounter—but is also thanks to the unforeseeable nature of its mission. Starfleet may well be out of communication range when a starship crew has to deal with a strange and unprecedented situation, but its written guidance still provides a framework for how best to proceed. Starfleet captains are expected to interpret and apply the rules with discretion, and may bend or break them in exceptional circumstances—provided they can justify their actions.

The best known encapsulation of Starfleet's ongoing mission is the oath taken by its captains (but echoed by Starfleet officers at all levels), with its pledge to: "explore strange new worlds, to seek out new life and new civilizations, to boldly go where no one has gone

before." This promise originated with the pre-Federation Starfleet, and some version of it has appeared on the dedication plaque of all its ships with the name *Enterprise*—starting with *Enterprise* NX-01.

Operational structure

Starfleet Command headquarters are in San Francisco, California, on Earth. This reflects the agency's

There are three things to remember about being a starship captain—keep your shirt tucked in, go down with the ship, and never abandon a member of your crew.
Kathryn Janeway

Starfleet before the Federation

In the era before the founding of the Federation, Starfleet was an off-shoot of UESPA—the United Earth Space Probe Agency. The two names were sometimes used interchangeably, though UESPA predates Starfleet by roughly 70 years. UESPA itself grew out of the International Space Agency, which landed the first Humans on Mars; and NASA, which put the first men on Earth's moon.

Many spacefaring ships were launched from Earth in the late 21st and early 22nd centuries, by UESPA and other agencies, each with limited exploratory or colonization objectives. But Starfleet's primary focus was to develop an armada of true starships, capable of crossing star systems in days or weeks instead of months or years.

With the successful launch of its first warp 5 vessels in the 2150s, Starfleet established its role as Earth's ambassadors on the final frontier.

origins as a Human-led initiative, and the strategic importance of Earth's location. Other facilities on Earth include Starfleet Academy on the other side of San Francisco Bay, with further Starfleet bases— or starbases—located on planets and space stations throughout the Alpha and Beta Quadrants.

Starfleet's command structure is similar to the rank system used by naval forces from Earth history, with the admiralty heading up the service, captains in command of ships, and ranks from commander down to enlisted personnel (non-commissioned officers) serving on board starships and starbases. All promotions are merit-based and—though many officers do aspire to become admirals—it is commonly accepted that the most rewarding and challenging role is to command a starship in deep space.

All Starfleet officers serve in one of three divisions—Command, Operations (Ops), or Sciences. The first of these is reserved for officers serving on the Command-track of starships, starbases, and Starfleet Headquarters. Department heads, such as chief engineers or security chiefs, may also be in this division, but are more likely to serve in Ops,

the division tasked with the day-to-day operational performance of a starship. The Sciences division includes specialists in an array of research fields, as well as medical personnel. Service in Operations or Sciences does not preclude an

officer achieving a Command role, such as captain of a starship.

Starfleet uniforms have seen many changes over the years, but the colors most often used for the divisions have been gold, red, and blue. Gold is the traditional color »

Status symbols The positions and titles of Starfleet personnel were based on those in the Earth naval forces. Their identifying insignia changed over the years with changes to the uniform, and included sleeve stripes, shoulder straps, and pips worn on the collar.

Main rank insignia, 24th century (worn on collar)

Ensign Lieutenant Junior Grade Lieutenant

Lieutenant Commander Commander

Captain

Admiral (Number of pips varies)

Main rank insignia, late 23rd century (worn on shoulder)

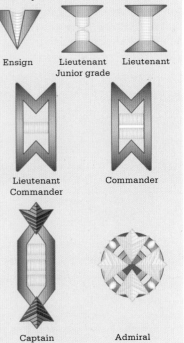

Ensign Lieutenant Junior grade Lieutenant

Lieutenant Commander Commander

Captain Admiral

Starship armada Starfleet ships were mostly used for independent missions, but at times a larger fleet was needed to protect Federation interests.

of Command, with red associated with Operations, though this was reversed during the 24th century. Blue uniforms have for the most part denoted Sciences.

The fleet

Since the days of its first deep-space explorer, *Enterprise* NX-01, Starfleet has hugely expanded its complement of vessels to include a wide array of starship classes suitable for different missions. Though these starships come in many shapes and sizes, the most common design builds on the template established by the NX class, with a saucer section to the front of the ship, and a secondary engineering hull below/behind it, projecting two warp nacelles on pylons to the sides. Examples of this formation include the various iterations of the *U.S.S. Enterprise,* and the *U.S.S. Excelsior,* while exceptions include *Constellation*-class ships (which have four warp nacelles), and the *Defiant* class (with its single hull and integrated warp nacelles).

The most famous name in the long history of Starfleet vessels is undoubtedly *Enterprise*—a title passed down through seven ships by the late 24th century. But the fleet has included many other notable starships, such as the *U.S.S. Defiant*—which played a vital role during the Dominion War and was the first Starfleet ship to be equipped with a cloaking device—and the *U.S.S. Voyager,* which became the first Federation starship to explore the Delta Quadrant.

> Starfleet could've sent a probe out here to make maps and take pictures, but they didn't. They sent us so that we could explore with our own senses.
> **Jonathan Archer**

By the 24th century it was not uncommon for larger starships to include crew members' families among their inhabitants, so that personnel did not need to be away from their loved ones for extended periods. Vessels such as *Galaxy*-class starships featured large living quarters, schools, and recreation facilities that made for comfortable environments in which to bring up a family. In the event of attack, civilians and non-essential personnel could be evacuated to the ship's

Starfleet and San Francisco

Since its inception as the space agency of United Earth, Starfleet has had its headquarters in San Francisco in the United States of America, overlooking the Golden Gate Bridge in San Francisco Bay. The complex grew considerably over the years, coming to include the campus of Starfleet Academy and spreading across both sides of the bay, including the former military base called the Presidio. This location has also been home to the Federation Council—the legislative branch of the United Federation of Planets.

San Francisco Bay was the site of a surprise attack by the Breen in 2375. Many Starfleet buildings and the Golden Gate Bridge were damaged beyond use, though all were repaired within a year.

In the timeline created by the Temporal Incursion of 2233, Starfleet Academy remained in the Bay area, while its HQ had been relocated to downtown San Francisco by the mid 2250s. This building was the target of two attacks by Khan Noonien Singh during 2259.

At ninth base Though Deep Space 9 was not a Federation outpost, Starfleet officers were posted to the station at the request of the Bajoran government.

saucer section, which would then be separated from the battle section, where senior personnel remained to address the enemy.

In addition to its array of starships, Starfleet maintains more than 500 starbases spread across Federation space and beyond. These facilities provide a more permanent presence than a starship and act as staging posts, rendezvous points, research stations, and command bases for the fleet. In the late 24th century, one of the most important Starfleet outposts was Deep Space 9, due to its strategic location at the mouth of the wormhole that connected the Alpha and Gamma Quadrants. A repurposed Cardassian station administered by the Bajorans, DS9 initially lay outside of Federation territory, and became a key tactical location during the Dominion War.

Intelligence gathering

Starfleet Intelligence is the branch of the organization that collects and analyzes information about threats to Federation security. This largely covert work is usually carried out by dedicated Starfleet Intelligence agents, though regular personnel may be assigned specific missions. Starfleet captains have access to some intelligence reports and can request others. The service uses numerous highly-placed informants in its intelligence gathering, and has been known to place agents in undercover roles on Starfleet ships.

Operating a covert body in an open society such as the Federation presents some challenges, and for that reason among others, Starfleet has an even more secretive level of operations known as Section 31. Whereas Starfleet Intelligence is answerable to Starfleet Command, Section 31 pursues its own agenda without oversight. Its existence is not officially recognized and it is, in practice, an autonomous body— in Starfleet, but also outside of it.

The Temporal Incursion

In 2233, the Kelvin Timeline was created when the Romulan mining ship *Narada* traveled back in time from 2387 and attacked the *U.S.S. Kelvin*. Starfleet was rocked by the attack, in which the *Kelvin* was lost, and began to direct more resources toward defense, while still pursuing its exploratory agenda. One result of this was that Section 31 started to take a more active role in Starfleet's research and development, working to create a new class of vessel that was effectively a warship. Factions within Starfleet saw this new ship as a vital defense in any future war with the Klingons, but in fact it was turned on Starfleet itself, and came close to destroying its headquarters in a suicide run by its creator, the genetically augmented war criminal Khan Noonien Singh. Following the attack, Captain James Kirk took the opportunity to restate the captain's oath, and Starfleet's commitment to peaceful, hopeful exploration above warmongering and fear. ∎

FROM THE STARS, KNOWLEDGE
STARFLEET ACADEMY

CAPTAIN'S LOG

NAME
Starfleet Academy

MAIN CAMPUS
San Francisco, Earth

MOTTO
***Ex Astris, Scientia* (From the Stars, Knowledge)**

BRIEFING
The senior officer of the Academy is the Superintendent, a role that has been held by Human, Vulcan, and Betazoid individuals

I am a graduate of Starfleet Academy. I know many things.
Worf

Reach for the stars Starfleet recruitment posters encourage members from across the Federation to join the organization.

Academy predates the United Federation of Planets by some years, but was established as the officer-training program for the wider fleet of the UFP upon its founding in 2161. It accepts applications from any planet in the Federation, and will consider candidates from non-member worlds if their application is sponsored with a letter of recommendation from a senior Starfleet officer.

All applicants to the Academy undergo rigorous examination to establish their suitability for officer training. Testing facilities such as the one on the planet Relva VII are located throughout the Alpha and Beta Quadrants, to ensure access for candidates across the Galaxy. If a potential cadet fails any of the mental or physical evaluations that make up the admissions process, they can retake the tests at a later date, provided their initial scores reached a certain threshold. Candidates with the skills and dedication to pass their evaluation

I n fulfilling the captain's oath to "seek out new life and new civilizations," Starfleet officers are expected to act as explorers, scientists, soldiers, and diplomats. The rigorous training program at Starfleet Academy prepares them for those varied roles. Most cadets spend four years at the Academy, but there are also opportunities to accelerate that process or to engage in more in-depth studies that can last up to twice as long.

As the training body for United Earth Starfleet personnel, Starfleet

Kobayashi Maru simulation

One of the most challenging tests undertaken by cadets at Starfleet Academy is the *Kobayashi Maru* simulation. Though a full bridge crew participates in the exercise, its primary focus is the reactions of the cadet in the role of captain.

The simulation presents the captain with a "no-win" scenario, in which a starship faces certain destruction no matter what course of action is followed. Its intended purpose is for the captain to keep control in the face of fear.

The *Kobayashi Maru* itself is the ship in distress at the heart of the scenario, which is located inside the Klingon Neutral Zone, along with a number of cloaked Klingon ships with the capacity and intent to destroy a starship.

The only cadet ever to beat the test was James T. Kirk, who reprogrammed the simulator to allow for a successful rescue of the *Kobayashi Maru* crew. His original thinking was rewarded with a Starfleet commendation.

are admitted to Starfleet Academy as cadets. They are issued a uniform and assigned to a campus where, alongside a core curriculum including Human history, Klingon military strategy, warp theory, and Starfleet General Orders, they can major in a wide variety of specialist subjects, including astrophysics, xenolinguistics, engineering, and exobiology. Medical trainees follow a specialized program at Starfleet Medical Academy—a separate but closely affiliated body with its own campus and facilities.

The main Starfleet Academy campus is located in San Francisco on Earth, on the other side of the Golden Gate Bridge from Starfleet Headquarters. Other campuses on Earth include one at the Marseilles Starfleet Base in France, and there are annexes on various Federation worlds. Study on training vessels or assignments on board starships also provide further opportunities for development in space.

Elite squadrons

Though every cadet is expected to excel, the Academy also operates elite programs for its very best and brightest. Such schemes have been beset with problems, however, due

to the intense pressure to succeed felt by the selected few. One such set was Nova Squadron—a group of cadets with expert piloting skills. In 2368, when a member of the squadron was killed during an unsanctioned maneuver during training, the other four members of the group conspired to cover up their part in the accident. Another, more wide-ranging elite group was Red Squad, whose members underwent extensive specialized training, but were unprepared for the realities of field duty when they

were thrust into action. Their unquestioning approach to duty contributed to an attempted coup on Earth in 2372, and to the eventual loss of most of the team during the Dominion War two years later. Fortunately, such incidents are so rare that they have not undermined the wider mission or standing of Starfleet Academy and its many illustrious graduates. ∎

Towers of knowledge Cadets on the main campus of Starfleet Academy in San Francisco, 25 years after the Temporal Incursion of 2233.

EXTRAORDINARY MEASURES

SECTION 31

CAPTAIN'S LOG

NAME
Section 31

STATUS
Classified—existence officially denied

AFFILIATION
Starfleet, United Federation of Planets

ESTABLISHED
Before 2150

HEADQUARTERS
Kelvin Memorial Archive, London (Kelvin Timeline)

KNOWN OPERATIVES
"Harris," Malcolm Reed (22nd century); "John Harrison," Alexander Marcus (23rd century, Kelvin Timeline); "Luther Sloan" (24th century)

BRIEFING
Section 31 operates on a similar covert level to the Romulan Tal Shiar and the Cardassian Obsidian Order

Beyond the open and honest dealings of daily Federation life lies a darker world that those in the know prefer to forget. It is not Starfleet Intelligence, the openly acknowledged covert arm of the Federation, but a more clandestine organization that has pursued its own agenda in the defense of Starfleet interests for hundreds of years. Those who know about this "black ops" division refer to it as Section 31.

The unit predates the founding of the Federation and exists thanks to the vague wording of Article 14, Section 31, of the Starfleet Charter, which states that "extraordinary measures" can be taken in "times of extreme threat." The result was an adjunct of Starfleet allowed to operate without official oversight or sanction for specific operations.

Section 31's work was brought to light during the Dominion War, when the group attempted to recruit Dr. Julian Bashir on the space station Deep Space 9. Bashir eventually exposed the organization's role in introducing the Dominion Founders to a deadly virus, and he began work to find a cure. His successful findings were instrumental in ending the war.

The Federation needs men like you, doctor. Men of conscience, men of principle. Men who can sleep at night.
Luther Sloan

The Temporal Incursion

Section 31 played a far more active role in Starfleet activities after the Temporal Incursion of 2233. Under the leadership of Admiral Alexander Marcus, it worked to develop new and dangerous weapons to protect Earth at all costs. Marcus used the destruction of Vulcan by the 24th-century ship *Narada* to justify his actions, going so far as to employ the amoral genius of 20th-century war criminal Khan Noonien Singh to develop a new warship, and then deploying that warship against the *Enterprise* in an attempt to cover up Khan's involvement with Section 31. ∎

TIME AND TIME AGAIN

THE DEPARTMENT OF TEMPORAL INVESTIGATIONS AND THE TEMPORAL INTEGRITY COMMISSION

CAPTAIN'S LOG

NAME
Temporal Prime Directive

PRECIS
No Starfleet personnel may interfere with the timeline of any alien life or society

RELATED GUIDANCE
Starfleet temporal displacement policy; Starfleet Regulation 157, Section 3, Paragraph 18 ("Officers shall take all necessary precautions to minimize participation in historical events.")

BRIEFING
In a possible version of the 29th century, the Temporal Prime Directive is enforced by Federation timeships with precise and powerful time travel capabilities

Since the mid-22nd century, numerous Starfleet personnel have become involved with incidents of time travel, whether on purpose or accidentally. In order to monitor and prevent damage to the timeline, Starfleet established time travel guidelines for officers to follow, and the Department of Temporal Investigations to police them.

When, in 2373, the *U.S.S. Defiant* traveled back to 2268, its crew was able to prevent the assassination of Captain James Kirk by another time traveler. The subsequent report by the ship's captain, Benjamin Sisko, led to two D.T.I. officers paying him a visit on board Deep Space 9.

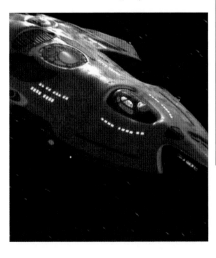

Captain Kirk had a particularly bad reputation within the D.T.I. as a result of 17 temporal violations on his file—a department record. However, the investigating officers for Sisko's encounter did not record it as a serious breach of regulations.

Another captain who garnered attention from the authorities owing to her temporal travels was Kathryn Janeway of the *U.S.S. Voyager*. She twice attracted the attention of the Temporal Integrity Commission— a Federation body from one possible version of the 29th century, which could be a future incarnation of the D.T.I. By this time, Starfleet's rules for time travel were known as the Temporal Prime Directive.

Further forward still, in the 31st century, an individual known only as Daniels traveled back to the 22nd century in an attempt to rectify the damage done to the timeline by the Temporal Cold War. Though he posed as a member of the *Enterprise* NX-01 crew, it is unknown whether he was truly affiliated with Starfleet or the Temporal Integrity Commission. ■

Time saver In 2375, the *U.S.S. Voyager* encountered the 29th-century timeship *Relativity* on a mission to save *Voyager* from being destroyed in its own past.

FIRST IN THE FLEET
ENTERPRISE NX-01

CAPTAIN'S LOG

NAME
Enterprise NX-01

LENGTH
225 meters

COMPLEMENT
83

BRIEFING
Enterprise NX-01 was launched in 2151 and decommissioned in 2161

More than 50 years after his first successful warp speed flight on board the *Phoenix*, Zefram Cochrane and the United Earth Space Probe Agency launched the Warp 5 Program. Its mission was to create an engine that could power a crewed vessel capable of deep space exploration. It took another 20 years for the technology to be developed that would allow them to move into the next phase: constructing the ship

that would house the warp engines. The NX Program was launched and the final result was *Enterprise* NX-01.

Prior to the launch of *Enterprise* in 2151, Humanity's main presence beyond Earth was the Earth Cargo Service, but those ships topped out at warp 2. Their journeys between star systems took years, which was far from conducive to Humankind's thirst to explore. With the advent of *Enterprise*, however, Humans could make similar journeys in days, if not hours. Even though *Enterprise* was theoretically capable of achieving a maximum speed of only warp 4.5 at launch, it went on to reach warp 5 during its first year in service.

A tour of NX-01
The design of *Enterprise* NX-01 established the look of Starfleet vessels for centuries to come. The command bridge sits atop a saucer-shaped hull, which is propelled by two warp nacelles at the stern. On the inside of the ship, the circular bridge centers on the captain's chair, which is surrounded by duty stations for security, engineering,

sciences, and communications. A briefing room or "situation room" adjoins the rear of the bridge and serves as a tactical center.

A unique feature of the ship that would become common in future starships is a matter transporter capable of moving people and materials via matter-energy conversion.

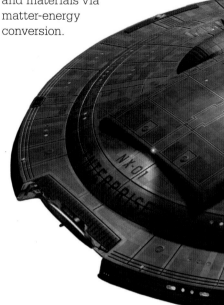

This process, known informally as "beaming," transforms objects into subatomic particles and then transmits those particles almost instantaneously to another location, where they are reconstituted as solid matter in its original form. Though the *Enterprise*'s transporter was approved for biological use (i.e. for beaming living beings), it was not immediately adopted for everyday use, with the ship's crew favoring *Enterprise*'s two shuttlepods for visits to planets and other vessels.

The seven decks of the ship initially carried a complement of 83 crew members—all Human except for the Vulcan observer Subcommander T'Pol, and the ship's Denobulan

doctor, Phlox. Like the transporter room and the shuttle bay, Phlox's sickbay would not look unfamiliar to subsequent starship personnel, though later Starfleet crews might be surprised by the compact living quarters, and by the food prepared by a chef in a galley—rather than replicated by technology similar to that used in transporters.

Enterprise's standard weapons at launch included phase cannons and spatial torpedoes. Two years into its mission, however, the ship underwent a refit to counter the threat from the Xindi, upgrading

> We're going to stumble, make mistakes... I'm sure more than a few before we find our footing. But we're going to learn from those mistakes. That's what being Human is all about.
> **Jonathan Archer**

its torpedoes to a new photonic design with a variable yield and a range more than 50 times greater than previously. The hull plating was also enhanced at this

time, and the universal translator was updated. A storage bay was repurposed as an additional command center, offering many functions that would become standard in later starships.

Enterprise: Year one
Final preparations for the launch of *Enterprise* were already under way when a Klingon ship crash-landed on Earth in Broken Bow, Oklahoma. The Klingon, named Klaang, was left in a critical condition after being shot by a Human, and *Enterprise*'s launch date was brought forward by the United Earth Starfleet in order to return Klaang to his own people on the Klingon Homeworld, Qo'noS »

First starship Earth's first warp 5 starship led an illustrious line of Starfleet vessels named *Enterprise*.

Enterprise NX-01

Earth's first warp 5-capable starship became the prototype of many Starfleet starships to come. Although the ships' functionalities were upgraded many times over the years, the basic features are duplicated in a number of the fleet's ships.

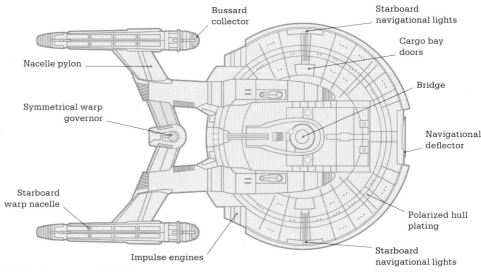

Bussard collector

Starboard navigational lights

Nacelle pylon

Cargo bay doors

Symmetrical warp governor

Bridge

Navigational deflector

Starboard warp nacelle

Polarized hull plating

Impulse engines

Starboard navigational lights

The ship launched from Earth's orbital drydock facility—where it was constructed—on April 16, 2151, with Captain Jonathan Archer in command. It successfully returned Klaang to Qo'noS, but only after the Klingon was briefly abducted from the ship. The kidnappers were later identified as Suliban agents in an elaborate "Temporal Cold War" being waged in secret against a number of species including Humans.

The Temporal Cold War plagued *Enterprise* throughout the first year of its voyage and beyond, but that did not keep the ship from reaching out to new worlds in the Alpha and Beta Quadrants. *Enterprise*'s crew

made Humanity's first contact with numerous species—most notably the Andorians, when they became inadvertently involved in a dispute between Andoria and Vulcan. The crew also recorded contact with a band of pirates from an unidentified species with a seeming obsession for acquiring material wealth. It was another 213 years until the Ferengi made official first contact with the Federation—during an encounter with the *U.S.S. Enterprise* NCC-1701-D under Captain Picard.

An era of conflict

Enterprise's second year in service was marked by yet more contacts

with unfamiliar species, including the crew's first interaction with the Tellarites, in the form of a bounty hunter who kidnapped Captain Archer. The ship also played host to a boarding party of Borg drones displaced from the 24th century—though these cybernetic attackers did not identify themselves to the crew. Nothing *Enterprise* encountered in space was enough to prepare the Earth for its first contact with the Xindi, however.

An alliance of four species from the planet Xindus in the Delphic Expanse of the Beta Quadrant, the Xindi made themselves known to Humanity with a space probe that

Enterprise NX-01 Timeline

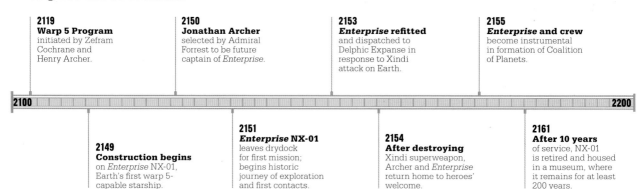

2119
Warp 5 Program
initiated by Zefram Cochrane and Henry Archer.

2150
Jonathan Archer
selected by Admiral Forrest to be future captain of *Enterprise*.

2153
***Enterprise* refitted**
and dispatched to Delphic Expanse in response to Xindi attack on Earth.

2155
***Enterprise* and crew**
become instrumental in formation of Coalition of Planets.

2100   2200

2149
Construction begins
on *Enterprise* NX-01, Earth's first warp 5-capable starship.

2151
***Enterprise* NX-01**
leaves drydock for first mission; begins historic journey of exploration and first contacts.

2154
After destroying
Xindi superweapon, Archer and *Enterprise* return home to heroes' welcome.

2161
After 10 years
of service, NX-01 is retired and housed in a museum, where it remains for at least 200 years.

launched an unprovoked attack on Earth. Cutting a path of destruction from Florida to Venezuela, it killed more than seven million people—including the sister of *Enterprise*'s chief engineer, Commander Charles "Trip" Tucker. Following the attack, *Enterprise*'s mission changed from one of exploration to defense, with Humans and Xindi pitched against each other as unwitting pawns in the Temporal Cold War. After almost a year of bitter conflict, it was the joint efforts of the *Enterprise* crew and a Xindi agent that succeeded in striking a decisive blow against their common enemy, signaling the beginning of the end of the war.

An era of peace

In its fourth year, *Enterprise* played an important role in averting a war between the Klingon Empire and Earth, after genetically augmented Humans hijacked a Klingon ship. Shortly afterwards, *Enterprise* was sabotaged by Klingons suffering from a virus derived from the DNA of the Human Augments—which Doctor Phlox was able to cure.

It was also during this year that *Enterprise* laid the groundwork for the United Federation of Planets, through Captain Archer's dealings

with the Andorians, Tellarites, and Vulcans. The Coalition of Planets that grew out of these encounters would play an important role in the Earth-Romulan war that followed.

Enterprise was decommissioned after ten years of service in 2161—the year that the United Federation

In the round Duty stations surround the captain's chair on the command bridge of *Enterprise* NX-01.

of Planets was founded. It went on to be displayed in a museum, in recognition of its role in the history of spaceflight and the Federation. ∎

Columbia NX-02

The second Starfleet vessel to be launched with a warp 5 engine was *Columbia* NX-02, commanded by Captain Erika Hernandez. The ship was superficially identical to *Enterprise* NX-01, but featured improved hull polarization, pulsed phase cannons, and ventral and dorsal torpedo launchers.

Columbia was set to launch in the summer of 2154, but remained in drydock until November of that year, owing to engine problems. These were eventually overcome by Commander Charles "Trip" Tucker, the ship's chief engineer, who transferred to *Columbia* from *Enterprise*.

One of *Columbia*'s earliest missions put it in close quarters with *Enterprise*, in a hazardous maneuver that saw Commander Tucker transferred back to his old ship via a tether while both ships were at warp 5.2. Not long after, both ships were reunited in battle against the Klingons as part of a rescue mission.

MODEL STARSHIP BUILDER

JONATHAN ARCHER

CAPTAIN'S LOG

NAME
Jonathan Archer

SPECIES
Human

BORN
2112, New York, Earth

PARENTS
Henry and Sally Archer

STARFLEET DIVISION
Command

BRIEFING
In his youth, Archer earned 26 merit badges and became an Eagle Scout in the Boy Scouts

It could be said that Jonathan Archer was raised to captain the first Starfleet ship capable of deep space exploration. He grew up making model spaceships with his father, Henry Archer, who was one of the main engineers working with Zefram Cochrane to develop a warp 5 engine. Though his father did not live to see him captain the first vessel capable of traveling at warp 5, Jonathan Archer knew that he was fulfilling his father's dream as well as his own.

Archer served as a commander in the NX Program to build Earth's first starship, and was recognized as one of its top test pilots. He was chosen to captain *Enterprise* NX-01, despite Captain A.G. Robinson being the favored candidate of the Vulcan ambassador to Earth, Soval. This did not endear the Vulcans to Archer, who already considered the

> The more I've experienced, the more I've learned that no matter how far we travel, or how fast we get there, the most profound discoveries are not necessarily beyond that next star—they're within us.
> **Jonathan Archer**

species responsible for holding back the NX Program.

Into the stars

With the launch of *Enterprise* in 2151, Archer's dreams of space travel were swiftly tempered by experience. On his first mission as captain, he returned an injured Klingon to the planet Qo'noS, only to face the ungrateful wrath of the Klingon High Council. His subsequent meetings and first contacts with many other species were to prove no less challenging. Through perseverance and patience, however, Archer made significant inroads for Humanity's standing in the Galaxy, not least in developing a mutually (albeit grudgingly) respectful relationship with the Andorian Imperial Guard commander Thy'lek Shran. Their burgeoning friendship was largely responsible for Humanity's receipt of Andorian assistance during the crisis caused by the Xindi attack on Earth in 2153, and was also integral to the later founding of the United Federation of Planets.

Archer established a model that Starfleet captains and other senior officers would follow for centuries to come. He was wholly committed to the ideals underlying Starfleet, but was not afraid to ask questions of his superior officers, or to bend the rules if his moral duty demanded it. A bold and popular leader, Archer shared a deep bond with his crew, but did not fail to exert authority where necessary. Aside from his dog, Porthos, his closest friend on board *Enterprise* was Commander Charles "Trip" Tucker, with whom he had worked during the test phase of the NX Program.

Archer was initially at odds with his Vulcan crew member, Subcommander T'Pol, but a bond slowly formed between them that positively influenced Human/Vulcan relations for years to come. Granted new insights into Vulcan history and philosophy, Archer was eventually instrumental in bringing about a new era in Vulcan society after he located the lost teachings of Surak, the "father" of Vulcan logic and reason. Archer earned many commendations during his career and following the Earth-Romulan war was one of the signatories to the charter that lead to the United Federation of Planets. Noted by history as the greatest explorer of the 22nd century, his name and legacy are still celebrated in Starfleet and the Federation, and two planets have been named in his honor. ∎

If the suit fits... Captain Jonathan Archer dons an EV suit for space walks and other inhospitable environments.

Where no dog has gone before

Rank has its privileges, and one that Captain Jonathan Archer claimed when he took command of *Enterprise* was to have Porthos, his faithful canine companion, on board.

Archer had owned a dog all his life, and he acquired Porthos from the mother of an ex-girlfriend when the puppy was just six weeks old. She gave him the pick of the litter of four male beagles, which she had already dubbed the "Four Musketeers."

Porthos was not the first dog in space, but he was the most well-traveled Earth pet of his era. He spent most of his time in Archer's quarters (staying alert to intruders and other anomalies), but was at times allowed to join landing parties—setting paw on new planets and "going" where no dog had gone before.

Despite such impulses, the voyages of the beagle lead to just one diplomatic incident—when the animal urinated on one of the planet Kreetassa's sacred trees. On this occasion, Archer was able to make up for the offense by performing an elaborate ritual apology, as required by the Kreetassans.

THE VULCAN OBSERVER
T'POL

CAPTAIN'S LOG

NAME
T'Pol

SPECIES
Vulcan

BORN
2088, Vulcan

MOTHER
T'Les

STARFLEET DIVISION
Sciences

BRIEFING
T'Pol initially employed a nasal numbing agent to reduce her heightened Vulcan sense of smell while serving with Humans on *Enterprise*

The needs of the two T'Pol and Koss are married in accordance with Vulcan tradition, having been betrothed since they were children.

Subcommander T'Pol was assigned to *Enterprise* NX-01 at the insistence of Soval, the Vulcan ambassador to Earth, in exchange for the starship being given access to Vulcan star charts. Starfleet was skeptical about this exchange—as was T'Pol herself—but she was present as the Vulcan "observer" when *Enterprise* set out on its very first mission—to return an injured Klingon to the planet Qo'noS. What no one anticipated was the effect she would have on the rest of the crew, or the effect that they would have on her and—as a result—all of Vulcan society.

Her own Vulcan
T'Pol first impressed *Enterprise*'s Human crew on that mission to Qo'noS. When Captain Archer was

injured, T'Pol took command and completed the mission, instead of returning to Earth as her Vulcan superiors would have wished. Later, when the *Enterprise* crew found evidence that the Vulcans were spying on the Andorians, T'Pol followed Archer's orders to reveal the information, despite the repercussions for the Vulcan High Command.

As is traditional for Vulcans, T'Pol was bonded with a future mate as a child. But when the time came to marry her betrothed, she went against tradition and her family's wishes, as marriage

Humans believe that sometimes you have to follow your instincts. Very illogical approach, but one I've come to embrace.
T'Pol

Before first contact

One of T'Pol's most prized possessions is a 1950s-era purse from Earth, inherited from her second foremother (great-grandmother), T'Mir. T'Pol's story about how T'Mir came by it challenges the prevalent Human belief that first contact between Vulcan and Earth took place in 2063.

T'Mir was part of a Vulcan survey team that was sent to investigate Earth in 1957 after the launch of *Sputnik*, Earth's first artificial satellite. When their ship malfunctioned, the Vulcans crash-landed in the United States of America. Not knowing if their distress call would be received, T'Mir and the two other surviving crew members had to find a way to survive. They disguised their Vulcan features and lived as Humans in the town of Carbon Creek in Pennsylvania. They made friends, found work, and one, Mestral, even started a romance with a Human.

A rescue ship arrived after three months, but by this time Mestral was infatuated with the Human race and chose to stay behind. He presumably lived out the rest of his life on Earth, while T'Mir returned home with a small souvenir.

Diplomatic dress As a member of the Vulcan Diplomatic Corps, T'Pol wears a simple jumpsuit in muted colors with subtle rank insignia on the collar.

would have ended her time on board *Enterprise*. She later agreed to marry for her mother's benefit, but still refused to leave the ship. Her husband, Koss, granted her an annulment after her mother died, knowing that the marriage was against her wishes.

A varied career

T'Pol was working as an aide to Ambassador Soval when she was chosen for the role of observer on board *Enterprise*. Prior to this, her long life (by human standards) had already included time as a covert agent for the Vulcan Ministry of Security, military service, duty at the Vulcan Ministry of Information, and service of the Science Council of the Vulcan High Command. It was not easy for T'Pol to adapt to

her new life on a Human-run vessel, but mutual respect developed to a point where, following the Xindi attack on Earth, T'Pol resigned her commission with the Vulcan High Command to continue serving with her Human crew mates. She later accepted a new commission in Starfleet, becoming a commander on board *Enterprise*.

A personal relationship

In her early days on *Enterprise*, T'Pol was often at cross-purposes with the emotional chief engineer, Commander Charles "Trip" Tucker, but circumstance slowly brought them closer together. One major factor in their growing bond was the support T'Pol gave Trip after the death of his sister. Another was the shared experience of discovering she and Trip had a daughter, (the child was a clone created without their permission, using their DNA) and the grief they shared as a result of the infant's death. ∎

TOUGH AS NAILS
CHARLES "TRIP" TUCKER

CAPTAIN'S LOG

NAME
Charles Tucker III

SPECIES
Human

BORN
2121, Panama City, Florida, Earth

FATHER
Charles Tucker II

STARFLEET DIVISION
Operations

BRIEFING
"Trip" Tucker was the unofficial morale officer on *Enterprise*, hosting regular movie nights

Commander Charles "Trip" Tucker was one of the first officers selected for the *Enterprise* crew. Part of Captain W.M. Jefferies' team on the NX Program that developed the ship, Tucker knew *Enterprise* inside and out and was already friends with Jonathan Archer, making him the ideal candidate for chief engineer. Prior to his posting on *Enterprise*, Tucker had visited just one planet beyond Earth, but he had a hunger to explore that would soon be fed.

His nickname reflected the fact that he was third in a triple line of Charles Tuckers, after his father and grandfather, and Trip was the name by which his crew mates knew him. His laid-back style and affable manner hid just how hard he had studied as a self-taught engineer, and how protective he was of *Enterprise*, and its engines in particular. His devotion to the ship was partly responsible for his initially tense relationship with

I'm the chief engineer. I spent years earning that position. I never had any intention of becoming a working mother!
Trip Tucker

Lieutenant Malcolm Reed, whose role as armory officer sometimes conflicted with Tucker's needs in engineering. The two eventually became friends in spite of Reed's buttoned-up manner, which was the opposite of Tucker's own.

Life and death

One of the strangest experiences of Tucker's life took place soon after *Enterprise* left Earth for the first time. An innocent encounter with Ah'len, a female Xyrillian led to him being the first Human male in recorded history to become pregnant. He had not been aware of the genetic transfer that caused the pregnancy, and it transpired that he was not the father, but merely the host. Yet he carried the unborn child, a girl, until she could be safely transfered to a Xyrillian host. Several years later, Tucker had another baby in unusual circumstances when his DNA and that of Subcommander T'Pol were unlawfully used to create a child. Part of a failed attempt to stir up xenophobic feeling by the terrorist group Terra Prime, the Human/Vulcan child did not survive, but lived long enough to bring Tucker and T'Pol closer together.

It's a girl! Surprised by Tucker's cross-species pregnancy, Ah'len scans his chest and discovers the embryo growing there is female.

Tucker's sister, Elizabeth, was among the seven million people killed in the Xindi attack on Earth in 2153. On the following mission to locate the Xindi superweapon, Tucker was plagued by sleepless nights and an intense desire for revenge. During this time, his relationship with T'Pol strengthened when she treated his insomnia using Vulcan neuropressure.

After ten years of service on *Enterprise* NX-01 (with a brief stint on *Columbia* NX-02), Tucker was killed in action on its final mission in 2161. Acting to protect Captain Archer when the ship was boarded, Tucker lured the intruders away to a plasma junction, where he set off an explosion. The blast killed the boarders and fatally injured Tucker. He died in *Enterprise*'s sickbay, knowing that his actions had saved his captain and ensured that Archer would be present at the ceremony to initiate the United Federation of Planets. ■

The life of Sim

In 2153, Trip Tucker was badly injured in an explosion on board *Enterprise*, while experimenting on the ship's warp core. Doctor Phlox identified extensive neural damage in the comatose officer, and proposed a controversial cure: a transplant of new brain tissue from a clone of Tucker.

The clone would be made by injecting Tucker's DNA into the body of a Lyssarrian desert larva. This would grow rapidly from a simple, egg-shaped creature into an identical copy of Tucker, but would live for just 15 days.

Captain Archer agreed to the procedure and a clone known as "Sim" was created. The ethical implications became clear as Sim grew from an infant into a child and then a man who shared Tucker's memories and personality. Sim planned to live by fleeing the *Enterprise*, leaving Tucker to die. When he chose to remain, he submitted to surgery willingly to save Tucker and the rest of the crew, who needed their crew mate's expertise. After his death, Sim was honored with a Starfleet funeral.

THE NAVY MAN
MALCOLM REED

Reed alert Reed established a range of new tactical protocols and security procedures on board *Enterprise*, many of which went on to inform regulations across the whole of Starfleet.

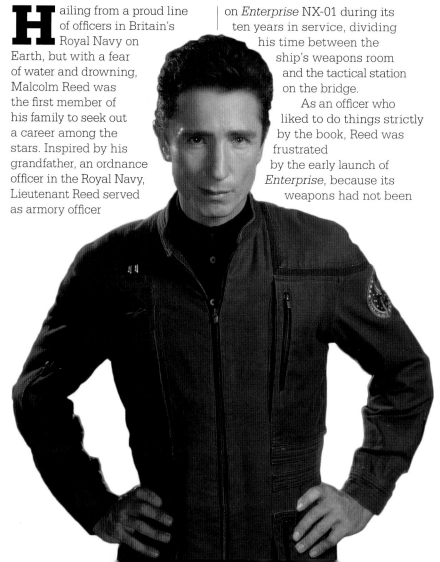

Hailing from a proud line of officers in Britain's Royal Navy on Earth, but with a fear of water and drowning, Malcolm Reed was the first member of his family to seek out a career among the stars. Inspired by his grandfather, an ordnance officer in the Royal Navy, Lieutenant Reed served as armory officer on *Enterprise* NX-01 during its ten years in service, dividing his time between the ship's weapons room and the tactical station on the bridge.

As an officer who liked to do things strictly by the book, Reed was frustrated by the early launch of *Enterprise*, because its weapons had not been

Reed and Section 31

Lieutenant Reed was always something of an enigma on board *Enterprise*, but none of his ship mates could have guessed the secret from his past that would come back to haunt him almost four years into his posting.

As a young ensign in Starfleet, Reed was excited to be recruited into Section 31, the secret "black ops" division of Earth security. It remains unknown what duties he carried out during that time, but he quickly lost his taste for covert operations, and chose to focus on his career as an officer.

Section 31 doesn't let go of its recruits so easily, though—and years later, in 2154, Reed's old supervisor contacted him with orders that required Reed to keep vital information from *Enterprise*'s captain and crew. Despite his misgivings, Reed carried out his orders—only to be exposed and detained in the brig. Reed committed to sever his link to Section 31, but later contacted them again with the permission of Captain Archer, in order to learn more about the terrorist group Terra Prime.

fully installed or tested prior to its first mission into Klingon space. In his first few years in charge of tactical functions on the ship, Reed was responsible for spearheading new defensive techniques and operational methods that Starfleet crews would follow for decades to come. After he and Commander "Trip" Tucker put their differences aside, the pair equipped the ship with phase cannons in a fraction of the time it would otherwise have taken the armory on Starfleet's Jupiter Station facility.

When it comes to our weapons frequencies, I wouldn't trust my own mother.
Malcolm Reed

Reed also perfected a stable electromagnetic barrier, effectively creating Starfleet's first functional force field, and developed tactical alerts that formed the basis of later red and yellow red alert protocols, after Captain Archer recommended their adoption across Starfleet. In the event of such an alert, the crew would report to battle stations and the ship was automatically made battle-ready—greatly improving response times that Reed had previously found inadequate.

Personal relations

A very private person, Reed was one of the last among the senior staff to ingratiate himself with his ship mates. He was reluctant even to share a meal with Captain Archer, because fraternizing with superior officers went against his natural instincts. He only chose to open up a little more following an encounter with a possible future version of *Enterprise*, where he learned that he had stayed single for his entire tour of duty.

Reed faced a different kind of challenge to his standing on board *Enterprise* in 2153, when the ship was working to defend Earth from the Xindi. As part of this mission, a MACO (Military Assault Command Operations) team was assigned to the ship, commanded by Major J. Hayes. Reed took the addition of the MACO team to *Enterprise* as a personal affront, particularly in light of the training sessions that Hayes recommended for the crew. The two men subsequently came to blows, resolving their tensions in the process. When Hayes was killed in the line of duty, Reed took command of the MACOs, leading them on a successful mission to destroy the Xindi superweapon that was threatening Earth. ∎

Power struggle T'Pol orders Reed and Hayes to plan the rescue of colleagues held captive by the Xindi, resulting in a clash between the two men.

SPACE BOOMER
TRAVIS MAYWEATHER

CAPTAIN'S LOG

NAME
Travis Mayweather

SPECIES
Human

BORN
2126, *E.C.S. Horizon*

MOTHER
Rianna Mayweather

STARFLEET DIVISION
Command

BRIEFING
Mayweather liked to find the zero-gravity "sweet spot" on board any ship, and then sleep in it

Born on a space freighter somewhere between the planet Draylax and the Vega colony, Travis Mayweather grew up among the stars and was a highly skilled pilot by the time he became helmsman on board *Enterprise*. He saw many worlds living and working on board the *E.C.S. Horizon*, but its journeys were long and slow. A top speed of warp 1.8 afforded the J-Class freighter little opportunity for exploration. For Mayweather to visit the star systems that he had dreamed of as a child, he would have to give up the life he knew and enrol in Starfleet on Earth.

Inspired by Starfleet captains of the past, and by his own father who was captain of the *Horizon*, Mayweather excelled in training. He earned the position of helm

I grew up on a J-Class...
And one thing I can tell you is that at warp 1.8, you got a lot of time on your hands between ports. That's how my parents wound up with me.
Travis Mayweather

officer on *Enterprise*, and was at the controls as the ship reached speeds previously unimaginable by Humankind.

Mayweather's achievements also went beyond the bridge, with the young ensign becoming one of the first Humans ever to land a shuttlepod on a comet. He was also part of the landing party that discovered the lost Earth colony of Terra Nova, an outpost that he had been fascinated to read about as a child. But one of his greatest challenges came when he had to maneuver *Enterprise* through a Romulan minefield—while one of the mines was attached to the ship, pinning Lieutenant Malcolm Reed to the outside of the hull.

Personal matters
Following the death of his father in 2153, Mayweather made a return trip to the *Horizon*, where his older brother, Paul, was now the captain. Tensions flared up between the two when the younger sibling applied his Starfleet knowledge to upgrade the freighter's systems, making it a more tempting target for pirates. The pair had to work together to fend off an attack on the ship they had grown up on, and overcame

Straight and steady

In naval tradition, the helmsman is responsible for steering a ship and maintaining a steady course. Similarly, the helm officer of a starship must be a skilled pilot and have strong and sturdy space legs.

Ensign Travis Mayweather had already clocked up more time in space than his captain when he came on board *Enterprise* NX-01. His spacefaring background gave him the dexterity and steely resolve needed to perform some of the most ambitious starship maneuvers ever attempted. During his flight training, Mayweather embraced a quote by 20th-century pilot Chuck Yeager: "I never let myself be afraid. I just focus on the dials and concentrate on flying."

The helm officer role evolved over time. By the 23rd century, the helm worked in concert with a separate navigational station. Centuries later, both posts were combined in one "flight controller" console.

their differences in the process, renewing their family bond.

When *Enterprise* was recalled to Earth for a meeting of the species that would found the Coalition of Planets, Mayweather was reunited with Gannet, a news reporter and

Locked up Mayweather is imprisoned by the Tandarans after straying into a military zone, and hatches a plan to free Suliban detainees from the complex.

former girlfriend of his. He gave her a tour of *Enterprise* and the pair rekindled their relationship, which had ended when he took up his post as helmsman. Gannet was later implicated as an agent of the terrorist organization Terra Prime, though Mayweather maintained that she was just doing her job as a reporter. In truth, she was working for Terra Prime, but on the orders of Starfleet Intelligence, working as a double agent to root out the real spy on board *Enterprise*.

Mayweather remained at the helm of *Enterprise* until the ship was decommissioned in 2161. For his next Starfleet posting, he was offered an assignment serving under Captain Stillwell, but Mayweather put off responding to the invitation until he learned where his captain of ten years, Jonathan Archer, was intending to serve next. ■

AN EAR FOR LANGUAGE
HOSHI SATO

CAPTAIN'S LOG

NAME
Hoshi Sato

BORN
2129, Kyoto, Japan, Earth

SPECIES
Human

STARFLEET DIVISION
Sciences

BRIEFING
Sato was skilled in the martial art of Aikido

When Starfleet revealed its plans for a starship capable of deep space travel, many officers competed for the chance to serve on board. Not so Hoshi Sato, however, who had a deep-seated fear of space travel. She had enrolled in Starfleet for the opportunities that it provided to study alien languages, but was very happy to do so on Earth. Yet Captain Jonathan Archer knew that *Enterprise* would need a very talented exolinguist to interpret the strange new languages they would encounter, and hand-picked Ensign Sato for the mission.

Sato was on leave, teaching as a professor of exolinguistics at the Amazon University in Brazil, when the launch of *Enterprise* NX-01 was moved forward, forcing her to cut her classes short. She was reluctant to abandon her students just two weeks before their final exams, but could not pass up the opportunity to become the first Human linguist to communicate with Klingons.

In the early days of *Enterprise*'s mission, Sato often had to combat her fear of space and the dangers it held. This led to occasional lapses in professionalism, which frustrated her more than anyone else on the

Hailing the communications officer

On a ship dedicated to seeking out new life and new civilizations, a communications specialist is a vital member of the bridge.

The comm officer is not only responsible for relaying incoming and outgoing transmissions to Starfleet Command and to other vessels, but also for facilitating comprehensible communications with other species, whether in person or via a viewscreen. In the early days of deep space travel, this called for a high level of expertise in exolinguistics (also known as xenolinguistics). The role required the study of morphology, phonology, syntax, and grammar, as well as knowledge of the full spectrum of electromagnetic and subspace frequencies. The mastery of universal translator technology was also essential, and remains so—though in 24th century the technology is so sophisticated and efficient that its use goes largely unnoticed by users.

Universal translator Ensign Hoshi Sato was the first Human to become fluent in Klingon, and could speak as many as 40 other languages.

> Anyone who tries to badmouth Captain Archer in front of me is going to get an earful—in any language they want.
> **Hoshi Sato**

Thanks to her varied experience interacting with new species while on board *Enterprise*, Sato was able to make significant advancements in universal translator technology. The device was still in its infancy when *Enterprise* launched in 2151, and would often fail completely—leaving the crew to rely solely on Sato's own expertise. But by 2155, the ensign had applied her skill and expertise to building a more reliable version of the translator, and in the 2160s she created the linguacode translation matrix, which remained in use 200 years later.

In her fourth year of service on *Enterprise*, Captain Archer put Sato in temporary command of the ship when the formation of the Coalition of Planets came under threat from the terrorist group Terra Prime. Her fear of space travel now far behind her, she skillfully managed the crisis from the captain's chair while an away team dealt with the terrorists' weapon. When Sato left Starfleet in the 2160s, she held the rank of lieutenant commander. ∎

ship. But with the support of her crew mates, she was never less than a first-rate communications officer, and by her second year on board, she was well-versed in almost 40 different languages.

Personal evolution
Sato's linguistic talents were in evidence from childhood, when she displayed a talent for picking up different languages. Years of private language tutoring led her to become isolated and made it

hard for her to make connections with people in later life—though her posting on *Enterprise* opened up her personal life as well as her academic horizons.

Sato's otherwise exemplary Starfleet record was marred by an incident during training in which she broke the arm of a commanding officer in a dispute over a game of poker. As a result, Sato was briefly discharged, but was allowed to return on probation because of her invaluable language skills.

THE DENOBULAN DOCTOR
PHLOX

CAPTAIN'S LOG

NAME
Phlox

SPECIES
Denobulan

BORN
Denobula

OCCUPATION
**Chief medical officer,
Enterprise NX-01
(member of Interspecies
Medical Exchange)**

BRIEFING
**Dr. Phlox holds academic
degrees in botanical
pharmacology, dentistry,
hematology, psychiatry
pharmacology, and
veterinary medicine**

The inclusion of Phlox as one
of just two non-Humans
among the *Enterprise* NX-
01 crew was largely a case of "right
place, right time." As a member of
the Interspecies Medical Exchange,
the Denobulan doctor was based
at Starfleet Medical on Earth when

Alien tongue Characteristics of
Denobulan physiology include long
tongues, wide smiles, striped toenails,
and ridges along the head and back.

an injured Klingon was brought in
for treatment. The launch date of
Enterprise was brought forward in
order to return the Klingon to his
Homeworld, and Captain Jonathan
Archer found himself in urgent need
of a chief medical officer. Based on
his skillful treatment of the Klingon
patient, Phlox was offered the post
for the initial mission and—on its
successful completion—signed up
for the ongoing journey.

Dr. Phlox's home planet,
Denobula, was noted among
Humans for its social structures
that markedly differed from those
of Earth. Having multiple spouses

was the norm, and Phlox himself
had three wives, each of whom had
three husbands. When one of Phlox's
wives, Feezal, made romantic
advances towards Commander
Charles "Trip" Tucker, the doctor
encouraged his crew mate to pursue
the relationship, in keeping with the
open nature of Denobulan marriages.

One of Phlox's most formative
experiences as a doctor occurred
many years before his assignment
to *Enterprise*, shortly after he had
obtained his medical degree. As
one of the first doctors on the scene
after a deadly explosion on a cargo

I must admit, I wasn't
planning to stay this long,
but the opportunity to
observe your species on
their first deep-space venture
has proven irresistible.
Phlox

Phlox's menagerie

Dr. Phlox's sickbay on *Enterprise* challenged conventional medical thinking, and played host to an array of exotic creatures the likes of which the Human crew had never seen before.

A star-shaped osmotic eel was Phlox's way to cauterize wounds, and he used Regulan bloodworms to filter toxins from the blood. He kept an Altarian marsupial for its valuable droppings, which he said were an unparalleled source of regenerative enzymes.

Phlox once transplanted the pituitary gland of a Calrissian chameleon into Captain Archer's dog, Porthos, to save his life. He also injected Commander "Trip" Tucker's DNA into a Lyssarian desert larva, in order to create a clone of the officer to serve as his own life-saving donor.

Phlox's diverse menagerie also included tribbles, which he used as food for other animals, and a Pyrithian bat, which he kept primarily as a pet.

ship, he saw many crew members that had been killed, including at least 17 dead on the bridge alone. His broad medical experience also included time working in a refugee camp on the planet Matalas, and in the Denobulan Infantry, but he was not outwardly jaded by his long career, retaining a genial and optimistic bedside manner.

Medical practices

Medical ethics on Denobula in the 22nd century were not identical to, but were fundamentally the same as, those on Earth. In 2154, Phlox admitted to two occasions during his 40-year career when he carried out practices that he considered unethical—which may or may not have included the cloning of Trip Tucker the previous year, an act which saved Tucker's life at the expense of the clone. Phlox's methods were certainly unorthodox by Human standards, and made full use of his many qualifications, including six degrees in veterinary medicine. He devised unusual treatments for various conditions, but sometimes refused to perform procedures on unfamiliar species if he could not be confident that his intervention would be of benefit.

During his fourth year with *Enterprise*, Phlox was kidnapped and made to work on a cure for a plague afflicting the Klingon Empire. The airborne illness had evolved from Klingon experiments to create genetically enhanced "Augments" of the kind that had caused Earth's Eugenics Wars in the 20th century. Thanks in part to his experience with Human Augments earlier that year, Phlox was able to reach a cure alongside a Klingon doctor called Antaak.

Like his Vulcan crew mate, Subcommander T'Pol, Phlox chose to remain on *Enterprise* during Earth's conflict with the Xindi, even though his species was not directly involved. He continued to act as chief medical officer on the ship for the entire ten years of its active service, including the duration of the Earth-Romulan war—which once again did not involve the Denobulans. When *Enterprise* was

Family doctor Phlox fathered three sons and two daughters with his wives before joining the crew of *Enterprise*.

decommissioned in 2161, Phlox returned to Earth, where he and his wives witnessed the historic ceremony that led to the United Federation of Planets. ∎

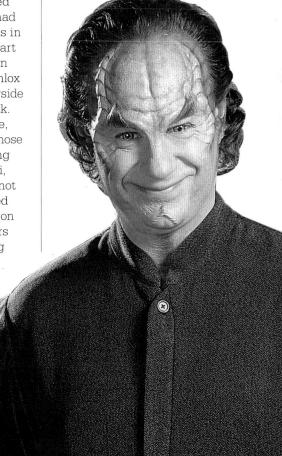

A STAR TO STEER HER BY
U.S.S. ENTERPRISE NCC-1701

CAPTAIN'S LOG

NAME
U.S.S. Enterprise

REGISTRY
NCC-1701

CLASS
Constitution

LENGTH
289 meters

DECKS
23

LAUNCH DATE
2245

BRIEFING
In standard operation, the Enterprise carried between 203 and 430 personnel, but could function with as few as five crew members

Sharing a name with the first Earth starship designed for deep space exploration, the *U.S.S. Enterprise* NCC-1701 began its voyages in the mid-23rd century and went on to become one of the most famous vessels in Starfleet's illustrious history. While under the stewardship of Captain James Kirk, the *Enterprise* journeyed to the far distant corners of the Alpha and Beta Quadrants; crossed the Great Barrier at the center of the Galaxy and the galactic barrier at its edge; and traveled through time on more than one occasion. Its crew made first contact with more new species and new civilizations than any of their contemporaries, and took the Starfleet oath to heart: boldly going where no one had gone before.

Design and capabilities

The *U.S.S. Enterprise* was a Class-1 Heavy Cruiser—one of at least a dozen, near identical, *Constitution*-class starships in the fleet. It takes its design cues from *Enterprise* NX-01, Captain Jonathan Archer's ship from a century before, with a saucer section containing the bridge and crew quarters, and a secondary or engineering hull housing the warp engines that power the port and starboard propulsion nacelles. To the fore of the secondary hull is the long-range sensor and navigational deflector, with the hangar deck or shuttlebay at the stern.

The command hub of the ship is the bridge, located on Deck 1—on top of the saucer section. At its center is the captain's chair, facing the main viewer from its slightly elevated position behind the helm control station. From this and the other bridge stations that surround the captain's chair, bridge officers can pilot the ship; fire its weapons; analyze sensor readings and other data; and send, receive, and monitor external communications.

Though the *Enterprise* is an exploratory vessel, it is equipped to defend against any threats it may encounter. A dozen phaser banks are located at various points on the ship, allowing the crew to target directed energy beams on all sides, above and below the vessel. Self-

propelling photon torpedoes can also be launched from six torpedo tubes—deploying a combination of matter and antimatter to highly explosive effect.

By the 23rd century, transporter science was far advanced from the developmental technology used on *Enterprise* NX-01. Beaming to and from the dedicated transporter room was the standard way to board or leave the ship—though occasional

malfunctions did still occur, with sometimes fascinating results. The shuttlebay provided an alternative means of transport, with 12 short-range craft including four Class-F shuttles with space for seven crew members or passengers.

Other design advancements for the *Constitution*-class *Enterprise* included tractor beams and a more powerful engine capable of taking the vessel to warp 9. The ship was

Designed to defend The *Enterprise* fires its forward phaser banks, located in front of the vessel's sensor dome on the underside of the saucer section.

updated at intervals throughout its working life, with upgrades made to its exterior and internal systems. In 2270, the *Enterprise* underwent a total refit, including a new bridge module, a new vertical-core warp engine, and new warp nacelles. »

Shuttlecraft of the *U.S.S. Enterprise*

Like other Federation starships of its size, the *Enterprise* NCC-1701 was equipped with a complement of shuttlecraft. Used for journeys outside of transporter range—or when beaming is unavailable or inadvisable—these small, highly maneuverable vessels are also essential for close examination of spaceborne phenomena.

The ship had 12 shuttlecraft, with names including *Columbus*, *Copernicus*, and *Einstein*. The *Galileo*, registry NCC-1701/7, was destroyed in service in 2267 and replaced by the *Galileo II*.

The names *Copernicus* and *Galileo* were also used for two shuttlecraft on the *Enterprise* NCC-1701-A. The former was destroyed and the latter badly damaged in 2287, during the *Enterprise*'s encounter with the renegade Vulcan Sybok. Years later, the *Enterprise* NCC-1701-D also had a shuttlecraft *Galileo*.

In the timeline created by the Temporal Incursion of 2233, the *Enterprise* NCC-1701 had an increased quota of shuttlecraft with names such as *Gilliam*, *Takayama*, and *Warrant*.

The five-year missions

Initially commanded by Captain Robert April and then Captain Christopher Pike, the *Enterprise* was in operation for almost two decades before Captain James T. Kirk took command in 2264. It was under his stewardship that the vessel undertook its final and most historic five-year mission, visiting more than 70 planets and making first contact with around two-dozen alien species, including the Organians, the Metrons, the First Federation, and the Gorn. The *Enterprise*'s science officer and second-in-command during this time was Commander Spock, who had also served on the ship during both of Captain Pike's five-year missions. The friendship that developed between Kirk and his first officer became fundamental to the success of the *Enterprise*'s often perilous mission, and is still regarded as one of the greatest and most respected partnerships in Starfleet history.

Among the ship's most notable encounters during Kirk's five-year mission were several engagements with the Imperial Klingon Fleet, and the first contact with Romulans for more than a century. The crew was responsible for discovering the first known silicon-based life-forms, and for destroying a giant "doomsday machine" capable of destroying entire planets. The ship was also the first to cross the Galactic Barrier that surrounds the Milky Way; the first to travel back through time using the slingshot effect; and the first to make contact with the alternative reality known as the mirror universe.

One event during the mission that would come back to haunt the crew was the discovery of the *S.S. Botany Bay*—an Earth sleeper ship launched in the late 20th century. Inside, the body of Khan Noonien Singh—a genetically engineered warlord from the Eugenics Wars—was held in suspended animation, along with those of his followers.

Cross that bridge The bridge of the *Constitution*-class *U.S.S. Enterprise* NCC-1701 follows the core design established with the NX-01 and continuing down the line for centuries to come.

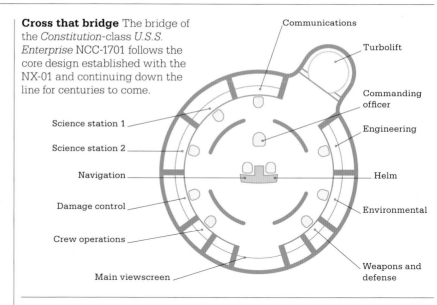

- Communications
- Turbolift
- Commanding officer
- Engineering
- Helm
- Environmental
- Weapons and defense
- Science station 1
- Science station 2
- Navigation
- Damage control
- Crew operations
- Main viewscreen

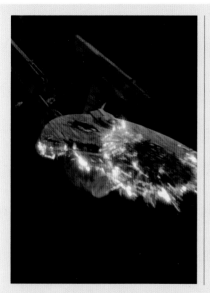

Code 0-0-0-Destruct-0

All Federation starships are equipped with an auto-destruct mechanism for use in extreme circumstances—most usually to prevent the vessel from falling into enemy hands. The destruct sequence is computer-controlled and can only be initiated by the commanding officer along with two other senior officers—each with their own memorized alpha-numeric authorization code.

In *Constitution*-class ships, the auto-destruct mechanism triggers explosive charges located throughout the vessel—starting on the bridge and spreading throughout the saucer section. Kirk started and aborted the *U.S.S. Enterprise*'s 30-second auto-destruct countdown in 2269 to thwart an attempted takeover of the vessel by Bele, an official from the planet Cheron. In 2285, a 60-second countdown ran to completion when the ship was commandeered by Klingons and abandoned by its Starfleet crew. As the ship exploded, Admiral Kirk and his crew watched sadly from the surface of the nearby Genesis planet, then beamed to safety aboard the virtually empty Klingon vessel orbiting above.

Burning bridges A Klingon boarding party is caught unawares by charges on the self-destructing *Enterprise* bridge.

The crew revived Khan, who later awakened the other sleepers, and with them, tried to take over the ship. When Khan was defeated, Kirk offered him and his followers exile on the uninhabited planet of Ceti Alpha V, where they could establish their own colony. Khan accepted the offer, which Kirk later came to regret.

Further voyages

When the *Enterprise* completed its five-year mission, it returned home to Earth, where the newly promoted Admiral Kirk recommended Willard Decker as its next captain. Decker oversaw a complete refit of the ship and was preparing to command its maiden voyage when Kirk resumed command in order to investigate an enormous alien object on course for Earth. Decker remained on board as first officer, but was recorded as missing following the mission, along with Lieutenant Ilia.

By 2285, Spock, now a captain, commanded the *Enterprise* while it served as a training vessel for Starfleet cadets. Kirk was on board when he received a message about a threat to the Federation's top secret Genesis Device, and

assumed command at Spock's insistence, setting course for the space station Regula I. En route, the ship was badly damaged in an attack by the *U.S.S. Reliant*— a Starfleet ship under the control of Khan Noonien Singh. Khan captured and detonated the Genesis Device, killing himself. He had hoped to destroy Kirk's ship, too, but *Enterprise* was able to escape the Genesis Wave as a result of Spock's work to reestablish warp power—exposing himself to fatal levels of radiation in the process. Spock's funeral was carried out on board the *Enterprise*, and his body was committed to space in a torpedo tube.

The end of an era

After 40 years' service, the battle-damaged *Enterprise* was set to be decommissioned. But when Kirk learned that there was a chance to reunite Spock's *katra*—his "living soul", which the Vulcan had stored within Doctor McCoy's mind— with what remained of his physical form, he sought Starfleet's permission to take the ship on one final mission to retrieve Spock's body. Kirk's request was denied— so he and his senior staff stole the *Enterprise* from spacedock. They found Spock alive on the newly formed Genesis planet, thanks to the revitalizing powers of the Genesis Wave, but came into conflict with a Klingon ship and its crew, who were eager to learn the secrets of the Genesis "weapon." Rather than let the *Enterprise* fall into enemy hands, Kirk and his skeleton crew had no choice but to initiate its self-destruct sequence—sending the ship to a fiery end. ∎

NCC-1701 Timeline

c. 2245
U.S.S. Enterprise
NCC-1701 launched from San Francisco Fleet Yards in Earth orbit, under command of Captain Robert April.

2264
***Enterprise* launches**
again under command of Captain James T. Kirk, begins historic five-year mission of unprecedented discovery, first contacts, and diplomacy.

c. 2282
Admiral Kirk retires
(temporarily); Captain Spock commands *Enterprise* as training vessel for Starfleet cadets.

2286
***Enterprise* NCC-1701-A**
commissioned; shakedown begins under command of demoted Captain Kirk; months of repairs and refits ensue.

2240   2300

c. 2251
Captain Christopher
Pike takes command of *Enterprise* for first of two five-year tours of duty. Personnel includes Science Officer Spock.

2270–2271
***Enterprise* begins**
extensive redesign and refit; command passes to Willard Decker. Kirk resumes command in V'Ger crisis; Decker goes missing.

2285
***Enterprise* significantly**
damaged in engagement with Khan Noonien Singh. 40-year history ends in self-destruct sequence over Genesis planet.

2293
***Enterprise*-A becomes**
integral in Khitomer peace talks with Klingons. Subsequently ordered back to Earth for decommissioning.

BY ANY OTHER NAME

U.S.S. ENTERPRISE NCC-1701-A

CAPTAIN'S LOG

NAME
U.S.S. Enterprise

REGISTRY
NCC-1701-A

CLASS
Constitution

LENGTH
305 meters

LAUNCH DATE
2286

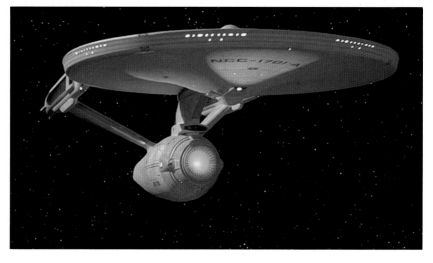

A fter stealing and blowing up the *Enterprise* NCC-1701, Admiral James Kirk and his senior staff faced a court-martial on Earth. They found the planet in turmoil, and took a Klingon ship back in time to save Earth from the actions of an unidentified alien probe. On their return to the 23rd century, their heroism earned them a reprieve from disciplinary action—with the exception of Kirk who was demoted to captain and given the command of a new ship: the *U.S.S. Enter*prise NCC-1701-A.

Though the new ship was very different on the inside, the exterior was almost identical to the NCC-1701, and made Kirk and his crew feel as if they had come home.

The *Enterprise*-A's shakedown cruise was not an auspicious event, as the ship was not fully prepared to leave spacedock. Chief engineer Montgomery Scott estimated that it would take weeks to bring the ship up to spec, but it was pressed into service while still undergoing repairs. Its first mission saw it penetrate the Galactic Core at the heart of the Milky Way—and become the first vessel ever to return from within it.

Six years later, the *Enterprise*-A was implicated in an attack on the

Two of a kind The *Enterprise*-A was almost identical to the refitted version of the *Enterprise* destroyed in 2285.

ship of Klingon Chancellor Gorkon. The attack was proved to be part of a conspiracy to undermine peace talks between the Federation and the Klingons. The *Enterprise*-A raced to the planet Khitomer, where Kirk and his crew exposed the conspiracy and saved the life of the Federation President. With the ship due to be decommissioned, Kirk ordered one last heading: "Second star to the right, and straight on till morning." ■

A NEW ENTERPRISE
U.S.S. ENTERPRISE NCC-1701 (KELVIN TIMELINE)

CAPTAIN'S LOG

NAME
U.S.S. Enterprise

REGISTRY
NCC-1701

CLASS
Constitution

LAUNCH DATE
2258 (Kelvin Timeline)

Following the unprovoked attack in 2233 on the *U.S.S. Kelvin* by a mystery ship—later identified as the 24th-century Romulan mining vessel *Narada*—Starfleet reallocated its resources to develop vessels better equipped for defense. This led to the *U.S.S. Enterprise* NCC-1701 launching in 2258 under Captain Christopher Pike—rather than 13 years earlier under Captain Robert April, as had been the case in the undisrupted timeline. The additional time was used to perfect significant design advancements, affecting both the exterior and interior look of the ship.

The *Narada*'s second attack on the Federation precipitated the ship's launch, when it was one of several starships sent to the planet Vulcan with emergency crews augmented by Starfleet Academy cadets. The *Enterprise* was the only ship not to be destroyed by the *Narada*, though Captain Pike was captured and tortured on board the Romulan ship, requiring first Commander Spock and then Acting Lieutenant James Kirk to take command of *Enterprise*. After Kirk and Spock rescued Pike and destroyed the *Narada*, Kirk was promoted to *Enterprise* captain and chose Spock as his first officer.

The next year, the *Enterprise* was badly damaged when it was attacked by the *U.S.S. Vengeance* in an attempt to suppress the truth about a conspiracy within Starfleet. The ship was saved by the actions of Captain Kirk, and the conspiracy was exposed. The *Enterprise* was then repaired in time for Kirk and his crew to embark upon a five-year mission of deep space exploration. ∎

Reconstitution class The Temporal Incursion of 2233 led to the building of a larger, more robust *U.S.S. Enterprise*.

OUT SAVING THE GALAXY
JAMES T. KIRK

CAPTAIN'S LOG

NAME
James Tiberius Kirk

SPECIES
Human

BORN
2233, Riverside, Iowa, Earth

BORN (Kelvin Timeline)
2233, *U.S.S. Kelvin*, near the Federation/Klingon Border

STARFLEET DIVISION
Command

BRIEFING
Kirk's middle name "Tiberius" comes from his paternal grandfather

Command chair James Kirk's seat on the bridge of the *U.S.S. Enterprise*, a *Constitution*-class starship, from where he monitors all operations on the ship.

James (Jim) Tiberius Kirk is considered one of the greatest captains in Starfleet history. Though he calls himself "a soldier, not a diplomat," his skill in dealing with even the most challenging species of the universe would prove otherwise. This is the reason that the logs of Captain James T. Kirk's missions are required reading for Starfleet Academy cadets serving into the 24th century.

Early career

Kirk excelled as a student at Starfleet Academy, despite facing constant bullying from an Irish upperclassman named Finnegan during his first year. The highlight of Kirk's education was becoming the only cadet ever to beat the *Kobayashi Maru* simulation—an exercise that tested a cadet in the role of captain. Kirk reprogrammed the scenario to ensure his victory, and although this was cheating, he earned a commendation for original thinking. Kirk served on board the *U.S.S. Republic* before being posted on the *U.S.S. Farragut* following his graduation.

In his personal life, Kirk became involved with Dr. Carol Marcus and they had a child named David. But professional obligations kept the couple apart and they ultimately ended their relationship as Kirk rapidly rose through the ranks to take command of the *U.S.S. Enterprise* NCC-1701 by the age of 32. Jim Kirk's success, however, kept him from seeing young David.

Fearless leader One of the most highly-decorated captains of Starfleet, Kirk was a bold leader, often bending the rules for the greater good.

Kirk enjoyed romancing women. One significant relationship took place 300 years before he was born, the result of a journey into the past through the Guardian of Forever—but he had to let his love die to avoid altering the timeline.

Kirk's bold command style often saw him rushing into danger, while at the same time doing everything possible to protect his ship and crew. Kirk repeatedly fought off various malevolent entities attempting to take over his ship and, occasionally, control of his body. He played cat and mouse with a Romulan, tangled with Klingons, and single-handedly fought off a Gorn.

Despite his many successes, Kirk was also the first Starfleet officer to face a court martial when he was charged with the death of the *Enterprise* records officer Lieutenant Commander Finney. Kirk was exonerated when it was discovered that Finney »

Like father, like son

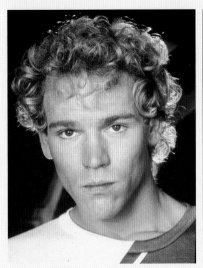

James Kirk was fortunate to know his father, though in his adult years he suffered the loss of his brother, George, on the planet Deneva in 2267. Later, however, the death of another family member whom he knew only briefly proved far more devastating.

Prior to his posting on the *Enterprise*, Kirk had a relationship with molecular biologist Dr. Carol Marcus which gave them a son, David. Jim and Carol's demanding career paths prevented them from ever being a couple, so at Carol's behest Jim stayed away, allowing Carol to raise David on her own, rather than have their son "chasing through the universe with his father."

David Marcus became a scientist and joined his mother's research team. Father and son were finally reunited some 20 years later and managed to form a bond. But their short time together came to a cruel end when the heroic young man was killed by Klingons. The tragedy led to Kirk's deep despair and a resentment toward Klingons that would last for many years.

Court-martial Charged with criminal negligence, Kirk faced a court-martial with the ship's computer as a witness.

had faked his death to frame the captain in a personal vendetta dating back to their time together on the *Republic*.

Following the *Enterprise's* first successful five-year mission, Kirk was promoted to rear admiral with a posting at Starfleet Headquarters. But Kirk was an explorer at heart and his desk job could not compete with the call of space. He returned to action when the Federation was threatened and little could keep him from the captain's chair.

Kirk returned to command the *Enterprise* when the highly

intelligent superhuman Khan Noonien Singh resurfaced. Although Kirk bested his old foe, he lost his best friend Spock in the process. The Vulcan sacrificed his life to save the *Enterprise*, embracing the Vulcan philosophy that "the needs of the many outweigh the needs of the few." Kirk then masterminded the theft of the *Enterprise* for an unsanctioned rescue mission to return Spock's living spirit—his *katra*—to his homeworld. Though the mission ultimately reunited him with his reborn first officer, it cost him his ship and the life of his son, David, who was killed by a Klingon raiding party. Kirk was punished by Starfleet for his actions by being demoted to captain, but was then rewarded for saving the world by awarding him the captaincy of the *U.S.S. Enterprise* NCC-1701-A.

After his retirement from Starfleet and while a guest at the launch of the *Enterprise*-B, Kirk was lost and presumed dead during a rescue mission. However, he had managed to survive, suspended in time in the nexus until he was called on to aid the captain of the *Enterprise*-D years later. This time, Kirk actually did give his life to stop a madman bent on gaining access to that nexus, which saved millions of lives.

Captain Kirk, I presume?
There's only one Captain James Kirk, but the Galaxy has spawned its fair share of imitators, including his similar-looking brother, two transporter duplicates (each with one half of Kirk's personality), and at least three identical imposters.

Passive Kirk created by transporter accident (2266)

Aggressive Kirk created by transporter accident (2266)

Android Kirk duplicate created by Roger Korby (2266)

Kirk's brother, George Samuel Kirk (2267)

Garth of Izar morphed to resemble Kirk (2268)

Shapeshifter Martia morphed to resemble Kirk (2293)

The Temporal Incursion
Growing up without his father following the Temporal Incursion of 2233 had a significant impact on young Jim Kirk's life. After his mother remarried, he was raised in Iowa on Earth, where he developed a rebellious streak and a contentious relationship with his step-father. As a boy, he stole his step-dad's classic car, taking it for a joyride that ended with the vehicle careening off a cliff. It was not

Against all odds...

When events in 2233 were altered by a bizarre twist of fate and time, young Jim Kirk's early life took a decidedly different course than it would have otherwise. But that life was made possible by the heroic actions of his father.

Lt. Commander George Kirk was first officer aboard the *U.S.S. Kelvin* when it suffered an unprovoked attack by a Romulan mining ship from the future. Kirk was left in command when Captain Robau traveled to the enemy vessel and was killed. Robau's last orders to Kirk were to evacuate the crew and use the auto-pilot to ram the starship into the aggressor, and then evacuate himself. But when the time came to execute those orders, Kirk found that the auto-pilot function had been destroyed. Kirk had no choice but to stay on board and operate the ship manually during its kamikaze strike. George Kirk may have been captain for just 12 minutes, but by sacrificing himself, he saved the lives of 800 crew members, including his wife and newborn son.

the only occasion that ended with Jim Kirk in police custody.

By the time Kirk reached the age of enlistment, he was—as Starfleet Captain Christopher Pike half-jokingly described him—the only "genius-level repeat offender

In the driver's seat Kirk's heroic actions, which saved Captain Pike, earned him the promotion to captain.

in the Midwest." It was during that first encounter with the captain that Jim Kirk's life took a dramatic turn. Once Pike realized that Jim was the son of George Kirk, he challenged the hot-headed young man to live up to his father's legacy and join Starfleet Academy. Not one to resist a challenge, Kirk accepted.

On the shuttle to the Academy, Kirk met Dr. Leonard "Bones" McCoy, who would later serve with him on the *Enterprise*. Kirk's three years at the Academy saw him achieve academic excellence, but his brash manner and womanizing ways earned him a bad reputation. It was here that Kirk came across the man who would later become his first officer: the Vulcan, Spock.

Rejecting the idea of a "no-win scenario," Kirk reprogrammed the *Kobayashi Maru* test designed by Spock to achieve a successful resolution. In response, Spock had Kirk brought up on charges of cheating and he was placed on academic probation. If it hadn't been for an emergency on the planet Vulcan—and the quick thinking of McCoy—Kirk might have been drummed out of the

Your father was captain of a starship for twelve minutes. He saved 800 lives, including your mother's and yours. I dare you to do better.
Christopher Pike

service. Instead, he joined the crew of the *Enterprise*, rising very quickly to the rank of captain through an unusual set of circumstances following Captain Pike's capture by Romulans.

Kirk and his Vulcan first officer worked together to rescue Pike and save Earth from meeting the same fate as Spock's homeworld. As a result of his efforts, Pike recommended Kirk for command of the *Enterprise*. ∎

THE HIGHLY LOGICAL VULCAN
SPOCK

CAPTAIN'S LOG

NAME
Spock

SPECIES
Vulcan/Human

BORN
2230, ShiKahr, Vulcan

DIED & REBORN
2285

STARFLEET DIVISION
Sciences

BRIEFING
Full Vulcan name is far too difficult for Humans to pronounce

The inscrutable first officer of the *U.S.S. Enterprise* under James T. Kirk, Spock bridges two worlds as a Vulcan-Human hybrid. The child of the Vulcan Ambassador Sarek and Human Amanda Grayson, Spock grew up on his father's world. His struggle to suppress his emotions may have been more difficult than it was for full Vulcans, but over his lifetime he managed to embrace his Human side while maintaining a commitment to logical pursuits.

As a child, Spock's Human side made him an outsider among his peers. He had a difficult time fitting in despite his determination to learn the ways of his father's people. In contrast, his older Vulcan half-brother, Sybok, turned his back on the Vulcan teachings and was eventually cast out of society for rejecting the tenets of logic.

A Starfleet officer

Possibly due to his outsider status, Spock decided to enroll at Starfleet Academy rather than attend the Vulcan Science Academy, a decision that would put a strain on his relationship with his father for years to come. Spock went on to serve on the *Enterprise* under Captain Christopher Pike for over a decade before Kirk took command. While on the original five-year

True blue Spock showed exceptional loyalty to both of the captains he served under, Christopher Pike and James Kirk.

mission under Kirk, Spock—in a tremendous display of loyalty— diverted the *Enterprise* to help his badly injured former captain. Risking court-martial, Spock returned Pike to the planet Talos IV where its inhabitants could use their mental powers to create convincing illusions that would allow the captain to live out the rest of his life free of the limitations of his disfigured body.

Spock was later forced to briefly return to his homeworld of Vulcan

Vulcan salute The V-shaped hand gesture is used by Vulcans when greeting or bidding farewell.

due to a biological urge to mate with his betrothed, T'Pring. When T'Pring announced that she did not wish to wed Spock and invoked the right of ritual combat, she chose Kirk as her champion.

Spock was manipulated to believe that he killed his captain in combat, and the shock helped suppress the overwhelming biological urges affecting him emotionally. Once he had regained composure, Spock and T'Pring agreed to part, since Spock could »

Fascinating.
Spock

"This simple feeling..."

Spock's spiritual nature has always been essential to his identity, but Spock has struggled with it throughout his life. Despite his dual parentage, in his youth he committed to put aside Human emotion and follow the Vulcan path of pure logic. Accordingly, after two decades in Starfleet, Spock returned to his home planet Vulcan to undergo *Kolinahr*, the ritual purging of all remaining emotion. But that process was interrupted when his Human side was stirred by another entity's consciousness, which was on a similar quest for answers.

When Spock later mind-melded with the living machine named V'Ger, he realized the barrenness of pure logic, and that emotions play an important role in the richness of life. Spock comes to appreciate the beauty and mystery of simple feelings, like the embrace of a friend.

During the course of his lifetime, Spock seems to have found that his answers lie in an integration of both Vulcan and Human ways. As he advised his younger self in 2258, sometimes one must "put aside logic" and just "do what feels right."

> Of my friend, I can only say this: Of all the souls I have encountered in my travels, his was the most... human.
> **James T. Kirk**

Fight to the death As T'Pring's nominated champion, Jim Kirk was forced to battle his friend Spock.

see the logic of living separate lives given that T'Pring was interested in another man.

Following the *Enterprise's* encounter with V'Ger, Spock was promoted to captain of the *Enterprise* while the ship served as a training vessel for Academy cadets. He stepped aside to allow Kirk to resume command in order to investigate Carol Marcus's communication about Starfleet's secret Genesis project. Unfortunately, Kirk realized too late that he was being led into a trap set by the superhuman Khan Noonien

Singh. During the mission, Spock gave his life when he exposed himself to the deadly radiation of the dilithium reactor room to restart the warp engines. His sacrifice allowed the ship and its crew to flee the blast radius of the experimental Genesis Device.

Unbeknownst to the crew, Spock's *katra* (living spirit) had been transferred into Dr. McCoy

before he died. Not long after, the Vulcan's body was launched into space, landing on the newly formed Genesis Planet. The planet, created by the experimental terra-forming device, had the unusual effect of regenerating Spock, but without his *katra,* he was a shell of his former self. Kirk and the *Enterprise* senior staff took Spock to Vulcan, where a gifted high priestess was able to reunite body with soul, effectively bringing Spock back from the dead. Kirk convinced the Vulcan that sometimes the needs of the one outweigh the needs of the many.

24th century Spock
Almost a century after his final mission on the *Enterprise*, Spock, now a Federation Ambassador, took on a secret mission to reunite the Vulcans and Romulans. This later brought him into contact with the crew of the *Enterprise*-D, and Captain Jean-Luc Picard who informed Spock of the death of his father, Sarek. Spock performed a mind-meld with Picard, which gave him some insight into his father's feelings for him, thanks to a previous telepathic bonding between Picard and Sarek. Once it was determined that Spock

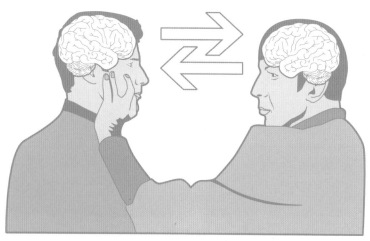

Mind-meld The Vulcan process of sharing thoughts requires physical contact and intense concentration, often achieved through ritual chanting.

would be safe with the Romulan underground, the *Enterprise*-D left him to continue his work.

In 2387, Spock developed a plan to inject red matter into a star that was about to go supernova and create a black hole to absorb the explosion. Although he succeeded in protecting the worlds of the Federation, he was unable to save the planet Romulus. A Romulan miner named Nero blamed Spock for the planet's destruction, and tried to attack the ambassador as both of their ships were dragged into the black hole Spock had made.

The Temporal Incursion

The black hole created by Spock sent both vessels back in time, triggered the Temporal Incursion of 2233, when Nero's ship emerged from the space-time phenomenon and began to make changes in the past. It took another 25 years for Spock to exit the black hole. During this time, his younger self experienced a childhood and adolescence very much like the one he'd already lived in his own unaltered timeline. Spock still dealt with childhood bullies, struggled with suppressing his Human emotions, and rejected the Vulcan Science Academy in favor of the Starfleet Academy.

It was after the elder Spock came through the black hole in 2258 that the younger Spock's life irrevocably changed. Nero planned to punish Spock by making him witness the destruction of his own planet, Vulcan. Realizing what was happening, the younger Spock rushed down to the planet to save his parents and the Vulcan elders, but could only watch helplessly as his mother lost her life on the crumbling world. The tragic event prompted an unusual angry outburst from Spock, convincing him that he was emotionally unstable, and to remove himself from command of the *Enterprise*.

Another major change wrought by the Temporal Incursion was in the relationship between Spock and Nyota Uhura. Although the pair seemed to occasionally flirt in the pre-incursion timeline, in the altered timeline they became emotionally involved while Uhura was still a cadet at the Academy.

Vulcan bond forged Spock and Kirk found common ground on an enemy ship while rescuing Captain Pike.

Spock's relationship with Jim Kirk was also different now, starting out quite antagonistically as he brought the cadet up on charges of cheating in the *Kobayashi Maru* test. Their subsequent posting together on the *Enterprise* saw them initially jockeying for a command position in a conflict between the hot-headed Kirk and the coldly logical Spock. They eventually overcame their differences, and when Kirk gave his life (temporarily) to save his ship and crew, Spock grieved openly at the loss of a "friend." ∎

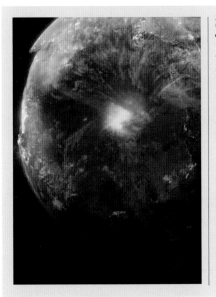

Saving the collective *katra*

Although the young Commander Spock was unable to save his home planet of Vulcan, he did succeed in preserving the essence of Vulcan culture, thanks to the unique telepathic abilities of his species.

Since ancient times, Vulcans have utilized their mind-melding technique to preserve the *katra*—or living spirit—of an individual before death by transferring it into another person or into a "katric ark." A katric ark can refer either to an individual artifact, or an entire chamber containing the collective knowledge of past souls—a chamber impenetrable to communications and even transporter beams.

When the destruction of their world was imminent, the elders of the Vulcan High Council gathered to retrieve that knowledge into themselves. Spock correctly predicted they would be unaware of the short time they had, so he beamed down to coax them out of the chamber and into transporter range. Most of the elders were saved by the *Enterprise*, but Spock's mother was killed when a cliff gave way beneath her.

THE OLD COUNTRY DOCTOR
DR. LEONARD "BONES" McCOY

For nearly 30 years, Dr. Leonard McCoy has served as the chief medical officer on ships that bore the name *Enterprise*. His service on the first *U.S.S. Enterprise* NCC-1701 began in 2266 under the command of Captain James Kirk, an officer who would become one of his closest friends in a crew that would come to be like family.

On the surface, McCoy has a fractious relationship with the ship's Vulcan first officer, Spock. The pair constantly bicker due to McCoy's more emotional personality versus Spock's logical demeanor. The doctor can often be heard boldly challenging the Vulcan's cold and detached nature, while Spock's commentary tends to be subtler, but equally biting. In truth, McCoy is as close to Spock as he is to Kirk, and they even spent shore leave together on a camping trip in 2287.

McCoy's relationship with technology is similarly conflicted. He celebrates the benefits of the medical advancements of his time, particularly compared with the methods practiced on Earth when he traveled back in time 300 years. Yet he is distrustful of other groundbreaking technology like transporters and androids. Still, he has considered the technologically advanced *Enterprise* his home for a considerably long time.

I'm a doctor! McCoy was ever quick to confirm that he is not a psychiatrist, physicist, or moon-shuttle conductor.

The real McCoy

A graduate of the University of Mississippi, McCoy faced one of his most difficult decisions early in his medical career when his father was stricken with a terminal disease. Rather than allowing his father to suffer, McCoy removed him from life support so that he could die in peace. Tragically, a cure for the illness was found shortly after and that fateful decision haunted McCoy for years to come.

McCoy was married for a time, though it ended before his posting on the *Enterprise*. Other romantic liaisons included a tryst with Emony Dax—a Trill symbiont— and a relationship with the future Mrs. Nancy Crater. On one mission, McCoy was reunited with the woman he believed was Nancy, but in reality it was the sole-surviving member of a species posing as his now-deceased former love.

McCoy faced many medical challenges during the first historic mission serving on the *Enterprise*, and was responsible for saving his crew mates on several occasions.

One of his own most notable personal health issues occurred when he was accidentally injected with a large dose of the chemical stimulant cordrazine. As a result, he suffered severe paranoid delusions that led to him leaping into a time portal and triggering a temporal disaster. Fortunately, Kirk and Spock were able to correct the damage and rectify the previously established timeline.

Later career

McCoy retired from Starfleet after the ship's initial five-year mission, but was conscripted back into service by Kirk when Earth came under threat from V'Ger, a space probe that developed a form of artificial sentience. As a member of the *Enterprise* crew once again, McCoy took part in many further adventures on the ship. One of the most emotionally challenging occurred during the crew's second encounter with the villainous Khan Noonien Singh, which led to the death of McCoy's friend and verbal sparring partner, Spock.

Spirited away Prior to his imminent death, Spock secretly transferred his *katra*, or living spirit, into Dr. McCoy.

Unbeknownst to McCoy, Spock used Vulcan techniques to render the doctor unconscious, transferring his *katra*—living spirit—into McCoy's mind so that it could be returned to Vulcan after Spock's death. Soon after the transfer, McCoy's behavior became erratic thanks to Spock's influence. After his return to Earth, he attempted to charter a ship to take him to the prohibited Genesis planet. At that point he was taken into Starfleet »

He's dead, Jim...
Leonard McCoy

The emotional argument

The success of the *Enterprise* missions under Kirk can be attributed not just to the confidence and charisma of her captain, but to a balanced consideration between the voices of logic and emotion. Dr. McCoy is the "old country doctor" with a home-spun warmth that contrasts starkly with Spock's cold intellect. Kirk values both perspectives in almost every situation where leadership is required.

Whether it is the bluntness of "Shut up Spock, we're rescuing you!" or the hyperbole of "My God, the man's talking about logic! We're talking about universal Armageddon," McCoy's passion—as irrational as it may seem at times—carries a truth that even Spock often cannot deny. Does one listen to the head, or the heart? The Kirk/Spock/McCoy dynamic proves the answer is yes, and yes.

custody. Once Kirk realized what had occurred, he and his crew broke McCoy out of lockup and traveled to the Genesis planet to retrieve Spock's surprisingly animate body and reunite it with Spock's soul.

For what ails you Despite having access to the most up-to-the-moment medical advances, the old country doctor continues to rely on his own brand of tried and tested remedies.

Mint Julep

Finagle's Folly

Romulan Ale

Baked Beans in Whiskey

Years later, McCoy was part of the delegation chosen to escort Klingon dignitaries to the Khitomer peace conference that would eventually unite the Federation with the Klingon Empire. Forces conspiring against the unification framed the *Enterprise* crew for the assassination of the Klingon chancellor Gorkon. When the doctor was unable to save the Klingon, he and Kirk were arrested for their involvement, placed on trial, and ultimately sentenced to the Klingon penal colony on the planetoid Rura Penthe. The *Enterprise* crew rescued McCoy and Kirk from their Klingon prison and discovered the true culprits— a cabal of disaffected officers, including Gorkon's own chief of staff, General Chang—clearing the men of their crimes.

Dr. McCoy finally left Starfleet with the rank of admiral. Though he was no longer in the service, the doctor still acted as a dignitary in ceremonial functions. On stardate 41153.7 at the age of 137, Admiral McCoy performed a walk-through inspection of the *U.S.S. Enterprise*-NCC-1701-D during its first mission. It was the latest starship to share the name of the vessels on which he had so proudly served.

> I'm a Doctor, not a brick layer!
> **Leonard McCoy**

The Temporal Incursion

Leonard McCoy's divorce was fresh on his mind when he enlisted in Starfleet years after the Temporal Incursion of 2233. He was still griping about the situation when he met Jim Kirk on the transport to Starfleet Academy. McCoy's friendship with Kirk developed during their time at the Academy with the good doctor often questioning his friend's rash decisions. When Kirk was finally threatened with expulsion and placed on inactive duty, it was McCoy's quick thinking that got the cadet onto the *Enterprise* as the ship was about to respond to a distress call from the planet Vulcan.

During the encounter with the Romulan mining vessel, the *Narada*, the *Enterprise*'s chief medical officer was killed and Dr. McCoy was promoted into the position.

Although McCoy vehemently disagreed with Spock's decision to maroon Kirk on a planet following the initial incident with the *Narada*, he did not stop his new captain. When Kirk returned to the ship and resumed leadership, McCoy was equally combative when Kirk's orders proved questionable, though he performed his role as instructed.

McCoy continued to serve as the ship's chief medical officer. He joined Kirk in rescuing a tribe on the planet Nibiru in what ultimately became a clear breach of the Prime Directive. During a later mission, while examining what was thought to be an experimental photon torpedo, McCoy accidentally activated the device and found that it housed a person in cryogenic stasis. The startling discovery helped explain the actions of the terrorist John Harrison, who was revealed to be Khan Noonien Singh.

McCoy's study of Khan's genetic makeup led to the discovery that his blood possessed near miraculous healing properties. When Kirk died after repairing the irradiated warp core reactor, McCoy injected him with a dose of Khan's blood. This totally unorthodox action saved Kirk's life, allowing the pair to continue together on future missions. ∎

> The ex wife took the whole damn planet in the divorce. All I've got left is my bones.
> **Leonard McCoy**

Blood and Bones McCoy takes a blood sample from Khan in order to find the source of his superhuman strength.

THE GREAT COMMUNICATOR
NYOTA UHURA

CAPTAIN'S LOG

NAME
Nyota Uhura

SPECIES
Human

BORN
2239, Africa, Earth

DIVISION
Operations

BRIEFING
***Uhura* means "freedom" in Nyota's native Swahili**

Nyota Uhura served as the communications officer on the *Enterprise* for close to 30 years. She is a talented linguist and technologically proficient, having trained to perform complex repairs of the communications system. On one occasion, Uhura rewired the entire communications system in order to cut through interference created by an explorer from the planet Pollux IV who claimed to be the Greek God Apollo. The *Enterprise* crew's initial five-year mission was Uhura's first Starfleet assignment.

Like most Starfleet officers, Uhura is capable of manning different stations on the bridge when the need arises, as she did when First Officer Spock was lost along with his crew on the shuttlecraft *Galileo* while studying the Murasaki 312 quasar. Uhura took control of the science station, leading the search for the spacecraft and locating the vessel and its surviving crew on the desolate planet, Taurus II.

In 2267, in a unique experience during her posting, Uhura was one of four senior members of staff transported to a parallel universe (or mirror universe) in which the Terran Empire exists. While there, she was forced to portray the role of her counterpart, getting

Hailing frequencies Uhura's role is key when in contact with unknown species.

Playing to a captive audience

Aside from her expertise in communications, Lt. Uhura brings to the *Enterprise* an accomplished singing voice, which she uses occasionally to soothe and entertain crew mates with cosmic love songs such as "Beyond Antares."

She has a knack for improvising lyrics. Once in the rec room she brought smiles by singing, "Oh on the *Starship Enterprise*, there's someone who's in Satan's guise," commenting on Spock's "devilish" sex appeal—as Spock himself accompanied her on the Vulcan lute. She then playfully teased young Charles Evans with "Oh Charlie's Our New Darling."

Uhura's talent has proven tactically useful. On the planet Nimbus III during the Paradise City crisis, she lured a lookout party away from their horses by singing "The Moon's a Window to Heaven." When the party was ambushed by Kirk she quipped, "Hello boys. I've always wanted to play to a 'captive' audience."

closer to the alternate version of Hikaru Sulu in an attempt to gain much-needed information, while still keeping the officer at arm's length. What she learned from her covert investigation aided the displaced landing party's return to their own universe.

Like many of the *Enterprise* crew, on several occasions Uhura fell under the influence of mind control during the initial five-year mission. In one such instance, she was forced to kiss her captain while being manipulated by telepathic beings. Another time, her mind was totally wiped by the Nomad space probe, requiring Dr. McCoy to assist her in being completely retrained in her memories. She disobeyed direct orders on another occasion when she disabled the communications panel while under the influence of plant spores from the planet Omicron Ceti III.

On stardate 4523.3, Uhura accepted a gift of a tribble from a trader named Cyrano Jones, but was unaware of the furry creature's high reproductive rate when she brought it back to the ship. Uhura unintentionally became responsible for an infestation as the tribble count multiplied rapidly. Fortunately, the crew found a humane way to dispose of them.

Uhura continued to serve on the *Enterprise* through its final mission at the Khitomer peace conference where she was instrumental in revealing a plot to sabotage the proceedings. At the time, she was supposed to be chairing a seminar at Starfleet Academy when Spock called her into service—along with the rest of the command crew—for the historic peace negotiations.

Mind wipe The space probe Nomad boarded the *Enterprise* and performed a mind wipe on Uhura.

The Temporal Incursion

The specific experiences that resulted in changes to Uhura's life path following the Temporal Incursion of 2233 are difficult to quantify, but there is no question that her life was altered prior to being stationed on the *Enterprise*. This was evident in her personal relationship with Spock, which began while she was still a Starfleet Academy cadet and he was one of her instructors. Though she had a mild flirtation with the *Enterprise* first officer prior to the Temporal Incursion, it was more a good-natured teasing on her part. This blossomed into a fully-fledged relationship during her time at the Academy when the history of the universe was rewritten. Spock is one of the few people who refers to Uhura by her first name, a name that she refused to reveal to her future captain, Jim Kirk, for years.

As her superior officer, Spock assigned Uhura to the *U.S.S. Farragut* as the vessels left Earth to answer the distress call on the planet Vulcan. His intention was not to show her favoritism by placing her on his ship, even though she had made it plainly known she had wanted to serve on it. **»**

When she insisted on joining the *Enterprise* because of its importance as the flagship of the fleet, Uhura made an impassioned and logical case for a transfer, convincing Spock to change his mind. The decision saved her life when the *Farragut* was destroyed by the Romulan mining ship, the *Narada*.

We're outnumbered, outgunned. There's no way we survive if we attack first. You brought me here because I speak Klingon. Then let me speak Klingon.
Nyota Uhura

Uhura was on the shuttlecraft from which Spock rappelled into an active volcano on the planet Nibiru. When his line was accidentally cut, Uhura was upset by Spock's order to be left behind rather than allow Kirk to violate the Prime Directive by revealing their presence to the planet's inhabitants. Uhura was grateful that Spock had been rescued, but could not understand how he could be so casual about his own life. Their relationship became strained until they had the opportunity to discuss the issue.

Linguistics expert
Uhura's study of exolinguistics and grasp of alien languages— in particular her ability to distinguish Romulan from Vulcan transmissions—ensured her early place among the *Enterprise*'s bridge crew at the communications station, under the order of Captain Pike.

In this version of the timeline, Uhura was well-versed in Klingon

Communication breakdown
Uhura finally convinces Spock of her value to the *Enterprise*.

as a cadet, whereas her counterpart in the unaltered timeline struggled with the language during a mission to free Kirk and McCoy from the Klingon prison planet. On that mission Uhura relied on a Klingon dictionary when trying to communicate with the species.

S.O.S. Uhura recognizes the distress call from the Klingon fleet under attack from the Romulan ship, the *Narada*.

Following the Temporal Incursion, Starfleet's new emphasis on defense had Uhura studying the language of one of the universe's larger threats early in her career. This came in handy when Uhura was able to intercept and translate

Educating Uhura In the wake of the Temporal Incursion, Uhura makes the study of alien languages her specialty.

> Lieutenant Uhura is unmatched in xenolinguistics. We would be wise to accept her conclusion.
> **Spock**

a Klingon broadcast indicating that a fleet of their ships had come under attack from a massive vessel. This turned out to be the same

ship, the *Narada*, that had been responsible for the death of Jim Kirk's father and the destruction of the *U.S.S. Kelvin* decades earlier.

Uhura's expert understanding of this challenging language was also instrumental in a mission that saw members of the *Enterprise's* senior staff secretly traveling to the Klingon Homeworld, Qo'noS, in an attempt to retrieve the terrorist later revealed as Khan Noonien Singh. When her handle on Klingon diplomacy failed to sway the enemy, she was quick with a phaser, prepared to rely on actions as well as words. Following that incident, Uhura continued to serve on the *Enterprise* as it began its first five-year mission. ■

Alien languages
The skilled linguist is familiar with many of the languages of the major political powers of the Alpha and Beta Quadrants.

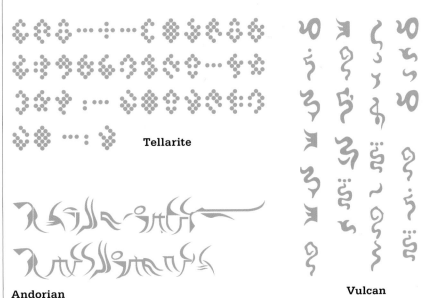

Tellarite

Andorian

Vulcan

Klingon

THE MIRACLE WORKER

MONTGOMERY SCOTT

CAPTAIN'S LOG

NAME
Montgomery Scott

SPECIES
Human

BORN
2222, Scotland, Earth

DIVISION
Operations

BRIEFING
Scotch is the drink of choice for this self-described "old Aberdeen pub-crawler"

Starfleet trains some of the best engineers in the known universe, but few have earned the reputation of "miracle worker." U.S.S. Enterprise chief engineer Montgomery "Scotty" Scott is one such miracle worker who has set the bar for decades to come. Over the course of Scott's 51-year career in Starfleet, he has served on eleven ships, including cruisers, freighters, and starships. The Enterprise is the first vessel on which he served as chief engineer, a post he held for almost 30 years.

By far the most important relationship Scott has had in his life has been with the original *Enterprise* and, to a slightly lesser degree, the *Enterprise*-A. The ships' engines are his babies and he takes any insult directed at the vessel personally. He once even started a fight when a Klingon compared the *Enterprise* to a "garbage scow"—a ship designed to carry waste. Conversely, Scott is certainly not afraid to look down on any ship that is not *his* *Enterprise*, even those he has worked on that may be more technologically advanced.

Scott's vaunted reputation is both earned and perhaps a little engineered on his part. According to the man himself, Scott often inflates his repair estimates so that he looks good when he completes a difficult job ahead of schedule.

A proud engineer

During the *Enterprise* crew's initial five-year mission, Scott served as chief engineer and acted as third in command, leading the vessel when both Kirk and Spock were on a mission or incapacitated. As chief engineer, he was responsible for the operation and maintenance of the ship's engines, transporter, and other key systems associated with the physical ship itself. He was an exemplary officer, but Scott did not pursue a command of his own, maintaining that he never

I've giv'n her all she's got Captain, an' I canna give her no more.
Montgomery Scott

wanted to be anything other than a respected engineer.

Proud of his role and reputation, Scott undertook many challenges that might have stymied lesser engineers. His list of achievements during emergency situations is impressive, including the many times that he saved the *Enterprise* from destruction at the risk of his own life. One such occasion occurred after the ship had been sabotaged and was flying at excessively dangerous warp speeds. Scott had to effect repairs to a fused matter-antimatter integrator in a procedure that was not intended to be performed while the device was in operation. His actions prevented the crew from being stranded in deep space had they been forced to eject the warp core before the ship was destroyed.

While on medical leave on the planet Argelius II, Scott came under suspicion for the murder of a local dancer when his own captain caught him holding the knife that had stabbed her. Scott had no memory of what had happened. During the course of the investigation, a female *Enterprise* crew member was also killed, stabbed by the knife that once again found its way into Scott's hands. When a third woman was murdered, Scott was threatened with harsh punishment and death. It was ultimately determined that an energy-based lifeform feeding off fear and terror was responsible for the murders. The entity had committed violent acts against women throughout history, including the victims of Earth's Jack the Ripper. Scott was acquitted and returned to duty.

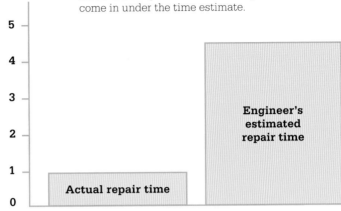

How to work miracles

Chief Engineer Scott multiplies all work estimates by a factor of four to maintain an enviable reputation when his repairs come in under the time estimate.

Engineer's estimated repair time

Actual repair time

An illustrious career

Scott oversaw the extensive refit of the *Enterprise* in the early 2270s under the command of Captain Willard Decker and then later served on the cadet training crew under Captain Spock. Scott was promoted to captain of engineering and transferred to the *U.S.S. Excelsior* when the *Enterprise* was to be decommissioned.

Although the *Excelsior* boasted the latest technological equipment, Scott did not care for the vessel or its captain. As such, he was more than happy to participate in the theft of the *Enterprise* to retrieve Spock's *katra*, rigging the ship to fly with only a skeleton crew. »

Hail to the chief engineer Scott takes the care of his ship more seriously than any other aspect of his life.

However, during the mission, Scott was forced to assist in initiating the auto-destruct sequence to keep the *Enterprise* from being taken by a Klingon crew. He then beamed down to the newly-formed Genesis Planet where he could only watch as his beloved ship was destroyed.

Scott was thrilled to discover that the crew's next posting would be on the *U.S.S. Enterprise* NCC-1701-A. He continued to serve as chief engineer on the starship until it was decommissioned, by which time Scott was planning for his retirement, having already bought a boat. He continued to attend Starfleet functions, most notably the launch of the *U.S.S. Enterprise* NCC-1701-B, before deciding to spend the rest of his days in the Federation retirement community on Norpin Colony. En route, Scott's transport vessel, the *U.S.S. Jenolan,* crashed and disappeared.

The fate of the ship wasn't revealed for another 75 years when it was discovered that Scott was still alive, having performed one last technological miracle.

Death on Argellius II Even after the knife had been found in his possession, Scott could not recall the murders.

Re-engineered retirement

Scott's retirement plans took a strange turn when the transport he was riding, the *U.S.S. Jenolan,* had a fatal encounter with a Dyson Sphere. He and one other survivor had inadequate supplies to await a rescue, so Scott jury-rigged the ship's transporter to hold their patterns in stasis. It was a stroke of engineering genius—but the plan worked for only one of them. Scott was picked up 75 years later by an entirely new generation of Starfleet.

The resurrected Scotty was like a kid in a candy store as he toured the *Enterprise*-D but he felt his attempts to help were interpreted as "getting in the way." Scott regained a sense of worth when he re-engineered the *Jenolan,* helped by his 24th-century counterpart Geordi La Forge, to rescue the *Enterprise* from being trapped inside the Dyson Sphere. The grateful crew gave him a shuttle to take wherever he wanted.

The Temporal Incursion

It was the elder Spock from the future that helped Montgomery Scott first board the *Enterprise* after they met on the frozen planet of Delta Vega, where Scott was stationed. Scott's desolate posting was a result of his long-standing desire to prove that a transporter beam's effectiveness could be expanded to allow for travel between star systems. Scott made the regrettable decision to use his commanding officer Admiral Archer's pet beagle as a test subject, but was unable to locate the dog following the experiment. Soon after, Scott received his posting where he had served for over six months with only crewman Keenser as company.

On the *Enterprise* Although the last member of the senior staff to join the crew, Scott quickly made it his home.

Undercover agent Scott infiltrated the *U.S.S. Vengeance* and managed to thwart a plot to destroy the *Enterprise*.

Once on board the *Enterprise*, Scott was vocal in his objection to several orders from his captain and Starfleet, starting with Kirk's plan to hide the ship on the planet Nibiru's sea bed. Even more problematic was the mission to Qo'noS in which the *Enterprise* carried 72 experimental photon torpedoes. When the engineer was forbidden to examine the weapons, he threatened to take a

> Do you have any idea how ridiculous it is to hide a starship on the bottom of the ocean?
> **Montgomery Scott**

leave of absence. Kirk accepted his offer. Scott's decision proved fortuitous as he was able to aid his crew by slipping onto the *U.S.S. Vengeance*, a prototype ship operated in complete secrecy by Section 31. After the incident, Scott returned to the *Enterprise* and served on the initial five-year mission. ∎

EVER UPWARD

HIKARU SULU

CAPTAIN'S LOG

NAME
Hikaru Sulu

SPECIES
Human

BORN
2237, San Francisco, Earth

DIVISIONS
Sciences, Command

DAUGHTER
Demora

BRIEFING
The name of Captain Sulu's ship, *Excelsior*, translates to "ever upward"

The noted *U.S.S. Enterprise* helmsman, Hikaru Sulu, did not begin his service in the position that became the signature of his career. Initially, Sulu served on the *Enterprise* in the sciences division as a physicist within the ship's astrosciences department. Early in the crew's first five-year mission he was transferred to the command division in the role with which he is most associated. Sulu sat at the helm throughout the historic five-year mission and was fourth in command, after Chief Engineer Scott. He remained with the *Enterprise* until 2290, when he was promoted to captain and awarded his own ship, the *U.S.S. Excelsior*.

Flower power Sulu tended Yeoman Janice Rand's carnivorous weeper plant, whom he liked to call Gertrude.

Man of many talents

Sulu is something of a Renaissance man with diverse interests, including botany, poetry, and even classic handheld weapons, being especially skilled in the sport of fencing. His experience with a foil was revealed to the crew when a virus, originating on the uninhabited planet Psi 2000, infected the crew. The primary symptom of this virus—known as polywater intoxication—was the suppression of all inhibitions. While under its effects, Sulu briefly held the bridge crew at bay with a foil, attempting to "rescue" Uhura prior to being subdued and sent to sickbay, where he was later cured.

Sulu's interest in botany proved valuable when the ship came under attack from a shape-shifting creature from the planet M-113. While tending a carnivorous weeper plant in the ship's arboretum, Sulu noted how the plant reacted when it came into contact

with the shape-shifter, which had adopted the form of crewman Green. It was an early indication that something was amiss on the ship prior to the discovery of a dead crew member.

Over the years, Sulu developed a close bond with Pavel Chekov, »

Bridge partners Stationed at the helm and navigation, Sulu and Chekov confronted many crises together.

Commanding the *Excelsior*

After many years serving under Captain Kirk, Hikaru Sulu was promoted to captain by 2290 and given command of the *U.S.S. Excelsior* NCC-2000. The ship had been a prototype in transwarp technology, but it was later converted to standard starship technology. Captain Sulu's initial assignment was a mission to catalog gaseous planetary anomalies in the Beta Quadrant. It was a pretty mundane tour of duty until the trip home, when the explosion of the Klingon moon Praxis thrust the *Excelsior* into a galactic conflict.

As a conspiracy unfolded to undermine peace talks between the Klingon Empire and the Federation, Sulu—in brazen defiance of Starfleet Command—inserted his ship into the fray. The *Excelsior* helped deal the final blow to the Klingon conspirator General Chang, and aided in exposing his non-Klingon collaborators.

Lost in place Sulu and Chekov learned that they were far more comfortable navigating space than Earth's forests.

the man who sat at the tactical station beside Sulu, beginning in 2267. They experienced many of the ship's greatest dangers while maintaining a light camaraderie, often joking or simply sharing a knowing smile when something happened on the bridge. Their friendship continued for decades after even when they were stationed on different ships.

One of the more embarrassing moments during the friendship occurred when the pair got lost hiking through a forest on Earth.

While navigating a forest is considerably different to charting a course through space, the friends were understandably reluctant to admit the truth to their crew mates. Uhura, the ship's communications officer, directed a shuttlecraft to retrieve them, promising not to share the details with anyone.

Saving the whales

When a whale probe threatened Earth, the *Enterprise* senior staff traveled back in time to the 20th century in an attempt to retrieve two extinct whales. Sulu took the opportunity to visit San Francisco, the city in which he was born. Here Sulu indulged in another interest by using a classic helicopter, the Huey 204, to deliver materials for Scotty to construct a tank for the whales. Sulu was later at the helm of a "borrowed" Klingon bird-of-prey when they returned to the 23rd century with the whales. The power systems failed and they crashed into San Francisco Bay where the creatures were released, unharmed.

Charges against Sulu and the crew for the theft of the *Enterprise* were dropped in light of their actions saving the Earth. Sulu had expressed an interest in working on the *Excelsior*, but when the senior staff arrived at their new ship, he was pleased to find it was the *U.S.S. Enterprise*-A. He served on the ship through its next mission, which took it into the Galactic Core. Three years later, his wish was fulfilled and he became captain of the *Excelsior*.

Unlike many of those he served with, Sulu found the time to raise

Don't call me Tiny.
Hikaru Sulu

Helm and navigation consoles

The joint consoles for helm and navigation on a *Constitution*-class Starfleet vessel are located at the front of the bridge.

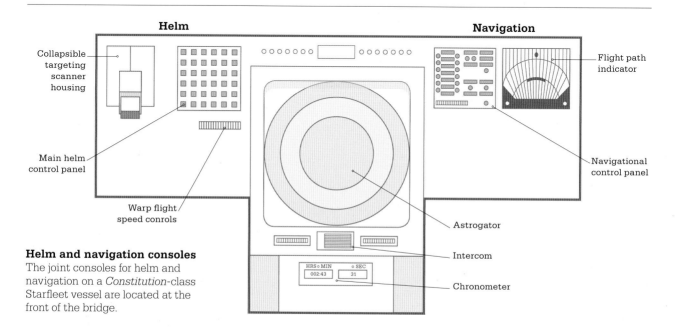

Helm

Collapsible targeting scanner housing

Main helm control panel

Warp flight speed conrols

Navigation

Flight path indicator

Navigational control panel

Astrogator

Intercom

Chronometer

HRS MIN 002:43   SEC 31

a family between space missions. Although his career often took him light years from home, his missions clearly had an impact on his daughter, Demora. The young woman followed in her father's footsteps serving as helm officer on the *U.S.S. Enterprise* NCC-1701-B. She was stationed on the bridge during its tragic maiden voyage.

The Temporal Incursion
The events associated with the Temporal Incursion of 2233 set Hikaru Sulu on a slightly different path, accelerating his acceptance of the *Enterprise* helm earlier than he had in the unaltered timeline. When the fleet was suddenly called up to answer the distress call from the planet Vulcan, Sulu was one of the cadets who found himself in a role for which he was not entirely ready. With the ship's regular helmsman, McKenna, suffering from lungworm, Sulu was placed at the controls.

His first act in the position was not auspicious when he failed to disengage the external inertial dampener, preventing the ship from entering warp speed. At Spock's suggestion, Sulu identified and corrected the issue, eventually sending the ship into warp drive. His mistake ultimately saved the ship and its crew, as the minor delay was enough to miss the initial engagement with the

You have two minutes to confirm your compliance. Refusal to do so will result in your obliteration. And if you test me, you will fail.
Hikaru Sulu

Captain Sulu Newly installed on the command chair, Sulu ordered the terrorist John Harrison to surrender.

Romulan vessel the *Narada*, which had destroyed the rest of the fleet that had been sent on ahead.

Sulu's fencing skills came in handy on this mission when he and Kirk fought off Romulans on the drilling rig stationed above Vulcan. Using a retractable blade, Sulu saved Kirk from an attacker before tumbling from the rig. Kirk went into freefall to reach Sulu and they were beamed to the *Enterprise*.

A year later, Sulu briefly gained command of the *Enterprise* when Kirk and Spock took a small team to Qo'noS to locate the terrorist Khan Noonien Singh, known at the time as John Harrison. Sulu's steely resolve in communicating directly with their target—and the fact that the *Enterprise* carried the supposed experimental weapons that held Khan's crew—were enough to convince Khan to surrender. ∎

THE RUSSIAN WHIZ KID

PAVEL CHEKOV

Ensign Pavel Andreievich Chekov joined the crew of the *U.S.S. Enterprise* as navigator while the ship was already in the midst of its first five-year mission under the command of James T. Kirk. It was the 22-year-old's first Starfleet posting.

Beyond his primary role as navigator, Chekov was also trained to serve at the science station, often filling in for Spock when the first officer was absent from the bridge. Additional duties included participating in landing parties, where Chekov performed the traditional functions of a science officer, using a tricorder to monitor the environment. Many of these planetary landing parties proved dangerous for him and his crew mates as they rarely knew what kind of situation they were beaming into. On one occasion, Chekov was the only member of a party unaffected by a rapid aging disease. After Dr. McCoy conducted a number of experiments, it was determined that a boost in Chekov's level of adrenaline when the rest of the team were infected by the disease had saved him from its effects.

It's a Russian invention...
Pavel Chekov

Russian roots

Chekov is intensely proud of his Russian heritage and frequently cites his background unprompted—although his grasp of his people's history is often colored by his personal bias. On more than one occasion, he has credited the Russian people with all manner of inventions or historically significant events, once even claiming that the story of Cinderella originated in his country.

Setting a course Despite his youth, Chekov's Starfleet training got the *Enterprise* out of a few tricky situations.

While at Starfleet Academy, Chekov met and became involved with the free-spirited Irina Galliulin. The fellow cadet of Russian descent did not adhere to the highly structured Academy life and she ultimately dropped out. Chekov and Irina often clashed over their different approaches to life, ultimately ending their relationship, though each credited the other with the breakup. Chekov would reunite with his ex-girlfriend after she had become a follower of Dr. Sevrin, a former professor who had rejected the modern technologies of society in search of the unspoiled planet Eden with its mythical healing properties. Sevrin and his team were apprehended by the *Enterprise*, having stolen the space cruiser the *Aurora* in their hunt for the elusive planet Eden.

While on the *Enterprise*, Irina used her connection to Chekov to learn about the ship's systems. She shared that information with Sevrin, allowing their group to seize control of the ship and steal a shuttlecraft to take them to the planet they believed to be Eden. Chekov was part of the landing party that retrieved Irina and her group when they discovered that the planet they thought to be Eden was in fact toxic to human life. Irina and the survivors were released to continue their search, and Chekov shared an intimate farewell with his former love.

Rising through the ranks
By the time the *Enterprise* had concluded its extensive refit in the early 2270s, Chekov had been promoted to lieutenant, serving as the ship's security chief and tactical officer. He continued to serve on the *Enterprise* until he was promoted to commander and transferred to the *U.S.S. Reliant* where he came across an old enemy of his former crew in 2285, Khan Noonien Singh. **»**

An unforgettable face

While the *Enterprise* was serving as a training vessel, Cmdr. Chekov transferred to the *U.S.S. Reliant* as first officer under Captain Clark Terrell. In 2285, the *Reliant* assisted Carol Marcus' Genesis Project by searching for suitable planets on which to conduct experiments. While investigating what they thought was a lifeless world, Chekov and Terrell came upon a shipwreck. Chekov feared the worst when he saw the name of Khan's old ship the *Botany Bay*.

In 2267, before being posted to the bridge, Chekov was on the original *Enterprise* when Khan Noonien Singh was revived and became a threat. Years later, Khan recognized Chekov's face and took the opportunity to reap revenge on his enemy Kirk. Khan used Ceti eels to control Chekov and Terrell's minds and have them lure Kirk into a trap. Terrell killed himself, but after Chekov overrode his eel's control, he was able to help Kirk defeat Khan.

Following the destruction of the *Reliant* and Spock's apparent death, Chekov temporarily assumed the position of science officer on the *Enterprise* as it was scheduled for decommissioning. Chekov was a key player in the plot by the senior staff to steal the ship for their mission to retrieve Spock's *katra*. During the incident, he was one of three officers providing the required authorization codes to activate the *Enterprise* self-destruct sequence to ensure the vessel did not fall into the hands of the warrior-like Klingons.

During a subsequent mission to the 20th century to retrieve a pair of whales, Chekov had a particularly difficult time due to his Russian heritage. Returning to Earth near the end of the Cold War between the United States and Russia, Chekov was captured as he was trying to siphon energy from the nuclear reactor on board the aircraft carrier *Enterprise* CVN-65. While attempting to escape U.S. Naval forces, Chekov was critically injured in a fall from the ship. The crew tracked Chekov to a local hospital, where Dr. McCoy was able to treat him and then slip him out in a brazen escape.

Upon their return to the 23rd century, Chekov and his crew mates were cleared of all charges related to the theft of the *Starship Enterprise*, and he was later assigned to the *Enterprise*-A.

During the *Enterprise*'s final mission to escort the Klingon chancellor Gorkon to the Khitomer Peace Conference, Chekov, acting as the ship's security chief, oversaw the investigation into Chancellor Gorkon's assassination.

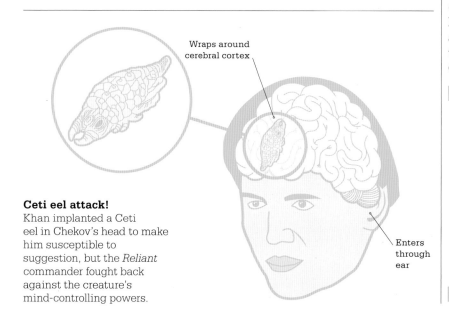

Wraps around cerebral cortex

Enters through ear

Ceti eel attack!
Khan implanted a Ceti eel in Chekov's head to make him susceptible to suggestion, but the *Reliant* commander fought back against the creature's mind-controlling powers.

A lot of people and things have tried to kill me. You'd be surprised.
Pavel Chekov

Chekov was later able to return a favor when he helped Kirk and McCoy escape the Klingon prison planet Rura Penthe, just as they had helped him escape the authorities in the 20th century. At the end of the mission, he was back at his navigation post when Kirk gave his final course heading. Chekov was also on hand at the launch of the *Enterprise*-B when Captain Kirk was tragically lost in an encounter with a rare spatial anomaly.

The Temporal Incursion

Pavel Chekov was the youngest member of the *Enterprise's* bridge crew during its original five-year mission, but following the events of the Temporal Incursion of 2233,

Quick thinking Chekov's great gift for calculating transporter coordinates saved Kirk and Sulu on the mission to Vulcan.

his relative youth was even more remarkable. In the altered timeline, the child prodigy accepted his posting at just 17 years old when the ship was summoned to deal with a crisis on the planet Vulcan.

Chekov proved his skill early on while calculating the coordinates for beaming Kirk and Sulu back to the *Enterprise* while they were

> ❝ Mr. Chekov, did you break my ship?
> **James T. Kirk** ❞

free-falling toward the planet. Soon after though, he was unable to save Spock's mother, Amanda, when the cliff she stood on crumbled beneath her as she was being beamed to the ship. He later devised a way for Kirk and Spock to beam over to the Romulan mining ship the *Narada*, while keeping the *Enterprise* hidden from the ship's scanners.

A year later, Chekov accepted a temporary field promotion to chief engineer when Montgomery Scott took leave after protesting at the mysterious cargo of experimental weapons technology. Now wearing the red uniform of an operations officer, Chekov identified a coolant leak in the warp core that seemed to be the result of sabotage. Once Scott returned to the ship, Chekov resumed his post on the bridge and continued his service on the vessel. ■

A GUIDING LIGHT
CHRISTOPHER PIKE

CAPTAIN'S LOG

NAME
Christopher Pike

SPECIES
Human

BORN
Mojave, California, Earth

Captain of the iconic *U.S.S. Enterprise* NCC-1701 from 2251 to 2262, Christopher Pike is celebrated for a tragically heroic act. After promotion to fleet commander, Pike was working on board a training vessel when he rescued numerous cadets from an area flooded with dangerous delta-particle radiation. He suffered crippling radiation poisoning that left him scarred, wheelchair-bound, and unable to speak.

Spock had served under Pike, and wanted to rescue his former captain from a life of pain and solitude. Acting against orders, Spock abducted Pike and directed the *Enterprise* to the forbidden planet Talos IV. It was potentially a court-martial offense but once Spock's intentions became clear,

Pike was permitted to live out the rest of his life on the planet. The Talosians used their telepathic powers to create an illusory life where Pike was free of the crippling effects of radiation on his body.

The Temporal Incursion
After the Temporal Incursion, Christopher Pike was an instructor at Starfleet Academy before taking command of the *Enterprise*. He is credited with persuading the young James T. Kirk to join Starfleet. After a distress call from the planet Vulcan, Pike was taken captive by the vengeful Romulan Nero, and tortured aboard Nero's ship, the *Narada*, in the hopes that he would reveal the security codes for Earth's defenses. Kirk rescued his injured captain and was rewarded with command of the *Enterprise* after Pike's promotion to admiral.

A year later, Pike was on the brink of returning Kirk to Starfleet Academy as the result of arrogantly ignoring the Prime Directive while rescuing the population of Nibiru from an active volcano. The rift between the two men was healed and Pike was scheduled to resume command of the *Enterprise* with Kirk as his first officer when

Khan Noonien Singh, in the guise of John Harrison, attacked Starfleet command. Pike was killed during the attack, motivating Kirk to seek his killer. ∎

Alternate reality Christopher Pike is promoted to the rank of admiral.

THE *ENTERPRISE* LEGACY
U.S.S. ENTERPRISE NCC-1701-B/C

CAPTAIN'S LOG

NAME
Enterprise NCC-1701-B

CLASS
Excelsior

LAUNCHED
2293

NAME
Enterprise NCC-1701-C

CLASS
Ambassador

LAUNCHED
2344 (presumed destroyed)

Enterprise NCC-1701-B

Just a few months after its predecessor's retirement, the *U.S.S. Enterprise* NCC-1701-B flew out of Earth's spacedock under the command of Captain John Harriman. This was the first *Enterprise* of the 23rd century not to be commanded by James T. Kirk. At the helm was Hikaru Sulu's daughter, Demora.

Carrying journalists and James Kirk, Montgomery Scott, and Pavel Chekov as honored guests, the maiden flight was intended to be a short one. The ship still lacked medical staff, tractor beam, and weapons. When it responded to a distress call from two Federation ships carrying El-Aurian refugees, it was ill-equipped to rescue them. The nexus ribbon ensnaring the ships trapped the *Enterprise* too.

With Captain Harriman unable to leave the bridge, Kirk volunteered to make an emergency modification

Don't let them do anything that takes you off the bridge of that ship, because while you're there you can make a difference.
James T. Kirk

to the ship's deflector system to escape the nexus. The mission was a success, but the section that he was in was destroyed by the nexus and Kirk was declared missing, presumed dead.

Enterprise NCC-1701-C

Launched in 2344, the *U.S.S. Enterprise* NCC-1701-C answered a distress call from a Klingon outpost near the planet Narendra III, where recorded history indicates that the ship was destroyed by Romulans who were attacking the outpost. However, an alternate timeline reveals that the *Enterprise*-C was pulled into a temporal rift sending the ship 22 years into the future. The ship's disappearance from the original timeline created a temporal incursion in which Starfleet did not intervene on the Klingons' part, and resulted in a future of unending war between the Federation and the Klingons.

Following an encounter in the future with the crew of the *Enterprise*-D, the *Enterprise*-C returned through the rift to repel Romulan ships attacking the Klingon outpost. Their valiant, self-sacrificing efforts paved the way for a peace alliance with the Klingons. ∎

HISTORY WILL NEVER FORGET
U.S.S. ENTERPRISE NCC-1701-D

CAPTAIN'S LOG

NAME
***Enterprise* NCC-1701-D**

CLASS
Galaxy

LENGTH
641 meters

COMPLEMENT
1012 (including families)

BRIEFING
***Enterprise*-D was launched in 2363 and destroyed in a crash landing on Veridian III in 2371**

Launched in 2363, the *Galaxy*-class *U.S.S. Enterprise* NCC-1701-D under the command of Captain Jean-Luc Picard remained in service for less than a decade, but carried its crew to the farthest known reaches of the Galaxy. This sixth Starfleet vessel to carry the proud name *Enterprise* made first contact with new species, took part in monumental scientific and historic discoveries, and defended the Federation against some of its most powerful threats.

Technical specifications

The primary construction of the *Enterprise*-D was carried out at the Utopia Planitia Fleet Yards orbiting Mars by a team overseen by Commander Orfil Quinteros. The ship's warp propulsion system was designed by Dr. Leah Brahms. It has a maximum sustainable speed of warp 9.6, which can be maintained for 12 hours.

Let's see what this *Galaxy*-class starship can do.
Jean-Luc Picard

As in most Federation starships, the bridge is located on Deck 1, along with the captain's ready room and a command conference lounge. The captain's chair is in the center of the bridge with the first officer's chair on the right on the same level. An additional seat for command officers and guests sits on the captain's left. The ship's counselor, an empath with a remarkable ability to read the emotions of other people (even those on other ships) usually occupies this post. Like most Starfleet vessels, the flight controller, or conn, is positioned between the captain and the main viewscreen. The chief of security's tactical station is slightly raised and sits just behind the captain.

The touch-sensitive computer stations that surround the bridge accept both physical input and vocal commands to connect the crew members with the Library Computer Access and Retrieval System (LCARS).

The *Enterprise*'s defensive systems include ten phaser arrays

Mission ready The *Enterprise*-D has sophisticated defenses and eight times the capacity of *Constitution*-class ships.

and two torpedo launchers, which are equipped with a standard complement of 250 powerful photon torpedoes. The high-capacity shield grid operates on multiple frequencies, offering protection from a wider array of weapons.

Because Starfleet is primarily an agency for scientific research and exploration, some vessels have the space to house families to make the longer deep space missions more tolerable for the crew, something unique to the Starfleet of this time period. One of the more notable features of the *Galaxy* class is the saucer section containing the primary hull, which can detach from the

engineering section in emergency situations. The temporary "battle bridge" in the secondary hull allows the command crew to operate this section of the ship independently from the saucer section. This feature makes the ship more hospitable for families of the crew as it isolates and protects them in dangerous situations. All non-essential personnel can be evacuated in the saucer section »

Shuttle roll of honor

A complement of 24 fully warp-capable shuttlecraft, plus smaller, impulse-only shuttlepods serve the *Enterprise*-D. Their names honor great explorers, scientists, and thinkers of Earth history, such as Einstein, Hawking, Feynman, Magellan, and Pike. Some craft have intriguing histories. When the *Fermi* was trapped in a molecular reversion field, its crew turned into 12-year-olds.

A Ferengi scientist modified the *Justman*, equipping it with metaphasic shielding that was later engaged in the struggle over the Vulcan Stone of Gol.

When Q was turned Human he seized the *Sakharov*. Later, a holographic simulation of the shuttle was given to Moriarty, leading him to believe that he would be able use it to roam the universe.

Scale models The first *Enterprise* ship, the NX-01, was home to a crew of around 80, whereas the latest craft, *Enterprise*-E, can carry 750 personnel.

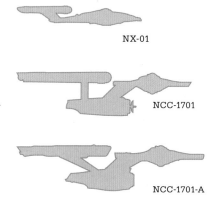
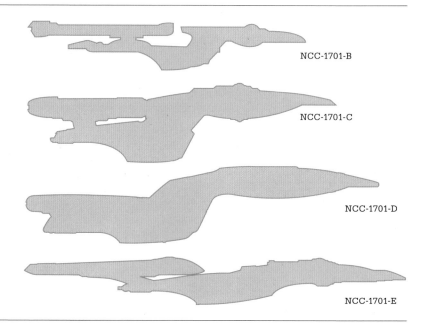

NCC-1701-B

NCC-1701-C

NCC-1701-D

NX-01

NCC-1701

NCC-1701-E

NCC-1701-A

while the crew in the secondary hull engage with an enemy.

Among the many advancements of the 24th century is a replicator system that uses transporter technology to shape matter into any requested form. If, for example, a crew member needs refreshment, a simple vocal command to the replicator will instantly produce whatever is asked for, such as a cup of coffee. The holodeck is another piece of breakthrough technology—it allows the crew to experience holographic recreations,

which can be used for their own entertainment or generated for mission-related purposes.

The seven-year mission

Even before the entire crew is fully assembled after the launch of *Enterprise* NCC-1701-D in 2363 on stardate 41153.7, their first mission brings them into contact with Q, an apparently omnipotent life-form. Q believes that Humans are a savage race unprepared for the mysteries of the universe, and places Captain Picard and his crew on trial for the

many crimes of Humanity. Picard and his crew prove Q wrong when they rescue an alien entity that has been subjugated and enslaved by the people of Farpoint Station on Deneb IV. Although Q allows the *Enterprise* to continue, he warns that he will keep an eye on them—a threat that turns out to have severe consequences during their mission.

For the seven years that the ship is in service, the crew continue to explore and reveal the remarkable variety of the Galaxy as well as facing fearsome opponents. During one of their most significant discoveries they find evidence of a species that might have been responsible for seeding the universe with the DNA building blocks for most humanoids. The crew also makes first contact with a number of other species, including the legendary Aldean civilization, Malcorians, Tamarians, and the first official contact with the Ferengi. Q is the instigator of the starship's deadly first encounter with the cybernetic species, the Borg, which causes the death of

NCC-1701-D Timeline

c. 2350
Development of *Galaxy*-class starship begins at Utopia Planitia Fleet Yards, Mars.

2364
Captain Picard assumes command and leads ship on its first mission, involving a first encounter with Q and a first high-warp saucer separation.

2371
Suffers warp core breach in Klingon attack, secondary hull destroyed, saucer section crash-lands on Veridian III with light casualties; rendered unsalvageable.

2345   2380

2363
Construction of *U.S.S. Enterprise* NCC-1701-D completed; after shakedown cruise, docked at Earth Station McKinley for final systems completion.

2367
Enterprise-D under command of William Riker destroys Borg cube responsible for massacre at Wolf 359, recovers assimilated Picard from collective.

Early encounter The crew is intercepted during their first mission to Farpoint Station.

18 crew members. This is just a taste of things to come: when the Borg later set their sights on the Alpha Quadrant, thousands will be lost at their hands.

The ship's mission is sometimes complicated by crew members' personal affairs, which can have galactic political repercussions. For example, thanks to the presence of the ship's Klingon chief tactical officer Worf, whose family had been unfairly discredited by a rival Klingon clan, the *Enterprise* crew becomes embroiled in the Klingon Civil War. When the Klingon High Council accused Worf's family of aiding the Romulans in their infamous attack on the Khitomer colony, Captain Picard stood by his side. Later Picard was called upon to act as the Arbiter of Succession when the head of the Klingon Council was assassinated.

Lieutenant Commander Data, an android, experiences a unique set of family problems when his "brother" Lore partners with a group of Borg who are trying to establish a new society free of the collective. And no one on the ship is ever fully prepared for a visit from Counselor Troi's overbearing mother, Lwaxana.

Cataclysmic events
The early indictment from Q and his people, the Q Continuum, is never lifted. They have declared Humans guilty and ordered their destruction. However, Q offers the *Enterprise* crew one last chance to prove themselves by sending Captain Picard through time to witness a potentially cataclysmic event. Working with the *Enterprise* crew in three different time periods enables Picard to expand his thinking to a remarkable degree and open himself up to previously unconsidered possibilities. His crew's response to the crisis saves the Galaxy from destruction and allows Humans to continue their mission of exploration.

The *Enterprise* crew members face a new threat to the universe in the form of an El-Aurian with a deadly quest. He plans to destroy a star system in order to attract a nexus of energy that will allow him to be united with the loved ones he can't forget. Captain Picard, aided by Captain James T. Kirk, who had previously been absorbed by the nexus, thwart the plan, but there are still terrible consequences. The *Enterprise*-D comes under attack from a Klingon ship, and although most of the crew survive, the starship is destroyed. ∎

See also: The Known Universe, Jean-Luc Picard, Holographic Technology, Where No One Has Gone Before, The Q Continuum

Death of a starship

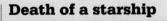

There were countless close calls, and even utter destruction in parallel realities and temporal loops, but the final demise of the Federation flagship *Enterprise*-D comes in a spat with the Klingons.

The Duras sisters, Lursa and B'Etor, in collusion with El-Aurian madman Soran, discover the *Enterprise*'s shield modulation frequency of 257.4 MHz and penetrate its defenses with their torpedo. The *Enterprise* manages to destroy their bird-of-prey, but suffers significant damage, leading to a warp core breach. The crew evacuate to the saucer section and separate from the secondary hull but cannot clear the antimatter explosion. The shock wave sends them hurtling into the planet Veridian III. The starship is unsalvageable.

DRIVE, DETERMINATION, AND COURAGE

JEAN-LUC PICARD

CAPTAIN'S LOG

NAME
Jean-Luc Picard

SPECIES
Human

BORN
July 13, 2305, **La Barre, France, Earth**

PARENTS
Maurice and Yvette Picard

STARFLEET DIVISION
Command

BRIEFING
One of Picard's ancestors fought at the Battle of Trafalgar. Another won a Nobel Prize

As a child, Jean-Luc Picard built model starships and dreamed of a life among the stars. This Starfleet officer, who went on to make first contact with 27 species and play a key role in some of the major turning points in galactic history, seemed destined for a life in his family's vineyard, in La Barre, France, Earth. At first Picard was denied entry into Starfleet Academy, but was accepted a year later and earned top academic honors. The hot-headed young cadet was often close to trouble and later in life expressed gratitude to Boothby, the Academy groundskeeper, who kept him on a straight path.

Shortly after graduation, Picard picked a fight with three Nausicaans and was critically wounded. The artificial heart that keeps him alive became a reminder of his foolhardiness as Picard grew into a calmer, more reasoned adult.

I always knew exactly what I wanted to do: be a member of Starfleet... Virtually my entire youth was spent in pursuit of that goal.
Jean-Luc Picard

Taking command

Picard earned his first command after taking control of the bridge of the *U.S.S. Stargazer* following the death of his captain. He then served as the ship's captain for 20 years until an unidentified vessel, which was later found to belong to the Ferengi, disabled the *Stargazer*. Picard managed to destroy the enemy ship using the *Stargazer's* warp engines (this unique tactic is later named the "Picard Maneuver"), but ultimately was forced to abandon his ship.

Although Picard's command of his next ship, the *U.S.S. Enterprise* NCC-1701-D, was briefer, lasting just seven years, it was marked by some of Starfleet's most notable missions, as well as bizarre and deadly encounters with the entity Q.

The most traumatic event Picard experienced while in command of the *Enterprise*-D, was his abduction and assimilation by the Borg. Cybernetic implants were added to his body, linking him with the shared consciousness of the Borg collective. His individuality and self-will suppressed, Picard became Locutus, a Borg drone. The evil did not end

Memory of a lost civilization

One of Picard's more remarkable experiences was triggered by a nucleonic beam, fired by a probe that was launched by a pre-warp humanoid civilization whose world died a thousand years earlier.

The beam transferred its memory record into Picard's cerebral cortex, causing him to experience, within 25 minutes, the memory of four decades of life as "Kamin," an iron weaver in the Ressik community on planet Kataan. Picard's identity as a starship captain became increasingly distant, as he experienced marriage, children, a rich community life, and old age. He even learned to play the Ressikan flute. The implanted memory was the civilization's only heritage and continues to endure, cherished in Picard's memory and his heart.

Space suit Picard wears an EV (environmental) suit for life support in inhospitable environments and space walks to inspect the ship's exterior.

there; the Borg used the captain's knowledge of Starfleet defenses to assist in the massacre at Wolf 359, the primary planet in the Wolf star system. Picard was forced to attack his own fleet, resulting in the destruction of 39 starships. Although he never fully recovered from the horror of this event, he was able to confront his ghosts when the *Enterprise* helped defeat a second Borg invasion on Earth, when the Borg tried to prevent the formation of the Federation by traveling into the past to change history.

Personal interests

Picard rekindled an earlier fascination with archaeology when he helped collect genetic samples that proved that ancient humanoids had once seeded primordial environments with the DNA that directed the evolution of all similar species.

The captain is something of a literature buff, keeping *The Complete Works of Shakespeare* in his ready room. He also likes to act out Dixon Hill detective novels on the holodeck starring himself in the lead role. Picard excels in fencing and horseback riding— and still likes to make scale models of Starfleet vessels. ■

Borg terror Picard's assimilation into the Borg collective reaches a grotesque climax when the captain becomes Locutus, a Borg drone, and is forced to massacre his own fleet.

NUMBER ONE
WILLIAM T. RIKER

CAPTAIN'S LOG

NAME
William T. Riker

SPECIES
Human

BORN
2335, Valdez, Alaska, Earth

PARENTS
Kyle and Betty Riker

WIFE
Deanna Troi

STARFLEET DIVISION
Command

BRIEFING
One of Riker's ancestors, Colonel Thaddius Riker, fought for the Union in America's Civil War on Earth

Optimistic, genial, and inventive, William T. Riker stands out for his unswerving loyalty to his crew and his captain, Jean-Luc Picard. Motherless from the age of two and raised by a cold, distant father in Alaska, planet Earth, he was left to fend for himself in his teenage years. It is unsurprising that for Riker, family life began when he graduated from the Starfleet Academy and became a member of the crew on his first ship.

A stalled career

During his initial posting on the *U.S.S. Pegasus*, Riker's loyalty was put to the test when Captain Erik Pressman began testing a phasing cloak device in direct conflict with the Treaty of Algeron. In spite of mutiny within the crew, Riker stood by his captain as they and a handful of crew mates escaped on a shuttle. The prototype ship went missing and was presumed destroyed. Years later, Riker exposed this illegal action when he admitted the truth about the ship's disappearance to Captain Picard.

Riker went on to serve on the *U.S.S. Potemkin* and was made executive officer on board the *U.S.S. Hood* before his transfer to the *Enterprise*-D. As first officer he was responsible for implementing his captain's orders, leading away missions, and taking command of the ship when the captain was away.

Riker took a nontraditional approach to problems, preferring to rely on creative tactics. What surprised many who considered him to be top choice to captain his own ship, was that he remained as first officer for the entire life of the *U.S.S. Enterprise* NCC-1701-D. He declined many offers of command—his bond with his captain keeping him content in his role as Picard's "Number One."

Multiple missions

Riker was a central figure in many adventures and in one notable mission, was gifted with Q Continuum powers while the rest

Will Riker, you have been my trusted right arm for fifteen years. You have kept my course true and steady…
Jean-Luc Picard

Double trouble

There are two William Thomas Rikers in the universe, each with an equal claim to the identity.

A bizarre transporter anomaly on Nervala IV caused the then-Lieutenant Riker to materialize in two places at once—on his ship, the *Potemkin*, but also back on the planet. The duplicate spent eight years in solitude until he was rescued by the *Enterprise*. The two Rikers were identical physically, but the one who left Nervala had become an experienced and self-disciplined commander, in contrast to the hot-headed duplicate lieutenant. The latter called himself Thomas and changed ship, but later left Starfleet to join the rebellious Maquis group. Captured during a mission to steal *Defiant* to fight the Cardassians, he was sent to a Cardassian labor camp.

of the senior crew were imprisoned in a deadly illusion world. Riker used his supernatural abilities to save them, and bring Lieutenant Worf and Wesley Crusher back to life.

During the time when Picard was abducted by the Borg, Riker was given a temporary field promotion to captain. He led the rescue of Picard and oversaw the ultimate disabling of the Borg vessel while it traveled to Earth.

As part of an officer exchange program, he was the first human to serve on a Klingon vessel.

Love interest

Over time Riker developed a personal interest in several of the entities he encountered in his travels, including a deep attachment to the holodeck character named Minuet. But no one eclipsed his love for ship's counselor, Deanna Troi. Their attachment formed on Troi's beautiful home planet Betazed, where she called Riker *imzadi*, the Betazoid word for "beloved." The rescue of Riker's duplicate (Thomas), created in a transporter error, complicated matters as Thomas tried to resume his affair with Troi. She flirted with the idea but soon realized that her future was not with Tom. She eventually married Will.

Not long after, Riker bid farewell to Picard and the *Enterprise* and took command of the *U.S.S. Titan*, where he promised to become the leader his captain had inspired him to be. ∎

Social scene Poker nights for the senior staff are hosted in Riker's quarters. Riker also plays trombone, loves jazz music, and is a skilled cook.

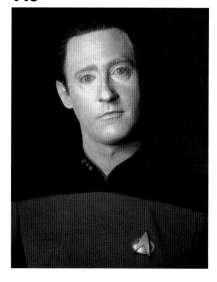

AN OFFICER AND AN ANDROID
DATA

CAPTAIN'S LOG

NAME
Data

SPECIES
Android

CREATED
**Omicron Theta
Science Colony**

ACTIVATION
2338 (by Starfleet)

DEACTIVATION
2379

CREATORS
**Dr. Noonian Soong
and Dr. Juliana Soong**

STARFLEET DIVISION
Operations

BRIEFING
**Data is one of the few crew
members to own a pet—a
devoted cat named Spot**

Changing Data The Borg Queen
attempted to transform Data by grafting
Human skin to his frame, allowing him
to experience the tactile sensations of
pain and pleasure for the first time.

Immune to virtually every
biological disease and
equipped with rapid-fire
processing and superhuman
physical strength, Data was
robotocist doctors Noonien and
Juliana Soong's fifth and finest
creation. The only android to
become a member of Starfleet, Data
was equipped with a sophisticated
positronic brain. This advanced
computing device, capable of
artificial sentience, allowed him
to learn from his experiences and
mimic Human behavior. Although
some facets of humanity—in
particular, emotional response—
remained beyond his grasp for
much of his existence, in his last
years he was considered to be the
only sentient artificial lifeform in
the Federation. After a Starfleet
hearing he was granted the full
breadth of civil rights.

Starfleet career
Data served as the second officer
and chief operations officer aboard
the starships *U.S.S. Enterprise*-D
and -E. Like all officers, he earned
his rank of lieutenant commander
through promotion after attending
and graduating from Starfleet
Academy. Nevertheless, throughout
his career he experienced some
prejudice against him as an
artificial intelligence.

Even though Data became
a beloved member of the crew,
developing a number of close
friendships, particularly with
Chief Engineer Geordi La Forge,
he faced many challenges in his
daily interactions. Humor often
escaped him and at times he was
too literal. Yet his lack of emotion
was often the envy of the crew
during terrifying missions.

The study of Human emotion
was an ongoing quest throughout
Data's posting on the *Enterprise*.
Through the powers of the
seemingly omnipotent Q, Data
experienced laughter for the very
first time. Later, the Borg Queen

The emotion chip

Data's struggle with the subtleties of Human behavior was a flaw in his design that his creator, Dr. Soong, had intended to correct. The cyberneticist spent 20 years perfecting a program module called an emotion chip for Data. But when Soong summoned him to install it, he was unaware that his earlier android creation, the problematic Lore, also received the homing signal. Lore stole the chip. In a later skirmish, Data disassembled Lore and retrieved his creator's gift. Fearing its power, he almost destroyed it, but engineer La Forge urged him not to.

When Data finally installed his emotion chip it caused erratic behavior, but he learned to control it to the point where he could turn his new emotional capabilities on or off at will.

offered to use the advanced technology of her people to make him more Human. Although he ultimately rejected her offer, he admitted to being tempted by it for 0.68 seconds. He noted this was nearly an eternity for an android.

Beyond the programming

Data was a member of the team that located a Soong android called Lore, who had been deactivated by his creator because of his dangerous emotional instability. After he was reactivated, Lore became a danger to the *Enterprise* crew over the years, attempting to take over the ship at one point. He was also a thorn in the side of Data, and manipulated him into partnering with the Borg against the Federation for a brief time.

In their later interactions, Lore used the emotion chip Dr. Soong developed as both a bargaining chip and a tool against his android "brother" Data.

Data attempted to follow in his creators' footsteps and used his own positronic brain template to create an android daughter named Lal, whose capabilities surpassed his own. Tragically a system-wide failure forced Data to deactivate her after just two weeks. In another attempt to continue the work of the Soongs, Data programmed B-4, an inferior prototype, and uploaded his own memories, creating a potential key to his own posterity.

On his final mission, Data sacrificed himself to save his crew from the explosion that destroyed the ship of Romulan Praetor Shinzon. While the crew mourned their android member, B-4 piped out the song that Data once sang at the Riker wedding; it was seen as a sign that his personality lived on. ∎

Special effects Able to breathe, blink, and even dream, Data was fitted with a program that simulated the external effects of aging.

I am the culmination of one man's dream. This is not ego or vanity, but when Doctor Soong created me he added to the substance of the universe.

Data

A NICE GUY AT HEART
GEORDI LA FORGE

CAPTAIN'S LOG

NAME
Geordi La Forge

SPECIES
Human

BORN
**February 16, 2335,
Mogadishu, Somalia, Earth**

PARENTS
Edward and Silva La Forge

STARFLEET DIVISION
Command/Operations

BRIEFING
**Excelled at engineering
at Starfleet Academy**

Geordi La Forge was born into a Starfeet family, traveling the Galaxy with his mother, a Starfleet captain, and father, an exobiologist Starfleet commander. He was blind at birth but after five years was fitted with VISOR technology that gave him superior visual and electromagnetic capabilities, which later enhanced his contribution as a crew member on Starfleet ships. Captain Jean-Luc Picard specifically requested him for the position of conn officer on the *Enterprise*-NCC-1701-D because of his impressive work ethic. La Forge was transferred from command to operations to become chief engineer and within a short time rose to the rank of lieutenant commander.

Technological ghosts
Memories from the past came to haunt La Forge during his missions on the *Enterprise*. While testing an experimental interface device for a probe, alien beings attempted to enlist his help through the technology, appearing to him in the form of a representation of his late mother, who died in the line of duty. Although he learned that it wasn't really her, the encounter allowed La Forge to say good-bye to his mother, something he had not had a chance to do in real life.

On another occasion, La Forge was rendered invisible through exposure to a new Romulan cloaking device. Assuming he was dead, his friends held a memorial ceremony, which he was able to attend and witness how those who loved him would bid him farewell.

Legendary engineer Montgomery Scott (Scotty) offered La Forge advice from another era after his rescue.

I've always thought that technology could solve almost any problem. It lets us travel across the Galaxy... even gave me my vision. But sometimes you just have to turn it all off.
Geordi La Forge

Close friendships

The android, Data, was La Forge's closest friend, and the pair often worked on engineering problems together. La Forge made it his personal mission to help Data in his quest to understand what it means to be Human. The pair often role-played in holodeck simulations of Sherlock Holmes stories, with Data assuming the role of Holmes and La Forge playing Dr. Watson.

In a complex struggle to enable the *Enterprise* to escape a Menthar booby trap, La Forge called on a holographic representation of Dr. Leah Brahms, the designer of the ship's warp drive, to assist him. In the process of solving the problem, he became more than a little infatuated with her. When given the chance to meet her in person he was disenchanted to find that the hologram had not prepared him for her true personality—or the fact that she had a husband.

Meeting legends

La Forge got the chance to meet some legends of engineering during his time on the *Enterprise* fleet. The crew picked up a distress call from the *U.S.S. Jenolan* and managed to rematerialize the former chief engineer of an earlier *Enterprise*, Montgomery Scott, who had been trapped in the transporter buffer for 75 years. La Forge exhibited an unusual reticence toward interacting with the overly helpful engineer, decades behind in technology, but grew to appreciate his elder's methodology. Later, a Borg-instigated trip through time allowed him to assist Dr. Zefram Cochrane with his historic test flight of the *Phoenix*. ∎

Morning glory La Forge is moved to tears watching his first ever sunrise after his eyes are regenerated temporarily by metaphysic radiation on the Ba'ku home planet.

The VISOR

At age five, Geordi La Forge was fitted with a Visual Instrument and Sensory Organ Replacement device, referred to as a VISOR, that enabled him to see for the first time. More than just a visual aid, it allowed him to perceive a broader range of the electromagnetic spectrum than visible light, including heat and radio waves. The device was worn across his eyes and attached on either side of his head to neural implants that transmit the device's input to his visual cortex. The VISOR caused La Forge constant pain, but he refused to accept drugs or surgery that might compromise the functionality of the device, even moderately.

Frequently La Forge's enhanced senses were used to good effect, and often made the difference in the success of a mission. But the VISOR also made him vulnerable to enemies who exploited the technology for their own ends.

On the *Enterprise*-E, La Forge traded his VISOR for advanced ocular implants— artificial eyes that offered him an equally wide range of sensory information.

AN HONORABLE MAN
WORF

CAPTAIN'S LOG

NAME
Worf

SPECIES
Klingon

BORN
2340 (Earth equivalent), Qo'noS

KLINGON HOUSE
Mogh (former)
Martok (current)

FOSTER PARENTS
Sergey and Helena Rozhenko

WIFE
Jadzia Dax (deceased)

SON
Alexander (mother K'Ehleyr)

STARFLEET DIVISION
Operations/Command

BRIEFING
As a child, owned a pet targ (a vicious creature)

Acourageous warrior, a dour colleague, a romantic with a gentle humor—Worf's personality reflected an upbringing that straddled two worlds. The Klingon was raised on a farm on Earth by adoptive parents after his birth parents died in the Khitomer massacre. Throughout his career as the first of his species to serve in Starfleet, he was loyal to the people who saved him but also desperate to embrace his lost Klingon heritage.

Distinguished career
Worf began his service on the *Enterprise*-D as a junior lieutenant in the bridge position of relief conn under the command of Captain Jean-Luc Picard. After Tasha Yar was killed by the Armus entity, he transferred to operations to become security chief and chief tactical officer and was promoted to lieutenant. The Klingon's time aboard the *Enterprise*-D was marked by heroics and tragedy,

Warrior sash Worf's Klingon sash, worn across his Starfleet uniform, is a symbol of his people's culture.

Alexander, son of Worf

An unlikely parent, Worf learned he had fathered a son, Alexander, after his affair with K'Ehleyr. Following K'Ehleyr's death, Worf became responsible for the boy and briefly passed him to his own adoptive parents, the Rozhenkos on planet Earth. But Alexander needed a father and was brought back to the *Enterprise*. Worf was troubled by the boy's behavior at school, and even more so by his disinterest in adopting Klingon warrior ways. But when he came of age, Alexander joined the Klingon Defense Forces and ended up serving alongside Worf in the Dominion War. Their arguments came to a head, but father and son were reconciled. Alexander was welcomed into the Klingon House of Martok.

> Sir, I protest. I am not a merry man.
> **Worf**

including combat with Borg drones, the rescue of Captain Picard from the Borg cube, and fantasy games with the dismissive Q. Promoted to lieutenant commander, he was engaged in the battle that led to the destruction of the *Enterprise*-D.

Worf was later summoned to Deep Space 9 to advise Captain Benjamin Sisko on a growing threat from the Klingon Empire. Sisko took the view that the only people who could handle Klingons were Klingons. For the first few years at DS9, Worf preferred to live aboard the *Defiant* and sometimes took command for missions if Sisko was otherwise occupied.

At the end of the Dominion War, Worf became Federation ambassador to Qo'noS at the request of Chancellor Martok.

Love and marriage

Early in his time on the *Enterprise* Worf had a relationship with K'Ehleyr, a Human-Klingon woman serving as an emissary between the Empire and the Federation. Although they never wed, K'Ehleyr gave birth to a son, who ultimately became Worf's sole responsibility. K'Ehleyr's death at the hand of his political enemy Duras plunged Worf and the *Enterprise* into the affairs of rival houses in the Klingon Civil War.

Worf also had a brief relationship with ship's counselor Deanna Troi, but following his transfer to Deep Space 9, found true love with Jadzia Dax, a joined Trill whose symbiont half had a past with the Klingon Empire. Jadzia's lively personality was often in conflict with the Klingon's reserved ways, but her playfully aggressive sexuality suited the instincts of his people.

The couple wed in Klingon style, but within a short time Jadzia was killed by Gul Dukat, who was possessed by a Pah-wraith. Worf struggled with his grief, especially after Ezri, the recipient of Jadzia's symbiont, joined the station. He found solace when a daring mission ensured his wife's place in *Sto-Vo-kor*, the Klingon afterlife. ∎

Klingon wedding Worf and Jadzia Dax wield *bat'leth* swords of honor in a traditional marriage ceremony.

THE EMPATH
DEANNA TROI

CAPTAIN'S LOG

NAME
Deanna Troi

SPECIES
Betazoid/Human

BORN
2336, near Lake El'nar, Betazed

PARENTS
Lwaxana and Ian Troi

HUSBAND
William Riker

SON
Ian Andrew (deceased)

STARFLEET DIVISION
Sciences

BRIEFING
Loves all forms of chocolate, and tales from Earth's ancient West

Surprise baby After she was invaded by a noncorporeal entity, Troi gave birth to a baby son within days. She raised the fast-growing child as her own, but his presence endangered the crew.

Ship's Counselor Deanna Troi's rare empathic abilities allowed her to sense emotions—the result of her mixed race heritage that is half Human and half Betazoid. The Betazoid possess telepathic powers and although Troi was not a full telepath like other Betazoids, she could communicate mentally with other members of the species, including her extrovert mother. During her childhood her Betazoid grandfather liked to tell her stories silently in his head, maintaining that "speech is for offworlders or people who don't know any better."

Troi grew up believing she was an only child, unaware that her elder sister, Kestra, had drowned. Her usually over-sharing mother blocked the painful event from her own mind and excluded any mention of Kestra from Deanna's life. Following Betazoid tradition, Troi was betrothed as a child to the son of family friends, but neither partner wished to commit to the relationship in adult life.

Troi's empathic skills came to the fore in her role as Starfleet counselor, especially in first contact situations, and encounters with hostile alien threats.

Extraordinary events

While Troi was serving on the *Enterprise*-D, a noncorporeal entity that wanted to experience a humanoid existence took up residence in her womb, and Troi became pregnant. She carried the life-form to term in a matter of days and gave birth to a male child. Although Troi did not fully understand the experience, she bonded with the baby and called him Ian Andrew Troi, after her father. Ian continued to grow at an accelerated rate but when he was approximately eight years old, the entity realized the radiation it emitted was placing its mother and

> If you're looking for my professional opinion as ship's counselor: he's nuts.
> **Deanna Troi**

Casual wear Troi's non-regulation unitards were later replaced by a standard Starfleet uniform.

the crew at risk. It sacrificed its own humanoid life for their survival.

The sensitive empath suffered another travesty when Federation ambassador Ves Alkar downloaded his dark thoughts and emotions telepathically to free up his diplomatic skills. The effect caused rapid aging and psychosis: Troi was an old woman close to death when Dr. Beverly Crusher saved her life.

Before the crash

In 2370 Troi passed the Bridge Officer's Exam and was promoted to commander. During the final mission of the *Enterprise*-D, Troi took the conn as the saucer section separated from the hull, which was about to suffer a warp core breach and explode. The blast's shockwave sent the saucer section hurtling into the planet Veridian III. Troi managed to bring the section in for a crash landing, saving most of the crew. ∎

Imzadi

On Earth we say "soulmate;" in the Betazoid language the person with whom you share your most intimate connection is your *imzadi*—it translates literally as "beloved."

Deanna Troi and Will Riker became mutual *imzadi* when the young Will was stationed on the planet Betazoid early in his Starfleet career. Troi taught Riker to "hear" her thoughts, an unusual feat for a Human. Once their spiritual bond was made, it endured even when the couple drifted apart, or betrothals and other relationships threatened to interfere. Although their romantic involvement appeared to end when Riker put his career ahead of his personal life and accepted a station on the *U.S.S. Potemkin*, their feelings were rekindled at a future date.

When the pair found themselves serving on both the *Enterprise*-D and later -E, they kept their emotional distance but occasionally remembered the unbreakable bond and called each other *imzadi*. Inevitably they married, and Troi joined her husband in his new post as captain of the *U.S.S. Titan*.

THE DANCING DOCTOR
DR. BEVERLY CRUSHER

Raised by her grandmother, Felisa Howard, after the death of both her parents, young Beverly had early experience of the power of medicine. Her grandmother was not a doctor, but was skilled in folk remedies handed down through the generations. Felisa's skills proved to be life saving for the survivors of a tragic incident at the Arvada III Colony when the usual medical supplies were exhausted. Watching her grandmother at work inspired Beverly to study medicine at the Starfleet Academy and later serve as chief medical officer on board the *Enterprise*-D.

The first tenet of good medicine is never make the patient any worse.
Dr. Beverly Crusher

Beverly met and married Jack Crusher early in her career and after his death was left to bring up their son Wesley alone. The *Galaxy*-class *Enterprise*'s family accommodations enabled her to stay involved in Wesley's upbringing while fulfilling the ship's needs. In fact she became so comfortable with her *Enterprise* family that she was able to leave the boy in their care for a year while she served as commander of Starfleet Medical on Earth. Remaining on the ship offered the best education to her technologically gifted son, who was later accepted into Starfleet Academy but eventually chose an alternative path.

Medical challenges
As chief medical officer, Dr. Crusher's primary focus is the sickbay, and through her career she built an extraordinary record. The many epidemics that ravaged the ship included a widespread case of polywater intoxication in 2364, which was a repeat of one that affected the crew of *Enterprise* NCC-

Taking command As a fully-certified bridge officer, Dr. Crusher can command the *Enterprise* when other senior crew members are absent or in danger.

The *U.S.S. Pasteur*

In an alternate future timeframe, the doctor was promoted to commander and served as Captain Beverly Picard on the Starfleet medical ship *U.S.S. Pasteur*. She had also married and divorced Jean-Luc Picard but kept his name following the split. Beverly agreed to chase down a temporal anomaly Jean-Luc had spotted in the neutral zone, despite her reservations about his mental state. After her ship crossed the Klingon border to scan the Devron system it was attacked by Klingon attack cruisers. An alternate future *Enterprise*-D, updated with a third warp-housing nacelle, and a powerful phaser below the saucer section, repelled the Klingon ships and rescued the *U.S.S. Pasteur* crew.

1701 nearly a hundred years earlier. This new intoxication called for Crusher to modify Dr. McCoy's original remedy. In the same year, students on a field trip to planet Quazulu VIII were infected with a deadly respiratory virus, which later spreads throughout the *Enterprise*. Beverly's antidote averted disaster.

Dr. Crusher treats individuals on and off the ship, although her concern for entire species has to be held in check by Captain Picard when it violates the Prime Directive. The doctor seized the chance to familiarize herself with Data's mechanisms when she helped reconstruct his brother android, Lore, after he was found abandoned on planet Omicron Theta.

Captain's crush

Dr. Crusher's close relationship with Captain Picard predates their time on the *Enterprise*. Picard had feelings for the doctor, but did not act on them out of respect for her late husband. There were some close calls. Dr. Crusher tried to seduce Picard when she was under the influence of the Psi 2000 intoxication. There was also a frisson when Picard invited her onto the holodeck for a Dixon Hill detective novel reenactment. Dr Crusher was an enticing vision in her 1940s garb.

Dancing is another passion, and although the award-winning tap and jazz dancer is sometimes embarrassed by her nickname "The Dancing Doctor," she did not hesitate to teach Data the basics of ballroom and tap. ■

Dancing with Data The doctor helps the android with a range of lifeskills, including learning to dance ready for his honorary role of father-of-the-bride at Keiko Ishikawa's wedding.

BOY GENIUS
WESLEY CRUSHER

CAPTAIN'S LOG

NAME
Wesley Crusher

SPECIES
Human

BORN
2349, Earth

PARENTS
Jack and Beverly Crusher

STARFLEET DIVISION
Command/Operations

BRIEFING
Wesley's prodigious talents were first identified by the Traveler but he warned Captain Picard not to reveal them. The boy needed to be left to cultivate his abilities without interference

Captain Picard is sometimes uncomfortable with the fact that there are children on board his ship, yet he allows Wesley Crusher to be the first underage person to set foot on his bridge. Over the years Picard had become something of a surrogate father to Wesley, the son of Dr. Beverly Crusher and Lieutenant Commander Jack Crusher, who died on a mission when Wesley was five years old. When Dr. Crusher accepts a year-long temporary command of Starfleet Medical, she leaves her fifteen-year-old son in the care of his *Enterprise* family. The boy had made his

Sir, in the past three years, I've lived more than most people do in a lifetime.
Wesley Crusher

intention to enlist at Starfleet Academy known from a young age, and the captain and crew do all they can to help him. At age 18, Wesley is given a micro-chip containing the holographic video message his late father recorded shortly after his son's birth.

Wesley is particularly gifted in science and technology, showing an impressive grasp of both from his early years, and often eclipsing noted adults in the field. He makes a stellar contribution on several missions, including helping the mysterious interdimensional Tau Alphan known as the "Traveler" to return the *Enterprise*-D to its own galaxy after a failed warp-drive experiment. An impressed Captain Picard gives Wesley the rank of acting ensign at the conn and the chance to watch and learn the ship's entire operations.

Academy upsets
Just before his sixteenth birthday, Wesley takes the Starfleet Academy entrance exams at Relva VII but fails to gain admission. He is ultimately accepted into the academy, but events on the *Enterprise*-D prevent him from joining immediately. In response, Captain Picard promotes

Lefler's Laws

As a handsome young cadet at Starfleet Academy, Wesley Crusher likely attracted plenty of female attention—yet his first romantic interlude occurs on the *Enterprise* during a break from his classes.

Young ensign Robin Lefler is working under Georgi La Forge as a mission specialist in engineering, when Wesley is assigned to help out with a scientific survey. Sparks fly while she advises him on how to manually calibrate some planetary detectors. Then she shares her own "Lefler's Laws," a personal code of conduct based on what she has learned from experience. Typical examples include: "You can only count on yourself," and "When all else fails, do it yourself."

Romance develops while the young couple collaborate to foil a plot by the Ktarians to take over the *Enterprise* (and ultimately the entire Starfleet), using an addictive game to gain control over the crew. After a dinner date in Ten-Forward, Wesley returns to school, adding another law to Lefler's list as he leaves: "A couple of light-years can't keep good friends apart."

Separation When Beverly Crusher leaves her son in order to accept a year-long post on Earth, she worries that his gifts will set him apart from his peers.

Wesley to full ensign, arranging for him to do coursework until he can continue his studies on campus.

While most of his work on board the *Enterprise* is of value, some of Wesley's experiments cause chaos. The ship is put in jeopardy after he creates small robots called nanites that replicate quickly and infiltrate the ship's systems, allowing them to take control.

During his time at Starfleet Academy, Wesley participates in the venerated Nova Squadron flight team. An attempt to perform a prohibited maneuver in preparation for the graduation ceremonies results in the death of Nova Squad member Joshua Albert. Wesley's participation, and collusion in a cover up, leads to a formal reprimand and an order to repeat his final year.

Different dreams

Another meeting with the Traveler in 2370 sets Wesley on a new path. While the *Enterprise*-D crew is ordered to forcibly remove colonists from planet Dorvan V to comply with redrawn borders created by the Federation-Cardassian Peace Treaty, Wesley becomes disillusioned with Starfleet. He resigns his commission, dropping out of the academy so that he can learn from the Traveler as they journey to other planes of existence. ∎

THE REPLACEMENT
DR. KATHERINE PULASKI

CAPTAIN'S LOG

NAME
Dr. Katherine Pulaski

SPECIES
Human

MARITAL STATUS
Divorced (three times)

STARFLEET DIVISION
Sciences

BRIEFING
Writes a seminal research paper, "Linear Models of Viral Propagation" early in her career

During Dr. Beverly Crusher's year-long post as head of Starfleet Medical, another doctor seized the chance to serve on the *Enterprise*-D. Dr. Katherine Pulaski placed her request for transfer to the ship as soon as the position became available.

Doctor Pulaski's bedside manner was markedly different from that of her predecessor. She had empathy with her patients but favored a brisk approach and had a stubborn streak, especially when forced to use forms of technology that she mistrusted. Like Dr. Leonard McCoy, her predecessor by some 80 years, Pulaski had a deep distrust of the transporter and preferred to travel by shuttle. Her refusal to engage with advanced systems also showed in her initial inability to interact on an equal level with Lieutenant Commander Data. She eventually overcame her prejudice and became friends with her sentient android crew mate after the two of them found themselves under attack from a holodeck recreation of Sherlock Holmes' arch rival Moriarty.

On the same side Pulaski initially distrusted Data but came to respect him during their tussle with Moriarty.

From a medical point of view, Pulaski's one year aboard the *Enterprise*-D was a mix of highs and lows. When she examined a youth carrying an advanced aging disease, she became infected herself and rapidly advanced into old age. Ironically, the cure involved using a strand of her hair for DNA and the transporter technology that she had always avoided.

As a physician she was called in when there were complications during Captain Picard's artificial heart replacement. Picard did not want the crew involved in what he considered to be minor surgery so Pulaski promised that she would keep the incident between themselves while she finished her spell of service on the *Enterprise*-D. ■

A LIFETIME OF STRUGGLE
NATASHA "TASHA" YAR

CAPTAIN'S LOG

NAME
Natasha Yar

SPECIES
Human

BORN
2337, Federation Colony Turkana IV (died 2364)

DAUGHTER
Sela

STARFLEET DIVISION
Operations

BRIEFING
An expert in Aikido, Yar participates in martial arts competitions with the crew

Lieutenant Tasha Yar's tragic short life was underwritten with violence. She was born into a failed Federation colony on planet Turkana IV and orphaned at the age of five shortly after the birth of her sister, Ishara. Left to fend for themselves, Tasha tried to care for her sister, scavenging for food and evading the gangs in a violent society. When she escaped the colony at age 15, Ishara stayed behind, and considered her sister a coward for leaving.

Yar joined Starfleet to seek out a better life for herself. Though she never escaped the memories of her youth, she enjoyed early success in her career, personally selected by Captain Picard to serve on the *U.S.S. Enterprise* NCC-1701-D. As security chief, Yar was the tactical officer charged with protection of the ship and its crew while on away missions. During her time as part of the away team on the planet Vagra II, a powerful life-form named Armus killed Yar in a senseless act of violence.

No good-byes. Just good memories. Hailing frequencies closed, sir.
Tasha Yar

Killed in action Tasha Yar died while on duty in Starfleet uniform, as she had predicted she would.

Another tragedy
In an alternate timeline with a similarly bleak outcome, Yar left the *Enterprise*-D to join the crew of the *Enterprise*-C—years before her actual birth—as the crew of that ship attempted to restore the timeline. The *Enterprise*-C was destroyed and Tasha and the rest of the crew were taken prisoner by the Romulans. The horrors of her childhood were revisited when she became the consort of a Romulan general who impregnated her. Yar gave birth to a daughter, Sela, who became the catalyst to her second tragic death. Aged four, Sela revealed her mother's escape plot to her father and Yar was executed. ∎

THE LISTENER
GUINAN

CAPTAIN'S LOG

NAME
Guinan

SPECIES
El-Aurian

BORN
Prior to Earth's late 19th century, El-Auria

OCCUPATION
Bartender, Ten-Forward, _Enterprise_-D

BRIEFING
Is given fencing lessons by Jean-Luc Picard and occasionally resorts to trickery to win

The bartender in the Ten-Forward Lounge on the _Enterprise_-D is as much a mystery as the uncharted species and territories the crew encounter on their missions. Guinan is an El-Aurian and one of the few remaining members of the self-described "Listeners" who became scattered throughout the Galaxy after a devastating Borg attack on their homeworld. Although she is

Historic encounter Data claims friendship with Guinan in the 19th century and asks for help to prevent Devidians harvesting Human energy.

a civilian crew member, she brings her experience of five or more centuries to Starfleet missions.

Guinan's "sixth sense" amounts to much more than a sensitivity to the needs of her bar patrons. When the _Enterprise_-D was caught in an alternate reality in which the vessel was a warship, she was the only crew member to sense that something was wrong. Captain Jean-Luc Picard had forged a close relationship with the El-Aurian and took her word as truth. Picard took

action to correct the timeline and return the _Enterprise_—and Starfleet—to its path of peaceful exploration. This is one of many occasions when the captain sought his bartender's advice.

A younger Guinan assisted the crew when Data and other senior staff members time traveled to the 19th century. Though Guinan had not met Data in this time, she trusted his story and helped him return to the 24th century.

Guinan has great insight into Q but is not forthcoming about their relationship, though their mutual dislike is clear to see. She is also handy with a weapon and keeps a phaser rifle behind the bar in case of emergencies. ∎

My name is Guinan.
I tend bar. And I listen.
Guinan

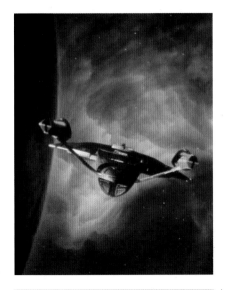

A SOVEREIGN CLASS

U.S.S. ENTERPRISE NCC-1701-E

CAPTAIN'S LOG

NAME
Enterprise NCC-1701-E

CLASS
Sovereign

LENGTH
685.8 meters

BRIEFING
Enterprise-E was launched in 2372 and remains in active service

After the *Enterprise*-D was destroyed in 2371, most of the original crew was transferred to a new *Sovereign*-class ship which, at the time of its launch, was the most advanced ship in the fleet. Unlike its predecessor, the *U.S.S. Enterprise* NCC-1701-E does not have a separating saucer section, nor does it accommodate families on board. It does, however, boast a Captain's Yacht—a luxury shuttlecraft for the captain's sole use.

The *Enterprise*-E followed in the warp path of the ships before it, engaging in one of its signature missions shortly after launch when crew members fought off a second Borg invasion into Federation space. After a Borg sphere entered a temporal rift that it had opened near Earth, Captain Picard ordered the *Enterprise* to follow the enemy back in time. The Borg plan was to stop the launch of Zefram Cochrane's warpship, the *Phoenix,* and prevent first contact between Humans and Vulcans—the earliest step in the formation of the United Federation of Planets. With the formation scrapped, the Alpha Quadrant would be ripe for Borg assimilation.

Borg infiltrated the damaged *Enterprise*-E, assimilating members of the crew along with parts of the ship. Picard ordered the surviving crew to abandon

Plenty of letters left in the alphabet.
Jean-Luc Picard

Superior starship A state-of-the art bridge helps make the *Enterprise*-E the most advanced ship of its time.

ship and initiated the ship's self-destruct, but the Borg Queen aborted the sequence, forcing a confrontation with Picard and Data while the crew assisted with the historic launch on Earth.

Returned to the 24th century, the *Enterprise*-E was repaired but relegated to diplomatic missions during the Dominion War. The crew inadvertently became involved in a Son'a plot to relocate the Ba'ku from their homeworld within the Briar Patch, which ran counter to the Prime Directive. Later, after a refit, the *Enterprise*-E thwarted Praetor Shinzon's plan to use the Romulan warbird *Scimitar* to destroy Earth. ∎

ACTION STATION
DEEP SPACE 9

CAPTAIN'S LOG

NAME
Deep Space 9

LOCATION
Denorios Belt, Bajoran system, Alpha Quadrant

RENAMED
2369

POLITICAL AFFILIATION
Bajoran Provisional Government, United Federation of Planets

BRIEFING
Deep Space 9 was the U.S.S. Voyager's last port of call before the ship was lost in the Delta Quadrant

Special Ops The Operations Center on board Deep Space 9 fulfills the role of a starship's bridge, conference room, and main engineering control hub.

When the Cardassian Union withdrew from the planet Bajor after 50 years as an occupying force, it also abandoned the uridium processing station and command post that its slave labor had built in orbit of the planet. The Cardassians did their best to trash the station as they left, but it remained a useable asset to a world emerging from occupation, and representatives of the Bajoran

Militia moved in. As part of the planet's petition to join the United Federation of Planets, the Bajoran provisional government also asked Starfleet to establish a presence on the station—running it jointly with a Bajoran liaison. Starfleet sent Commander Benjamin Sisko to pave the way for Bajor's entry into the Federation with Major Kira Nerys as his Bajoran first officer. The station, which had previously been called Terok Nor, reopened under a new name: Deep Space 9.

The Bajoran wormhole
For all these changes, the biggest was still to come. Urged on by the Bajoran spiritual leader, Kai Opaka, Sisko and Lieutenant Commander Jadzia Dax set out to discover the source of the nine powerful orbs, or "Tears of the Prophets" that had appeared in the skies of Bajor over several millennia. What they found was a stable wormhole—the only one known to exist—offering fast, safe passage to the far-off Gamma Quadrant. Sisko would later learn that this was no fluke—and that his

Power of three Cardassian design is typified by curves and triangles, often in threes, as seen with Deep Space 9.

That's one of the great things about this station. You never know what's going to happen next, or who you're going to meet.
Benjamin Sisko

fate had been inextricably linked to the wormhole before he was born. The immediate implication was that DS9 was no longer just an aging space station—it would begin a new era as the gateway to a new frontier of exploration.

DS9 was taken out of Bajor's orbit and positioned near the entrance to the wormhole. It became a hub for research and trade in the Gamma Quadrant and a tactical location in the Alpha Quadrant.

Design and layout

As a Cardassian-designed outpost, DS9 differs dramatically from most other Federation space stations. Its basic structure is circular, with two concentric rings linked by bridges that converge on a central core. The inner ring is for habitation, and the outer ring enables smaller ships to dock. Six curved docking pylons for larger vessels extend above and below the outer ring.

The central core is home to the station's Operations Center—also known simply as Ops—which is the closest equivalent DS9 has to a starship's bridge. From here, the command crew can control internal systems, communicate with ships, oversee the docking and departure of vessels, monitor the surrounding area of space, and deploy weapons »

Terok Nor

Before it became known as Deep Space 9, the Cardassian station Terok Nor spent almost 20 years as a uridium ore processing center. It was built and operated by slave labor from the planet Bajor, which was under Cardassian rule.

The station was commanded by the Cardassian Prefect of Bajor, Gul Dukat, and its main function was to process 20,000 tons of ore a day, for use in the construction of Cardassian ships. Conditions for laborers were oppressive, with summary executions for any wrongdoing, and the abuse of Bajoran "comfort women" by Cardassian officers.

Some Bajorans and others were allowed to run shops and bars on the station, but when the Cardassians left Bajor, they ransacked Terok Nor, leaving most of the proprietors with nothing, while some of them were even killed.

The Promenade The shopping district is the figural heart of Deep Space 9 where residents can enjoy the amenities of space station life while mingling with the many guests that visit from all over the Galaxy.

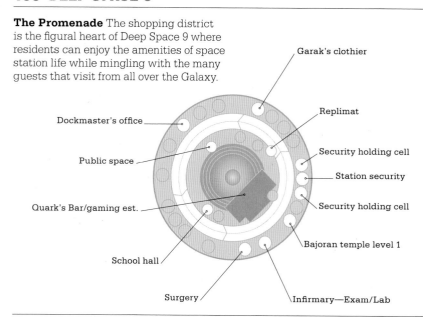

Dockmaster's office
Public space
Quark's Bar/gaming est.
School hall
Surgery

Garak's clothier
Replimat
Security holding cell
Station security
Security holding cell
Bajoran temple level 1
Infirmary—Exam/Lab

to maintain the station's position in orbit above Bajor, but were used to relocate the station to the mouth of the Bajoran wormhole following its discovery in 2369.

Life on the frontier

Within months of DS9 establishing itself as the gateway to the Gamma Quadrant, the station had played host to many previously unknown species from the other side of the wormhole, including the Wadi, the Rakhari, the Parada, and the Tosk. The station also became the focus of tensions relating to Bajor's anticipated future as part of the Federation. In 2370, a Bajoran rebel group, The Circle, seized control of DS9 as part of a plan to free Bajor from off-world influences. Their

You don't think Starfleet took command of this space station without the ability to defend it, do you?
Kira Nerys

to defend the station from attack. There is a viewscreen, transporter facilities, and an elevated private office—designed for a Cardassian prefect to look down on his or her personnel. The touchscreen control panels use a Cardassian interface, giving them a distinctly different look from Starfleet displays.

Below Ops in the central core, a three-level thoroughfare known as the Promenade is the station's social and commercial center. The range of services on offer includes shops, restaurants, replicators, an infirmary, a school, and a temple, as well as Quark's Bar, Grill, Gaming

House, and Holosuite Arcade—one of the most popular establishments on the station.

The habitat ring provides living quarters for thousands of residents and visitors, and also includes the station's armory. Three weapons arrays project from the structure—echoing the curved shape of the larger docking pylons—and there are six landing pads for small craft such as the station's complement of Starfleet runabouts.

The outermost ring features 12 docking ports and is mostly given over to cargo storage. Six thrusters on the docking ring are designed

Deep Space 9 Timeline

2369
Cardassian station Terok Nor ceded to Bajor and renamed Deep Space 9. Federation presence established at request of Bajoran government.

2371
U.S.S. Defiant assigned to DS9 in response to the Dominion threat. Station commander Benjamin Sisko promoted to captain.

2372
Captain Sisko temporarily reassigned from DS9 to Earth as chief of Starfleet Security.

2374
Allied Federation and Klingon forces retake DS9 in Operation Return. Lieutenant Commanders Jadzia Dax and Worf are married on the station.

2375
Captain Sisko marries Kasidy Yates on DS9.

2369 | 2377

2370
Bajoran extremist group The Circle assumes temporary control of DS9 as part of attempted coup on Bajor.

2371
U.S.S. Voyager departs from DS9 immediately prior to its seven-year journey in the Delta Quadrant.

2373
The Dominion War begins as Cardassian and Dominion forces seize control of the station.

2374
Jadzia Dax is killed while in command of DS9. Colonel Kira Nerys takes command while Captain Sisko takes a leave of absence.

2375
The Dominion War ends with the surrender of the Dominion. Colonel Kira Nerys takes command of DS9.

Celestial shortcut As well as being a shortcut to the Gamma Quadrant, the Bajoran wormhole is also the gateway to the Celestial Temple of Bajoran lore.

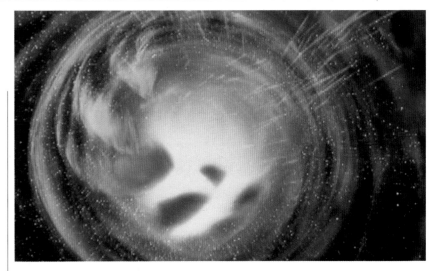

coup fell apart when it was found that they were being armed by the Cardassians. With DS9 peacefully returned to joint Federation and Bajoran control, relations between the planet and its Starfleet partners continued to grow stronger.

The newly formed Maquis—a resistance group that opposed the forced resettlement of Federation citizens from their homes along the nearby Cardassian border—chose DS9 as the location for their first attack, destroying a Cardassian freighter, but otherwise the station's future looked largely peaceful.

That all changed when the *U.S.S. Odyssey*, a *Galaxy*-class Federation starship, was destroyed while in the Gamma Quadrant by the forces of the Dominion—the dominant power on the other side of the wormhole. To help combat the Dominion threat, DS9's weapons and shields were upgraded, and the station was assigned a defensive starship—the heavily armed *U.S.S. Defiant*. However, when Dominion forces did enter the Alpha Quadrant, they did not attack DS9, but

massed their ships in territory belonging to the Cardassians, with whom they had formed an alliance. When the Dominion finally attacked the station, it did so en masse. DS9 destroyed more than 50 Cardassian and Dominion ships, but despite their efforts the station eventually fell to the enemy forces.

Once again under the control of the Cardassians, DS9 reverted to its old name, Terok Nor. Owing to a non-aggression pact between Bajor and the Dominion, the station remained officially Bajoran territory, with many Bajoran Militia officers still on board. However, in practice, it became the base from which the Dominion and

the Cardassians directed their war efforts against the Federation.

After several months, Starfleet and its allies succeeded in retaking the station with help from a newly formed secret resistance group on board. DS9 then became the base for the Ninth Fleet of the Federation Alliance, and served as a vital staging post for forces engaged in the fight against the Dominion. When the war was over, Colonel Kira Nerys took command of DS9, following the departure of Captain Sisko with the wormhole aliens. ∎

See also: Benjamin Sisko, The Bajorans, The Cardassian Union, The Dominion War, The Prophets

Runabouts

Larger than a standard Federation shuttlecraft but much smaller than a starship, runabout vessels were commissioned in 2368 and became the primary form of transportation for the crew of DS9 until the arrival of the *Defiant* in 2371.

Compared to shuttlecraft, the runabouts were suited to a wider range of missions—with greater operational range, living quarters, transporters, and mission-specific modular midsections.

All named after rivers on Earth, the station's original complement of three runabouts comprised the *Ganges*, the *Yangtzee Kiang*, and the *Rio Grande*. Only the last of these was not destroyed in service, with the others replaced by the *Mekong* and the *Orinoco*. Other runabouts in service at various times include the *Rubicon*, the *Shenandoah*, the *Gander*, the *Volga*, and the *Yukon*.

ONE TOUGH LITTLE SHIP
U.S.S. DEFIANT NX-74205

CAPTAIN'S LOG

NAME
U.S.S. Defiant

REGISTRY
NX-74205

CLASS
Defiant

COMPLEMENT
50

LAUNCH DATE
**2370: Original *Defiant*
2375: Renamed
replacement *Defiant***

BRIEFING
**Lieutenant Commander
Worf commanded the first
Defiant in battle against
the Borg in 2373**

Officially referred to as an "escort vessel," the *U.S.S. Defiant* was designed to be Starfleet's first ever warship. It was intended for combat against the Borg, and featured none of the family facilities or research cargo found on board many 24th-century starships. Its engines and firepower far exceeded the capabilities of any other ship of its size, and as a result it almost shook itself apart when it was tested at full power. This led to the prototype being mothballed by Starfleet as the Borg threat receded.

First assignment
Commander Benjamin Sisko worked on the *Defiant* prototype prior to his posting on Deep Space 9. When the threat posed to the station by the Dominion became clear, Sisko requested that the ship be assigned to DS9. It boasted numerous unique features that would serve it well in defense of the station, most notably ablative armor, designed to dissipate blasts from directed energy weapons, and a cloaking device on loan from the Romulan Star Empire. The Treaty of Algeron prohibited other Starfleet ships from using cloaking devices, but for the *Defiant*, the Federation worked out a special amendment with the Romulans.

The ship's first mission was to locate the Dominion's Founders in the Gamma Quadrant and convince them that the Federation was not its enemy. The mission did not go well, and the *Defiant* was attacked and boarded by Dominion forces. On its return to DS9, the ship underwent a two-week overhaul to address its inherent design flaws.

Major engagements
In 2371, the *Defiant* was stolen by the Maquis and used to attack the Cardassians. The following year, it was forced into battle with another Starfleet ship—the far larger *U.S.S. Lakota*, whose crew believed that the *Defiant* was under the control of Changelings. A year after that, the *Defiant* was disabled by a cascade

It's funny—I've served on half a dozen ships, and none of them have had cloaking devices except the *Defiant*. Now that we're not using it I feel... naked.
Miles O'Brien

A history of *Defiants*

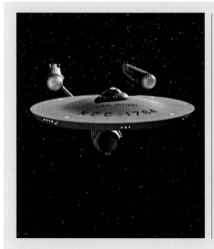

100 years before Commander Benjamin Sisko took command of the *U.S.S. Defiant* NX-74205, the *Constitution*-class *U.S.S. Defiant* NCC-1764 responded to a distress call in Tholian space and became trapped in an interphase between two universes. When it was found by the *U.S.S. Enterprise* NCC-1701 three weeks later, the crew had all been driven mad by the effects and had killed one another.

The *Defiant* was later pushed all the way through the rift, into the "mirror universe," where the Tholians from that reality took control of it. It was then seized by a Terran raiding party and used to stage a coup within the Terran Empire on Earth.

In an echo of these events, Terrans from the mirror universe later coerced Sisko to help them develop a 24th-century *Defiant* for use in their struggle against the Klingon-Cardassian Alliance that had overthrown the Terran Empire many years before.

virus introduced to its systems by a Maquis agent when he was part of DS9's Starfleet personnel.

During the Dominion War, the *Defiant* was involved in numerous engagements under the command of Lieutenant Commander Jadzia Dax, while Sisko served as adjutant to Vice Admiral William Ross. Later Sisko formulated a plan to retake DS9 from Dominion control. The *Defiant* was the lead Starfleet ship in the First Battle of Chin'toka, which dealt a major symbolic blow to the Dominion, but was destroyed alongside 300 other ships when the Dominion reclaimed the Chin'toka system the following year.

In late 2375, the *U.S.S. Sao Paulo* was assigned to DS9 and renamed *U.S.S. Defiant*. Though superficially identical to its namesake, this new ship boasted redesigned shielding to counteract the Breen weaponry that had torn through the fleet in the Second Battle of Chin'toka. The new *Defiant* joined the fleet for the decisive Battle of Cardassia, which proved to be the final battle of the Dominion War. ∎

See also: Deep Space 9, Benjamin Sisko, The Dominion War

Small ship, big guns The *Defiant* was equipped with exceptional phaser and photon firepower.

THE EMISSARY
BENJAMIN SISKO

CAPTAIN'S LOG

NAME
Benjamin Lafayette Sisko

SPECIES
Human

BORN
2332, New Orleans, Louisiana, Earth

PARENTS
Joseph and Sarah Sisko

STARFLEET DIVISION
Command

BRIEFING
When Sisko traveled back in time to 2268, he managed to get Captain James Kirk's autograph by asking him to sign a crew manifest

Ben Sisko was the first officer of the *U.S.S.* Saratoga when it was destroyed by the Borg in the Battle of Wolf 359. Sisko and his son, Jake, made it to an escape pod in time, but his wife, Jennifer, was already dead from injuries she sustained in the battle. He went on to raise his son alone, but constantly replayed his wife's death in his mind.

Two years later, in 2369, Sisko was given a new assignment as commander of Deep Space 9—an old Cardassian mining station in orbit of Bajor, which was to be jointly run by Starfleet and the Bajorans in advance of Bajor's anticipated entry into the United Federation of Planets. Sisko did not want the job, and was even thinking about quitting Starfleet, but the role took on an unexpected appeal when Sisko and Lieutenant Jadzia Dax discovered a wormhole connecting Bajoran space to the distant Gamma Quadrant.

Spiritual leader
Inside the wormhole, Sisko made contact with non-corporeal beings who existed outside linear time. The Bajorans knew these beings as the Prophets, and because of Sisko's communication with them, many Bajorans believed Sisko to be the "Emissary of the Prophets"—a spiritual leader who would save Bajor. At first, Sisko was skeptical, but the Prophets continued to speak to him and send him visions, and eventually confirmed that he was, indeed, their emissary. At times this conflicted with his Starfleet responsibilities—most significantly when he advised Bajor not to join the Federation, after he saw the planet destroyed in a vision.

Wartime commander
By staying out of the Federation, Bajor was able to remain neutral in the Dominion War—a major focus in Sisko's latter years on Deep

It's easy to be a saint in paradise.
Benjamin Sisko

Baseball has been very good to Ben

Benjamin Sisko was always happy to talk baseball, though the game had not been played professionally on Earth since the 2040s. He even kept an antique ball on his desk.

When he first encountered the Prophets in the Bajoran wormhole, he used baseball as a metaphor to explain the concept of linear time. "Every time that you throw a ball," he enthused, "a hundred different things can happen." Not knowing which it would be is what makes the game worth playing.

The game had something of a revival in the 24th century, even among some Vulcans, such as Sisko's former Academy class mate, Solok. When Solok's ship, the *U.S.S. T'Kumbra* docked at DS9, his all-Vulcan team played Sisko's hastily assembled team in a holosuite ballpark. Solok's "Logicians" beat DS9's "Niners" 10-1, but somehow that single run gave Sisko's team a greater sense of victory than a win could ever have done.

Space 9. After making first contact with the Dominion in the Gamma Quadrant, Sisko realized that they posed a serious threat. He convinced Starfleet to fortify DS9 with the *U.S.S. Defiant*, as the station would be on the front line in the event of Dominion forces coming through the wormhole. Not long after, he was promoted to captain, and served briefly as the chief of Starfleet Security when it became clear that Dominion agents were working on Earth. When war was declared, Starfleet was forced to abandon DS9, but Sisko led the eventual assault to retake it. Faced with unbeatable Dominion forces, he invoked the help of the Prophets to defeat them.

Sisko suffered several crises of conscience during the Dominion War, not least when he colluded in a conspiracy to draw the Romulans into the conflict. When Jadzia Dax was killed in battle, he took a leave of absence on Earth, unsure if he

would ever return to DS9. However, a vision revealed to him that the Prophets were responsible for his birth, and his destiny lay with Bajor.

At the end of the war, Sisko was drawn to the Fire Caves on Bajor, where he was forced to surrender

his corporeal, linear existence and take his place among the Prophets. He left Jake and his pregnant wife, Kasidy Yates, behind, but promised to return one day. ■

See also: Deep Space 9, Jake Sisko, The Battle of Wolf 359, The Prophets

Tribble on deck After returning to DS9 from the 23rd century with a tribble, Sisko and his crew face an infestation of the creatures as they overrun the Promenade and Quark's Bar.

REBEL OFFICER
KIRA NERYS

CAPTAIN'S LOG

NAME
Kira Nerys

SPECIES
Bajoran

BORN
**2343, Dahkur
Province, Bajor**

PARENTS
Taban and Meru

OCCUPATION
**Bajoran liaison to
Deep Space 9 (later
station commander)**

BRIEFING
**Like all Bajorans, Kira's
family name precedes
her given name, so her
close friends called
her "Nerys"**

Kira Nerys was born during the Cardassian occupation of Bajor and spent much of her early life in a labor camp on the planet. She got involved with the Bajoran Resistance at the age of 12, and spent her teens participating in raids, ambushes, and bombings against the occupying forces. Her expertise in guerilla warfare served her well in later life, though some of her resistance work still gave her nightmares many years later. When Cardassian forces left Bajor in 2369, the provisional Bajoran government awarded Kira the rank of major in the newly reformed Bajoran Militia.

Starfleet liaison
At the Bajoran government's request, Kira was assigned to Deep Space 9, a former Cardassian mining station above Bajor, as liaison officer to the Starfleet personnel assigned to the station. She was initially skeptical about the benefits of inviting more outsiders to Bajor, but slowly came to see the Federation newcomers as valued colleagues and even friends. She enjoyed a close friendship with Lieutenant Jadzia Dax, and even carried Keiko and Miles O'Brien's baby to term after Keiko was hurt, moving in with the O'Briens during the latter part of the pregnancy.

Secrets and lies Security Chief Odo was secretly in love with Kira Nerys for many years, even though she had lied to him about a murder that took place when she was a resistance fighter.

Kira, Bareil, and Bareil

Kira became involved with Vedek Bareil Antos when she stayed at his monastery. She consulted one of the Orbs of the Prophets at the monastery and it showed her a vision of her and Bareil as lovers. The vision came true and Bareil and Kira were together until his death as a result of an explosion.

Three years after Bareil died, his counterpart from the "mirror universe" arrived on board Deep Space 9, reigniting Kira's feelings for the man that she had lost.

In his universe, he was one of the lovers of Kira's counterpart—the sadistic Intendant Kira—and he had traveled to DS9 to steal one of the Orbs of the Prophets. But after an Orb vision of his own, he saw another way of life—raising a happy family with the Kira from DS9. Ultimately, he left the station empty-handed, and returned to his own universe, convinced that if he stayed with Kira on DS9 he would only end up hurting her.

Born leader Renowned for her tactical and strategic skills, Kira rose from refugee to commander of Deep Space 9.

The Dominion War

During the Dominion War, DS9 fell into the hands of the Cardassians once again. Kira remained on the station as Bajor's liaison with the new administration, while secretly operating a resistance movement that helped Starfleet to retake the station. She was later promoted to colonel and took command of DS9 when Captain Benjamin Sisko took a leave of absence.

Toward the end of the war, Kira took the difficult step of teaching the guerilla tactics she had used during the occupation to her old enemies, the Cardassians, when some of them began to rise up against the Dominion. In order to earn their trust, she accepted a Starfleet commission from Sisko, and donned a Starfleet uniform. In the final battle of the war, Kira led a Cardassian team in an attack on the Dominion command center on Cardassia Prime.

The aftermath

The end of the war saw Sisko depart DS9 for a new life with the Prophets, leaving Kira in full-time command of the station. Kira had a deep respect for Sisko, both as a commander, and as a spiritual guide—the "Emissary of the Prophets." But he was not her greatest loss. As part of the peace with the Dominion, Odo, her lover, had returned to the Great Link—his home among fellow shape-shifters.

Kira had first met DS9's security chief, Odo, during the occupation of Bajor, and over the years he had fallen in love with her. Odo hid his feelings well, certain that Kira did not love him back. When she finally learned the truth, Kira revealed that she felt the same way, and the two began to make up for lost time. After several months together, Kira took Odo home to the Great Link, where they said their final goodbyes. ■

See also: The Mirror Universe, Odo, The Bajorans, The Cardassian Union, The Prophets

I'm always diplomatic!
Kira Nerys

A NEUTRAL PARTY OF ONE

ODO

CAPTAIN'S LOG

NAME
Odo

SPECIES
Changeling

BORN
Founders' homeworld, Gamma Quadrant

OCCUPATION
Security chief

BRIEFING
Odo had to regenerate every 16 hours, when he would revert to his natural gelatinous form and rest in a bucket

Odo came from a species of shape-shifters called the Founders—though he was unaware of this for most of his life, spent among "solids," which is how the Founders refer to non-Changeling life-forms. Odo came to live among the residents of Deep Space 9 when he was found adrift in his natural, gelatinous form near Bajor. The Cardassians sent the peculiar substance for study by the Bajoran scientist Dr. Mora Pol. Not realizing that the sample was even alive, Mora labeled it as *odo'ital*, which means "nothing" in Cardassian, and subjected it to harsh experiments. Only when it lashed out in the form of a tentacle, which then took the shape of a laboratory beaker, did Mora appreciate that he was torturing a sentient being.

When he left Mora's lab behind, Odo kept the name that the doctor had given him, considering it apt for someone with no friends and no past. He modeled his appearance on Mora's own, and found a home on Terok Nor—an ore-processing space station in orbit of Bajor, built as part of the ongoing Cardassian occupation of the planet.

Life on Terok Nor
Being neither a Bajoran worker nor a Cardassian overseer, Odo found a role for himself as a neutral arbiter in disputes on Terok Nor. Asked to investigate a murder on the station, he identified the prime suspect as the Bajoran Kira Nerys. Much later, she would become the person who most defined his life, but her major impact on this first meeting was to give him the nickname "Constable."

Odo eventually became chief of security on Terok Nor, and grew to value the differences between simply keeping order and ensuring justice. When the occupation came to an end, the Bajorans asked him to stay on board the station.

Life on Deep Space 9
Operating as security chief under the new Bajoran/Federation regime brought new challenges. Odo was not used to Starfleet regulations, and the discovery of the Bajoran wormhole brought new threats to the station—now called Deep Space 9—on an almost daily basis. However, the wormhole also gave Odo a chance to investigate his origins. When he did locate his

> Being an outsider isn't so bad. It gives one a unique perspective.
> **Odo**

Solid connections When Odo returned to the Great Link, he said he would miss everyone on Deep Space 9, even Quark, the troublesome Ferengi barkeeper.

people in the Gamma Quadrant, he was shocked to learn that they held a deep hatred for solid life-forms, and that they were the Founders of the tyrannical Dominion.

With the Federation and the Dominion on the brink of war, Odo unwittingly infected his people with a deadly virus created by Starfleet's black ops division, Section 31. When all-out war was declared, Odo sided with his friends on DS9—who were able to find a cure for the virus that was also killing Odo. He was able to end the war by offering to cure the Founders and then stay with them in the Great Link on their home planet.

Returning to his own people was painful because it brought an end to Odo's loving relationship with Kira. His long-concealed feelings for her had blossomed in his last year on board the station. Kira escorted Odo on his final journey to the Great Link, and as a parting gift, he shape-shifted his usual attire into formalwear—she had said that he always looked good in a tuxedo. ■

See also: Section 31, Kira Nerys, Quark, The Dominion, The Dominion War

Dr. Mora Pol

Dr. Mora Pol was the closest thing Odo had to a father. The Bajoran scientist taught him to live among humanoids, but also studied him and performed unpleasant tests on him before he realized he was a sentient life-form. Even when he knew Odo's true nature, he made him perform shape-shifting tasks in the name of science—and less academic party pieces such as the "Cardassian neck trick."

Odo came to resent Mora and they went their separate ways. But when the two of them cared for an infant Changeling many years later, Odo saw how Mora's sometimes harsh methods had their merits. The two reconciled their differences and agreed to see each other again. They may not have parted as father and son, but Odo had a renewed appreciation of his old mentor.

NINE LIVES
JADZIA & EZRI DAX

CAPTAIN'S LOG

NAME
Jadzia Dax

SPECIES
Trill

BORN
**2341, Trill
(joined 2367)**

FATHER
Kela

STARFLEET DIVISION
Sciences

NAME
Ezri Dax

SPECIES
Trill

BORN
**2354, New Sydney
(joined 2374)**

MOTHER
Yanas Tigan

STARFLEET DIVISION
Sciences

Inside every joined Trill is a symbiont: A sentient, slug-like life-form that links with its humanoid host to create a new, interdependent being with a shared consciousness. Symbionts can live for hundreds of years by outliving their hosts and joining afresh, and each new host acquires the memories of their predecessors. Dax is one such symbiont, and had already lived seven other lives when it joined with Jadzia, a female Trill and Starfleet officer.

Jadzia Dax
When Lieutenant Jadzia Dax was assigned to Deep Space 9, she was reunited with Commander Benjamin Sisko, a close friend of the previous Dax host, Curzon. The pair picked up their friendship where it had left off, and Sisko continued to call her by the nickname "old man."

Though she had been quiet and shy before joining with Dax, Jadzia liked to socialize in Quark's Bar on DS9, playing games of tongo with the Ferengi staff long into the night. She also enjoyed the company of Klingons, and renewed Curzon's friendship with three old warriors to fulfill a Klingon blood oath. Her knowledge of Klingon culture

Jadzia Dax After being joined with the Dax symbiont, Jadzia demonstrated the habits of its previous hosts, such as enjoying a lively party.

and skill in Klingon martial arts greatly impressed Lieutenant Commander Worf when he joined the station staff during Jadzia's

Dax's blood oath

A joined Trill is not obligated by debts and commitments incurred in the symbiont's previous lives, but Jadzia Dax felt she it owed to Curzon to honor the "blood oath" that he made with three Klingon friends—Kor, Kang, and Koloth.

Years ago, a criminal known as "the Albino" had murdered the eldest sons of these three elderly warriors, including Dax, Curzon's godson. They swore vengeance on the Albino, and after decades of searching, he was finally found.

The four reunited on DS9 for one last, glorious battle—even though Curzon was dead. They traveled to the Albino's heavily guarded compound, and Jadzia disabled all its energy weapons, giving the old *bat'leth* masters a fighting chance. It was Kang who dealt the death blow to the Albino—but not before he and Koloth were mortally wounded, to Jadzia's grief. It was a good day to die, but there is never a good time to lose a friend.

fourth year on DS9. The pair fell in love and were eventually married, with plans to start a family.

Despite being a science officer first and foremost, Jadzia stepped up to vital command duties during the Dominion War. Promoted to the rank of lieutenant commander, she captained the *U.S.S. Defiant* during many missions and battles against Dominion forces, and also assumed command of DS9 when Sisko was leading a Federation offensive into Cardassian territory.

Jadzia was killed in the Bajoran temple on DS9 after she went there to give thanks for the news that she

and Worf could have children. She was attacked by a Pah-wraith while trying to defend the sacred Bajoran Orb of Contemplation that was kept in the temple, and died shortly after.

Ezri Dax

Though Jadzia was killed, the Dax symbiont was saved. It was sent to Trill to be joined with a new host, but its health deteriorated badly en route. The only way to save it was for Dax to join with the only Trill on the ship—the reluctant Ezri Tigan, who agreed to the procedure, even though she had never intended to become joined.

While most joined Trill undergo lengthy training before receiving their symbiont, Ezri Dax had no preparation. A Starfleet ensign, she sought out Sisko, who gave her a promotion to lieutenant and made her counselor on board DS9. This made life hard for Worf, who was mourning Jadzia, but in time the two were able to get along. Ezri later began a

relationship with Dr. Julian Bashir—a long-time admirer of Dax's previous host, Jadzia. ■

See also: Worlds of the Federation, Benjamin Sisko, Worf, Dr. Julian Bashir, The Klingon Empire

> ❝
> It's a strange sensation, dying. No matter how many times it happens to you, you never get used to it.
> **Ezri Dax**
> ❞

The new host After Jadzia's death, Ezri Tigan became the ninth host of the Dax symbiont, known as Ezri Dax.

OUR MAN BASHIR
DR. JULIAN BASHIR

CAPTAIN'S LOG

NAME
Julian Subatoi Bashir

SPECIES
Human

BORN
2341

PARENTS
Richard and Amsha Bashir

STARFLEET DIVISION
Sciences

BRIEFING
As a child, Bashir's most prized possession was his teddy bear, Kukalaka

D r. Julian Bashir arrived on Deep Space 9 with dreams of "frontier" adventures on one of the Federation's most remote outposts. Straight out of Starfleet Medical Academy, he cut a slightly brash, even irritating figure next to his more seasoned colleagues—not least Lieutenant Jadzia Dax, who had lived whole lifetimes before he was born, but whom he still tried to romance. However, experience came quickly and his commitment to his work soon earned him the respect of his crew mates. After he helped save the life of Chief of Operations Miles O'Brien, the two men formed a close bond, spending time together playing darts, or recreating famous battles from Earth history in the holosuites above Quark's Bar.

Early intrigue
Another friend made by Bashir soon after his arrival on Deep Space 9 was the Cardassian tailor, Elim Garak. Though he claimed to be a plain, simple man, Garak fascinated Bashir from the first time he invited himself to lunch. Bashir was convinced that Garak was a spy, and had his suspicions all but confirmed when he saved Garak's life by removing a cranial implant installed by Cardassia's ruthless secret service, the Obsidian Order. He also allowed

A doctor, not a hologram Bashir was briefly considered as the model for a Long-term Medical Hologram by Dr. Lewis Zimmerman.

Garak to join in another of his favorite holosuite programs—an Earth spy story with Bashir cast as the dashing secret agent hero.

The war doctor

In the run-up to the Dominion War, Bashir was taken prisoner by the Dominion while a Changeling took his place on DS9, which went unnoticed by the crew for more than a month. When the real Bashir escaped, with help from Garak and Lieutenant Commander Worf, he alerted DS9 to the presence of the double, who was about to detonate a star and destroy the Federation fleet.

The year after Bashir's capture by the Dominion, he was abducted again, but this time ostensibly by

I'm a doctor. You're my patient. That's all I need to know.
Julian Bashir

On target Dr. Bashir's genetic enhancements gave him the edge over O'Brien in dart games.

his own side. Section 31, Starfleet's black ops division, had identified him as a potential asset, and subjected him to a simulation of DS9 where he was suspected of being a traitor, to test his loyalties. When Bashir passed this test, Section 31 offered him a job, but he refused—appalled that such a group could exist in Starfleet.

As the Dominion War unfolded, Bashir and O'Brien discovered that Section 31 was responsible for the virus that was killing the Founders of the Dominion—and their friend Security Chief Odo. He succeeded in luring a Section 31 agent to DS9, and worked with O'Brien to extract the cure from the operative, using illegal Romulan mind probes. This not only saved Odo's life, but also led to peace with the Dominion.

The end of the war saw Bashir in a relationship with Lieutenant Ezri Dax, a joined Trill with all the memories of the recently deceased Lieutenant Jadzia Dax. Bashir had been infatuated with Jadzia since his first day on the station, and tried to avoid Ezri at first. But they soon admitted to a mutual attraction and remained together on DS9. ∎

See also: Section 31, Jadzia & Ezri Dax, Miles O'Brien, The Dominion

Bashir's secret history

Dr. Julian Bashir's mental acuity and physical precision were in large part thanks to the illegal form of genetic enhancement he underwent as a child. Knowing that if this secret came out it would end his Starfleet career, Bashir told no one, and grew up thinking that his parents had been ashamed of him.

The truth was revealed when Bashir's estranged parents paid a visit to Deep Space 9, and his father, Richard, spoke candidly to a hologram of his son, under the impression that it was the real Bashir. The doctor thought that he would have to resign, but his father insisted on taking all responsibility and accepted a two-year prison sentence, in exchange for which Starfleet took no action against Bashir.

The incident also led to a reconciliation between Bashir and his parents, who explained that all they had done had been born out of love, not shame.

CHIEF AMONG THEM
MILES O'BRIEN

CAPTAIN'S LOG

NAME
Miles Edward O'Brien

SPECIES
Human

BORN
2328, Killarney, Ireland, Earth

FATHER
Michael O'Brien

STARFLEET DIVISION
Operations

BRIEFING
O'Brien had a daughter, Molly, and a younger son, Kirayoshi, with his wife Keiko

By the time Miles O'Brien came on board Deep Space 9 as chief of operations, he had already spent 22 years serving on six different starships, including the *U.S.S. Enterprise* NCC-1701-D. Though his father had wanted him to become a concert cellist, he joined Starfleet as an enlisted crew

Family guy Miles O'Brien juggled his duties as DS9's chief of operations with his responsibilities as the father of two children, including his firstborn, Molly.

member, and saw extensive combat duty in the Federation-Cardassian Wars. One of his defining memories from this time was a massacre on the Federation colony of Setlik III, where O'Brien saved 13 lives using a field transporter and led an assault against a Cardassian regiment— becoming known as the "Hero of Setlik III" in the process. After the wars, he retained a deep dislike of Cardassians, but later admitted that what he really hated was what they had made him become.

Family matters

O'Brien married Keiko Ishikawa on board the *Enterprise* in 2367, and she and their daughter Molly came with him to DS9 two years later. Keiko set up a school while O'Brien set to work repairing the extensive damage that was done to the station's systems when the Cardassians evacuated. Though Keiko found it hard to adjust to life on DS9, while O'Brien relished the technical challenges, the pair were deeply attached and went on to have another baby on board the station. This second pregnancy was not without drama, as Keiko was injured on board a runabout, and their unborn son had to be transferred to a surrogate— Major Kira Nerys, the Bajoran liaison officer. When he was born, the couple named him Kirayoshi in the major's honor.

The O'Briens faced another challenge to their parenting skills when eight-year-old Molly fell into an alien time portal. It was only a matter of hours for the O'Briens until she was rescued, but for Molly it was ten years, which she spent living a feral existence on an uninhabited

O'Brien and the *Enterprise*-D

Miles O'Brien served on board the *U.S.S. Enterprise* NCC-1701-D under Captain Jean-Luc Picard from its very first mission, when he was assigned to the bridge as relief flight controller. During his tenure he most often served as the transporter chief, but also undertook security and tactical duties on occasion.

It was on the *Enterprise* that O'Brien was introduced to Keiko Ishikawa, by their mutual friend Lieutenant Commander Data.

The pair were later married on board the ship, and a year later their first child, Molly, was born. O'Brien was not present at the birth, as he was trapped on the bridge by a systems failure.

O'Brien was also reunited with Captain Ben Maxwell, his commanding officer from the *U.S.S. Rutledge*, while on board the *Enterprise*. He convinced Maxwell to give himself up after the captain tried to reignite the Federation-Cardassian wars.

world. When the teenage Molly proved unable to cope with life on DS9, her parents made the difficult choice to return her to the world she knew—and were reunited with the younger Molly as a result.

Hard times

For all the comfort his family provided, O'Brien endured many difficult experiences on DS9. In 2369, he was infected by a weaponized virus, known as the Harvesters, and would have died without Dr. Julian Bashir's intervention. In 2370, he was framed and put on trial by the Cardassian state. In 2371, he died from accidental exposure to delta radioisotopes; fortunately the accident also served to shift O'Brien a few hours forward in time—and the O'Brien of a few hours hence was able to

> ❝
> I am very much alive and I intend to stay that way.
> **Miles O'Brien**
> ❞

take the original's place. In 2372, he was given simulated memories of a 20-year prison sentence. During the Dominion War, he was sent undercover to infiltrate the criminal Orion Syndicate, and became good friends with Liam Bilby, a syndicate operative whom he was later forced to betray. It is hardly surprising that after the war, O'Brien returned to Earth with his family to take the post of professor of engineering at Starfleet Academy. He left behind a scale model of the Alamo for Dr. Bashir, who became his best friend during their time together on board DS9. ■

See also: *U.S.S. Enterprise* NCC-1701-D, Deep Space 9, Dr. Julian Bashir

Handheld device O'Brien uses a PADD (Personal Access Display Device) to log and access data.

THE USUAL SUSPECT
QUARK

CAPTAIN'S LOG

NAME
Quark

SPECIES
Ferengi

BORN
2333, Ferenginar

PARENTS
Keldar and Ishka

OCCUPATION
Proprietor, Quark's Bar, Grill, Gaming House, and Holosuite Arcade

BRIEFING
Despite his self-centered reputation, Quark sold food to the Bajorans at reduced prices during the Cardassian occupation of their planet—along with the occasional alibi

Named as the nagus Quark briefly became leader of the Ferengi Alliance after Grand Nagus Zek faked his own death as part of an elaborate scheme.

The arrival of the Federation on the former Cardassian space station Deep Space 9 nearly convinced Quark to leave. When the station had been known as Terok Nor, Quark had run a thriving bar business, plus illegal sidelines, but as the Federation doesn't use money, Quark couldn't see the profit in sticking around. The station's new Starfleet commander, Benjamin Sisko, knew that DS9 would need businesses to survive, and put pressure on Quark to stay. He did, and the bar went from strength to strength, despite having to operate (for the most part) on the right side of Federation and Bajoran law.

Worthy adversaries

From the day they first met on Terok Nor, Odo was a regular thorn in Quark's side. The shapeshifter, who, with the arrival of Starfleet, became DS9's chief of security, disliked Quark's dishonesty, but came to respect his cunning over the years. The respect was mutual; the two liked to trade insults while trying to catch each other out. They saved each other when they were marooned on a barren planet, and when Odo finally left DS9, Quark sought him out to say goodbye.

Indeed, compared to his main adversary in business, Liquidator Brunt from the Ferengi Commerce

Quark's Bar

Food, drink, gossip; *dabo*, *tongo*, *dom-jot*; holosuites; even darts. Visitors to the Promenade on Deep Space 9 could find it all at Quark's Bar, Grill, Gaming House, and Holosuite Arcade.

Thirsty? Try the Aldebaran whiskey, Saurian brandy, Tranya, or Kanar. Recommended cocktails include the "Black Hole" and the "Warp Core Breach," while non-alcoholic options take in root beer, *raktajino*, Slug-o-Cola, prune juice, and even Enyak's milk.

Hungry? Why not try some groatcakes, or the "Kai Winn soufflé"—named in honor of the Bajoran religious leader. Or, if what you really hunger for is adventure, book a holosuite to experience the famous Battle of the Alamo, the Battle of Klach D'Kel Brakt, kayaking, baseball, ion surfing, or a secret agent story with you as the hero. All it takes is a few slips of latinum, and Quark can make all your fantasies come true!

Association, Odo was more like a best friend to Quark.

Quark met Brunt when the latter was investigating Quark's mother, Ishka, who broke the Ferengi law prohibiting females from earning profit. Brunt showed up again to punish Quark when he failed to prevent his bar staff from forming a trade union (also against Ferengi rules). Brunt bought Quark's body parts when Quark auctioned them off in the mistaken belief that he was dying, and then put Quark out of business when he reneged on the deal by surviving.

Quark twice foiled Brunt's plans to become grand nagus—leader of the Ferengi people—and on the second occasion posed as a female to secure support for the real nagus's newfound passion for female rights. Ishka was now the power behind the nagus's throne, and though Quark harbored dreams of assuming the nagus title one day, the role eventually went to his brother and business partner, Rom.

Frontier Ferengi

Quark was one of the first Ferengi to meet a Human, when he, Rom, and Rom's son, Nog, accidentally traveled back in time to Earth in

> All I ask is a tall ship
> and a load of contraband
> to fill her with.
> **Quark**

the 1940s. He was also among the first Ferengi to travel to the mirror universe, and to encounter the main Dominion species—the Founders, the Vorta, and the Jem'Hadar.

When the Dominion War broke out and Starfleet was forced off DS9, Quark continued to run his bar. Despite his supposed dislike of the Federation, he passed information to the

Emissary of the profits

Quark prided himself on having the lobes for business and was prepared to bend—or break—the law in search of a good deal.

rebels and helped Starfleet to retake DS9. After the war, Quark remained on the station. ∎

See also: Odo, Rom, Nog, and Leeta, The Ferengi Alliance

WAR CORRESPONDENT

JAKE SISKO

CAPTAIN'S LOG

NAME
Jake Sisko

SPECIES
Human

BORN
2355

PARENTS
Benjamin and Jennifer Sisko

OCCUPATION
Writer

BRIEFING
Jake's early writing projects included a semi-autobiographical novel called *Anslem* and the short story, "Past Prologue"

Just like his father, Benjamin, Jake Sisko had a narrow escape from the *U.S.S. Saratoga* when it was destroyed by the Borg. His mother, Jennifer, was killed in the attack, uniting the 11-year-old and his father in grief.

When Commander Sisko was assigned to the distant space station Deep Space 9 three years later, both father and son were unenthusiastic—though the elder Sisko did his best to put a brave face on it. It was only when Jake befriended a young Ferengi boy called Nog that he began to settle in. Jake's father did not approve of the friendship at first, but over time Jake taught Nog to read and encouraged him to join Starfleet. The two had their fallings-out, but their bond endured over many years and they eventually came to share quarters.

War writing
Jake had ambitions to become a writer and was traveling with DS9's doctor, Julian Bashir, to gather information for an article when the Federation colony on Ajilon Prime came under attack. While Bashir attended the wounded on the colony,

Ballpark father figure Jake and his father, Benjamin Sisko, enjoyed playing baseball and recreating famous games in the holosuites on Deep Space 9.

> Why can't we live on the planet instead of some old space station?
> **Jake Sisko**

Jake got his first taste of the brutal reality of war. Caught in an assault on a hospital, he fired a phaser in panic and brought down a ceiling, halting the attack. He was hailed as a hero, but explored the truth in an article about the fine distinction between cowardice and courage.

Later, when Starfleet was forced to relinquish control of DS9 during the Dominion War, Jake chose to remain on the station, serving as a reporter for the Federation News Service. With his dispatches being suppressed by the Dominion, he joined a resistance cell formed by Major Kira Nerys, and helped the Federation Alliance to retake DS9 by disabling its weapons.

Mom in the mirror

Six years after Jennifer Sisko died, Jake experienced her loss all over again when her counterpart from the alternative reality known as the mirror universe abducted him. Her intention was to secure Benjamin Sisko's help in the rebellion against that reality's Klingon-Cardassian Alliance, but she and Jake became close during his time in a universe where the mirror version of Benjamin and Jennifer did not have a son. However, the relationship was cut short when Jennifer was killed defending Jake from disruptor fire.

Prom pals Jake and Nog spent many happy hours watching the world—and the women—go by on DS9's Promenade.

Back in his own universe, Jake later served as best man at his father's wedding to Kasidy Yates, a freighter pilot whom he had introduced to Benjamin. When his father left DS9 for a new life with the Prophets, he promised Kasidy and Jake that he would return eventually. ■

See also: Benjamin Sisko, Rom, Nog, and Leeta, The Dominion War, The Battle of Wolf 359.

The future rewritten

In an alternative timeline, Jake Sisko lost his father to an energy discharge from the warp core of the *U.S.S. Defiant*. Though he was not dead, Captain Sisko was left in a temporal limbo falling in and out of time. Nothing could be done to retrieve him, and Jake had no choice but to move on with his life.

Years later, when Jake was a successful and happily married author, his father appeared to him and expressed pride at his son's achievements. Jake then gave up writing and dedicated the rest of his life to bringing his father back. His obsession cost him his marriage, but after 50 years, he was able to speak to his father again. Distraught that Jake had sacrificed so much, Benjamin urged him to return to writing.

When Jake realized that his own existence was trapping his father in time, he killed himself. This returned Benjamin to his own time, where he was able to avoid the warp core accident.

FAMILY BUSINESS
ROM, NOG, AND LEETA

Quark's younger brother, Rom, was not a traditional Ferengi. He did not possess the business skill for which his species is famed and—after the birth of his son, Nog—signed away all of his assets to the family of his wife, who then left him. He allowed himself to be cheated out of his fair share of profits while working in his brother's bar, and even established a trade union for Quark's staff—in direct contravention of Ferengi law. Worst of all in his brother's eyes, Rom allowed Nog to attend a Federation school, learn to read, and eventually enrol at Starfleet Academy.

What Rom lacked in traditional Ferengi thinking, he made up for in prodigious engineering talent. His

I've always been smart, Brother. I've just lacked self-confidence.
Rom

skills saw him rise swiftly through the ranks when he joined the Deep Space 9 maintenance team. When the Dominion began to mass its forces in the Alpha Quadrant, it was Rom who designed the mines that successfully barricaded their passage through the wormhole for several months.

Rom fell in love with Leeta when she was working at the *dabo* tables in Quark's Bar, but he did not find the courage to tell the Bajoran woman how he felt until she was about to leave the station forever. When he discovered that she reciprocated his feelings, the two were married within a year.

Rom eventually became grand nagus—the most powerful figure in the Ferengi Alliance. This was not in spite of his unconventional approach to life, but because of it, and came as a result of his mother's increasing influence in reforming Ferengi society.

Starfleet's first Ferengi
Rom's son, Nog, lived on DS9 with his father and proved to be just as nonconformist, if not more so. His friendship with the Human youth Jake Sisko introduced him to new experiences such as reading and

Morn

In a bar where everybody knows your species, you can always rely on one particular stool being filled by Quark's most frequent customer: Morn.

Morn is a Lurian whose life is more colorful than one might suspect from looking at him. He ships mundane cargoes such as beets for a living, but he once took part in a heist at the Central Bank of Lissepia, stealing 1,000 bricks of gold-pressed latinum. He stored the liquid latinum in his second stomach for years, causing his hair to fall out. He then faked his death to throw his fellow thieves off his trail.

Morn also aided Starfleet in the war against the Dominion by passing intelligence on to Captain Benjamin Sisko.

Morn's presence at Quark's Bar is such a fixture that when he's not there, business drops. That's why Quark created a hologram of him to fill his stool whenever the barfly is away.

formal education, which led him to pursue a career in Starfleet. As the first ever Ferengi to wear a Starfleet uniform, Nog fought bravely in the Dominion War, and lost one of his legs in battle. He was given a new biosynthetic leg, but struggled to cope with the emotional distress

Engine ears Nog's time as a Starfleet cadet included a field commission as chief engineer on the *U.S.S. Valiant*—a ship crewed entirely by cadets.

> Can you believe it? They made me an ensign!
> **Nog**

caused by the injury and thought about resigning his commission. He chose to remain in Starfleet while on medical leave on DS9, and was promoted to lieutenant junior grade at the end of the war.

Not just a *dabo* girl

Dabo girl Leeta's light-hearted air belied a hidden depth beneath her beauty. Her first relationship on DS9 was with Dr. Julian Bashir, and later she considered leaving the station to start a new life with another Starfleet doctor, Lewis Zimmerman. But Rom learned of her plans and confessed his love for her, which convinced her to stay. Captain Benjamin Sisko officiated at their wedding just a short time later—an honor for the bride, given Sisko's spiritual significance among Bajorans as the Emissary of the Prophets.

The Dominion War forced the newlyweds to part briefly, but they were soon reunited in resistance against the Cardassians and their Dominion allies. When Rom was made grand nagus of the Ferengi Alliance, Leeta became the "first lady" of Ferengi society. It seemed unlikely that she would ever wait on another *dabo* table again. ∎

See also: Quark, The Bajorans, The Ferengi Alliance

Bar association Rom and Leeta met when they were both working for Rom's brother, Quark. Together they formed a trade union, and later a romantic one.

THE VOYAGE HOME
U.S.S. VOYAGER NCC-74656

CAPTAIN'S LOG

NAME
U.S.S. Voyager

REGISTRY
NCC-74656

CLASS
Intrepid

LENGTH
343 meters

DECKS
15

LAUNCH DATE
2371

BRIEFING
Voyager had a crew complement of 141 before it was pulled into the Delta Quadrant

The U.S.S. Voyager was just over half the size of its contemporary, the Galaxy-class Enterprise-D, but it was faster (with a top speed of warp 9.975), and equipped with more advanced computer and sensor systems. The Intrepid-class ship was also capable of making landfall, and was among the first to be equipped with an Emergency Medical Hologram, or EMH. These advances proved vital when the ship became stranded in the Delta Quadrant, 70,000 light-years away from its last known position—as did the ingenuity and tenacity of its Starfleet crew, and the Maquis rebels it absorbed into its number. Over seven years, the ship overcame many new threats and incredible odds before returning to Earth with a hero's welcome.

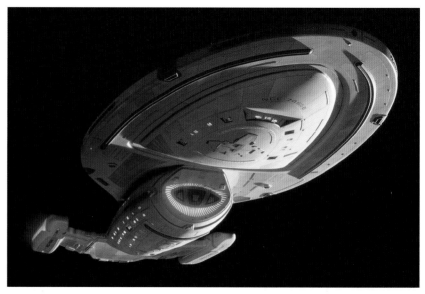

Delta dealings During seven years in the Delta Quadrant, the U.S.S. Voyager made contact with dozens of species previously unknown to the Federation.

How to land a starship

Most starships are built in space and designed to stay in space—their crew traveling to planets by transporter or shuttlecraft. But *Intrepid*-class starships have the unique ability to enter a planet's atmosphere and touch down upon its surface.

Prior to landing, the *U.S.S. Voyager* crew goes to code blue status. The warp core is taken offline and all plasma is vented from the nacelles. Atmospheric controls are placed on standby, landing mechanisms are brought online, and the inertial dampers are set at maximum. As the flight controller takes the ship into the atmosphere of a planet, compensations are made for turbulence and gravity. Once the landing site is visually confirmed, landing struts are extended from the engineering hull and locked in place. On touch down, the engines are disengaged and the thruster exhaust is secured.

The crew also assumes its code blue stations for take-off, which is achieved using anti-grav thrusters until it is safe to use the impulse engines and reengage the warp core.

Technical specifications

Intrepid-class starships were the first Starfleet vessels to make use of bio-neural gel packs instead of isolinear circuitry in their primary systems. Bio-neural cells within the gel packs processed data more efficiently than isolinear chips for faster computer response times. Owing to their biological nature, however, these cells proved to be susceptible to infection, leading the crew of *Voyager* to investigate more traditional alternatives during their time in the Delta Quadrant.

Another feature that debuted on board *Intrepid*-class vessels, and which went on to become standard issue, was the Emergency Medical Holographic program. Designed to act as a supplement to, or temporary replacement for, the medical staff of a starship in times of crisis, the EMH Mark I installed on *Voyager* was quickly retired on other ships owing to its poor bedside manner, but became essential to *Voyager*'s survival when its original team of medics were all killed during its unplanned journey to the Delta Quadrant. This particular EMH not only saved lives on many occasions, but also surpassed the limitations of his original programming to become a valued crew member.

Voyager had a duranium hull in a streamlined iteration of the usual Starfleet formation of saucer section and secondary, engineering section with two warp nacelles. Unlike most starships, *Voyager*'s warp pylons were able to pivot—repositioning the nacelles for maximum efficiency in and out of warp. The ship's defenses included multiphasic shields, several phaser banks, and a pair of photon torpedo launchers, but over the course of its journey through the Delta Quadrant, the vessel received a variety of non-standard upgrades. Access to Borg technology enhanced not only the ship's defenses, but also its power relays, warp engines, and sensors—cutting its estimated journey time back to Earth by around 20 years. »

An intrepid voyager The *Intrepid*-class *U.S.S. Voyager* is one of the latest 24th century starship designs. Smaller and sleeker than the *Galaxy*-class, it boasts one of the most advanced computer systems in the fleet.

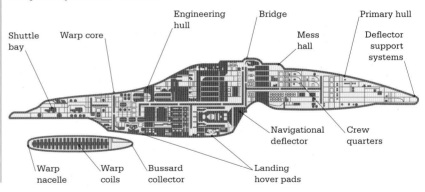

Shuttle bay · Warp core · Engineering hull · Bridge · Mess hall · Primary hull · Deflector support systems · Navigational deflector · Crew quarters · Warp nacelle · Warp coils · Bussard collector · Landing hover pads

Handle with care "Caretaker" was a name given to a powerful member of the Nacene species who protected the Ocampa species.

The Caretaker

Voyager's long isolation in the Delta Quadrant was due to a being known to them as the Caretaker. The ship set out to locate Lieutenant Tuvok, a Vulcan Starfleet officer who had gone missing on his mission to infiltrate the Maquis, a resistance group fighting against the terms of the Federation's treaty with the Cardassian Union. When Captain Kathryn Janeway pursued Tuvok's Maquis ship into a region of anomalous space known as the Badlands, *Voyager* was struck by a displacement wave that sent the ship 70,000 light-years off course—badly damaging it in the process.

After identifying their new location as the Delta Quadrant, the *Voyager* crew found both the Maquis ship—which had suffered the same displacement—and the Caretaker, a life-form that was retrieving vessels from across the Galaxy in search of a compatible mate. The Caretaker was responsible for the wellbeing of a species called the Ocampa, but was about to die. He feared leaving the Ocampa to the mercy of the rapacious Delta Quadrant sect the Kazon-Ogla. In his dying moments, he convinced Janeway to destroy his base, rather than let it fall into Kazon hands—even though this would mean destroying the most expeditious means of sending *Voyager* and the Maquis vessel back home.

With two crews now stranded in the Delta Quadrant, and the Maquis ship lost in battle with the Kazon, Janeway welcomed the Maquis on board *Voyager*, assigning them all to standard crew duties. Tuvok resumed his role as Janeway's security officer, while the Maquis leader, Chakotay, became her first

This ship is a match for any vessel within a hundred light-years. And what do they do with it? Well, let's see if we can't find some space anomaly today that might rip it apart.
Neelix

officer. The new crew set a course for home—some 75 years away.

The Delta Quadrant

During its passage through regions never before charted by Federation vessels, *Voyager* sought out spatial and temporal anomalies that might shorten its journey home, and made first contact with more species than any ship since the *U.S.S. Enterprise* NCC-1701. Its early encounters with unfriendly Delta Quadrant species such as the Kazon and the Vidiians

The *Delta Flyer*

After five years traversing the hostile Delta Quadrant, the *U.S.S. Voyager* had lost a number of its original complement of shuttlecraft in the line of duty. When a specialized vehicle was required to retrieve a probe from within a gas giant, Captain Janeway authorized the construction of the *Delta Flyer*—a vessel that had been conceived by Lieutenant Tom Paris. His 24th-century "hot rod," complete with dials and levers inspired by Paris's science fiction-based "Captain Proton" holodeck program, boasted retractable warp nacelles, a tetraburnium alloy hull with parametallic plating, unimatrix shielding, and photonic missiles.

After a successful mission inside the gas giant, the *Flyer* was deployed many times—traveling through a quantum slipstream and underwater—before it was destroyed during an assault against the Borg.

A replacement was built and named *Delta Flyer II*, and went on to compete in the Antarian Trans-stellar Rally.

were made more challenging by the tensions that existed between the Starfleet and Maquis personnel, but in time the two crews became one coherent unit. Together they shaved whole decades off their journey time, and staved off threats from the likes of the Krenim and the Hirogen.

There were births and weddings on board, and regular scientific discoveries and technological advancements. The vessel even reestablished contact with the Federation after four years. But one threat continued to loom large: They were traveling through the region of the Galaxy that was home to the Borg.

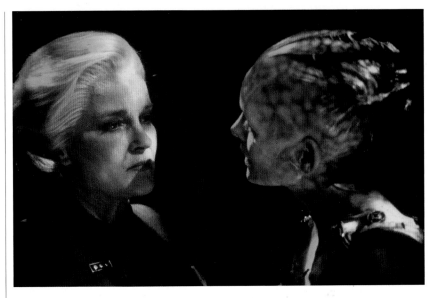

Borg space

Voyager's first indication of Borg activity came two years into their journey, when the crew discovered the remains of a Borg drone, and then an entire derelict Borg cube. When *Voyager* finally encountered active Borg vessels, the crew learned that the Borg were at war with a powerful extra-dimensional species known as Species 8472. Concluding that this species posed a greater threat to the Galaxy than the Borg collective, Janeway made an alliance with the Borg—helping them to banish Species 8472 to its own fluidic realm in exchange for *Voyager*'s safe passage. Once their enemy was defeated, the Borg broke the alliance and tried to assimilate *Voyager*, but the crew was prepared and escaped, taking with them a single Borg drone who later became an important member of the crew.

After seven years in the Delta Quadrant, *Voyager* finally returned home thanks to the use of a Borg transwarp hub in Unimatrix 01— the heart of Borg space. Though Janeway had originally chosen to avoid this Borg stronghold, she was convinced to reconsider it by a version of herself from a future where it had taken the ship 23 years to get home. The future Admiral

Future shock An older version of Admiral Janeway sacrificed herself to defeat the Borg and get *Voyager* back to Earth, erasing her established timeline.

Janeway equipped *Voyager* with advanced weaponry to fend off the Borg and then sacrificed herself in order to infect the Borg with a neurolytic pathogen. This enabled *Voyager* to destroy the transwarp hub while inside it, emerging close to Earth in the Alpha Quadrant, with no way for the Borg to follow. ∎

See also: The Known Universe, Kathryn Janeway, Chakotay, Seven of Nine, The Maquis, The Borg Collective, Species 8472, The Nacene

U.S.S. Voyager Timeline

2370
Kathryn Janeway is chosen to command the *U.S.S. Voyager* NCC-74656.

2372
Naomi Wildman is the first child to be born on *Voyager*. The ship is briefly hijacked by the Kazon and the crew left stranded.

2374
Voyager allies with the Borg against Species 8472. The former Borg drone Seven of Nine joins the crew. Contact is made with Starfleet.

2376
Starfleet's Pathfinder Project, led by Admiral Owen Paris on Earth, establishes regular datastream contact with *Voyager*.

2378
Voyager returns to Earth via a Borg transwarp hub, with help from a future version of Janeway. Miral Paris, Torres and Paris' daughter, is born on the ship.

2370   2380

2371
Voyager is transported to the Delta Quadrant on its first mission. Maquis personnel join the crew for the 70,000-light-year journey back to Earth.

2373
Starfleet Command declares *Voyager* officially lost. The ship travels to Earth in 1996 and later enters Borg space.

2375
The *Delta Flyer* launches. *Voyager* traverses large expanses of space using a Borg transwarp coil, a quantum slipstream, and a subspace vortex.

2377
The *Delta Flyer* is destroyed. Lieutenants Tom Paris and B'Elanna Torres are married and take their honeymoon on board its replacement, the *Delta Flyer II*.

THE CAFFEINE-FUELED CAPTAIN
KATHRYN JANEWAY

CAPTAIN'S LOG

NAME
Kathryn Janeway

SPECIES
Human

BORN
May 20, Bloomington, Indiana, Earth

PARENTS
Edward and Gretchen Janeway

STARFLEET DIVISION
Command

BRIEFING
Captain Janeway likes her coffee black—and as often as possible

The daughter of a Starfleet admiral, Kathryn Janeway was captain of the *U.S.S. Voyager* when it was flung 70,000 light-years across the Galaxy, along with a ship of Maquis separatists. Faced with a choice between returning home using powerful technology that would fall into the

Renaissance woman As a scientist, Captain Janeway enjoyed discussions with a holodeck recreation of the artist and inventor Leonardo da Vinci.

hands of a hostile alien species bent on harm, she chose to destroy the equipment. With both her ship and that of the Maquis stranded in the Delta Quadrant, Janeway integrated the Maquis on her Starfleet vessel. Though well out of communication range with Starfleet Command, she insisted that all on board should follow Starfleet regulations because discipline was their best chance of reurning home in one piece.

As a scientist, Janeway relished the chance to explore uncharted regions of space on board *Voyager*, but as a Starfleet captain, she was well aware of her responsibility to get her crew back home. During

seven years in the Delta Quadrant, she formed close bonds with her ship mates, but denied herself the luxury of a romantic relationship, despite the mutual attraction she shared with her Maquis first officer, Commander Chakotay. She enjoyed a longstanding friendship with her Vulcan security chief, Tuvok, from before their time on *Voyager*, and served as a mentor and a role-model for her junior officers and the former Borg drone Seven of Nine.

Personal heroes
Janeway was affected deeply by the death of her father, and the depression that followed. Her sister helped her to recover, and Janeway went on to excel as the scientist that he had inspired her to be. Janeway was similarly inspired by an ancestor, Shannon O'Donnell, whom she believed had a role in Earth's space program during the 21st century. This turned out to be untrue, but served as the impetus for Janeway's enrolment in Starfleet.

An unusual set of circumstances also gave Janeway the chance to meet her biggest idol—the Human pilot Amelia Earhart, who had been presumed dead in 1937. In fact, her disappearance was the result of

Janeway assimilated

Like her fellow captain Jean-Luc Picard, Kathryn Janeway had her fair share of encounters with the Borg and their Queen, and was even assimilated to become part of their collective. Unlike Picard however, Janeway deliberately allowed herself to be turned into a drone, along with Lieutenant B'Elanna Torres and Lieutenant Commander Tuvok.

The three officers hoped to infect the collective with a virus that would give Borg drones the power of independent thought. With their bodies assimilated but their minds protected by an inoculation, they succeeded in deploying the virus, though Tuvok succumbed to the power of the hive mind and Janeway was captured. They survived with help from the drones freed by the virus—initiating a Borg civil war. All three crewpersons returned to *Voyager*, where the Emergency Medical Hologram removed their Borg implants.

abduction by aliens from the Delta Quadrant, where Earhart survived in suspended animation.

Coming home

In 2378, Janeway met a version of herself from a future where it had taken *Voyager* 23 years to get back to Earth, at great personal cost to the crew. This older Janeway had identified a point in time where the ship could get home much sooner, and was equipped with technology from her own time to help them do so. The younger Janeway was very reluctant to change the timeline, but eventually agreed to a plan that would take the ship home and deal a significant blow to the Borg. Her future counterpart sacrificed herself to achieve this, submitting to Borg assimilation in order to infect the collective with a highly destructive neurolytic pathogen. In the newly created timeline, *Voyager* returned home safely—seven years after it set out. Its captain was promoted, and became Admiral Janeway, just as her father had been before her. ■

See also: *U.S.S. Voyager* NCC-74656, Holographic Technology

Brave leader Captain Janeway often risks personal safety to save her crew.

THE CONTRARY COMMANDER

CHAKOTAY

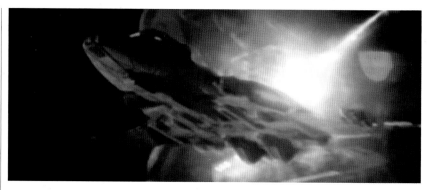

CAPTAIN'S LOG

NAME
Chakotay

SPECIES
Human

BORN
2329, Federation colony world near the border with Cardassian space

FATHER
Kolopak

STARFLEET DIVISION
Command

BRIEFING
Chakotay professes a passion for anthropology and paleontology

Several generations before Chakotay was born, his Native American ancestors left Earth to live a spiritual life far removed from modern technology. Growing up in the colony they founded, Chakotay struggled to fit in and longed to embrace modernity over tradition, taking inspiration from stories of space pioneers. His father described him as a "contrary," citing his breech birth as evidence of non-conformity. At age 15, Chakotay proved his father right by applying to Starfleet Academy.

Starfleet and beyond
Chakotay proved himself an able pilot at the Academy—as well as an accomplished boxer. He served on board a starship after graduating, and moved up the ranks to become a lieutenant commander. However his Starfleet career was cut short after 13 years, when his father was killed defending their colony from Cardassian attackers. A Federation treaty with the Cardassians left the colonists unprotected by Starfleet. Angered by a Starfleet policy that killed his father, Chakotay resigned

Under fire Chakotay's Maquis raider, the *Val Jean*, comes under Cardassian attack shortly before being transported to the Delta Quadrant.

his commission and joined with the Maquis—a resistance group fighting for all the colonists affected by the treaty. Chakotay's ancestors had been forced off their land on Earth long ago, and he was unwilling to see history repeated. During this time he began to embrace the beliefs and traditions of his tribe, decorating his brow with a tattoo in honor of his father.

In the Delta Quadrant
With his command experience, Chakotay was soon put in charge of a Maquis ship. He did not know that his crew included spies for the

Seska

Chakotay was hurt to find that Tuvok—one of his fellow Maquis fighters—was an undercover Starfleet officer. But the betrayal paled next to the discovery that his former lover, Seska, was a Cardassian spy.

Seska had been genetically altered to appear Bajoran and had tricked her way into the Maquis and Chakotay's affections. Once on board *Voyager*, she cared only about getting home, and made deals with species in the Delta Quadrant behind Chakotay and Captain Janeway's backs. Her Cardassian nature was revealed following an accident, and she defected to the Kazon-Nistrim.

As part of this warlike tribe, Seska continued to plot against *Voyager*. She used her newborn son to lure the ship into a trap—claiming that Chakotay was the child's father—and successfully seized control of *Voyager* with the Kazon. She was killed in the battle to retake the ship.

Federation and the Cardassians, but when his ship was pulled into the Delta Quadrant, the *U.S.S. Voyager* followed in pursuit of its undercover operative. Stranded and faced with unknown threats, Chakotay agreed to cooperate with Captain Kathryn Janeway of *Voyager* for the benefit of both their crews. When *Voyager* came under attack, he destroyed his own ship to protect the Starfleet vessel, leaving the Maquis in need of a new home. Chakotay took responsibility for his crew on board *Voyager*, and Captain Janeway awarded him the vacant position of first officer, provisionally ranked commander—a sign of trust and cooperation within the newly combined Maquis and Starfleet crew.

Commander Chakotay lived up to the standards he had learned at Starfleet Academy and set a strong example to the rest of the Maquis crew. Over time, he forged a lasting bond with Captain Janeway, but was not afraid to challenge her, or to stand up for the non-Starfleet personnel on the ship. He did not neglect his spirituality in his new role, and during one away mission communicated with a species that had visited his tribe in the form of "Sky Spirits" 45,000 years before.

When the former Borg drone Seven of Nine joined the crew of *Voyager*, Chakotay found it hard to trust her. But the pair grew closer and he helped her reconnect with her Human emotions. They began a romantic relationship just in time for the ship's safe return to Earth. ∎
See also: Kathryn Janeway, B'Elanna Torres, Seven of Nine, The Maquis

Family ink Chakotay's tribal tattoo honored his dead father and the Native American heritage they shared.

My people taught me that a man does not own land. He doesn't own anything but the courage and loyalty in his heart.
Chakotay

MR. VULCAN
TUVOK

CAPTAIN'S LOG

NAME
Tuvok

SPECIES
Vulcan

BORN
**2264, Vulcanis
Lunar Colony**

MOTHER
T'Meni

STARFLEET DIVISION
Operations

BRIEFING
**Tuvok is married to T'Pel,
with whom he has three
sons, one daughter, and a
grandchild named T'Meni
after Tuvok's mother**

Lieutenant Tuvok was not on board *Voyager* when it was dragged 70,000 light-years away from home. Instead, he was already in the Delta Quadrant—serving undercover on the Maquis ship that had suffered the same fate, and which *Voyager* had been sent to locate. With both vessels stranded, he resumed his role as *Voyager*'s security officer, reuniting with his friend Captain Kathryn Janeway, and revealing his betrayal to the Maquis. As the two factions became one on board *Voyager*, the Maquis leader, Chakotay, became Janeway's first officer, while Tuvok served as her second officer—an arrangement that the 107-year-old Vulcan respected as logical.

Unlikely friendships
Despite his Vulcan reserve—or perhaps because of it—Tuvok

When Tuvok met Neelix Whereas Tuvok might favor a Vulcan salute, the Talaxian Neelix has no reluctance to greet new acquaintances with a hug.

formed bonds with two emotional Delta Quadrant inhabitants who joined the *Voyager* crew from the outset of their long journey home. The Talaxian chef Neelix, who set himself up as *Voyager*'s unofficial morale officer, took an immediate liking to Tuvok, calling him "Mr. Vulcan" from their first meeting. When Tuvok lost his memory and his emotional control, Neelix helped him recover, and Tuvok admitted to some reciprocal affection for the Talaxian. Later, the two were fused into one being by a transporter accident, and lived for more than a month as the hybrid "Tuvix."

Tuvok also developed a close bond with Neelix's partner, Kes, an Ocampan with strong mental capabilities. Tuvok helped Kes to harness her powers using Vulcan techniques such as mind-melds. When she progressed beyond the level of corporeal existence and left the ship, he marked her loss through meditation.

Mental trauma
Kes was not the only member of *Voyager*'s crew to undergo a mind-meld with Tuvok. He melded with Lieutenant Tom Paris to prove him innocent of murder. Conversely,

Tuvok and the *Excelsior*

Almost 80 years before he served on *Voyager*, Tuvok had another, brief Starfleet career as an ensign on board the *U.S.S. Excelsior*.

On one memorable occasion, he had just made Captain Hikaru Sulu a Vulcan blend of tea when the Klingon moon Praxis blew up, initiating a huge shift in galactic politics. As part of these events, Captain Sulu ordered his ship to assist his former ship mates from the *Enterprise*—in defiance of orders from Starfleet Command.

Tuvok vehemently disagreed with this course of action, but received a dressing down from his captain, who told him there was far more to serving on the bridge of a starship than simply following orders.

After three years serving on the *Excelsior*, Tuvok resigned his commission and returned to Vulcan to teach and to pursue the *Kolinahr* ritual. He rejoined Starfleet 50 years later, realizing that he still had much to learn.

when the Betazoid crewman Lon Suder was found guilty of killing a colleague, Tuvok joined with him in an attempt to understand his motives. However, the meld with Suder caused Tuvok to become violent himself, and he required medical treatment to restore his emotional balance.

A year later, Tuvok and Janeway shared a mind-meld after he experienced a series of debilitating and disturbing memories. They established that the memories

were not his own, and identified the cause as a virus, which was curable with bursts of radiation.

Tuvok required further medical attention after he, Janeway, and B'Elanna Torres submitted to Borg assimilation as part of a plan to destabilize the Borg collective. Despite being inoculated against the mental effects of assimilation, Tuvok succumbed to its control.

Although he did not reveal it to the rest of the crew, it transpired that Tuvok suffered from a serious

We often fear what we do not understand. Our best defense is knowledge.
Tuvok

degenerative mental condition that called for treatment in the Alpha Quadrant. In a timeline where it took *Voyager* 23 years to return to Earth, he suffered incurable brain damage. However, that outcome was averted by a future version of Janeway, who was determined that Tuvok would get the care that he needed in time. ∎

See also: The Vulcans, Kathryn Janeway, Neelix, Kes, Transporters

Exploring memory Tuvok and Neelix help Chakotay search for the symbols of his ancestors on an apparently uninhabited planet.

FLY BOY
TOM PARIS

CAPTAIN'S LOG

NAME
Thomas Eugene Paris

SPECIES
Human

FATHER
Owen Paris

STARFLEET DIVISION
Command

BRIEFING
Paris enjoys eating 20th-century junk food such as hotdogs, pizza, and popcorn

Not many Starfleet officers are recruited from penal settlements, but Thomas Eugene Paris was a special case. The son of a Starfleet admiral, his own Starfleet career had been cut short by his involvement in a fatal accident and its subsequent cover-up. Looking for a fight, he sought out the Maquis and joined in their rebellion against the Federation-Cardassian treaty, but was quickly caught. He was serving out an 18-month sentence in New Zealand when his fortunes changed thanks to Captain Kathryn Janeway.

Janeway needed help to locate a Maquis vessel, and saw this as a chance to redeem Paris—having served with his father before she became a captain. Paris agreed to join the mission, but only because it would mean a favorable report at his next review.

Paris came on board the *U.S.S. Voyager* as an observer only, but when the ship was swept into the Delta Quadrant, Janeway restored the lieutenant junior grade rank

Personal capital During his time on *Voyager*, Tom Paris won back his self-respect, and earned the crew's trust.

he had held before he was ritually dismissed. As an accomplished pilot, he was assigned to the flight controller's station, and was also able to put his basic medical training to good use during support duties in sickbay. His checkered past did not inspire everyone's confidence, however, and it took time for him to win the trust of the entire crew.

Ship mates Harry Kim and Tom Paris cemented their friendship while held captive together in an underground prison on the planet Akritiri.

A man of many parts

Paris's hobbies included a passion for 20th-century culture, especially science-fiction films. He created various holodeck programs that he shared with the rest of the crew, among them the "Captain Proton" series of sci-fi adventures, and a recreation of the bar in Marseilles, France, where he had spent time as a cadet. His skill as a mechanic extended from 20th-century Earth automobiles to warp-capable craft, and he was largely responsible for the development of the *Delta Flyer*, an advanced shuttlecraft designed specifically for the Delta Quadrant. In another shuttlecraft, he was also the first person ever to cross the transwarp threshold—reaching warp 10. This experience caused him to mutate into an amphibian life-form, but he recovered.

Personal relations

The first friend that Paris made among *Voyager*'s crew was Harry Kim, a young ensign who did not share the bias against him shown by some more senior officers. He also grew close to Kes, for whom he felt some romantic affection, causing tension with her partner, Neelix. Paris did not act on these feelings, however, and in time he and Neelix also became friends.

But it was Paris's relationship with *Voyager*'s chief engineer, B'Elanna Torres that defined his time on board the ship. It took more than two years for them to admit their feelings for each other—when they were close to death during an away mission—but after this their relationship progressed to the point where they were married and had a daughter, Miral, in time for their return to the Alpha Quadrant. ∎

See also: Time Travel, B'Elanna Torres, Harry Kim, The Maquis, Warp Drive, Holographic Technology

If we don't get more power to the warp drive, we're going to have to get out and push.
Tom Paris

Admiral Owen Paris

Tom Paris had resigned himself to being a disappointment to his father. A Starfleet admiral, Owen Paris expected his son to excel, but the high bar he set always left Tom feeling like a failure, despite his many exceptional talents.

When he became stranded in the Delta Quadrant, Lieutenant Paris seemed more than happy to leave his whole life in the Alpha Quadrant behind. But when the *Voyager* crew began to receive datastreams from home, he was forced to admit that he hoped to find a letter from his father among them. There was, but it proved impossible to access. He could only take Lieutenant Torres's advice and assume it said that his father loved him and was proud of him.

Torres was right about the admiral, and back on earth Owen was heading up the Pathfinder Project—dedicated to making contact with the ship that had his son on board.

THE DIVIDED SELF
B'ELANNA TORRES

CAPTAIN'S LOG

NAME
B'Elanna Torres

SPECIES
Human/Klingon

BORN
**2349, Federation
colony on Kessik IV**

PARENTS
John Torres and Miral

STARFLEET DIVISION
Operations

BRIEFING
**A group of Klingon
pilgrims worship
Torres' daughter, Miral,
as the *kuvah'magh*—
a prophesized savior
of the Klingon Empire**

Born to a Klingon mother and a Human father, B'Elanna Torres struggled with her heritage throughout her youth and into adulthood. Her father left when she was young, compounding her insecurities about her Klingon temperament and features, and she was victimized by bullies at school. Years later, as a cadet in Starfleet Academy, she struggled to fit in, and faced four disciplinary actions and a suspension in the space of two years. Despite her clear academic talents, she dropped out of the Academy and eventually found a place among the rebellious Maquis, where she finally began to feel at home.

A new beginning
In the Maquis, Torres grew close to her cell leader, Chakotay, who helped her deal with some of her turmoil using Native American

Get this cheese to sickbay.
The Doctor should look at
it as soon as possible.
B'Elanna Torres

Emotional space Facing death in the depths of space, B'Elanna Torres shares her true feelings for Tom Paris.

meditation techniques. Both she and Chakotay were on board the Maquis ship *Val Jean* when it was pulled 70,000 light-years across space, along with the Federation starship *Voyager*. Circumstances forced the two ships to join forces, and Torres found herself back in a Starfleet uniform. She made her objections to this arrangement very clear—even going so far as to punch a senior officer—but went on to prove her great engineering skill when *Voyager* was trapped in a quantum singularity. This led Captain Kathryn Janeway to make her the ship's new chief engineer on Chakotay's recommendation.

Identity crises

Torres continued to wrestle with her identity on board *Voyager*, and on one occasion was even forced to become two separate beings—one Human, one Klingon—as the result of DNA experiments by the Vidiians. This unique experience gave Torres a greater appreciation of her Klingon side—with which she was eventually reunited.

Two years later, Torres' Klingon mating instincts were triggered by the Vulcan crew member Vorik, who was undergoing his own *Pon farr* mating drive. This resulted in a passionate kiss between Torres and Lieutenant Tom Paris. It was another year before Torres allowed this relationship to go any further, finally admitting to Paris that she was in love with him when the two were close to death—hanging in space far away from *Voyager*. Torres and Paris were married in their final

Time shift When *Voyager* is thrown into its past, Torres helps a fellow Maquis rebel defeat one of the Kazon.

If you tell me to relax one more time, I'm gonna rip your holographic head off!
B'Elanna Torres

year on board *Voyager*, when she was pregnant with their daughter. Memories of her unhappy childhood led her to try to alter her unborn child's appearance, but her husband was able to change her mind. Their daughter, Miral, was born with her mother's Klingon forehead ridges as *Voyager* made its return to the Alpha Quadrant. ■
See also: Chakotay, Tom Paris, The Maquis

The Barge of the Dead

When Lieutenant Torres was rendered comatose during a mission, she believed that she was on the Barge of the Dead, the ship that took dishonored souls to *Gre'thor*—the Klingon equivalent of Hell. Before the Doctor was able to revive her, she met another "dishonored soul"—her own mother, Miral.

Concerned that Miral was being punished for her child's dishonor, Torres insisted on returning to a comatose state so that she could go back to the ship and save her mother. However, when she did find herself back on the Barge, she and Miral argued about the choices that Torres had made. She made a deal with Kortar, the captain of the Barge, and her mother was released to *Sto-Vo-kor*, the Klingon Heaven, in exchange for Torres going to *Gre'thor* in her place.

In *Gre'thor*, Torres found a strange version of *Voyager*, where her crew mates listed her perceived failings, and her mother appeared to her again, telling her to "choose to live" and to free herself. When she awoke in sickbay, Torres had worked through many of her personal demons—wherever it was that she had been.

FRESH OUT OF THE ACADEMY

HARRY KIM

CAPTAIN'S LOG

NAME
Harry S.L. Kim

SPECIES
Human

BORN
2349, South Carolina, Earth

PARENTS
John and Mary Kim

STARFLEET DIVISION
Operations

BRIEFING
Kim formed the jazz band "Harry Kim and the Kimtones" with other *Voyager* crew members, playing saxophone and clarinet

He'll always have Paris Harry Kim finds that Tom Paris is also on Earth in an alternative reality where neither of them ever served on board *Voyager*.

Harry Kim graduated from Starfleet Academy as class valedictorian and a sports champion. For his first posting, he requested the *U.S.S. Voyager*, and was awarded the role of operations officer in charge of internal systems controls, sensors, and comms. His eagerness to assume the role meant that he forgot to pack his clarinet.

Nervous and a little naïve, Kim also left behind his parents, with whom he enjoyed weekly contact, and his girlfriend Libby. Though he struggled to cope with being so far away from his loved ones after *Voyager* became stranded in the Delta Quadrant, he struck up an unlikely friendship with the rather more worldly Tom Paris. He also earned the respect of former Maquis crew mates such as B'Elanna Torres, who nicknamed the by-the-book ensign—"Starfleet."

Alternative lives

Kim's wish to return to Earth was granted when he woke one morning to find himself in San Francisco—now engaged to Libby and working in starship design after his request to serve on *Voyager* was rejected. This alternative reality was caused by Kim passing through a temporal anomaly in a shuttlecraft, and while it held its appeal for Kim, he could not accept it as real. With help from one of the beings that lived inside the anomaly and the unhappy Tom Paris from this timeline, Kim was able to return to his life on *Voyager*.

Not long after this, the entire *U.S.S. Voyager* was duplicated by a spatial scission that began to drain both ships of vital antimatter supplies. With each ship unaware of the other's existence, one fired a proton burst that damaged the other, killing Kim and the newborn Naomi Wildman. The undamaged *Voyager* was later destroyed by its own crew to save the damaged

Another time, another Kim

When *Voyager* was fitted with a new quantum slipstream drive, the crew hoped it would reduce their journey time from years to hours. For the ship to navigate the slipstream, Ensign Harry Kim traveled ahead of *Voyager* in a shuttlecraft, transmitting course corrections. However, Kim made an error in his calculations, and *Voyager* crashed on an icy world, killing everyone on board.

Fifteen years later, the guilt-ridden Kim returned to the wreck of *Voyager* and used its sensor logs and stolen Borg temporal technology to send new data back in time to *Voyager*, saving it from destruction.

As a result, a new timeline was created and the version of Kim that destroyed—and then saved—the ship ceased to have ever existed. A message that he recorded for his younger self did survive though—a small space-time paradox that left Ensign Kim thoroughly awestruck.

ship, but not before its Kim had swapped ships, taking the healthy Wildman baby with him. It was ultimately impossible to say which had been the "real" *Voyager*—or the "real" Kim.

Kim in command
Though he remained an ensign for his entire seven years on *Voyager*, Kim stepped up to far more senior duties on numerous occasions.

He commanded the ship for the first time when a temporal distortion sent it back to Earth in the 1990s and the senior officers went on an undercover away mission in Los Angeles. He did so again when the bulk of the crew was kidnapped by a species called the Quarren and then brainwashed to serve as a workforce.

In a version of the future, Kim became captain by the year 2404, in command of the *Nova*-class *U.S.S. Rhode Island* on a four-year mission. Captain Kim assisted Admiral Janeway in her mission to change history and return *Voyager* to Earth in seven years rather than 23. When she succeeded, this version of Kim's future ceased to exist. ∎

> Why does everyone say 'relax' when they're about to do something terrible?
> **Harry Kim**

Staying focussed Ensign Kim works alongside ex-Maquis crew mate B'Elanna Torres, who comes to respect his attention to detail.

EMH-MARK 1
THE DOCTOR

CAPTAIN'S LOG

NAME
The Doctor

SPECIES
Humanoid hologram

INITIALIZED
2371, *U.S.S. Voyager*

CREATOR
Dr. Lewis Zimmerman

STARFLEET DIVISION
Sciences

BRIEFING
The Doctor is an accomplished opera singer who developed a short-lived fanbase on the planet Qomar

A holiday for the Doctor A mobile emitter from the 29th century allows the Doctor to take his first steps outside the *U.S.S. Voyager* on Earth in 1996.

An Emergency Medical Hologram (EMH) that grew far beyond the limitations of his original programming, the Doctor (as he is simply known), proved essential to the crew of *Voyager* after a powerful alien dragged it into the Delta Quadrant, inadvertently killing its entire medical staff.

Versed in millions of possible treatments collected from 2,000 medical texts as well as the experience of 47 physicians, the Doctor was designed to run for two months at most, functioning within the confines of *Voyager*'s sickbay or its holodecks. In fact, he remained online in the Delta Quadrant for the better part of seven years—earning the rights and privileges of a flesh-and-blood crew member. He also gained freedom of movement after obtaining a mobile holoemitter—a piece of 29th-century technology from the timeship *Aeon*.

Growing and learning
In the early days however, the EMH was treated as little more than a piece of equipment, being turned on and off as required, and left out of the loop about important ship's business. It was his assistant, Kes, who brought his dissatisfaction to the attention of Captain Kathryn Janeway, who responded by granting him more autonomy and more respect as an individual. In return, the Doctor did his best to temper his brusque bedside manner and began to make friends.

In pursuit of personal growth beyond his coded parameters, the Doctor began to explore recreational activities such as opera, and even created his own holographic family. With his permission, Lieutenant B'Elanna Torres reprogrammed his overly perfect wife and children, so that he could better experience real

Dr. Lewis Zimmerman

The Doctor's physical appearance was based on that of his inventor: the Human scientist Dr. Lewis Zimmerman. When the Doctor found out that Zimmerman was dying, he got Captain Janeway's permission to travel to the Alpha Quadrant to treat him.

As a Mark I EMH, the Doctor was the last person Zimmerman wanted to see. Every other Mark I had been swiftly removed from medical duties and reassigned to waste management—all wearing his face, much to his shame and embarrassment.

As Zimmerman's only non-holographic friend, Lieutenant Reg Barclay asked Counselor Deanna Troi to intervene. She reconciled the pair to the point where Zimmerman consented to be treated by the Doctor, and in their interaction the inventor was able to see that one of his holographic lookalikes had gone on to achieve great things.

When the Doctor returned to *Voyager*, Zimmerman was set to make a full recovery. The two parted on good terms, posing for a "father-son" photograph.

family life. Similarly, when he gave himself a simulated dose of flu, Kes secretly introduced extra realism.

He had his first love affair with the Vidiian scientist Denara Pel, and later developed a crush on crew member Seven of Nine.

New horizons

When *Voyager*'s crew encountered a Hirogen communications network leading beyond the edge of the Delta Quadrant, the Doctor played a vital part in reestablishing contact with Starfleet. He traveled through the network to a Starfleet ship that had been captured by Romulans and, after defeating them with help

from that ship's EMH, let Starfleet Command know that *Voyager* and its crew were in the Delta Quadrant and heading home.

Toward the end of *Voyager*'s journey, Captain Janeway awarded the Doctor a commendation for protecting the ship from raiders, and gave permission for emergency command protocols to be built into his program. These allowed him to captain the ship if the senior officers were incapacitated. The protocols were activated twice before *Voyager* returned safely to Earth, though he remained—in every sense—the Doctor. ■

See also: *U.S.S. Voyager* NCC-74656, Kes, Holographic Technology

Doctor who? The Doctor never chose a name on board *Voyager*, but called himself "Joe" in one version of his future.

Please state the nature of the medical emergency.
The Doctor

A TALAXIAN OF ALL TRADES

NEELIX

CAPTAIN'S LOG

NAME
Neelix

SPECIES
Talaxian

BORN
Rinax, moon of Talax

OCCUPATION
Chef, morale officer, ambassador

BRIEFING
Neelix introduced the crew of *Voyager* to the Talaxian holiday Prixin, a celebration of family that he hoped would be an annual event

It will be my job to anticipate your needs before you know you have them. And I anticipate your first need will be me.
Neelix

Guide, trader, cook, morale officer, talk-show host—Neelix brought his many talents to bear when he joined the crew of the *U.S.S.* Voyager. A Delta Quadrant native, Neelix met the displaced Federation starship near the Ocampa homeworld where his beloved Kes was held prisoner. Seeing his chance to rescue her,

Neelix offered to serve as the crew's guide on the planet. Once Kes was free, he extended his offer, promising to act as guide to the entire region in exchange for Captain Kathryn Janeway letting him and Kes join the ship on its journey. To further sweeten the deal, he also offered to cook for the crew, turning part of the ship into a kitchen to save on replicator use.

Neelix's life on *Voyager* proved an escape from his lackluster career as a junk scavenger, and contrasted sharply with the grim experiences he had endured throughout his life.

His optimistic disposition hid the fact that his entire family had been killed in an attack on the moon he had once called home. Neelix felt guilt that he was not there when it happened because he had fled to avoid serving in the war. Along with Kes, the friends that he made on *Voyager* were the closest thing he had to a family.

Conflicting emotions

Neelix's relationship with Kes was complex. When he met her he did not know that she was an Ocampa with an expected lifespan of nine years. He grew jealous of her friendships on board *Voyager*, and even fought over her with Lieutenant Tom Paris, but their greatest challenge came when Kes entered her fertile stage—the *elogium*—prematurely, and Neelix was forced to consider the prospect of fatherhood. The *elogium* faded, and was deemed to be a false alarm, perhaps brought on by the nearby presence of an unknown alien species, which had somehow kickstarted Kes's hormonal drive. Kes later broke off her romantic relationship with Neelix, though the pair remained close friends for the rest of her time on *Voyager*.

Heeeere's Neelix

Among his many other roles, in his second year on board *Voyager*, Neelix also became a TV star. His daily program, *A Briefing With Neelix*, was available on screens across the ship, and featured news, music, interviews with crew members, and gossip.

His first guest was Ensign Baylart—a juggler who could keep hyposprays, PADDs, and phasers in the air for several minutes at a time. He asked the Doctor to host the "Hints for Healthful Living" segment, and the hologram conceived all sorts of topics, including "How To Keep Your Nostrils Happy."

However, the big story was an investigation into who among the crew had been secretly communicating with the Kazon-Nistrim. All the evidence pointed to Tom Paris, but Captain Janeway had to take Neelix aside to reveal this was a ruse to uncover the real traitor. After the truth came out, Neelix set the record straight in a glowing interview with Paris about his exploits. Sadly, this left no time for the Doctor's nostrils report.

I'm not a fighter. I'm just a cook who sometimes imagines himself to be a diplomat.
Neelix

Trials of life

Neelix's life on *Voyager* was not without its traumatic events. On one of his first away missions, his lungs were removed from his body by Vidiians. With no way to replicate such complex Talaxian organs, *Voyager*'s Doctor created holographic lungs to keep Neelix alive. A permanent solution was found when the Doctor transplanted one of Kes's lungs into Neelix.

On a later mission, Neelix and Lieutenant Tuvok were fused into one being as a result of a transporter accident. The newly created being, Tuvix, was happy to remain in his combined form, but Captain Janeway insisted the two men be restored so they could live out their individual lives.

Later still, Neelix was killed in an accident then brought back to life by the former Borg drone Seven of Nine using nanoprobes from her own body. The event rocked Neelix's faith in an afterlife and sent him into a deep depression, which he overcame with the help of Commander Chakotay.

When *Voyager* encountered a Talaxian colony, Neelix left the ship to start a new life with his own people. Captain Janeway appointed him ambassador to the Delta Quadrant shortly before the *Voyager* returned to its own part of the Galaxy. ∎

See also: Kes, Tuvok, Talaxians, The Ocampa

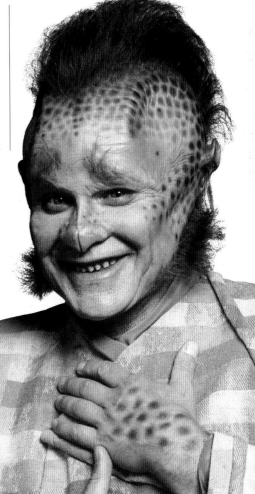

Talaxian tailoring

Neelix favored bright, multicolored outfits that matched his lively personality—if nothing else.

A LIFE LESS ORDINARY

KES

CAPTAIN'S LOG

NAME
Kes

SPECIES
Ocampa

BORN
2370, Ocampa homeworld

PARENTS
Benaren and Martis

BRIEFING
After giving birth, Kes's mother wished that someday her daughter would see the sun

With a lifespan of around nine years, Kes was just two years old when she joined the crew of *Voyager* but was already a fully grown adult. Like the rest of her people, the Ocampa, she had been raised underground, watched over by a kindly but overprotective "Caretaker." The Ocampa had been forced to live like this since visiting Nacene explorers inadvertently destroyed the atmosphere of their planet. In recompense, the Nacene installed the Ocampa in an underground city with a Caretaker to provide for their every need.

Kes was eventually able to leave this world with help from Neelix—a Talaxian trader she fell in love with—after she helped the crew of *Voyager* rescue Ensign Harry Kim and B'Elanna Torres from the Caretaker's clutches.

Life among the stars

When Neelix and Kes joined the crew of *Voyager*, Neelix became chef, while Kes found her place growing food and training to be a nurse. Having spent her life underground with little access to water, she was adept at growing fruit and vegetables with limited resources in the ship's cargo bay. Her medical training with the ship's holographic Doctor gave the crew access to a medic who could leave sickbay, and also provided the Doctor with an on board friend.

Kes demonstrated her love for Neelix when she donated one of her lungs to him after his organs were harvested by the Vidiians, but her other on board friendships provoked his intense jealousy.

Their relationship was tested when Kes prematurely entered the *elogium*—the only time in her life when she could conceive a child. At first she wanted to have Neelix's baby, but he was slow to accept the idea; then Kes changed her mind. In the end, the *elogium* seemed to have been a false alarm. Kes eventually broke off the relationship, but the pair remained friends.

Going beyond

On board *Voyager*, Kes started to exhibit the mental powers that had lain dormant among her people for generations. After the ship located

On my homeworld, it's so much simpler. You choose a mate for life. There's no distrust, no jealousy, no envy, no betrayal.
Kes

Forced to decide Kes is thrown into an early *elogium* (fertility phase) by life-forms surrounding *Voyager*, and asks Neelix to have a child with her.

a colony of Ocampa with advanced telepathic abilities, its leader, Tanis, tutored Kes in their use. But when she demonstrated her newfound skills to Tuvok she nearly killed him. When he recovered, Tuvok became her mentor, helping her to control her powerful impulses.

Later, after Kes communicated telepathically with Species 8472, she experienced a huge leap in her mental abilities—unintentionally doing serious damage to *Voyager*. She eventually chose to travel from the ship in a shuttlecraft, as she transformed into a non-corporeal being. As a parting gift, she used her powers to push *Voyager* 9,500 light-years closer to home.

The crew's final encounter was with an elderly Kes seeking revenge for what she remembered as the ship's abandonment of her. But a recording made by her younger self, reminded her that her choices had been all her own, and she returned to her homeworld, once more on good terms with the crew. ■

See also: Neelix, The Ocampa

Life in reverse

In a timeline where *Voyager* was badly damaged in a conflict with the Krenim and exposed to time-altering chroniton particles, Kes eventually married Tom Paris. The pair had a daughter called Linnis who aged at the normal rate for an Ocampa and grew up to marry Harry Kim, giving Tom and Kes a grandson called Andrew.

When Kes was nine years old and close to the end of her natural life, the Doctor tried to rejuvenate her using a bio-temporal chamber.

This procedure reactivated the chronitons in Kes's body and sent her back through her own timeline, reliving experiences but also changing them.

She moved further back in time until the Doctor was able to stabilize her in 2373 using antichronitons. Having seen the consequences of the Krenim's attack in the possible future she had experienced, Kes was then able to warn Captain Janeway about the threat that lay ahead.

DISCONNECTED
SEVEN OF NINE

CAPTAIN'S LOG

NAME
Seven of Nine (formerly Annika Hansen)

SPECIES
Human with Borg implants

BORN
2350, Federation Tendara Colony

PARENTS
Magnus and Erin Hansen

BRIEFING
One of Seven's ancestors is 22nd-century prize fighter Sven "Buttercup" Hansen. Seven herself is skilled in the Norcadian martial art of *Tsunkatse*

When Captain Kathryn Janeway formed an uneasy alliance with the Borg collective, a drone was assigned to the *U.S.S. Voyager*. Its Borg designation was "Seven of nine, tertiary adjunct of Unimatrix 01." The Borg collective broke off collaboration as soon as they had what they wanted from Janeway and company, and directed the drone to assimilate *Voyager*. The crew had anticipated this, however, and initiated a plan to sever "Seven of Nine," as they called her, from the collective. The plan was a success, and the ship acquired a new resident.

Becoming Human
Voyager's holographic Doctor was able to remove most of the drone's cybernetic implants, restoring the appearance of the Human female

Drone alone Seven of Nine is cut off from the Borg collective when Captain Janeway initiates *Voyager*'s "Scorpion" defense against assimilation.

who had existed before. Starfleet records revealed that she was born Annika Hansen and had been assimilated, along with her parents, at the age of six. Having only known life as a Borg, she was not a willing addition to the crew, and longed to return to the security of the collective. She refused to go by the name Annika, agreeing to be simply "Seven."

Over time Seven grew slowly more comfortable with her forced return to Humanity. Though she retained a few Borg parts, deemed crucial to her survival, and

I am no longer Borg, but the prospect of becoming Human is unsettling. I don't know where I belong.
Seven of Nine

The Borg children

Seven explored the maternal side of her Humanity when Captain Janeway made her guardian to a group of four Borg children who had been disconnected from the collective. At first, she devised a rigid schedule for the children, with severe punishments if they disobeyed her. When this proved unsuccessful, Chakotay told her that children also need variety and spontaneity, after which she learned to embrace "disorder" in their daily routine.

Three of the children were eventually returned to their home planets, but the eldest, Icheb, remained with *Voyager* after it was discovered that his people had engineered him as a weapon against the Borg. He and Seven became friends and he donated one of his own Borg implants to her when her life was at risk. Icheb survived the dangerous procedure and later went on to pass the Starfleet entrance exam.

regenerated in a Borg alcove rather than sleeping, she began to feel more at home among individuals, and even started to make friends. Crew members who had viewed her with suspicion came to value the contribution she made to the ship, while Captain Janeway and the Doctor took a special interest in developing her Human side.

One of Seven's more unlikely friends was Naomi Wildman—the first child to be born on *Voyager*—who, like Seven, had no memories of life in the Alpha Quadrant. At first, she disapproved of the girl's fascination with her, but went on to instruct her in astrometrics and join her for games of *kadis-kot*.

Echoes of the Borg

A year after she joined *Voyager*, Seven was contacted by the Borg Queen, who told her that the ship and its crew would be assimilated if she did not rejoin the collective. Having embraced her Humanity, Seven agreed reluctantly, but was soon rescued by her crew mates.

Full metal jacket Assimilated at the age of six, Annika Hansen spent five years in a Borg maturation chamber before emerging as an adult drone.

Not long after, she started to exhibit multiple personalities—the disturbing echoes of the individuals she had assimilated as a drone. The voices were silenced when Lieutenant Tuvok performed a Vulcan mind-meld with her.

During *Voyager*'s final year in the Delta Quadrant, Seven was upset to learn that one of her vital implants would shut down if she experienced a strong emotion, such as love. The Doctor found a way to remove the implant and Seven took her first steps toward a romantic relationship on a date with Commander Chakotay. ■
See also: Kathryn Janeway, The Borg Collective, Species 8472

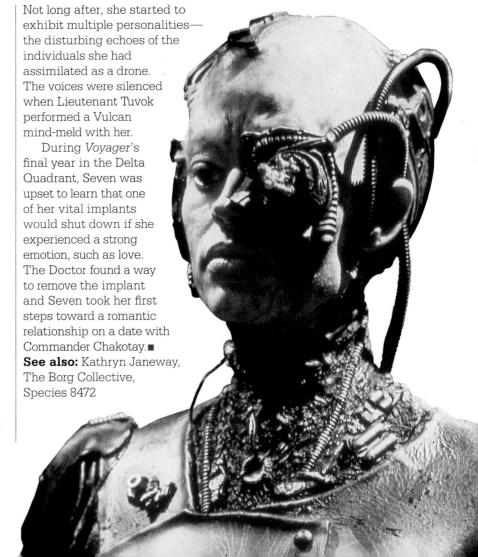

FEDERAT
ALLIES A
ENEMIES

ION
ND

In the vast Galaxy, political alliances can shift on a whim with enemies becoming friends and allies turning to adversaries. The United Federation of Planets is only one galactic power in a universe filled with Empires, Alliances, and Unions. Other races found in all four Quadrants have their own interesting relationships with the Federation that are as unique as the lifeforms that populate these diverse planets.

IN THE HANDS OF THE PROPHETS
THE BAJORANS

CAPTAIN'S LOG

PLANET
Bajor (B'hava'el VII)

CLASS
Class-M planet

LOCATION
**Bajoran System,
Alpha Quadrant**

MOONS
**Five (including Derna
and Jeraddo)**

POLITICAL AFFILIATION
**United Federation of
Planets (applicant)**

BRIEFING
**Most Bajorans wear
ornamental earrings as
a display of their faith**

The Bajoran civilization has flourished for hundreds of thousands of years, and was once renowned for its art and architecture. Although never a major political power in the Alpha Quadrant, in the 24th century the Bajorans endured one of the darkest periods in their history when the Cardassians occupied their planet.

Rich in resources

Bajor is one of two inhabited worlds among the 14 planets of the Bajoran system. It is located in the Alpha Quadrant along the border of Cardassian space and the former Demilitarized Zone that separates Cardassia from the Federation. The planet is rich in mineral resources, which is why Bajor became a tempting target for the Cardassians.

According to legend, Bajorans first explored space during Earth's 16th century. Their early vessels, or lightships, did not rely on warp propulsion or impulse engines, but on solar-sails, invented by the ancient Bajorans. Vessels using these massive reflective sails

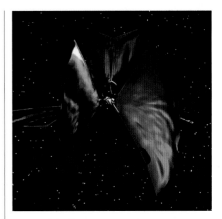

Ship of light Benjamin Sisko proved the legends true by reaching Cardassian space using a solar sail.

propelled by solar winds were said to be able to travel faster than light and to reach as far as Cardassia. This was proven by Commander Benjamin Sisko in 2371 when he constructed one of these vessels using ancient plans.

A deeply spiritual people

For the past 10,000 years, the Bajorans have believed that their gods—a group of non-corporeal, extra-dimensional beings that they

Our religion is the only thing that holds my people together.
Kira Nerys

refer to as the Prophets—once sent them nine orbs, found in orbit of their planet, to share their wisdom with the inhabitants of Bajor. These are known as the "Tears of the Prophets," and can be used to provide insight into the past, and, in some cases, prophecies of the future. These visions, seen as either direct or indirect communication with the Prophets, were often interpreted by high-ranking Bajoran clerics, or vedeks.

Each of the nine orbs has a special significance, which is reflected in its name. For instance, there are orbs of Contemplation, Time, Wisdom, Prophecy, and Change. It is not necessary to be Bajoran to attempt to communicate through the orbs, but many who connect with the Prophets will fail to have an Orb Experience. Those who do succeed may continue to be visited by visions, or Orb Shadows, long after the experience ends.

The Bajoran spiritual leader is known as the kai, an elected position that is bestowed on its holder for a lifetime. Although Bajorans have a secular government, their religious leadership is a »

Divine rule As the religious leader of the Bajorans, the kai's authority is rivalled only by the Emissary of the Prophets.

powerful political force—the Vedek Assembly is a spiritual congress of 122 members who work under the kai's leadership. Both the kai and the vedeks have a voice in legislative issues, taking part in diplomatic missions and endorsing treaties.

Political leaders

Although Bajor existed in peace with the neighboring planet of Cardassia for many centuries, the militaristic Cardassians seized their chance to conquer Bajor in the early part of the 24th century. More technologically advanced than the Bajorans, the Cardassians faced little resistance as they increased their military presence in the star system and ultimately annexed the planet. For 50 years, the Cardassian Union maintained an iron grip over the Bajoran people, committing terrible acts of genocide while enslaving the people and forcing them to strip their own planet of its rich natural resources.

Resistance and freedom

A Bajoran resistance movement grew during the occupation, using tactics referred to as "terrorist" by the Cardassians, but seen as heroic by many Bajorans. At first, these actions were brutally put down, but when a new gul, or Cardassian commander, called Dukat became the Prefect of Bajor, he instituted a gentle touch—or at least claimed to do so. He reduced the death rate in the Bajoran labor camps, but this did not weaken the resistance's resolve.

After a while, the combined pressure of the resistance and the Cardassian's long-running war with the Federation led the Cardassian Central Command to withdraw from Bajor. The world they left behind was a shadow of its former self—denuded of its resources and with much of its farmland

now hopelessly toxic, its people struggled to determine a future for themselves and their planet.

The Bajorans formed a provisional government to oversee its transition to freedom. This was made up of a chamber of ministers led by a first minister, who was elected every six years. Although it was officially a secular form of government, the kai and Vedek

Religious leaders Bareil Antos (right) withdrew his candidacy for kai to clear the way for Winn Adami (left).

Federation emissary Benjamin Sisko (right) served a dual role as commander of DS9 and Emissary to the Prophets.

Assembly held great sway over the political landscape of the planet, effectively forming two equal branches of government. A few years after the Cardassians' withdrawal, Vedek Winn Adami defeated her rival, Bareil Antos, to lead Bajor as their first elected kai after the occupation.

An early action of the new government was to petition to join the United Federation of Planets and ask for help from the interstellar government to rebuild their world. This was not an entirely popular decision among Bajorans, as the Federation had largely refrained from intervening during the occupation, citing the Prime Directive. On the other hand, pressure from the Federation had been integral in forcing the Cardassians to free Bajor.

Deep Space 9

The Federation took command of the Cardassian space station that was positioned in Bajor's orbit and

D'jarra

During the Cardassian occupation, the Bajoran religious leaders put aside certain practices to allow more citizens to become soldiers. Chief among these was the D'jarra caste system, which dictated a person's work according to their family name and created social stratification. For instance, the Ih'valla held higher status than Te'nari, and those who prepared the dead for burial were said to be "unclean." Bajorans could be killed for defying their D'jarra.

When a historical figure calling himself Emissary of the Prophets emerged from the wormhole and took power, the D'jarras were reinstituted. This was divisive among Bajorans and a problem for the Federation, as caste-based discrimination would disqualify Bajor's petition for membership. D'jarra was abandoned again after Benjamin Sisko consulted the Prophets, and the "other" Emissary returned to his time.

renamed it Deep Space 9. It soon became an established outpost run by a combined crew of Starfleet and Bajoran personnel. Benjamin Sisko made one of the greatest discoveries in Bajoran history when he and his science officer, Jadzia Dax, located a stable wormhole near the station. As far as anyone in the Federation is aware, this permanent bridge to the Gamma Quadrant is entirely unique in the Galaxy.

The wormhole was believed to be the home of the Prophets, and became known to the Bajorans as the Celestial Temple. Commander Sisko was deemed the Emissary of the Prophets—a prophesied leader who had been sent to save the Bajoran people and unite the planet. As a reluctant Emissary, Sisko learned more about the Bajoran faith as the Prophets communicated with him by sending visions via the orbs.

If he dies, then peace with Cardassia dies with him.
Kia Winn on Vedek Bareil

On the eve of Bajor accepting Federation membership, Sisko received a vision warning him to convince them to reject it. They acted as he instructed, which allowed Bajor to sign a treaty with the Dominion and save themselves from being occupied again as the Dominion War escalated. The planet avoided many of the atrocities that affected other Alpha and Beta Quadrant worlds, and the Bajoran people survived to renew their application for membership in the Federation following the war. ■
See also: Deep Space 9, Benjamin Sisko, Kira Nerys, The Maquis, The Cardassian Union, The Prophets.

Space-time tunnel A wormhole connects two separate locations—and occasionally two different times—by joining through sub-space rather than normal space.

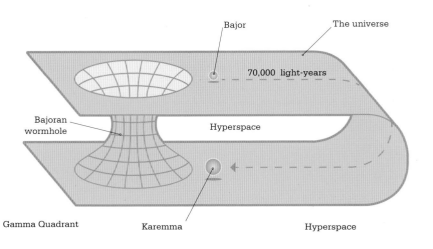

Bajor

The universe

70,000 light-years

Bajoran wormhole

Hyperspace

Gamma Quadrant

Karemma

Hyperspace

THERE ARE NO SAINTS, JUST PEOPLE
THE MAQUIS

CAPTAIN'S LOG

NAME
The Maquis

FORMED
2370

BASE OF OPERATIONS
**The Badlands,
Alpha Quadrant**

DESTROYED
2373

BRIEFING
The name "Maquis" originated on Earth as a name for a band of French resistance fighters during World War II

The Federation-Cardassian Treaty of 2370 brought a temporary end to hostilities that had raged between the two governments for more than 20 years. The treaty established a new boundary between the intergalactic superpowers and created a Demilitarized Zone in which no outposts could be built nor military vessels permitted to enter. Another consequence of the new border was that some established Federation colonies now found themselves in Cardassian space—this meant they had to be relocated even though many of them did not want to leave their homes.

While Starfleet was in the process of negotiating to remove the colonists from the planets, the Cardassians applied increasing pressure to have the worlds vacated as stipulated by the terms of the treaty. This was problematic—the Federation did not want to forcibly remove its colonists but could not ignore the treaty. Eventually, the Federation sidestepped the matter by leaving some of the colonies to their fate, in spite of the fact that the Cardassians did not want them to stay. Tensions between Cardassians and the colonists gave rise to a paramilitary resistance organization that became known as the Maquis.

Mounting a resistance

The Maquis resistance movement consisted of members of the former Federation colonies as well as sympathizers for their cause. Some of the fighters were former members of Starfleet, and a rare few were still active members, participating covertly. Like the Bajoran resistance, the Maquis operated as separate cells, with only the leaders of each cell in contact with one another, to reduce the chance of information leaking in the event of capture. The Maquis used the Badlands as their base of operations as this area of space is plagued by plasma storms, making it hard for starships to navigate.

The Maquis fighters announced themselves with early missions that included destroying a Cardassian freighter, abducting the prefect Gul Dukat, and stealing the starship

> If you can't have victory, sometimes you just have to settle for revenge.
> **Michael Eddington**

U.S.S. Defiant. During the conflict, the Maquis obtained ships and weapons that allowed them to make considerable inroads into countering the Cardassians' power. But everything changed when the Cardassians signed a treaty with the Dominion, who then came into the Badlands. Before long they had wiped out almost all of the Maquis and put a decisive end to the threat.

A surviving cell

During the conflict, both the Federation and the Cardassians placed spies within the Maquis organization. They even positioned some aboard the Maquis' raider crafts, such as the *Val Jean*, which flew under the command of former Starfleet officer Chakotay. When the *Val Jean* was pulled into the Delta

Quadrant, the crew included Tuvok, a Vulcan Starfleet officer, and a disguised Cardassian spy named Seska who would later join the Kazon when her identity was revealed. The *Val Jean* was destroyed while fighting a Kazon ship alongside the *Voyager*. Its surviving crew—almost all that remained of the Maquis—were incorporated into the crew of the Starfleet ship and they all set off for home aboard the *Voyager*. ■

See also: Deep Space 9, *U.S.S. Voyager* NCC-74656, Chakotay, B'Elanna Torres, The Cardassian Union, The Dominion War.

Mind games The Maquis briefly took control of *Voyager* when subconscious mental programming was activated years after the Maquis was destroyed.

Michael Eddington

One person's "terrorist" is another's "freedom fighter," and even loyal Starfleet officers can see the other point of view. As Miles O'Brien, chief of operations on Deep Space 9, once said: "One day they're trying to eke out a living on some godforsaken colonies on the Cardassian border, the next day the Federation makes a treaty handing those colonies over to the Cardassians. What would you do?"

For some, feelings run far deeper. Michael Eddington, a Maquis leader who was formerly an officer on Deep Space 9, says to Commander Benjamin Sisko: "We've never harmed you, and yet we're constantly arrested and charged with terrorism... Why? Because we've left the Federation, and that's the one thing you can't accept... In some ways you're worse than the Borg. At least they tell you about their plans for assimilation." Unfortunately this has no effect, and Sisko ensures that the traitor is locked away.

THE STARS ARE MADE OF LATINUM
THE FERENGI ALLIANCE

CAPTAIN'S LOG

PLANET
Ferenginar

CLASS
Class-M planet

LOCATION
Ventarus Idrilon system, Alpha Quadrant

POLITICAL AFFILIATION
Ferengi Alliance

BRIEFING
The planet Ferenginar experiences an average yearly rainfall that is much higher than elsewhere in the Ventarus Idrilon system. The precipitation is so intense and prolonged that the Ferengi language contains 178 different words for "rain"

Not every species in the Alpha Quadrant can be identified as both friend and foe of the United Federation of Planets. Like the Klingons, the Ferengi occasionally shift their allegiance. They are a mostly self-serving people who dislike making declarations of support for any side, as they fear these may get in the way of making profit. The Ferengi are far more interested in setting up trade relations with other galactic entities, as this satisfies their uppermost priority—the accumulation of wealth.

The government is known as the Ferengi Alliance, and its agency for overseeing business and trade laws is the Ferengi Commerce Authority. This agency is the most powerful organization in a society intensely focused on financial gain. The grand nagus, who serves as Master of Commerce, is the leader of the Ferengi people. As both a political and economic leader, he oversees all the planet's business transactions with other species from his office in the majestic Tower of Commerce. He is also available for personal consulting if an appropriate payment of respect is forthcoming.

Ferengi sensitivities
Ferengi tend to be shorter than the average humanoid, and their most notable physical features—enlarged skulls and oversized ears—give them a keen sense of hearing. The Ferengi's distinctive ear lobes are considered an erogenous zone and an essential part of the species' seduction ritual. However, the lobes' acute sensitivity also means that they feel intense pain, making them the focus of attention for torturers.

Seal of authority
The Ferengi Commerce Authority oversees all business practices and enforces all trade by-laws.

The Ferengi belief system centers on the Great Material Continuum, also known as the Great River, which is thought to be the force that binds the universe together. This belief is the closest thing the Ferengi have to a religion, and at its core is the idea that the millions of worlds in the universe are each filled with too much of one thing, but not enough of another. The Continuum flows through the Universe like a river, so it is believed that a skilled Ferengi could navigate along it and fill his ship with everything his heart desires. The focus on acquisition means that the wealthy are the most respected members of Ferengi society.

Valuable latinum

The monetary unit of Ferenginar is gold-pressed latinum (latinum being a highly valued liquid encased in worthless gold). Latinum is an especially valuable commodity because it cannot be replicated by technological means, so it is near impossible to counterfeit. The various denominations of gold-pressed latinum range from the low-rated slip, through the strip and bar, up to the brick, which is the highest unit of Ferengi currency. Ferengi are one of the few species in the

Greed is great An entrepreneur with shifting values and allegiances, Ferengi Quark owns a lucrative bar on Deep Space 9.

You've proven yourself a true Ferengi. You've betrayed friends and family for personal gain.
Ishka

known universe that continue to rely on a monetary system, as much of the Federation has foregone the need for material wealth.

Sexist society

The male of the species dominates Ferengi society to the point that women are effectively considered property. This brand of misogyny exhibits itself in many ways, like the fact that females are forbidden »

Equal rights The efforts of Quark's mother, Ishka, were vital in starting to reform the Ferengi's misogynistic attitudes and practices.

> Humans used to be a lot worse than the Ferengi: slavery, concentration camps, interstellar wars. We have nothing in our past that approaches that kind of barbarism. You see? We're nothing like you. We're better.
> **Quark**

from entering into business agreements and even barred from wearing clothing. Marriages are seen as business contracts between father and husband, and they are entered into for periods of five years, while pregnancies are termed as rentals with the husband acting as the holder of the lease. However, Ferengi opinions on these oppressive beliefs finally start to shift as they enter the latter part of the 24th century.

First contact

Rather than waste time and resources developing their own forms of warp-capable ships, the Ferengi simply purchased the technology as an expedient way of expanding their business opportunities. The technology enabled the Ferengi to experience several instances of first contact with members of the Federation, occasions that were less than auspicious. Ferengi visited Earth as early as the mid-20th century, thanks to a time travel mishap that sent Deep Space 9 residents Quark, Rom, and Nog back in time, where they ended up being briefly held by the U.S. military.

A second instance occurred in the 22nd century when the crew of an unidentified Ferengi vessel briefly took control of *Enterprise* NX-01. The third, and most violent, confrontation happened in the 24th century, when a Ferengi ship attacked the *U.S.S. Stargazer*, and forced its captain, Jean-Luc Picard, to abandon his vessel. At the time of the incident, the attacking ship was unidentified, but in 2364 it was revealed to be a Ferengi Marauder when Picard had a second, face-to-face encounter with the Ferengi.

Fierce contact In 2364, an aggressive group of Ferengi officially encounter Starfleet officers for the first time when they are both trapped in Delphi Ardu.

The event came to be considered the first official contact between the two powers.

On this occasion, Captain Picard, now in command of the *Enterprise*-D, engaged with an unusually violent segment of the Ferengi population on a planet in

The Ferengi Rules of Acquisition

The Ferengi have a guiding set of doctrines known as "The Rules of Acquisition," which were drawn up 10,000 years ago by the first grand nagus, Gint. By the 24th century there are 285 of these sacred precepts, including:
#3: Never spend more for an acquisition than you have to.
#10: Greed is eternal.
#21: Never place friendship above profit.
#34: War is good for business.
#35: Peace is good for business.

#48: The bigger the smile, the sharper the knife.
#59: Free advice is seldom cheap.
#62: The riskier the road, the greater the profit.
#75: Home is where the heart is, but stars are made of latinum.
#98: Every man has his price.
#211: Employees are the rungs on the ladder of success. Don't hesitate to step on them.
#285: No good deed ever goes unpunished.

Ferengi hand gestures
Ferengi culture grew out of its economic system, and its three most used hand gestures communicate key "deal-making" messages.

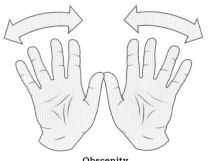

Obscenity
Waving hands above head

Greeting or submission
Wrists together, hands apart, fingers curled inward

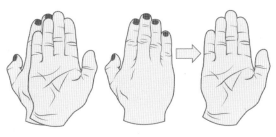

Agreeing a deal
A Ferengi puts the back of their hand against that of another and pulls it away to the side

have no business sense. However, Rom is one of the few Ferengi to support Zek's progressive views and so he is deemed the proper person to oversee the planet Ferenginar's transition to a more open society. The appointment is given the full backing of the Congress of Economic Advisers, a legislative body that was created to limit the powers of the office of the grand nagus. ■

See also: Time Travel, Jean-Luc Picard, Deep Space 9, Quark, Rom, Nog, and Leeta.

Change of heart Once the upholder of traditional values, Zek changed Ferengi society forever after falling in love with Ishka.

the Delphi Ardu system. When both ships experienced a power-system failure they were forced to cooperate to identify the source of the problem. Although they managed to free themselves from the planet's hold, they could not be considered allies after their departure.

Ferengi relations with other species took a considerable turn in the early 2370s when Starfleet accepted shared control of Deep Space 9. Although there were only a handful of Ferengi on the station at the time—most notably the bar owner, Quark—it was Quark's connections with the grand nagus that led to Starfleet having deeper and more positive interactions with the Ferengi.

A time of change
The Ferengi Alliance experiences a dramatic shift in its beliefs in the late 24th century under the

leadership of Grand Nagus Zek. This occurs because Ishka, the mother of Deep Space 9 residents Quark and Rom, provides financial advice to the grand nagus that is highly beneficial to the Alliance— a move that is unheard of amongst the patriarchal Ferengi. Ishka's guidance is the first step in a plan to allow women to have more of a voice in their society. Ferengi women are not even allowed to put on clothing without first seeking approval from a male, but when Ishka dresses without permission, it inspires Grand Nagus Zek to amend the Bill of Opportunities so that all females are granted the right to wear clothes.

When Zek's son proves unfit to lead the Ferengi Alliance, Zek is forced to look elsewhere for his successor. He chooses an unlikely candidate in Quark's brother, Rom, who has always been thought to

SPIRITUAL STORYTELLERS
TALAXIANS

CAPTAIN'S LOG

PLANET
Talax

CLASS
Class-M planet

LOCATION
**Talaxian system,
Delta Quadrant**

POLITICAL AFFILIATION
**Haakonian Order
(annexed)**

MOON
Rinax

BRIEFING
**In the ancient Talaxian
language, "Vaadwaur" has
come to mean "foolish,"
reminding people that they
had once been foolish
enough to trust another
species (the aggressive
Vaadwaur people)**

Talaxians, formerly known as Talax-ilzay, are an ancient people of the Delta Quadrant who have been capable of warp-powered travel for centuries. They are a generally genial species, though there have been dark periods in their history. A spiritual people, Talaxians believe that after death they go to the Great Forest, where their ancestors wait for them at the Guiding Tree.

Storytelling is an important part of their culture, and during meals diners are regaled with a tale about the preparation process.

Coming home Neelix (left) finds a new family with the young Talaxian Brax and his mother Dexa thousands of light-years from his tragic past.

Talaxians do not have a positive history of encounters with other beings, such as the Vaadwaur in ancient times and, more recently, the Haakonian Order. A decades-long war with the Haakonian Order ended in 2356 with the deployment of a devastating weapon of mass destruction on the inhabited moon Rinax. The Metreon Cascade killed over 300,000 Talaxians and the government issued an unconditional surrender the next day.

While the *U.S.S. Voyager* never visited the Talax system during its time in the Delta Quadrant, it did take on a Talaxian crew member named Neelix. Some of the *Voyager* crew also partnered with a small fleet of Talaxians in a mission to retake their ship when it was seized by the Kazon.

Toward the end of *Voyager*'s journey in the Delta Quadrant, the crew came across a group of Talaxian exiles who fled their homeworld during the war. After helping to protect the colony from miners trying to take over their asteroid home, crew member Neelix left *Voyager* to live among his people once more. ∎
See also: *U.S.S. Voyager* NCC-74656, Neelix.

BRIEF LIVES HALF LIVED

THE OCAMPA

CAPTAIN'S LOG

PLANET
Ocampa

CLASS
Class-H planet

LOCATION
**Ocampa System,
Delta Quadrant**

POLITICAL AFFILIATION
None

BRIEFING
**Most of the Ocampa's
physiological development
occurs in the first six
months of life; they reach
adolescence toward the
end of their first year**

The Ocampa only have an average lifespan of nine years, although some have been known to live for 14 years or more. In ancient times, the Ocampa homeworld was struck by an ecological disaster, accidentally caused by a group of extragalactic explorers called the Nacene. Two of these non-corporeal beings stayed behind to protect the unintended victims of their travels. Ultimately only one remained, who became Caretaker to the Ocampa. Realizing the Ocampa could not survive the harsh surface conditions caused by the Nacene, the Caretaker moved the endangered species underground, providing over 500 generations of Ocampa with all they required for their subterranean home.

Although the Caretaker's intentions were good, the Ocampa became severely limited by a lifestyle in which everything was provided for them; they even lost their advanced mental powers. In 2371, the Caretaker died, leaving the Ocampa with just enough power to sustain their people for five years, after which they will be forced to return to the planet's surface.

That same year, a young female Ocampa named Kes joined *Voyager* and during her travels came across another colony of her people, whose ancestors had left the planet with the Caretaker's partner. These Ocampa have fully embraced their mental powers and live longer lives as a result of the freedoms they experience. Although Kes decides not to remain with this colony, she continues to explore her mental abilities until she evolves to possess powers far beyond traditional humanoid capabilities. ■

See also: *U.S.S. Voyager* NCC-74656, Kes, The Nacene

Superior powers Tanis, a proud Ocampa in full possession of his psychic abilities, encouraged Kes to leave the *Voyager* and develop her mental powers.

KHAAAAAAA-AAAN!
KHAN NOONIEN SINGH

CAPTAIN'S LOG

BORN
Mid-20th century, Earth

WARLORD
1992–96

ABANDONED EARTH
1996

DISCOVERED
2267

DIED
2285

DISCOVERED (KELVIN TIMELINE)
Classified

DIED (KELVIN TIMELINE)
Classified

BRIEFING
Khan lost his beloved wife Marla and 19 other followers when parasitic eel creatures attacked his people on Ceti Alpha V

Khan Noonien Singh is the most dangerous and calculating enemy the crew of *U.S.S. Enterprise* NCC-1701 encounters in any timeline. He is a warlord from Earth's past who was genetically engineered to be part of a superior Human race.

Khan's people rose up at the end of the 20th century to overthrow those who had created them in the Eugenics Wars. As leader, Khan took control of the lands of South Asia and the Middle East for four years, before he was eventually defeated by traditional Humans who were reclaiming their world. Khan and his followers escaped on the *S.S. Botany Bay*, a sleeper ship that kept them in suspended animation until the 23rd century. Khan slept for almost three centuries, until he was awakened when the *Starship Enterprise*, under James T. Kirk, came across the *Botany Bay*.

Man and superman
Unaware of Khan's true identity, the *Enterprise* crew was unprepared for his attempt to take over their ship, but they managed to subdue him. Kirk allowed Khan and his people to live in exile on the planet Ceti Alpha V rather than imprison them, but this was a decision that he came to regret.

Hostile takeover Khan's inexperience with the *Reliant*'s systems ultimately led to his doom.

Genetic engineering

Earth has learned through bitter experience that for every positive change that results from genetic engineering, there is a potentially negative one—such as creating a "superhuman" like Khan whose ambition and thirst for power was enhanced, along with his intellect.

Beyond the devastating wars of the 20th century, eugenics reared its ugly head again in the 22nd century, when Dr. Arik Soong raised people from embryos of genetically enhanced Humans (Khan's brethren). Known as the "Augments," their aggression and treachery nearly led to war with the Klingons.

The Klingons themselves then decided to experiment with eugenics, with disastrous results—much of the Klingon population was left disfigured for more than a century.

In the Federation, genetic manipulation has since remained illegal except in cases of serious birth defects.

Almost 20 years later, Khan and his followers on Ceti Alpha V experienced an environmental catastrophe when a neighboring world exploded. Taking advantage of Starfleet personnel investigating the planet, Khan seized control of their ship, the *U.S.S. Reliant,* and stole the experimental Genesis Device from the Regula I Space Laboratory. Kahn's followers killed most of the researchers, and lured Kirk and the *Enterprise* to the site. Khan's revenge plot against Kirk wasted many lives, including Spock who forfeited his own to save his ship.

Ultimately, Kirk outsmarted Khan, but rather than surrender to his old nemesis, the dying Khan set off the Genesis device, destroying

himself—and, he hoped, the *Enterprise* crew. Fortunately, Spock's sacrifice made it possible for Kirk and his crew to escape in time.

The Temporal Incursion

In the alternate timeline created by Nero's incursion, Starfleet Admiral Marcus conscripts Khan into service for Starfleet's black ops division, Section 31, by holding his cryogenically frozen people hostage as leverage. The genetically enhanced Khan helps Section 31 create groundbreaking technology and weaponry. But then he turns on

Game play Khan surrendered to the *Enterprise* crew on Qo'noS and is then taken aboard the ship.

his captors, destroying Section 31's London headquarters.

Marcus sends James Kirk and the *Enterprise* on a mission to retrieve Khan, without revealing that the 72 "experimental weapons" on the ship are really stasis chambers containing Khan's followers. With both Marcus and Khan working against them, Kirk ultimately sacrifices himself to save his crew, but a quick-thinking Leonard McCoy revives him using Khan's genetically enhanced blood. ∎

See also: United Earth, The Temporal Incursion of 2233, *U.S.S. Enterprise* NCC-1701, *U.S.S. Enterprise* NCC-1701 (Kelvin Timeline), James T. Kirk, Spock.

You are a pawn, Kirk. You can't even guarantee the safety of your own crew.
Khan Noonien Singh

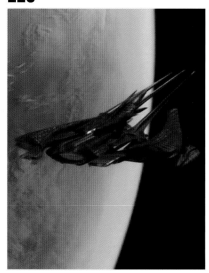

FIVE DISTINCT SPECIES
THE XINDI

CAPTAIN'S LOG

NAME
The Xindi

SPECIES
Aquatics, Arboreals, Insectoids, Primates, Reptilians, and Avians (extinct)

TERRITORY
Delphic Expanse

FORMER HOMEWORLD
Xindus (destroyed 2030)

BRIEFING
Prior to its destruction, Xindus was the lone planet in its star system

The Xindi were once a collection of six diverse species, all of which had evolved on the same homeworld of Xindus in the Delphic Expanse. The six shared common DNA characteristics, but had dramatically different physical traits and personalities.

Xindus is a seismically active planet, and during a civil war, weapons were detonated beneath eight of its largest fissures. This destroyed the planet and wiped out the technologically inferior Avian species, leaving the five remaining (Aquatics, Arboreals, Primates, Insectoids, and Reptilians) intact but homeless. The post-destruction era is known as the Great Diaspora, and it saw the surviving species scatter across the Delphic Expanse in a struggle to survive.

Guardian gods
The majority of the Xindi species was saved from extinction by a group of time-traveling, extra-dimensional beings known as the Guardians, who guided them to new homeworlds within the Delphic Expanse. The Xindi treated the Guardians as gods, and responded positively to their encouragement to form a united government. As a result, representatives of the five surviving species came together to form the Xindi Council, though tension between the species continues to simmer beneath the surface.

The seemingly all-knowing Guardians also warned the Xindi about a violent future in which Humans would be responsible for their extinction. The trusting Xindi did not realize that their "gods" were manipulating them to avoid a future in which the United Federation of Planets defeat a Guardian invasion as the Temporal Cold War evolved into actual warfare.

Attacks on Earth
In 2153 the Xindi launched a devastating attack on Earth, using a particle-beam probe created with the help of the Guardians. This carved a swath of destruction from Florida to Venezuela, killing seven million Humans. The survivors were understandably devastated by the horrific and unprovoked attack. In response, United Earth recalled the

If you ever question the Guardians again, your skin will adorn the bow of this ship.
Commander Dolim, Xindi-Reptilian

starship *Enterprise* NX-01 for system upgrades and supplemented its crew with Military Assault Command Operations (MACO) personnel. The crew's primary responsibility became the defense of Earth. A year of conflict between Humans and Xindi was to follow.

As tensions mounted between Humans and Xindi, Captain Jonathan Archer and his crew discovered that the Guardians had been using the Xindi as pawns in a Temporal Cold War. They were

Five remain The Xindi species shared the same homeworld but evolved in vastly different ways.

Avians (extinct)

Aquatics

Primates

also responsible for altering space in the Delphic Expanse to resemble their own dimension.

The more aggressive species—Reptilians and Insectoids—refused to believe the information, but Archer persuaded representatives from the Primates, Arboreals, and Aquatics. Together, Humans and their allies stopped a new super weapon and enacted a truce. Information supplied from another time-traveling operative suggests that the Xindi will become a member of the Federation by the 26th century, if not before. ∎

See also: United Earth, Time Travel, *Enterprise* NX-01.

Insectoids

Arboreals

Reptilians

The Delphic Expanse

The Delphic Expanse was an area of space superficially reminiscent of the mythic Bermuda Triangle on Earth: many ships entered it, but only a few returned and before they did, bizarre things happened.

For instance, a Vulcan crew that entered the Delphic Expanse went insane and destroyed their own ship. A Klingon vessel emerged from the Expanse with every crew member anatomically inverted, their bodies splayed open, but still alive. It was as if the laws of physics no longer applied.

In fact, they didn't. That region of space had been tampered with by the Xindi's Guardians. They are also known as "Sphere Builders," because they reconfigure space in this universe to be habitable for themselves, as a prelude to invading it several centuries in the future.

Enterprise NX-01 entered the Expanse—2,000 light-years across and three months from Earth at warp 5—based on a tip from a faction of the Temporal Cold War. After one year of targeted destruction of the space-altering Spheres, the Expanse ceased to exist.

A CRIMINAL SYNDICATE
THE ORIONS

CAPTAIN'S LOG

NAME
Orion

CLASS
Class-M planet

LOCATION
Pi 3 Orionis system, Alpha Quadrant

BRIEFING
Following the Temporal Incursion of 2233, at least two Orion women are known to have joined Starfleet, though relations between the two worlds remain unclear

On the surface, the Orions seem to be a neutral power in the Galaxy. This is largely pretense: It is a ploy to cover up the criminal activities undertaken by its people. In reality, the people of the planet Orion are extremely duplicitous and they are responsible for one of the most powerful criminal organizations in the known universe.

Orion natural charms
The green-skinned Orions are humanoid in appearance. The women tend to be more animalistic in demeanor and boast some unique physiological features, including the ability to emit a pheromone that makes them highly attractive to most humanoid males. These pheromones are known to cause aggression in males while at the same time placing them in a delusionary state that renders them highly open to suggestion. The same pheromones have a different effect on humanoid women (largely causing headaches), and Denobulan males, who experience interrupted sleep cycles. Vulcans seem to be immune to the effects.

This physiological quirk has led to the practice of selling women as slaves. In fact, this has handed more power to the women, who use their abilities against their new masters, ultimately enslaving them.

The Orion Syndicate
Of all the criminal organizations working in the Alpha and Beta Quadrants, the chief one is the Orion Syndicate, based in the Orion sector. It is engaged in all types of criminal activity including assassination, blackmail, extortion, piracy, and the slave trade. Members are required to offer a portion of their income to the organization as a "fare" for the higher-ranking members, and in the rare event that anyone is suspected to have betrayed the Syndicate that person will pay a high price, perhaps even death. If a person guilty of betraying the organization cannot be located, their family may be killed instead.

In the days leading up to the founding of the Coalition of Planets,

The Orion Syndicate tried to kill me. They never kill their own. They don't need to. Any one of them would take their own life before they'd testify against the Syndicate.
Quark

the Orions are a key subject in the discussions, even though they are not part of the meeting. One of the Tellarites' primary requests for the Coalition is that they place a trade embargo on the Orions because their people are suspected of raiding Tellarite freighters. This is opposed by the Coridans, because they have been successfully trading with the Orions for centuries. This is a problem that often arises.

Over a century later, when the Coridans finally petitioned to join the United Federation of Planets, tensions still existed between the Federation and Orions. A Federation presence in the Coridan system would greatly affect the Orion's dilithium smuggling operation. While Federation ambassadors are en route to Coridan on the *U.S.S. Enterprise*, the ship comes under attack but ultimately foils an Orion plot to disrupt the Federation. ■
See also: The United Federation of Planets, The Temporal Incursion of 2233

Orion "animal women"
Orion females have powerful natural pheromones that make their mere presence hypnotic to humanoid males.

It's not easy being not-green

The formation of the Federation united several species with whom the Orions have periodic run-ins, which may be why, after the 22nd century, the Orions rarely show their faces. Instead, they have expanded their Syndicate to include all stripes and colors, and let those members interface with the interstellar community.

One such unit of the Syndicate is a motley crew of humanoids including Farian gangsters, a Bolian bartender, and a Human named Liam Bilby. They engage in fairly standard offenses like online bank robbery and arms running, until an insidious collaboration between the Syndicate and the Dominion entangles them in a plot to kill a Klingon ambassador.

When Bilby learns that his confidant "Connelly" (Miles O'Brien) is actually a Starfleet infiltrator, and that he himself is about to step into a death trap, he goes through with it anyway to keep the Syndicate from killing his family.

DEATH BEFORE DISHONOR
THE KLINGON EMPIRE

CAPTAIN'S LOG

NAME
The Klingon Empire

HOMEWORLD
Qo'noS

CLASS
Class-M planet

LOCATION
Sector 070, Qo'noS system, Beta Quadrant

MOON
Praxis

POLITICAL AFFILIATION
Klingon Empire

BRIEFING
Qo'noS is less than 90 light-years from the Sol system

Historic hall The revered Great Hall of Qam-Chee was the setting for the marriage of Kahless and Lukara.

The Klingon Empire is a political superpower located in the Beta Quadrant, which has acted as both an ally and an enemy to the United Federation of Planets at various times. Its governing body is the Klingon High Council, which consists of approximately 24 representatives from the most honored Klingon Houses, led by a single Chancellor. The Council has, on occasion, led its people into periods of turmoil when motivated by their own political needs rather than the good of the Empire.

Kahless the Unforgettable
Around the time of Earth's 9th century, Kahless the Unforgettable slew Molor, a hated tyrant who ruled Qo'noS, and conquered his longstanding enemies the Fek'lhri people. He then united his people

The Sword of Kahless

Like the Holy Grail on Earth, the Sword of Kahless is a sacred icon and the object of a great quest.

According to legend, it was the first *bat'leth* ever forged. Kahless thrust a lock of his hair into the lava of the Kri'stak volcano, then plunged it into the lake of Lusor and twisted it into the sword that he used to kill the tyrant Molor.

After Kahless' death the *bat'leth* was wrapped in a shroud and revered on Qo'noS, until some 500 years later when it was stolen by the invading Hur'q of the Gamma Quadrant. When the "Shroud of the Sword" was unearthed a millennium later, *Dahar* master Kor set out to find the sword itself with Starfleet officers Worf and Jadzia Dax. They succeeded, but the discord that arose over the artifact threatened to divide the Klingon Empire. So they kept the sword's discovery secret and left it adrift in space. It may be found again in another thousand years.

by founding the Klingon Empire. The Klingons have no gods (they killed them), but they revere their great leader Kahless with a devotion bordering on the spiritual. His teachings on honor and strength continue to inspire this warrior race in the 24th century, as they pride themselves on behaving with honor above all else. Those who die honorably are celebrated as heroic warriors who will gain entrance to the Klingon afterlife of *Sto-Vo-kor*. Those who die in dishonor are said to end up on the Barge of the Dead, where they are ferried to *Gre'thor*, the Klingon version of hell.

There are many tales of Kahless winning great battles, but his marriage to the Lady Lukara is one of the greatest love stories in Klingon history. Together, they are said to have held off 500 of Molor's warriors who were attacking the Great Hall of Qam-Chee at the start of their historic romance. The vows they made to each other there are often repeated by couples during modern marriage ceremonies. »

Kahless the Unforgettable The founder's promise to return is fulfilled when his clone, Kahless II, is appointed Ceremonial Emperor.

Klingon warrior Klaang was investigating a Suliban plot against the Klingons when he fell to Earth.

Upon his death, Kahless promised he would return. This later inspired some 24th-century clerics to produce a leader which they claimed was Kahless returned. The ruse was soon discovered: "Kahless" was revealed to be a clone made from preserved cellular material taken from Kahless's blood. Nevertheless, the clone was accepted as a representation of the great leader and called Kahless II. He was also named Ceremonial Emperor, a symbolic post to remind Klingons of their honorable past.

Contacting the Federation

First contact between the Klingon Empire and Humans occurred when a Klingon crash-landed on a farm in

A Klingon's honor is more important to him than his life.
Worf

Broken Bow, Oklahoma on Earth in 2151. Klaang was being hunted by two Suliban soldiers, who were trying to retrieve evidence of a Suliban plot to destabilize the Klingon Empire. Klaang killed them by blowing up a corn silo with them inside. Thinking his farm was under attack, the Human farmer shot the Klingon. Critically wounded, Klaang was put on life support at Starfleet Medical, and the launch of *Enterprise* NX-01 was brought forward by three weeks so he could be returned to his homeworld, Qo'noS. This marked the beginning of Human exploration into deep space.

As the *Enterprise* crew returned Klaang to his people, Captain Archer and Subcommander T'Pol discovered that the Klingon was carrying information about the Temporal Cold War in his DNA. Yet rather than showing gratitude for Klaang's return, the Klingon High Council sent the Human crew on their way with words that are better left untranslated.

Klingon Augments

In 2154, the chief medical officer of *Enterprise* NX-01, Dr. Phlox, was abducted and taken to the Klingon

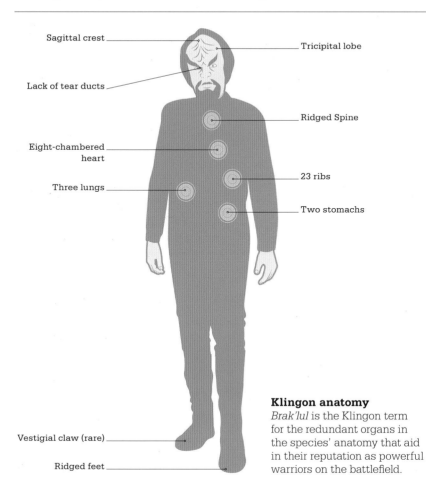

Sagittal crest

Lack of tear ducts

Eight-chambered heart

Three lungs

Vestigial claw (rare)

Ridged feet

Tricipital lobe

Ridged Spine

23 ribs

Two stomachs

Klingon anatomy
Brak'lul is the Klingon term for the redundant organs in the species' anatomy that aid in their reputation as powerful warriors on the battlefield.

colony of Qu'Vat to assist Klingon scientist Dr. Antaak. Phlox was placed in charge of a research operation to combat an infection that was affecting millions of Klingons, and had the potential to lead to their extinction. Honor prevented the Klingons from asking Starfleet for assistance, fearing it would make them appear weak, so they had taken the doctor forcibly, knowing of his research into viral propagation and metagenics.

Phlox determined that the Klingons were suffering from a mutated form of the Levodian flu, but the more important discovery was that the problem was self-inflicted. The virus included DNA that could be traced back to the Eugenics Wars on Earth in the late 20th century. It became clear that the Klingons were attempting their own eugenics experiments, and were trying to breed super-warriors using DNA samples from the Human Augments created during Earth's 20th century.

The Klingon test subjects in the Augment experiments lost their cranial ridges and became very aggressive, then their neural pathways degraded, resulting in violent deaths. One of the test subjects who was suffering from the Levodian flu spread the virus

It is more honorable to give one's life to medical research than to die for no purpose!
Antaak

Killer virus Levodian flu spread from a Klingon Augment. These genetically produced warriors lost facial ridges and suffered fatal brain damage.

among the Klingon people, where the plague ran unchecked until Dr. Phlox found a cure. Although he saved the Klingons from extinction, some effects of the virus—such as the loss of facial ridges—were passed on to their descendents.

A fragile peace
Relations between the Klingon Empire and the Federation began to improve at the Khitomer peace conference of 2293. This was not a matter of free choice: the Empire was forced to ask for Federation assistance when over-mining caused the moon Praxis to explode. The devastating loss of a prime energy-production facility and the environmental effects on the Klingon Homeworld of Qo'noS, »

moved Chancellor Gorkon to propose peace with the Federation. The Federation sent the *U.S.S. Enterprise* NCC-1701-A to escort the Chancellor's ship to the peace conference, where a welcoming dinner revealed deeply held prejudices on both sides. When the Chancellor was assassinated shortly afterward, Captain Kirk and Dr. McCoy were tried and

The Klingon who kills without showing his face has no honor. He must not lead the Empire. Such a man would be capable of anything—even war with the Federation.
Chancellor K'mpec

ultimately convicted of his death. But with the help of the *Enterprise* and *Excelsior* crews, Kirk and McCoy revealed the true culprits: a coalition of Federation and Klingon operatives. Chancellor Gorkon's daughter, Azetbur, was persuaded to continue her father's work as chancellor, forming an alliance between the two powers that was known as the Khitomer Accords.

A time of unrest

The Klingon Empire maintained an uneasy peace with the Federation over the next 70 years while also experiencing turmoil within its own ranks. The Klingon High Council finally reached breaking point in 2367, when the Empire was thrown into civil war after the poisoning of Chancellor K'mpec.

K'mpec's murder was seen as a dishonorable act in Klingon society, and the battle to fill his seat threatened to tear the Empire apart. It did not help that, prior to his death, K'mpec had chosen a Human to act as his Arbiter of Successor. In this

unusual rite, orchestrated by Federation Ambassador K'Ehleyr, Captain Jean-Luc Picard of the *Enterprise*-D took the role of Arbiter.

When Gowron became the lead candidate for the position of Chancellor, the powerful House of Duras attempted to block his ascension. Although records showed that Duras's father Ja'rod had betrayed the Empire by assisting the Romulans in the Khitomer massacre of 2346, this awkward truth had been buried. Duras falsely accused the House of Mogh of the act of treason, and specifically the father of *Enterprise*-D security officer Worf. The slur brought the Starfleet officer to Qo'noS to deny the accusation, and Worf later challenged and killed Duras in a *bat'leth* duel. The House of Duras continued to fight for the succession, pushing the Empire into a brief civil war, suspended when Starfleet exposed the house's link with the Romulans, and Gowron finally came to power.

The Dominion War

The Klingons later launched an attack on the Cardassian Union, fearing that within the Union, Dominion Founders had replaced high-ranking officials with Changelings. But the Klingons were unaware that a shape-shifter had replaced their own General Martok. When the Federation spoke out against the unprovoked Klingon attack and provided sanctuary aboard Deep Space 9 for the Cardassian leadership, Gowron revoked the Khitomer Accords.

The conflict with the Cardassian Union lasted for a year, after which

General Martok welcomed Worf into his House and took part in the traditional Klingon version of a bachelor party, which emphasizes mental and physical challenges over debauchery.

How to speak Klingon

The Klingon language, sometimes called "Klingonese," is composed of 80 dialects constructed on an adaptive syntax. All are notably guttural, sounding harsh, abrupt, and severe, as suits the character of this warrior race. Common words and expressions include the following:
- *HIja'* or *HISlaH*, means "yes."
- *ghobe*, means "no."
- *Qapla*, means "success."
- *Suvwl*, means "warrior."
- *maj ram* means "good night."
- *petaQ* or *p'tak* is a general form of expletive.
- *jol yIchu*, means "activate beam."
- *par'Mach* is a word for "love" (with rough, playful undertones).
- *Heghlu'meH QaQ jajvam,* means "today is a good day to die."
- *taHqeq*, means "liar."
- *bortaS bIr jablu'DI' reH QaQqu' nay*, famously means "revenge is a dish best served cold."

Cardassia was so weakened it agreed to ally with the Dominion, giving them a stronger foothold in the Alpha Quadrant. Gowron was forced to reinstate the Khitomer Accords and work with the Federation to defend their space. After Martok's Changeling doppelganger was exposed, the real general took command of Klingon forces, but Gowron felt threatened by his successes. He issued orders to Martok that resulted in a slew of failed missions, threatening both the Klingons and the Allied Forces.

When Worf became aware of the Chancellor's dishonorable actions, he challenged Gowron for leadership, killing him in *bat'leth* combat. However, Worf refused to accept the title of Chancellor, passing it to Martok who then worked with the Federation to defeat the Dominion. ■

See also: *Enterprise* NX-01, *U.S.S. Enterprise* NCC-1701-A, The United Federation of Planets, Worf, B'Elanna Torres.

New ambassador After the war, Worf was asked to serve as the Federation Ambassador to the Klingon people as they entered a new (and probably brief) period of peace.

BEWARE ROMULANS BEARING GIFTS
THE ROMULAN STAR EMPIRE

CAPTAIN'S LOG

NAME
Romulus

CLASS
Class-M planet

LOCATION
**Romulus system,
Beta Quadrant**

POLITICAL AFFILIATION
Romulan Star Empire

DESTROYED
2387

NAME
Remus

CLASS
Class-Q planet

LOCATION
**Romulus system,
Beta Quadrant**

POLITICAL AFFILIATION
**Romulan Star Empire
(former)**

In the known Galaxy there are few species that have been at odds with the United Federation of Planets longer or more consistently than the Romulan Star Empire. This species is colder and more calculating than the Klingons, preferring covert means of attack rather than face-to-face combat. In fact, very few members of the Federation dealt directly with a Romulan during the first century of aggressions between the superpowers, so fought an entire war without seeing the face of their enemy. And yet, Romulans also

Capital city Located on Romulus, the capital of the Romulan Star Empire houses the Senate at its center.

possess their own code of honor that makes them noble warriors while still being duplicitous foes.

Split from the Vulcans
The Romulan nation was born on the planet Vulcan as a sect that turned its back on the teachings of the philosopher Surak. Rather than following the path toward pure logic, these Vulcans chose to abandon their home planet, in a

Working relations Romulan commanders (right) need to keep senators such as Tal'aura (left) on side.

Bird of prey The emblem of the Empire features a bird of prey clutching the sister planets Romulus and Remus.

Earth's warp-capable space flight led indirectly to the formation of the Coalition of Planets, when a scheme to create discord between Andorians and Tellarites had the opposite effect. The Earth–Romulan War that took place between 2156 and 2160 further cemented the relationship when Andorians, Tellarites, and Vulcans came to the aid of their Human allies. The Federation itself was formed shortly after the cessation of hostilities.

The Romulan Neutral Zone was also established at the end of the war. This defines the border between the United Federation of Planets and the Romulan Star Empire. For several centuries it became a violation for either side to cross the Neutral Zone. Both the Romulans and Federation heavily »

time before warp-capable flight, and set off to find a new home. Their journey was long and arduous, but they eventually came to settle on the planets of Romulus and Remus in the Beta Quadrant. Here they were free to continue to express their emotions and explore the darker tendencies of their people. These former Vulcans were said to have marched under the banner of the raptor, which became the symbol of the Romulan Star Empire.

Physiologically, Romulans are similar to their Vulcan cousins. They too have pointed ears, upswept eyebrows, and copper-based green blood. Many Romulans also possess a pair of ridges above their nose as a lone visible trait distinguishing them from Vulcans. Anatomically speaking, the

Romulans have slightly different internal organs, which means that traditional Vulcan remedies do not always work to cure them of certain diseases.

The true source of power

The Praetor is the highest-ranking leader in Romulan government, above the Proconsul, Vice-Proconsul, and the Romulan Senate. Together, these serve as the governing body of the Empire, though the Senate is the true seat of power. It drafts the laws of its people and engages in interstellar relations. Even some of the more mundane decisions of the Empire must pass through the Senate for approval, as the senators maintain a tight control on their people.

The Romulan Empire is said to be partially responsible for the founding of the United Federation of Planets. This is because their actions during the early days of

Our people are warriors, often savage. But we are also many other pleasant things.
Romulan Commander

The Romulan Neutral Zone

A demilitarized area between the Federation and the Romulans, the Neutral Zone crossed through Sector Z-6. Seven Federation outpost stations were set up on their side of the zone.

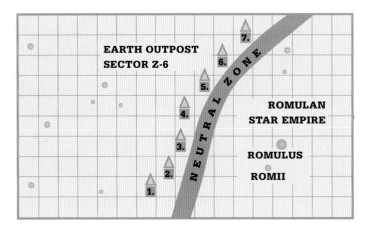

EARTH OUTPOST
SECTOR Z-6

NEUTRAL ZONE

ROMULAN
STAR EMPIRE

ROMULUS

ROMII

7.
6.
5.
4.
3.
2.
1.

monitor that area of space, and are vigilant for any infraction that could be considered an act of war.

In the century following the Earth-Romulan war there was little contact between the two peoples until a Romulan warship attacked Federation outposts along the Neutral Zone in 2266. It was stopped by the *Starship Enterprise* under James Kirk's command, and he was ultimately forced to set his critically damaged vessel to self-destruct. Aside from a few other minor conflicts, the two galactic powers stayed clear of one another for a century or so after this incident.

From enemy to ally

In 2364, a Borg attack along the Neutral Zone opened a new phase of face-to-face interactions between the two powers. Tension continued, but Federation ambassador Spock made overtures for peace in a covert mission, embedding himself in a Romulan underground faction that was working to end hostilities. The crew of the *Enterprise*-D were briefly pulled into his mission on the Romulan homeworld, but

eventually left the ambassador to continue his work on his own.

The Dominion War broke out in the following years, while Spock was still working toward the reunification of the Vulcans and Romulans. The Romulans were initially persuaded to sign a treaty of nonaggression with the Dominion, preferring to avoid the conflict that it had seen weakening its enemies.

However, they were eventually drawn into the battle when evidence of Cardassian involvement was discovered in the death of a senator. The Romulan Star Empire then joined the Federation and Klingon allied forces unaware that a Cardassian ex-patriot who was working for the Federation had manufactured the murder evidence. The Romulan contribution to the war effort was impressive, and they proved to be a powerful ally to the eventual victors in the conflict.

An empire falls

In 2379, a Human clone of Captain Jean-Luc Picard, known as Shinzon, was held captive on Romulus's neighboring planet of Remus. From this vulnerable position he managed to rise up and take over the Romulan Empire by assassinating virtually the entire Romulan Senate. Now Praetor, Shinzon lured the *Enterprise*-E to Romulus under the guise of peace.

Romulan betrayal Spock overpowers Romulan commander Sela when he learns of her plans to attack Vulcan.

In fact, it was the opening gambit for an attack on the Federation and an attempt to gain access to the blood of the man the Romulans had used to clone Shinzon: Captain Picard. The *Enterprise* crew thwarted Shinzon's plan, but at the cost of Commander Data's life.

The Empire was still rebuilding its political power when it was faced with its greatest threat less than a decade later. A star close to Romulus threatened to become

Romulan Senate Visitors face the Praetor and Continuing Committee.

a supernova, and this prompted the Romulans to forge another alliance with the Federation in the hope of stopping the potential disaster before it destroyed much of the Galaxy. Ambassador Spock devised a plan to use red matter to create a singularity within the star so that it would be absorbed into a black hole. As Spock traveled to Romulus

to enact his plan, the star turned into a supernova. Although Spock was able to stop the supernova's shock wave before it traveled beyond Romulan space, he was too late to save the planet Romulus from being destroyed. ■

See also: The United Federation of Planets, The Temporal Incursion of 2233, *Enterprise* NX-01, Spock

Romulan script The written form of the Romulan language consists of square and rectangular symbols.

The Tal Shiar

It seems that almost every major power in the Galaxy has some super-secret organization that is authorized by its government but operates outside it—it may even operate outside the law. In the Romulan Star Empire, that organization is the Tal Shiar.

Domestically, the Tal Shiar enforces loyalty among the Romulan citizens and the military. Agents are seen to exercise broad discretionary powers and can overrule field commanders with little fear of reprisal. Many Romulans feel the Tal Shiar's tactics are unnecessarily brutal,

but such views are rarely voiced for fear of retribution, such as the sudden "disappearance" of family members.

As the Empire's elite intelligence service, the Tal Shiar operates its own fleet. In 2371, the Tal Shiar joined forces with the Cardassian Obsidian Order to mount a pre-emptive strike against the Dominion. However, the Tal Shiar had unknowingly been infiltrated by the Founders, and the combined fleet was ambushed and annihilated, rendering the Tal Shiar virtually extinct.

NO QUARTER, NO CAPTIVES
THE EARTH-ROMULAN WAR

CAPTAIN'S LOG

NAME
The Earth–Romulan war

DURATION
2156 to 2160

ALLIED FORCES
United Earth, Vulcans, Andorians, Tellarites

DECISIVE BATTLE
Battle of Cheron

Shortly after Humans began their mission of deep space exploration in 2151, the Romulan Star Empire put its own covert plans into action. Their aim was to limit the growth of the major political powers in the Alpha and Beta Quadrants: United Earth, the Vulcans, the Andorians, and the Tellarites. As the Romulan Star Empire was then the largest political entity in known space, it viewed any potential union between other worlds as a threat. Initially the Romulans attempted to sow discord between the various species, but when this failed, they declared war in 2156.

Starbase 1 triggers war

The Coalition of Planets was founded in 2155, one year before the Romulans declared war. This alliance between eight species of the Alpha and Beta Quadrants forged interstellar cooperation, and allowed Earth's Starfleet to make ever-increasing footholds in space. As Starfleet expanded its reach, with additional starships and colonies spreading throughout the two quadrants, it quickly became obvious that the great distances between star systems meant that a more permanent operation needed

Starbase 1 The first Starbase space station had a large central living area, surrounded by space docking stations with retractable docking clamps.

to be established throughout the Galaxy. One of the most ambitious plans was the development of Starbase 1, a United Earth outpost intended to support deep space missions and Human colonies.

Starbase 1 opened above the planet Algeron in 2156 and immediately proved useful as a support and trading post for Earth as well as the other Coalition

United Earth The peace between Vulcans, Andorians, and Tellarites brought about by United Earth was seen as a threat by the Romulans.

planets. However, Algeron is on the border of Romulan space, so the Romulans viewed it as a sign of a growing threat.

The Romulan Empire reacted by falsely claiming that the planet Algeron was part of their territory and must be vacated immediately. The Humans refused to abandon the prime location, having already invested a tremendous amount of resources, so the Romulans launched an attack on the outpost, catching Starfleet off-guard. The space station and two Starfleet vessels

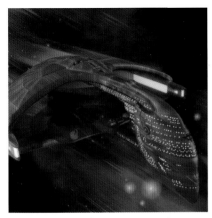

Romulan Warbird Romulan ships, some of the most powerful in the Alpha and Beta Quadrants, have names that echo the avian theme of their emblem.

were destroyed in the attack, but they managed to get a message to Earth alerting Starfleet Command to the danger.

Alliances form

The Humans initially tried to find a diplomatic resolution to the conflict but failed, leading to a declaration of war. Vulcans, Andorians, and Tellarites (part of the Coalition) were quick to support their Human allies, but other Coalition planets hesitated, even when Denobula became an unwitting victim in the fray. There was never any ship-to-

Earth believes the Romulans to be warlike, cruel, treacherous; and only the Romulans know what they think of Earth.
Spock

ship communication, allowing the Romulans to hide their appearance from their enemy, and war waged on for four years using weapon systems that future generations of Starfleet would consider primitive.

In 2160, the Battle of Cheron delivered a decisive victory to the allied forces. Romulans retreated to their side of the border, and following the war they closed off all forms of communication with the newly formed Federation for over a century. ∎

See also: The United Federation of Planets, United Earth, *Enterprise NX-01*, The Romulan Star Empire

The Treaty of Algeron

Following the decisive Battle of Cheron in 2160, a Neutral Zone was established in talks via subspace communication. This zone was to delineate the area of space that neither Humans nor Romulans would be allowed to cross. The demarcation was honored by the Federation upon its formation and then strictly enforced, remaining unviolated until the Romulans crossed into Federation space in 2266.

After this, all was quiet in the Neutral Zone until hostilities erupted once again between the Romulan Empire and the Federation in an explosive battle that became known as the Tomed Incident of 2311. Thousands of lives were lost. The incident led to the Treaty of Algeron, which reaffirmed and redefined the Romulan Neutral Zone, and also reiterated that its violation by either party without adequate notification would be considered an act of war. This treaty also forbade the Federation from developing or using cloaking technology in its starships. This particular provision of the Treaty was eased in 2370 during the Dominion threat.

ENEMIES MAKE DANGEROUS FRIENDS
THE CARDASSIAN UNION

CAPTAIN'S LOG

NAME **Cardassia (Cardassia Prime)**

CLASS **Class-M planet**

LOCATION **Alpha Quadrant**

MAJOR SPECIES **Cardassians**

POLITICAL AFFILIATION **The Cardassian Union, Dominion 2373–2375**

BRIEFING **The planet Cardassia Prime is located five light-years from the planet Bajor**

By the middle of the 24th century the Cardassian Union had grown to be one of the more powerful political forces in the Alpha Quadrant, quietly absorbing other worlds into its Union while the Federation was occupied in clashes with the Romulans and Klingons. But the Federation was not blind to the Cardassians' aggressive actions; its own conflict with the species had stretched on for 20 years. Although the Federation-Cardassian war ended in 2366, tensions never diminished in spite of a treaty intended to bring peace to the warring factions. A new, more devastating war was on the horizon, one that would deeply affect the Federation and leave the Cardassian Union a shadow of its former self.

Expanding their reach
Cardassia, also known as Cardassia Prime, is the capital planet of the militaristic Alpha Quadrant species. Once known as a civilization that was rich in art

Union of warriors The emblem of the Cardassian Union mirrors the design of their *Galor*-class warship, highlighting the militaristic aspect of their species.

and architecture, the archeological ruins of the planet were considered treasures throughout the known universe. Tragically, the inhabitants had hardened as they struggled with starvation and disease in the face of the planet's diminished natural resources. These once-spiritual people become soldiers

enslaving other worlds as the Union spread across the Galaxy in search of resources. Over time, Cardassians began to plunder their own once-revered archeological treasures to support themselves and build military strength as they sought to grow through planetary domination rather than nation-building.

Cardassians don't make mistakes.
Dukat

The government of the Union was divided into three branches: the Cardassian Central Command; the Obsidian Order; and the Detapa Council. Although the civilian Detapa Council was technically the head of government, it was effectively a powerless figurehead. The true might in the Union rested in the military authority of the Central Command and the Obsidian Order intelligence agency. These two factions were often at odds with one another as they relied on very different methods to accomplish their goals. Central Command tended toward overt acts of aggression; the Obsidian Order preferred subtler tactics.

Massacre on Bajor
In the early part of the 24th century, the Cardassian Union expanded its reach to the planet Bajor in a

Imperfect prefect Gul Dukat's regime as Cardassian Prefect of Bajor saw the deaths of millions of Bajorans.

neighboring star system. The Bajorans were unable to defend themselves against the overpowering forces of the Union, and their planet was eventually annexed. The Cardassians stripped Bajor of its resources while subjugating its people, killing millions. Though the Bajoran resistance movement successfully weakened the Cardassian hold on their planet, they were not strong enough to win back Bajor on their own. It wasn't until the Union became weakened by war with the Federation that it withdrew from Bajor to strengthen its own forces. The Cardassians left devastation in their wake, with Bajor a shell, and its people beaten, but resilient. »

An uneasy peace

The Cardassians entered into a tenuous peace treaty with the Federation in 2367, but it did not bring an end to the hostilities. The Federation-Cardassian Treaty established a Demilitarized Zone with redrawn borders that caused several colonies to be displaced. Some inhabitants strongly opposed this imposed political agreement which they had no say in creating. Their anger gave rise to the Maquis, a resistance movement of colonists—including many former Starfleet officers—who went on to engage in terrorist activities in order to keep their homes. There was an increase in Maquis attacks in the years following the Treaty, until the Cardassians enlisted new allies in the Dominion—a major power originally from the Gamma Quadrant—to help eradicate them.

The Cardassians proved early on that they had no intention of adhering to the Treaty when their military started rebuilding its forces. These covert acts drove Starfleet captain Benjamin Maxwell of the *Starship Phoenix* to violate

Ready for war The Cardassian buildup of warships and military forces puts an end to their peace treaty.

the Treaty in an effort to prove the Cardassians were engaged in illicit activities. In so doing, Captain Maxwell destroyed a Cardassian outpost and two vessels. He was forced to surrender to Starfleet for prosecution.

A while later, the Cardassians made an even bolder move when Gul Madred lured Captain Jean-Luc Picard into a trap and tortured him

cruelly for information on Starfleet's defensive operations. Picard did not yield during the interrogation, but he came close to breaking before Madred was forced to return him to his ship. After several more years the Treaty was finally revoked.

A lost opportunity

When Cardassian forces withdrew from Bajor in 2369, they failed to anticipate the huge strategic mistake they would be making. The discovery of the Bajoran wormhole shortly after they abandoned their space station, Terok Nor, became a missed opportunity for Cardassians to establish a tactical location and open up relations with the Gamma Quadrant. Following their departure, the Cardassians maintained deeply strained relations with Bajor in spite of a peace treaty they signed with Kai Winn Adami in 2371. In fact, their relationships with most worlds in the Alpha and Beta Quadrants was destined to suffer for years to come.

Obsidian Order

This highly efficient and ruthless intelligence organization represents the ever-vigilant eyes and ears of the Cardassian Union. It has been said that a Cardassian citizen cannot sit down to a meal without each dish being noted and recorded by the Order. Even the Romulan Tal Shiar agency cannot boast such efficiency in obtaining intelligence.

In theory, the Obsidian Order answers to the political authority of the Detapa Council, but in practice—like the military— it runs its own affairs and has worked in this way for 500 years.

The Obsidian Order was run by Enabran Tain for 20 years, the only chief to live long enough to retire. Tain was so callous that he exiled his own son and protégé, Elim Garak, to the space station Terok Nor (later Deep Space 9) for some unknown misdeed, and later even ordered his assassination.

Tain came out of retirement to mastermind a first strike— combining forces with the ships of the Romulan Tal Shiar intelligence agency—against the Dominion. This act ended in disaster for both organizations.

Into the Badlands The location of the treacherous area of space known as the Badlands made it a strategic location for the Maquis to launch their campaign against Cardassians.

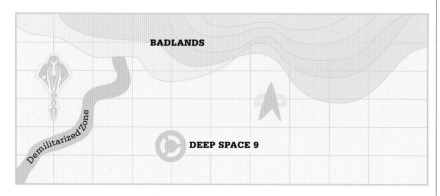

align with the Dominion was initially beneficial to the Union, and especially to Gul Dukat who was named leader of his people for arranging the alliance. Dukat eventually lost his position when the non-corporeal entities known as the Pah-wraiths began to consume his thoughts. The Dominion brought the weaker Gul Damar into power, but it was not long before he realized that his people had become oppressed.

A rebellion sparked among the Cardassian people, but it was quickly quashed by the merciless Dominion regime. Rather than silencing the Cardassian voices, however, it led to an uprising that helped destabilize the Dominion's position in the war. In response, the Dominion brutally attacked Cardassia, leveling cities and killing over 800 million people before fleeing the planet. Though the Cardassian Union had won its freedom, the cost had been huge. ∎

See also: Deep Space 9, The Bajorans, The Maquis, Elim Garak, Dukat, The Dominion War

There is no dilemma that cannot be solved by a disciplined Cardassian mind.
Dukat

The Cardassians revolt

The conflict severely weakened the Cardassian Union. Faced with no other option, the Union agreed to ally with the Dominion in 2373. Among the Dominion's first acts was to find and destroy all the Maquis cells that had been fighting the Cardassians. The decision to

The Klingons from the Beta Quadrant launched an attack on Cardassia in 2372, when they suspected that shape-shifting Founders had taken over the Detapa Council. Gul Dukat rescued the members of the council, fleeing to the Federation-controlled space station Deep Space 9, where it was proved they had not been replaced.

Fallen Union The Dominion left devastation in its wake when it pulled out of Cardassia and punished the people for betraying the alliance.

A SIMPLE TAILOR
ELIM GARAK

CAPTAIN'S LOG

NAME
Elim Garak

SPECIES
Cardassian

OCCUPATION
Tailor, Garak's Clothiers

BRIEFING
This skilled liar offers multiple reasons for his exile from Cardassia, including tax evasion and murder

Aformer top agent in the Obsidian Order—the Cardassian intelligence organization—Elim Garak ended up in exile on Deep Space 9, where he ran a tailor's shop. Garak was the son and protégé of the former leader of the agency, Enabran Tain, and was highly skilled in the art of deception. All his life, he had been forced to hide his relationship with his father so it would not weaken Tain's standing in the Order. It was only on Tain's deathbed that he finally acknowledged his son.

It is difficult to quantify Garak's career in espionage because he is so talented at covering up evidence of his work. But he is likely to have been responsible for a number of killings, particularly of high-ranking Romulans during his time working as a gardener in the Cardassian Embassy on planet Romulus.

Following the Cardassian withdrawal from the planet Bajor, Garak was exiled to Deep Space 9 where he set up Garak's Clothiers. But his espionage skills were not

Outcast or spy? Secretive about his past, Garak may be using his tailoring skills as a cover up for his continued espionage activities.

> Do you know what the sad part is, Odo? I'm a very good tailor.
> **Elim Garak**

redundant and proved useful when he arranged an assassination to help the Federation draw the Romulans into the Dominion War.

While on the station, Garak formed a tentative friendship with several residents, including the genetically enhanced Dr. Julian Bashir, who once had his own dreams of what it meant to be a spy. But Garak's most notable relationship was with Tora Ziyal, the half-Bajoran daughter of his bitter enemy Gul Dukat. Garak never quite understood what the open and innocent young woman saw in him, but he regretfully never had the chance to find out as she was killed during the Dominion War. ∎

ONE MAN'S VILLAIN IS ANOTHER MAN'S HERO
DUKAT

CAPTAIN'S LOG

NAME
Dukat

SPECIES
Cardassian

BRIEFING
Dukat has fathered at least nine children by three different women. One of them is Tora Ziyal, his half-Bajoran daughter

As the final prefect of Bajor before the Cardassian withdrawal, Gul Dukat oversaw numerous atrocities and Bajoran massacres, but never expressed remorse. Dukat showed little regret for the cruelty he inflicted during his rise through the ranks of Central Command.

One of Dukat's many Bajoran enemies was Kira Nerys, a former resistance fighter stationed on Deep Space 9. Though she felt nothing but hatred for the man, she worked with him to rescue his half-Bajoran daughter, Tora Ziyal, from a Breen encampment.

The revelation that Dukat had a Bajoran daughter weakened him in the eyes of the Cardassian Union, but he eventually regained his standing and hosted secret talks with the Dominion to form an alliance between their peoples. This union made them a powerful force in the Alpha Quadrant and allowed Dukat's rise to lead the Cardassian government. However, Dukat fell from grace again following the death of his daughter, his subsequent breakdown, and his capture by the Federation.

Pah-wraith power
Dukat escaped and called on the Pah-wraiths—non-corporeal entities who were enemies of the Bajoran Prophets—to aid him in the Dominion conflict, eventually

Everything I have lost, I will regain.
Dukat

Daddy's girl Dukat's love for his half-Bajoran daughter, Tora Ziyal, costs him his high standing in Cardassian society.

forming a cult in their honor.

While the Pah-wraiths possessed Dukat's body, they caused the death of Starfleet lieutenant commander Jadzia Dax among other tragic events. At the end of the Dominion War, Dukat was working to free the Pah-wraiths from their captivity in the fire caves of Bajor when the Emissary, Benjamin Sisko, came to disrupt his plan. The two fought, falling into the fire caves where Dukat is presumed to have died. ∎
See also: Deep Space 9, Kira Nerys, The Cardassian Union, The Dominion War, Pah-wraiths

VICTORY IS LIFE
THE DOMINION

CAPTAIN'S LOG

NAME
Founders

LOCATION
Founders' homeworld, Omarion Nebula, Gamma Quadrant (until 2371)

CLASS
R-class planet (until 2371)

BRIEFING
The Founders rule over a large population, "The Dominion," supported by forces including the Vorta and Jem'Hadar

They are called "The Founders" by the Gamma Quadrant species that follow them, but their true name is unknown. This ancient civilization of shape-shifters, or Changelings, once explored the Galaxy, but found the "Solids" of the universe to be fearful of them and, as a result, dangerous. Consequently the Founders decided to isolate themselves on a planet in the Omarion Nebula to protect themselves from attack. But that did not stop them from expanding their reach. From that planet they built the Dominion, exercising their oppressive control over hundreds of star systems in the Gamma Quadrant through fear and intimidation via their surrogates, the Vorta and Jem'Hadar.

These shape-shifters consider adopting the form of another object to be a spiritual experience that allows them to fully understand that object. Skilled Changelings can fully mimic the form of other species down to the cellular level, making it nearly impossible to identify them. But when a body part becomes separated from the whole it will revert to its natural gelatinous state, revealing the Changeling's true form.

From their homeworld, the Founders continued to explore the Galaxy in their own way, sending out a hundred young Changelings into the Galaxy. These infants were unaware of their mission, but they were programmed to return in a future century to share what they had learned in their travels. Deep Space 9 Security Chief Odo was one of those explorers. His

The Founders *are* gods.
Weyoun

premature reunion with his people came soon after the opening of the Bajoran wormhole—a cosmic tunnel connecting the Alpha and Gamma Quadrants—an event that ultimately led to war.

In light of past experience with Solids, the Founders had become a xenophobic species that saw the opening of the wormhole as a precursor to an invasion force from the Alpha Quadrant. Their concerns were proven true in 2371 when a combined fleet of the Cardassian Obsidian Order and Romulan Tal Shiar set out to destroy the Founders' original homeworld. But the Founders' intelligence operatives had warned them that the force was coming and they relocated to another planet, springing a trap on the invading fleet. It was not long before war broke out between the Dominion and those in the Alpha Quadrant.

At first, the Founders and their allies proved a formidable force, but the balance of power shifted, bringing their race to the edge

of extinction. Once Starfleet operatives were pushed beyond their limit, they introduced a virus into the Founder community that threatened their lives. In the end, it took one of their own children, Odo, to unite the Founders in their Great Link—the intermingling of Changelings in their natural gelatinous form—to heal their people as they tried to move beyond this time of war.

The Vorta

While the Founders could use their shape-shifting abilities to hide among their enemies, they preferred to rely on enslaved intermediaries and soldiers to enact their plans and fight. The Vorta served as the Founders' **»**

Vorta vows Field Commander Kilana sacrifices the lives of herself and her crew when they are unable to rescue a Founder from a downed starship.

> I tried to deny it. I tried to forget. But I can't. They're my people… and I want to be with them… in the Great Link.
> **Odo**

Family reunion Although Odo is an outsider among his people, he ultimately becomes their savior.

> The Dominion has endured for two thousand years and will continue to endure long after the Federation has crumbled into dust.
>
> **Weyoun**

liaisons to the universe, directing their allies in war and dealing with enemies of the Dominion. The Vorta do not consider themselves slaves, rather they see the Founders as gods and will do anything to protect them, including sacrificing their own lives.

Vorta worship of the Founders dates back to the earliest days of their primitive species. They were once small and timid apelike creatures residing in hollowed-out trees, living in fear of the many predators that preyed on them. One day a family of Vorta gave help to a wounded Changeling who was hiding from a group of Solids. The Changeling promised that one day the Vorta would be transformed into powerful beings who would become an important part of a great new interstellar empire. This shape-shifter was a member of the species that would eventually become the Founders, and saw to it that the promise came true.

White knights Jem'Hadar soldiers are fed carefully monitored portions of the substance ketracel-white through supply tubes in their necks.

The Vorta have been genetically altered with enhanced abilities to better serve the Founders. This form of engineering also helped create a race the Founders could control with targeted weaknesses that have made the Vorta more dependent. The Vorta's religious devotion to the Founders has been programmed as a part of them, just like their physical attributes. Vorta have enhanced hearing, but their eyesight is poor, they lack aesthetic sense, and are tone deaf. They also have a limited sense of taste, and are only really able to enjoy rippleberries and kava nuts. But they can appreciate the different textures of foods and are immune to most forms of poison.

The Founders have cloned the Vorta, creating numerous versions of their more trusted followers. This is particularly useful as the Vorta each have a termination implant—a device attached to the brain stem—that allows them to kill themselves in the event of capture.

Jem'Hadar

The Jem'Hadar is another genetically-engineered species that serve as the soldiers of the Dominion. They have been bred for combat by the Founders and believe this is their one purpose in life. Before a battle, they perform a ritual chant asserting their belief that they are already dead and will only reclaim their lives through the fight. Like the Vorta, the Jem'Hadar also see the Founders as god-like beings and do all that it takes to protect them.

Having been bred for battle, it is the fight that the Jem'Hadar live for and the sole reason for their existence. There are no women

> I am dead. As of this moment, we are all dead. We go into battle to reclaim our lives. This we do gladly, for we are Jem'Hadar. Remember: victory is life.
> **First Omet'iklan**

in Jem'Hadar society as they are created in birthing chambers, where they mature at a rapid rate and are ready to serve within three days upon their exit. They do not need food or rest and only require one substance to keep them going: the isogenic enzyme ketracel-white.

To ensure their loyalty, the Founders engineered the Jem'Hadar to lack ketracel-white. The Vorta tightly control this substance, providing it through

White light Ketracel-white usage is carefully monitored to ensure that Jem'Hadar soldiers remain addicted to the enzyme and compliant to orders.

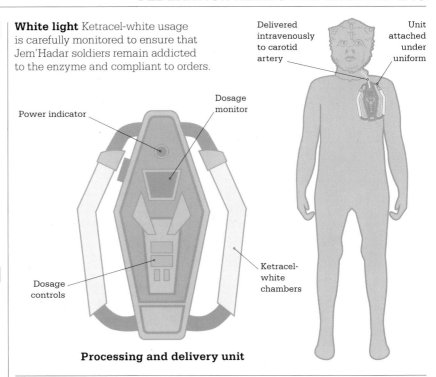

Power indicator
Dosage monitor
Dosage controls
Ketracel-white chambers

Delivered intravenously to carotid artery
Unit attached under uniform

Processing and delivery unit

a delivery system that injects the drug into the necks of the soldiers. The Jem'Hadar have become fully dependent on this drug, though they had proved their loyalty to their leaders even when ketracel-white became unavailable during the war when Federation allied forces destroyed the sole production plant in the Alpha Quadrant. ■

See also: Deep Space 9, Benjamin Sisko, Odo, The Cardassian Union, Weyoun, The Breen Confederacy, The Dominion War

The Great Link

For such cold-blooded tyrants, the Founders, or Changelings, are spiritual people. They would be an inspiration, were it not for their unrelenting belief in their own superiority.

The Great Link of the shapeshifters, who founded the Dominion, is analogous to what many traditions call Heaven—the bliss of interconnectedness with other souls that exist together as one. The Great Link gives meaning to the Changelings' existence: the merging of form and thought and the sharing of ideas and sensations.

The Link is the Changelings' natural state, manifesting as a vast golden sea on the Founders' homeworld. For millennia, this was a rogue planet situated in the Omarion Nebula, until the Founders relocated in a trap to annihilate Alpha Quadrant forces.

The Founders' greatest advantage proves to be their greatest downfall when a morphogenic virus is introduced to the Link, threatening their extinction. Deep Space 9 security chief Odo, a Changeling, rejoins his people in order to provide them with a cure.

A TRUSTED SOLID
WEYOUN

CAPTAIN'S LOG

NAME
Weyoun

SPECIES
Vorta (multiple clones)

AFFILIATION
Dominion

DECEASED
2375 (all known clones)

BRIEFING
At least ten copies of Weyoun were known to exist. Weyoun became the most well-known Vorta in the Alpha Quadrant during the Dominion War

Weyoun is the name given to a succession of at least ten Vorta clones who served the Founders in the late 24th century. Weyoun played a key diplomatic role in relations between the Dominion and the Federation before and during the Dominion War. The Female Founder considered Weyoun her most loyal follower, placing him as liaison to the Cardassians and promising that he would oversee Earth and the Federation once the war was won.

Prior to the war, Weyoun attempted to negotiate a peace

My loyal Weyoun...
the only Solid
I have ever trusted.
Female Changeling

deal with Captain Benjamin Sisko of Deep Space 9, but the plan failed. Another Weyoun clone returned to take control of the station with an armed force of Dominion and Cardassian ships. He served on the ruling council with the Cardassian military leader, Dukat, overseeing operations on the renamed Terok Nor until it was retaken by the Federation. Afterwards, a Weyoun was posted on Cardassia where he appointed Damar as leader of the Cardassian Union to replace Dukat, who showed signs of losing his grip on reality because of his growing dependence on the malevolent Pah-wraiths.

Most of the Weyoun clones met with tragic deaths at the hands of others such as Jem'Hadar soldiers or enemy agents. Weyoun #5 was killed in a suspicious transporter accident, while defective Weyoun #6 questioned the actions of the Founders in the war and offered to defect—taking his own life to keep Odo (a Founder and therefore a god) from being killed. The Obsidian Order agent Garak killed Weyoun #10 at the end of the war, bringing the line to a close. ∎

See also: Deep Space 9, Odo, The Dominion, The Dominion War

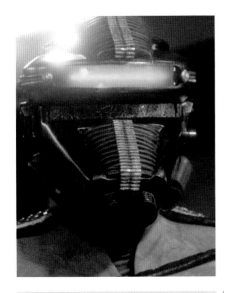

NEVER TURN YOUR BACK ON A BREEN
THE BREEN CONFEDERACY

CAPTAIN'S LOG

NAME
Breen

LOCATION
**Breen System,
Alpha Quadrant**

AFFILIATION
**Breen Confederacy,
Dominion**

BRIEFING
**During the Klingon
Second Empire, Chancellor
Mow'ga sent a fleet to
conquer the Breen
homeworld. The ships
never returned**

With hearts as cold as the frozen planet from which they hail, the Breen Confederacy is a mysterious and dangerous species. Federation doctors confirm that very little is known about them. The frigid climate of the Breen homeworld is cited as the reason its people have no blood in their veins. Since they do not leave their planet without being fully covered in refrigeration

Mean Breen The Breen do not hesitate to capture and torture prisoners to further their cause.

suits, few know what the Breen look like under their masks. What is certain is that they torture captives and force innocent civilians to work in their dilithium mines.

When the Breen formed an alliance with the Dominion in a war that pitted species from three quadrants against one another, it was backed with the promise that they would be rewarded with the Federation territory, including Earth, once victory was assured. It was a pledge the Dominion was unlikely to keep.

The Breen's alliance with the Dominion shifted the balance of power for a time during the war

when they launched a devastating attack against Starfleet Command on Earth. Their ships incorporated biological components and possessed cloaking technology similar to that used by the Klingons and Romulans. The vessels were armed with disruptor weapons and an energy-dampening device that proved valuable in battle until Starfleet developed a method for negating its effects.

Although the Cardassians eventually withdrew their support for the Dominion, the Breen remained committed to the war effort until the final battle. ■

See also: The Dominion, The Dominion War

Captain, every species has its weakness. They're no exception.
Martok

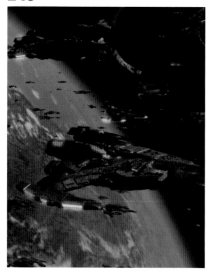

IN TIME OF WAR, THE LAW FALLS SILENT

THE DOMINION WAR

CAPTAIN'S LOG

NAME
The Dominion War

DURATION
2373 to 2375

FEDERATION ALLIANCE
**United Federation
of Planets, Klingon Empire,
Romulan Star Empire**

DOMINION ALLIANCE
**Dominion (Founders),
Cardassian Union,
Breen Confederacy**

With the opening of the Bajoran wormhole into the Gamma Quadrant, it became possible to initiate relations with previously unknown species—such as those who made up the combined forces of the Dominion. These were led by the xenophobic Founders, who possessed a deep-rooted hatred for all Solids. By replacing key figures in the Federation, Klingon Empire, and other political powers with Changelings, the Dominion was able to affect the power structure of the Alpha Quadrant and even to manipulate the Klingons into a war with the Cardassians.

Deep Space 9 taken

In 2373, the Cardassian Gul Dukat formed an alliance between his people and the Dominion. This resulted in a vast offensive against all of Cardassia's enemies—the Maquis were annihilated within just three days and the Klingons

War begins The first skirmish of the Dominion War was focused on Deep Space 9, as the Federation fight to keep control of the space station.

were forced out of Cardassian space. Realizing the danger posed by this new union, the Federation joined with the Klingon Empire. Starfleet placed self-replicating mines at the opening of the Bajoran wormhole to prevent Dominion reinforcements from entering the Alpha Quadrant.

In response, the Dominion launched an attack on Starfleet and Deep Space 9. Starfleet was forced to abandon the station, but by disabling its power and computer systems, handed the Dominion a useless victory. Meanwhile, a combined Starfleet and Klingon taskforce entered Dominion territory and attacked the shipyards at Torros III. Over the following months, both sides in the Dominion War had some success in battle, and Starfleet took back the station with the help of the Bajoran Prophets.

The war widens

In 2374, the war escalated when the Dominion invaded and took control of Betazed, a strategic location in the Alpha Quadrant. This meant they could threaten core worlds within Federation territory. In response, Starfleet drew the Romulans into the conflict

Sisko's gambit

War demands many sacrifices, and sometimes these include an officer's self-respect.

After the Dominion captured Betazed, the commander of Deep Space 9, Captain Ben Sisko, knows the only way to gain the offensive is to bring the Romulans into the war, but they already have a non-aggression pact with the Dominion. To convince them to switch sides, Sisko needs proof of Dominion duplicity. Consulting his resident Cardassian ex-spy, Garak, he realizes that the only course of action open to him is to manufacture the evidence.

This moral compromise gnaws away at Sisko, but he perseveres, believing that the cause is just. Romulan Senator Vreenak comes to hear the evidence, but decides it is fake. Meanwhile, Garak sabotages Vreenak's shuttle to cause his death and ensure that the forged evidence ends up in the hands of the unwitting Romulans.

in support of the Federation. The newly combined fleet—made up of the Federation, Klingons, and Romulans—presented a strong unified front.

The Founders began to show signs of a degenerative disease. It was later discovered that its cause, a morphogenic virus, had been created by the rogue Federation agency Section 31. A cure was discovered, but the Federation Council decided to withhold it from the Founders—an act that many felt went against their values.

The Dominion then made another push into the Alpha Quadrant, aligning with the

We're losing the peace, which means a war could be our only hope.
Benjamin Sisko

Breen Confederacy and launching an attack on Earth. The new leader of the Cardassians, Damar, saw the new partnership as proof of his people's weakened position and started his own small rebellion against the Dominion.

The Dominion pulled their forces back to Cardassian space, but the Federation and its allies did not allow their enemy to regroup. The Federation attacked, and at the same time a Cardassian uprising severely weakened the Dominion. The Cardassians paid a high price for their actions—the

Bajor Treaty The Treaty of Bajor marked the end of the Dominion War. It was signed on Deep Space 9 by representatives from both sides.

Dominion laid waste to their homeworld, killing over 800 million Cardassians while the Federation closed in. As the Dominion fell, Constable Odo offered them the cure to the virus in exchange for their surrender. ■

See also: Section 31, Deep Space 9, Benjamin Sisko, Elim Garak, Dukat, The Dominion, The Breen Confederacy

RESISTANCE IS (NOT) FUTILE
THE BORG COLLECTIVE

The Borg collective is a large interconnected group of cybernetic beings that share a single consciousness. They propagate through the forced assimilation of other species in an effort to add to their biological and technological distinctiveness. The collective has one goal: To achieve perfection by taking what they deem best from every other species in the Galaxy and discarding that which is useless to them.

Once assimilated by the Borg, an individual becomes a Drone and part of the collective consciousness. The assimilation process suppresses the individual's personality as that person becomes one among many, and their knowledge is absorbed by the collective in its unending quest for perfection. The link between Drones allows them to share information, make decisions, and plot out a course of action immediately as one unit, without conflict or indecision.

Little is known about the history of the Borg collective except that it originated in the Delta Quadrant. What is clear is that this single-minded society has spread across the Galaxy over many centuries, via transwarp hubs that allow them to cross great distances faster than warp speed. The closest thing the collective have to a homeworld is the primary Unicomplex, a vast Borg structure

Faster babies The Borg use maturation chambers to accelerate the growth of babies who have been assimilated.

in space, which is composed of thousands of connected structures. This complex serves as their base of operations in the Delta Quadrant.

First Federation contact
The Federation had experienced minor interactions with the Borg species at various times over the course of its history, but the first notable encounter occurred in 2365. A mysterious entity known as "Q" was rejected as a guide by

Captain Jean-Luc Picard and in response, Q hurled the *Enterprise*-D into the path of a primary Borg vessel, a Borg cube. The Starfleet ship was quickly overwhelmed by the cube, and Picard was forced to beg Q for assistance. Although the crew survived the encounter, 18 lives were lost. After this first interaction with the Borg, Starfleet began to prepare for an attack, certain that the collective would set its sights on the Federation in the future.

Shared consciousness

The Borg collective's shared consciousness allows its members to adapt immediately to any threats across the collective. For instance,

Captain Jean-Luc Picard was assimilated by the Borg in 2366 and became its Locutus, or spokesperson.

any energy weapon that is fired against a Borg drone is promptly studied, and defensive systems are adjusted to protect against a future attack from that energy setting. The best way for its enemies to counter this defense is to use weapons that have variable energy settings or to mount a physical attack disabling the biological component of the body.

Borg weapons' systems are as adaptive as their defenses, able to cut through starship defensive shields with ease. Their ships can also travel at high warp speeds, making it impossible for Starfleet vessels to outrun them. Despite being in possession of these facts, Starfleet were caught out by the first Borg invasion of the Alpha Quadrant in 2366, during which Captain Jean-Luc Picard was assimilated and his knowledge used to destroy 39 Starfleet ships.

After Picard's assimiliation, the Borg took the unusual step of designating him as Locutus: »

You can't outrun them, you can't destroy them. If you damage them the essence of what they are remains; they regenerate and keep coming. Eventually you will weaken, your reserves will be gone. They are relentless.

Q

Biological distinctiveness Borg victims are chosen to further the quest for perfection. For example, Ferengi enhanced hearing and Vulcan protective inner eyelids make them promising targets.

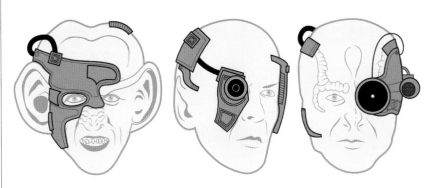

| Ferengi | Vulcan | Cardassian |

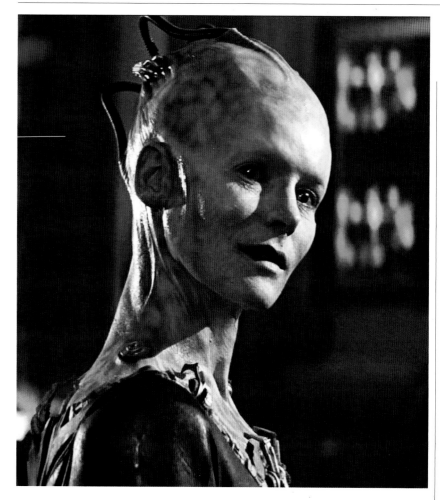

The Borg Queen As head of the Borg, the queen is said to be "the one who is many."

the malevolent android brother of Lieutenant Commander Data.

Years later, the crew of the *Starship Voyager* have more success when they free the drone Seven of Nine from the collective, though integrating her into the crew is a challenge initially.

The Borg Queen

Within the shared consciousness of the collective, there is one voice that brings order to the chaos of the many thoughts of the drones—the Borg Queen. Although she seems to function as an individual, she is simply another part of the whole, and apparently can be replaced if her body is destroyed. In 2373, the Borg Queen offered Data the opportunity to achieve his own form of perfection, by assimilating him and adding Human biology to his android body. Data was tempted and briefly considered the offer before rejecting it so that he could remain an individual.

Strength is irrelevant. Resistance is futile. We wish to improve ourselves. We will add your biological and technological distinctiveness to our own. Your culture will adapt to service ours.
The Borg

A liaison between the Borg and Humanity to be used to expedite the assimilation of Earth.

The first known instance of a drone becoming free of the collective occurred when the *Enterprise* crew managed to recapture their captain. Picard's personality reasserted itself intermittently to instruct them on how to fight the Borg, and as the Borg ship exploded, Picard's implants shut down and he was returned to normal.

When the *Starship Enterprise* crew came across a crashed Borg scout ship on a later mission, they took an injured drone on board to see what else they could learn

about the collective. When the drone began to exert his individuality—even adopting the name Hugh—it became morally difficult for the crew to use him as a weapon against the Borg, which had been their plan. So they released him back into the collective with his individuality intact, hoping it would spread throughout the hive.

Unfortunately, when Hugh's individuality did spread, the Borg members who were affected by it were severed from the collective. Forced to make new lives for themselves separate from the Borg, the former drones came under the evil influence of Lore,

A blow for the Borg

The *Enterprise* crew under Jean-Luc Picard made great strides in weakening the Borg collective, but it is Captain Janeway of the *Starship Voyager* who deals the most devastating blow.

Finding themselves alone in the Delta Quadrant, the *Voyager* crew initially unite with the Borg against a common enemy: a nameless, xenophobic non-humanoid species, labelled Species 8472 by the Borg. The alliance, however, is not destined to last.

The Borg attempt to assimilate the *Voyager* but are thwarted by Janeway, who has anticipated their actions. *Voyager* escapes with Seven of Nine, who has been serving as a liaison with the Borg, still on board. As the drone begins to interact with the crew, she shares her knowledge of the Borg and its technology. Eventually the crew, working in conjunction with a version of Janeway from the

Joining forces Captain Janeway (left) and drone Seven of Nine (right) worked together to save *U.S.S. Voyager* from an attack by Species 8472.

future, outwit the collective by using one of its own transwarp hubs to return home. In the process, the crew infects the collective with a neurolytic pathogen designed to "bring chaos to order." A new incarnation of the Borg Queen is

My people encountered them a century ago. They destroyed our cities and scattered my people across the Galaxy. They're called the Borg. Protect yourself, Captain, or they'll destroy you. ∎
Guinan

destroyed along with the primary Unicomplex and the transwarp hub itself, helping to protect the Federation from future incursions. The *Voyager* emerges from the wreckage of a Borg sphere vessel and is welcomed back to Earth. ∎
See also: *U.S.S. Enterprise* NCC-1701-D, Jean-Luc Picard, *U.S.S. Voyager* NCC-74656, Seven of Nine, The Q Continuum

The United Federation of Planets

The start of the 24th century had seen an unprecedented period of peaceful exploration for the United Federation of Planets, with old adversaries such as the Klingons becoming allies. But this period of peace was brought to an abrupt halt within a decade when the most powerful and destructive force in the Galaxy, the Borg, invaded the Galaxy.

The collective's brutal agenda for assimilation of all species ran directly contrary to the principles and values of the Federation which had been in effect for more than 200 years. These were first established in the Charter of the United Federation of Planets, a document that sealed a new alliance between Earth, Vulcan, Andoria, and Tellar. Their purpose was to "save succeeding generations from the scourge of war" and "reaffirm faith in the fundamental rights of sentient beings… [and] the dignity and worth of all life-forms." Caste-based discrimination was forbidden, as was interference in the internal affairs of any sovereign power.

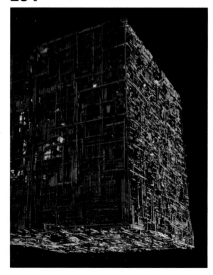

THE FIRST BORG INVASION
THE BATTLE OF WOLF 359

CAPTAIN'S LOG

NAME
The Battle of Wolf 359

WAR DECLARED
2367

WARRING PARTIES
The Borg versus the United Federation of Planets and the Klingons

BRIEFING
39 Federation starships and 11,000 lives are lost

I n terms of losses, the Battle of Wolf 359 pales in comparison with the Dominion War, but it was a significant milestone in Federation history. It was one of the most violent conflicts that Starfleet ever engaged in, and opened Federation eyes to undreamed of perils in space exploration.

The first sign of trouble occurred in 2367 when the *Enterprise*-D arrived on planet Jouret IV to find that the colony of New Providence had been totally destroyed. An away team found evidence of weaponry that was similar to that found by the *U.S.S. Enterprise* a year earlier during their initial encounter with the Borg. The devastation at outposts along the Romulan Neutral Zone pointed to a Borg incursion into Federation space.

As Starfleet prepared for an invasion, the *Enterprise* responded to a report of a strange cube-shaped vessel in the vicinity. The Borg offensive was contained in this single massive Borg cube.

With the rest of the fleet at least six days away, the *Enterprise* was forced to engage the vessel on its own. Its captain, Jean-Luc Picard, was captured and assimilated and then selected as a spokesperson for the Borg, and given the designation "Locutus of the Borg."

Picard's assimiliation had disastrous consequences. His knowledge of Starfleet defenses became shared with the Borg, who then used the information to attack his former crew. Although the *Enterprise* managed to temporarily weaken the cube during the encounter, they were ultimately no match for the vessel and their former commander. The cube escaped, leaving the *Enterprise* behind to work on repairs to its damaged systems.

The battle begins
While the *Enterprise* succeeded in briefly delaying the cube, Starfleet gathered its forces almost eight light-years from Earth and prepared to take a stand. Reinforcements were sent from the Klingon Empire, and Starfleet considered requesting aid from the Romulans, but this support would have come too late.

Picard's tactical knowledge had become a part of the collective, and this, combined with the cube's superior firepower, allowed the Borg

We've mobilized a fleet of 40 starships at Wolf 359, and that's just for starters. The Klingons are sending warships. Hell, we've even thought about opening communications with the Romulans.
Hanson

The death of Jennifer Sisko

Many Starfleet families suffered losses during the Battle of Wolf 359, and Benjamin and Jake Sisko were among them. Benjamin Sisko, first officer of the *U.S.S. Saratoga*, his wife Jennifer, and their son were on board when the starship was called to fight the Borg cube. The *Saratoga* was hit with a cutting beam that breached its warp core, giving the crew just five minutes to abandon ship. Jennifer died in the attack, but Ben managed to rescue Jake and flee in an escape pod, only to see the starship destroyed.

The loss left Sisko bitter and more than a little resentful toward Picard, aka Locutus. He strongly considered resigning his Starfleet commission, but then had an emotional catharsis during an encounter with the Prophets of the Bajoran wormhole. Finally he was able to mourn Jennifer and make the decision that Deep Space 9 was the place where he belonged.

to launch a devastating attack. The battle did not last long. When the *Enterprise* finally arrived, 39 ships had been lost at the cost of over 11,000 lives. Countless Starfleet officers were assimilated as the Borg cube journeyed toward Earth.

Self-destruct As the Borg cube enters Earth's orbit and prepares to attack, the *Enterprise* crew's subversive instructions cause it to self-destruct.

The *Enterprise* crew under acting Captain William T. Riker took up the chase and, arriving in Earth orbit, managed to retrieve the captain. Back on board, Picard still suffered from the effects of his assimilation, but was able to break his connection to the collective for long enough to suggest a plan for stopping the invasion. As the Borg cube prepared to attack Earth, the crew of the *Enterprise* managed to transmit a series of subversive commands through Picard's connection to the collective, instructing the drones to start regeneration. As the cube shut down, it initiated a self-destruct sequence, destroying itself before it could launch the attack. ∎

See also: *U.S.S. Enterprise* NCC-1701-D, Jean-Luc Picard, Benjamin Sisko, Jake Sisko, The Borg collective

CHANGING SECTS

THE KAZON ORDER

CAPTAIN'S LOG

NAME
The Kazon Order

LOCATION
Delta Quadrant

BRIEFING
Also known as the Kazon Collective, its notable sects include: Halik, Hobii, Mostral, Nistrim, Ogla, Oglamar, Pommar, and Relora

The Kazon Order is a humanoid, patriarchal species in the Delta Quadrant, divided into warring sects, each led by a first maje. When young men come of age in Kazon society, they are subjected to a trial in which they earn their adult name. This test often involves the killing of an enemy, but may end in a heroic death in battle.

The Kazon were formerly slaves to the Trabe, a society that exercised power by pitting the various Kazon sects against one another. Although they overthrew their oppressors, tension between the sects has prevented them from uniting under a single government. In 2372, when they encountered the Federation starship *U.S.S. Voyager*, there were 18 sects, but the number is thought to be constantly shifting.

Kazons are aggressive warriors, who are constantly looking for ways to expand their power base, despite their lack of technological knowledge and advancements. In their sector natural resources are scarce, which

We must begin to forge alliances. To survive, we must have powerful friends. The Kazon-Nistrum were willing to be our protectors in return for some minor technology.
Seska

Kazon script Having a common script has failed to stop the various Kazon sects from fighting each other for control of the quadrant's resources.

often puts the sects at odds with one another as they struggle and scrounge to meet their needs.

Although they are warp-capable and possess energy weapons the Kazon are greatly impressed by advanced equipment, such as replicators and transformers, on the Starfleet ship from the Alpha Quadrant, and covet its superior technology. This sets them against the *Voyager* crew, who refuse to share their technology because it would violate the Prime Directive.

The Borg consider the Kazon one of the few species unworthy of assimilation, judging them to have very little in the way of biological or technological distinctiveness, and hence nothing to offer the collective. ∎
See also: *U.S.S. Voyager* NCC-74656, Chakotay

NECESSARY MEASURES
THE VIDIIAN SODALITY

CAPTAIN'S LOG

NAME
The Vidiian Sodality

SPECIES
Vidiian

LOCATION
Delta Quadrant

BRIEFING
Vidiian technology includes a combined weapon, medical scanner, and surgical instrument

The Vidiians are a Delpha Quadrant species who were once known for their nobility, and their impressive art and culture. However, everything changed when they were struck by a disease known as the Phage. This horrific virus affects the genetic codes of its victims, attacking on a cellular level and forcing the body to consume itself, so that it appears as if it is decaying on the outside. For 2,000 years the disease ravaged the Vidiians without a cure being found—those affected were saved by the replacement of affected organs. At first, they relied on transplanted organs from the deceased, but as the plague spread through their society they began to resort to abduction and the harvesting of body parts from unwilling victims.

Sophisticated device Compatible organs and tissue are harvested into the transporter and then transplanted into a needy Vidiian recipient.

To reduce the risk of spreading the disease, Vidiian ships were designed to operate with a minimal crew. Most vessels functioned under the direction of a pair of officers—a commander and a Honatta, a specialist in organ-harvesting. These ships scoured the Galaxy in search of victims.

When they encountered the *Voyager* crew, they harvested the lungs of Talaxian crew member Neelix, forcing him to rely on a pair of holographic replacement organs until Ocampan crew member Kes donated her lung to save him. The Vidiians also kidnapped Chief Engineer B'Elanna Torres when they discovered that Klingon DNA is resistant to the disease. They temporarily split her into her Human and Klingon halves in a misguided attempt to find a cure for the Phage.

Although they were considered enemies by the *Voyager* crew, one of their physicians, Dr. Danara Pel, struck up a relationship with the Doctor as she worked to find a means of combating the disease. Ultimately, a cure was found with the assistance of an alien think-tank that excels at problem-solving. ∎
See also: *U.S.S. Voyager* NCC-74656, B'Elanna Torres, The Doctor

HUNTER AND PREY

HIROGEN

CAPTAIN'S LOG

NAME
Hirogen

LOCATION
Delta Quadrant

BRIEFING
The Hirogen's advanced hunting weapons include a device that reveals the bio-data of their prey

Hirogen are hunters who have been engaged in the search for prey for thousands of years. The need for the hunt is so ingrained in this species that they eventually abandoned their homeworld in search of more elusive prey. As a result, they now live as nomads in the Delta Quadrant, traveling in small numbers (from only two members to a few ships).

Hirogen are loyal to their traveling packs and particularly their pack leader, who is known as the Alpha-Hirogen. They have no formal government and have effectively abandoned all scientific and technological research aside from that associated with creating superior hunting weaponry. Their only interest in other species is as prey and they use the spoils of the hunt (from personal possessions to bones and body parts) to decorate their ships.

The ultimate hunt

In 2374, the Hirogen took control of the *U.S.S. Voyager* and discovered that the holographic technology on board offered a new way to engage in the hunt. They found they could

Armed for the hunt Hirogen body armor offers its wearers internal life support, so they can hunt in even the most hostile environments.

Capable prey make the hunt more challenging.
Hirogen Hunter

use the ship's holodecks to play out various hunting simulations, using the crew members as prey. This allowed them to test out a limitless variety of hunt scenarios.

With most of the crew held captive and brainwashed into believing the holodeck scenarios are real, the Doctor was forced to patch them up and send them back into the hunt, with all holodeck safety devices turned off. Eventually Captain Janeway reluctantly proposed a truce and offered up the holotechnology to the Hirogen as a trophy. ∎

See also: *U.S.S. Voyager* NCC-74656, Holographic Technology

WHAT'S IN A NAME?

SPECIES 8472

CAPTAIN'S LOG

NAME
**Unknown
(designated Species 8472
by the Borg)**

LOCATION
Fluidic space

BRIEFING
**A life-form with a dense
genetic structure and
powerful immune system**

Species 8472 is the Borg designation for a tripedal species that exists in a dimension of fluidic space separate from the known universe. These beings have an extraordinary immune response whereby anything that penetrates the cell membrane is instantly destroyed. This makes Species 8472 one of the rare few that the Borg cannot assimilate; it means that they pose a huge threat to them. Their cells can also act as a weapon, infecting other beings and consuming a body from the inside.

When the *Voyager* crew began to suspect that Species 8472

intended to destroy all life in the known universe, Captain Janeway made the unusual decision to partner with the Borg to defeat the mutual threat. While working together she found out that it was the Borg's attack on Species 8472 that pulled them out of fluidic space and brought them into the Delta Quadrant. The Borg admire the species for their powerful bioships and consider them to be the peak of biological evolution.

Although the *Voyager* crew never learn the true name of the species, they experience a more direct confrontation with them in the future, when they find a perfect replica of Starfleet Academy created by Species 8472 inside a

The weak will perish.
Species 8472

Three-legged beings Species 8472 boast a biological technology that is superior even to the Borg, who suffer huge losses under their attack.

terrasphere in the Delta Quadrant. The replica is part of a plan for the species to invade the Alpha Quadrant and infiltrate the Federation. Janeway uses her diplomatic skills—and an offer of Borg nanoprobe technology—to convince a representative of the species that the Federation means them no harm. She forms a truce and persuades them to return to fluidic space. ■
See also: Starfleet Academy, *U.S.S. Voyager* NCC-74656, The Borg collective

SCIENCE
TECHNO

AND
LOGY

Exploration doesn't stop at the stars. New technologies are discovered or created every day on a wide scale, ranging from enormous starships to microscopic nanites. Scientific advancements can enhance lives, space travel, and defense, but these incredible technologies are not always a gift. In the wrong hands, they can be more destructive than the forces of nature, and far deadlier.

ENGAGE
WARP DRIVE

Zefram Cochrane invents warp drive; begins adapting Titan missile as launch vehicle.

c. 2061

Earth begins launching low-warp vessels into interstellar space, including the starships *Valiant* and *Conestoga*.

c. 2065

Starfleet's NX Program breaks warp 2 barrier, and soon after, warp 2.5.

2143

Enterprise NX-01 launched with maximum theoretical speed of warp 4.5.

2151

Warp 7 engine developed.

2161

2063

Cochrane's flight of the *Phoenix* inaugurates Humanity as a warp-capable species.

2119

Warp 5 Complex established to develop an engine that enables more practical interstellar flight.

2144

NX Program achieves warp 3.

2152

Enterprise NX-01 engine achieves warp 5.

c. 2245

Fleet of *Constitution*-class starships launched with maximum cruising speed of warp 8, emergency speed of warp 9.

Space is vast. This may be obvious, but what is also clear is that to travel across the great distances between star systems requires a powerful engine to take ships at speeds previously considered unimaginable. The development of warp speed travel is a significant milestone in the technological advancement of any planet, opening up a civilization to the greater intergalactic community. Generally, it is a sign that a species has reached a level of development that makes them ready to embrace a life among the stars and all that it has to offer.

Not every species that achieves warp-capable flight intends to use it for beneficial purposes, but there is a reason why the United Federation of Planets considers it a key factor in determining if a planet is worth considering for membership. Generally speaking, those who have not achieved warp flight tend to lack technological proficiency in other areas. The Federation is opposed to interfering with the natural evolution of a civilization, and the possibility of sharing such advanced technology is a prime factor in this decision. There are

those who question the timing of the initial interactions with warp-capable races. For example, the Vulcans eventually came to express concerns over the haste of making first contact with Humans within only a day of Earth's first warp test flight.

Traveling at warp speeds is not a simple process. Every civilization comes to an understanding of the technology in its own time. For the Vulcans and Bajorans it took centuries for their species to transition from subwarp capable interstellar flight to more advanced means of travel.

Through alien intervention, *U.S.S. Enterprise* achieves speeds of warp 11 and warp 14.1 in separate instances.

2268

Warp theory revised and warp factor scale recalibrated to place warp 10 at theoretical maximum.

c. 2300

Test with multiple simultaneous injector streams increases warp energy output on *Galaxy*-class vessel.

2366

Warp fields deemed a threat to certain areas of space, speed limit of warp 5 imposed by Federation pending further study.

2370

Tom Paris crosses warp 10 threshold in Delta Quadrant on shuttlecraft *Cochrane*; transwarp effect proven harmful to living beings.

2372

2284

Starfleet experiments with transwarp propulsion; prototype test on *U.S.S. Excelsior* fails, experiments abandoned.

c. 2350

Galaxy-class starship developed with speeds up to warp 9.6 sustainable for 12 hours.

c. 2367

Class 7 warp drive developed for *Defiant*-class starships, capable of warp 9.5.

2371

Intrepid-class starships equipped with variable-geometry warp drive nacelles to prevent damage to subspace continuum; sustainable cruise velocity of warp 9.975.

Humans made the leap from launching Earth's first satellite to warp flight in slightly over 100 years, though it took another century-worth of research to perfect the technology.

Achieving warp flight does not simply involve producing a powerful engine. The design for the ship that houses that engine is just as important. Precautions must be taken to protect the ship's crew from the abrupt stopping and starting of a vessel that travels at extreme velocities—something that humanoid bodies were not necessarily designed to experience.

The warp scale used by Starfleet has been adjusted over time, but the generally accepted top speed is just under warp 10. By the 24th century, the average Starfleet vessel can achieve a maximum warp somewhere between warp 9 and warp 10, though only in extreme cases. Speeds at the lower end of the warp scale are still incredibly fast, but it is generally agreed that warp 5 and above is ideal for deep space exploration. Travel at these velocities will cut a journey that once took months or even years, down to days and hours.

As advanced as warp travel can be, it still has its limitations. Even the fastest Starfleet vessels cannot outrun the advanced propulsion system of a Borg cube. When the *U.S.S. Voyager* was pulled 70,000 light-years away into the Delta Quadrant, the crew still had to rely on transwarp corridors to bring them home faster than the anticipated 70-year journey would have taken at top warp speed. So Starfleet continues to experiment with technology in the hope that the next breakthrough will take them further into discovering the mysteries of the universe. ∎

CAPTAIN'S LOG

APPROXIMATE WARP SPEEDS
in kilometers per hour

Standard Orbit
9600

Full impulse (¼ light speed)
270 million

Warp factor 1
1 billion

Warp factor 2
11 billion

Warp factor 3
42 billion

Warp factor 4
109 billion

Warp factor 5
229 billion

Warp factor 6
421 billion

Warp factor 7
703 billion

Warp factor 8
1.10 trillion

Warp factor 9
1.62 trillion

Warp factor 9.2
1.77 trillion

Warp factor 9.6
2.05 trillion

Warp factor 9.9
3.27 trillion

Warp factor 9.99
8.48 trillion

Warp factor 9.999
214 trillion

Warp factor 10
Infinite

Various early forms of interstellar space travel, belonging to different species from throughout the Galaxy, relied on basic technology that required generational ships capable of spending decades, or even centuries, in space. One of the few known pre-warp technologies that allowed for more expedited flight between star systems was the Bajoran solar-sail. This form of transport—considered only to be theoretical until the 24th century—relied on propulsion provided by enormous sails that caught solar winds. Although these ships could reach faster-than-light speeds, the velocity of their journey relied heavily on external factors like the reflection of protons combined with the presence of tachyon eddies—naturally occurring flows of sub-atomic particles in space—in the region and was not a consistently reliable mode of transportation.

Warp core dynamics A newly redesigned warp core was a key enhancement of the refit *U.S.S. Enterprise* NCC-1701.

The modern development of warp drive allows starships to travel at faster-than-light speeds through a controlled matter/antimatter fusion reaction, providing a considerably more consistent form of propulsion through space. This relatively recent technology generates warp fields that form a subspace bubble surrounding a starship. That bubble distorts the local space-time continuum, enabling the starship to move at velocities that exceed the speed of light.

Basic Warp Design is a required course at the Academy. The first chapter is called 'Zefram Cochrane.'
Geordi La Forge

Inertial dampers

The extreme acceleration and deceleration rates of starships require counteracting forces to protect crew members from— to use engineering parlance— getting crushed into chunky salsa on the ship's walls. These counterforces are "inertial dampers," field manipulators that compensate for the g-forces generated when a space vehicle changes speed or flight direction.

In theory, inertial dampers are only necessary at impulse (sublight) speeds, given that at warp the "subspace bubble" moves spacetime around the ship rather than the ship itself. However, in practice a starship often has to maneuver a great deal while at warp, or enter warp from a gravity well such as a planet, which can create inertial forces similar to that of impulse motion.

The effects of inertial damping are not always instantaneous, especially in the case of unexpected stresses on the starship like weapons fire, when the crew may experience a momentary rocking motion.

The warp core is the engine that powers the starship. The matter/antimatter reaction takes place within the core, annihilating matter and sending power to the warp coils within the ship's nacelles. In standard Starfleet design, a pair of nacelles are located on extended wings positioned port and starboard of the engineering hull. The warp coils create the subspace displacement field that propels the ship. In Starfleet vessels it is possible to travel at warp speed if one of the nacelles is non-functional, though the ship will not be able to reach the same speeds as it would with both nacelles active.

A navigational deflector is built into the bow of Starfleet vessels, usually located in the secondary hull of ships in the 23rd century and beyond. This important piece of technology generates a force-beam that diverts debris from the path of the vessel, where even microscopic particulates could cause serious damage.

Magic carpet ride Human inventor Zefram Cochrane's warp test brought a pair of future visitors from the *Enterprise*-E along for the ride.

The warp factor refers to the unit of measurement tracking the velocity of the ship as it travels faster than the speed of light. In the 23rd century, Starfleet vessels traveled at a cruising speed of warp 6 with a generally accepted top speed of warp 8. On rare occasions, and with the assistance of alien technological intervention, a vessel like the *Constitution*-class *Starship Enterprise* was able to reach speeds of up to warp 14. By the 24th century, the warp factor scale was recalibrated to accept the theoretical warp 10 as the maximum speed, though Starfleet vessels generally cannot exceed warp 9.8 without some type of external intervention.

United Earth warp research

Founding members of the United Federation of Planets, such as the Vulcans and Andorians, were traveling between star systems centuries before United Earth had the capability to journey beyond its nearest planetary neighbors. It is unclear when Vulcans developed vessels that could travel at faster-than-light speeds. »

However, they were clearly warp-capable by the middle of Earth's 20th century as the launch of the satellite *Sputnik* drew their initial interest in Humans. Formal contact between the two civilizations, however, was still over a hundred years away.

In the 21st century on Earth, Human inventor Zefram Cochrane used Albert Einstein's Theory of Relativity as the building block for his theories on warp travel. Following the conclusion of Earth's Third World War in 2053, Cochrane repurposed the shell of a nuclear weapon for the booster stage of the vessel he named the *Phoenix*, which would go down in history as the planet's first warp-capable vessel. What historians did not record was that the crew of the *U.S.S. Enterprise* NCC-1701-E, under

the command of Captain Jean-Luc Picard, assisted the inventor with his groundbreaking launch.

During an attack on the Alpha Quadrant in 2373, the *Enterprise* crew followed a Borg sphere scout ship back in time to 2063 when the species of cybernetic beings intended to alter the course of history by destroying the *Phoenix*. This act would then avert the first contact between Humans and Vulcans, potentially destroying the founding of the Federation and making that region of space far more susceptible to Borg assimilation. What the *Enterprise* crew found when they arrived in the small American town of Bozeman, Montana, was not the revered inventor depicted by history, but an intoxicated genius who had given up on his invention

> Warp drive has been around for three centuries. It's a proven technology.
> **Geordi La Forge**

following a Borg attack that damaged the prototype.

While Cochrane's associate, aeronautic engineer Lily Sloane, was briefly taken aboard the *Enterprise* during a Borg invasion, an away team worked to sober up the inventor and help him complete work on his vessel. The *Phoenix* launched on April 4, 2063. As recorded by history, a Vulcan survey ship detected the signature of the warp trail and altered its course, landing on Earth and making first contact with the inventor and the Human species.

Fifty years after the launch of the *Phoenix,* the United Earth Space Probe Agency established the warp 5 program to develop the first warp engine capable of deep space travel. Cochrane served as lead scientist in the program that included Henry Archer—the father of the future captain of *Enterprise* NX-01, Jonathan Archer. Although members of the technologically advanced Vulcan species helped oversee the program, many Humans felt that the cautious Vulcans were intentionally slowing the development of the engine. It took over 20 years for the warp 5 engine to be ready to enter the testing phase.

Picard maneuver This battle maneuver was named in honor of Jean-Luc Picard during his time as captain of the *U.S.S. Stargazer*. He developed the tactic in a last ditch effort to fight off an attack from an unidentified vessel.

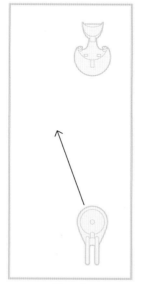

Phase 1
Initiate a short burst of warp speed.

Phase 2
The sudden move will confuse enemy ship's sensors into believing the vessel is in two places at once.

Phase 3
Fire on enemy ship as soon as you come out of warp, before their sensors have time to adjust.

Following the warp 5 engine reaching test phase, the United Earth Space Probe Agency initiated the NX Project to design the ship that would house it. Overseen by Commodore Forrest, the NX Project had a bumpy start when the test of the NX-*Alpha* captained by A.G. Robinson exploded shortly after successfully reaching warp 2.2. The captain only survived by jettisoning in an escape pod. At that point, the Vulcans convinced Starfleet to suspend the program.

Unhappy with the decision, other members of the project— namely test pilot Jonathan Archer and design engineer Charles "Trip" Tucker III—believed the ship to be structurally sound. They located the cause of the explosion and, along with Robinson, stole the NX-*Beta* prototype to perform a successful test of the engine. Though they were going against orders, their actions spurred on a renewed interest in the program at Starfleet. The Vulcans still insisted on further tests before signing off Earth's completion of the program, delaying the launch of *Enterprise* NX-01 by seven years.

Big issue Hekaran scientists Rabal and Serova were first to point out the ecological dangers of warp flight.

The dangers of warp travel

Warp technology continued to evolve into the 24th century. Although it has been perfected to reach almost the top speed possible for physical travel, there are still dangers associated with this type of propulsion system. The entire process relies on the use of highly combustible antimatter, so any damage to the system can result in a cataclysmic warp core breach that could destroy a ship. For that

reason, Starfleet has developed an emergency system by which a warp core can be ejected in the event of an explosion. Once clear of the blast zone, the ship must rely on its impulse engines and travel at sublight speeds.

A greater issue was revealed in 2370 when scientists from the planet Hekaras II found that the cumulative effect of warp drive on a given area of space was capable of causing subspace rifts that would eventually make that location impassable. As a result, the Federation Council stated that any areas of space found to be susceptible to warp fields would be restricted to essential travel only. For a time, all Federation vessels were to be limited to a speed of warp 5, except in emergencies. Of the major political players in the universe, the Klingons agreed to the terms, but the Romulans did not. Starfleet quickly developed a means of neutralizing the warp field effect and its vessels were soon able to use maximum warp speeds again. ■

See also: United Earth, *Enterprise* NX-01, *U.S.S. Enterprise* NCC-1701-E, The Bajorans

---

Warp 10 threshold

By the 24th century, warp theory was revised in such a way that warp factor numbers did not represent a simple exponent of c, the speed of light, as they had in the 23rd century, but rather fell along a "curve" that approached infinity toward warp 10. Thus the difference between, say, warp 9.6 and 9.975 was significantly greater than the difference between warp 8 and 9. Warp 10 is considered "infinite velocity," a theoretical state occupying every point in the universe

simultaneously. This would hypothetically allow travel anywhere instantly, since time and distance have no meaning.

The discovery of a new form of dilithium in the Delta Quadrant led Tom Paris of the *U.S.S. Voyager* to attempt to cut short the 70-year journey home the crew faced, by trying to cross the warp 10 threshold. He succeeded, but the transwarp effect caused a bizarre "evolution" of human cells, making such travel untenable.

ENERGIZE
TRANSPORTERS

CAPTAIN'S LOG

NAME
Transporter

STARFLEET APPROVED
FOR BIO-TRANSPORT
2151

FIRST RECORDED
TRANSWARP BEAMING
2258 (Kelvin Timeline)

PRIMARY USES
- **Personnel transport**
- **Cargo transport**
- **Emergency transport**

Beginning with the first Starfleet vessel to roll off the line, every starship in the fleet has included at least one transporter capable of moving people or objects from one place to another through matter-energy conversion. This advanced form of transportation is more convenient than landing a shuttle on a planet or docking with another vessel.

The technology not only supports missions, but it can also save numerous lives in an emergency.

Technical parameters

Transporters work by temporarily converting a person or material into energy and then beaming that energy to another location where it is reconstructed in its original form. Although *Enterprise* NX-01 was equipped with a transporter approved for bio-transport, the technology was considered so new at the time that most Starfleet officers were uncomfortable with its use. Centuries later, some crew are still concerned with how the technology breaks down the physical body into energy.

Most transports are initiated in a transporter room where a platform with multiple individual pads is located. A transporter chief oversees the process of beaming an individual from a transporter pad by first scanning the target area and achieving a coordinates lock. The subject is then dematerialized into a matter stream that transfers through the pattern buffer, which acts as a failsafe in case of a malfunction. In an emergency, a pattern stored in the buffer can be diverted to a different location for rematerialization. The matter stream is then transmitted to the other location, where the object is rematerialized. This technology can also beam an individual from one location to another, bypassing the transporter platform in what is known as site-to-site transport.

I signed on this ship to practice medicine, not to have my atoms scattered back and forth across space by this gadget.
Dr. Leonard McCoy

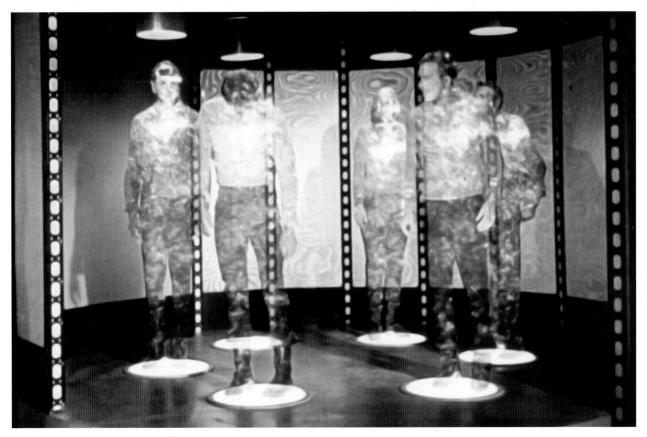

Beaming effect The materialization process takes a brief moment to reconstruct the crew of the *U.S.S. Enterprise* NCC-1701.

By the 24th century, the standard *Galaxy*-class starship has six personnel transporters and eight low-resolution transporters for moving cargo. An additional six emergency transporters allow for mass evacuation from the vessel through high-volume scan-only phase transition coils. These transporters are only capable of beaming from the ship, and do not carry individuals or objects into the vessel.

Transwarp beaming
As advanced as transporter systems have become by the 24th century, the technology still has some limitations. Most Federation and non-Federation transporter systems require a ship's deflector shield to be deactivated while beaming as the matter stream cannot transmit through the forcefield. The maximum distance for safely beaming objects is approximately 40,000 kilometers, and optimal conditions require the transport of a subject between two stationary bodies.

These challenges are addressed in the transwarp beaming formula developed by engineer Montgomery Scott, which Ambassador Spock brought back into the past after the Temporal Incursion of 2233. Transwarp beaming allows the transporter to beam objects into distant star systems light-years away, as well as onto ships traveling at high warp speeds.

The core concept required Scott to consider space itself as the moving component in the process.

Transporter malfunctions
Transporters are equipped with numerous safety features and are overseen by personnel trained in a variety of protocols to compensate for the unexpected. And yet unanticipated problems still arise with the technology. Transporter malfunctions have often been responsible for numerous unusual incidents befalling Starfleet crews. As a result, some experience transporter phobia, a fear that is not always irrational.

In the three centuries that Starfleet has been in existence, crews have logged several more extreme cases of transporter malfunctions. These incidents »

Beam me up Transporter technology allows for Starfleet crew members to move across great distances through a near instantaneous method of travel.

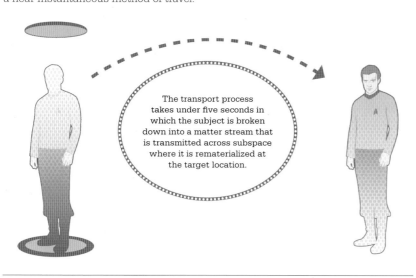

The transport process takes under five seconds in which the subject is broken down into a matter stream that is transmitted across subspace where it is rematerialized at the target location.

Transporting really is the safest way to travel.
Geordi La Forge

include pattern degradation causing death, objects merging with the subject of transport, or simply people rematerializing without any clothes.

DoppelKirker After a transporter malfunction the outrageous behavior of Kirk's bold, aggressive half endangers members of the crew.

One common form of transporter accident results in identity-related issues. In the 23rd century, an alien ore interacted with the transporter on the Starship Enterprise causing Captain James T. Kirk to be duplicated, creating two entities, each with a distinct set of characteristics—one meek and gentle, the other bold and

animalistic. A variation on this splitting effect happened almost a century later when a distortion field affected a transporter beam carrying officer Will Riker while he served on the U.S.S. Potemkin. The matter stream split into two beams, one of which was redirected to the planet while the other continued to the ship. In this case, each beam created an identical version of Riker and the Potemkin crew unknowingly abandoned one Riker on the planet to live alone for eight years. In the case of Kirk, the crew was able to reintegrate the disparate sides of Kirk into one. As for Riker, both men continued to live out their separate lives, with one deciding to go by his middle name, Thomas.

Transporters have not only separated individuals; they have also caused them to merge. Such was the case in 2372 when the *Starship Voyager* was transporting crew members Neelix and Tuvok with an alien orchid. Lysosomal enzymes within the orchid affected the transporter process so that the two crew men were combined into one individual who became known as Tuvix. Carrying both men's personalities in one body, Tuvix developed as an individual, bonding with the crew as they worked to

Rascals Keiko O'Brien, Guinan, Ensign Ro Laren, and Captain Jean-Luc Picard reverted to their childhood bodies but kept their adult minds.

reverse the damage. By the time a solution was devised, Tuvix had established a life for himself that he did not want to sacrifice for Neelix and Tuvok. Captain Janeway had to order Tuvix to undergo the procedure to restore her two original crew men.

Transporters have also been responsible for accidents that have affected groups of individuals. In 2369, the members of an away team on the *Enterprise*-D were significantly reduced in age when their DNA was affected during transport through an energy field that had enveloped their shuttle. Another time, an explosion of a microscopic singularity interfered with the beaming process, causing the transporter to beam members of Deep Space 9's senior staff 300 years into Earth's past.

A more common accident relating to the transporter is its role as a portal to the parallel universe at one time dominated by the so-called Terran Empire. Four crew members of the *Starship Enterprise* under Captain Kirk were the first sent to this mirror universe when they beamed up to the ship during an ion storm. A century later, members of the Deep Space 9 crew were brought into the same universe—now home to the Klingon-Cardassian Alliance—via a multidimensional transporter device that made travel between the universes more common. ■

See also: The Mirror Universe, *U.S.S. Enterprise* NCC-1701, William T. Riker, Deep Space 9, Neelix, Tuvok

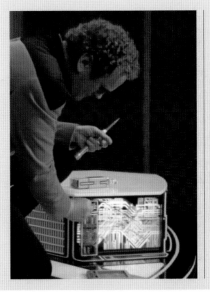

The Heisenberg compensator

The transporter is an extremely complex device with many components. When a body is converted into billions of kiloquads of data and transmitted through subspace, there can be no margin for error. That is why one vital component of the system removes the "uncertainty" inherent in the quantum mechanics of the process.

The Heisenberg compensator was named after Earth physicist Werner Heisenberg, a pioneer in quantum theory who, in 1927, postulated his famous "Uncertainty Principle."

The theory suggests that on a subatomic level, it is possible to know either the motion or the position of a particle, but not both. Further, the more accurate the measurement is in one observable quantity, the greater uncertainty of other quantities in the equation.

During the beaming process, the Heisenberg compensator creates a map that derives both the vector and positional data of particles to the same degree of accuracy, ensuring the matter stream remains coherent and not a single atom is out of place.

FREEZE PROGRAM
HOLOGRAPHIC TECHNOLOGY

CAPTAIN'S LOG

NAME
Holographic technology

POPULAR HOLODECK
PROGRAMS
- *Enterprise* **NX-01 historical record**
- **Leonardo da Vinci simulation**
- **Battle of the Alamo**
- **Battle of Britain**
- *The Adventures of Captain Proton*
- *The Adventures of Flotter*
- *Beowulf*
- *A Christmas Carol*
- **Dixon Hill detective novels**
- *Henry V*
- *Kahless and Lukara*
- **Sherlock Holmes mysteries**
- *The Tempest*
- *The Three Musketeers*
- *Vulcan Love Slave* **(Parts 1, 2, & 3)**

Holographic technology has made great advances in the 24th century, creating fully immersive life-like simulations through the projection of three-dimensional visual displays. As a result, holodecks have become standard issue on Starfleet vessels, serving as a valuable tool for crew training exercises and examination programs for Starfleet cadets and officers. The technology has also led to the creation of the Emergency Medical Hologram, a supplement to a ship's staff on Starfleet vessels.

Holodecks and holosuites

The holographic environment simulator—housed in either a holodeck or holosuite—creates almost any setting possible in a virtual manner that is nearly indistinguishable from reality. The physical holodeck is a large room lined with holographic projectors that create a fully immersive environment of three-dimensional backgrounds that can transform the finite space into what seems like an area with unlimited dimensions.

All aspects of a simulation are limited to the holodeck and will cease to exist if taken through the exit out of the holographically-generated environment.

The holodeck technology relies on a system similar to a replicator, using matter conversion to add physical objects to the holographic environment. The combination of matter conversion with holographic projections gives these objects and people physical form and they are able to become solid or insubstantial on command.

The holodeck makes excellent use of finite space.
Jean-Luc Picard

Doorway to another world The holodeck on a Federation starship can take crew members to any time or any place in history.

Training and fun

Holodecks serve important operational purposes on a starship. Sporting programs keep the crew in good shape while phaser target practice hones their skill with weaponry. Various training programs ensure a crew keeps abreast of the latest operational procedures and field training exercises. Holodecks are also useful for testing purposes, for example, practical simulations in the Bridge Officers' exam give candidates command experience without endangering the ship.

Beyond their official applications, holodecks have become an integral part of life on a starship, often providing an escape for crew members, as serving on a vessel of deep space exploration leaves little time for shore leave. The technology was essential in maintaining the morale of the *U.S.S. Voyager* crew when they were lost in the Delta Quadrant. »

This includes realistic simulations of humanoids or other life-forms operated, in part, by computer-controlled tractor beams. Forcefields are employed to add substance to the environment, and to further enhance the simulation, audio speakers and atomizers add sound and scent for a complete sensory experience.

When the holodeck is operating within normal parameters, a person using the room has full control of the simulation. That person can change the environment at will or simply adjust one element of the hologram with a voice command. Simulations can be paused mid-program and saved for later or elements can be replayed and revised allowing a user to experience alternate scenarios.

As holodecks work with a combination of visual and solid material, simulations can present various degrees of danger for the occupants. To ensure that no one is harmed while in a simulation, holodecks are equipped with safety protocols that protect the user from harm. More adventurous participants have occasionally turned the safeties off, at which time the simulation becomes just as dangerous as it would be in a real world setting.

A sporting time The holodeck provides countless entertainment and physical activities in the limited confines of a starship.

The big chill A sudden change in scene helps convince the participants in the Dixon Hill holoprogram that the holodeck is not functioning properly.

One of the most popular forms of entertainment to derive from this technology is the holonovel, which allows users to watch or become actively involved in their favorite stories. From Sherlock Holmes to Shakespeare, these tales engage the participant in an existing narrative, either by following the script or by creating an alternate tale of their own. Depending on the chosen perspective, holodeck users can be an active part of the simulation or a passive viewer. However, as entertaining as these diversions are, they can also be fraught with danger.

Holo pursuits Holodecks incorporate a variety of technologies from holographic projectors to replicator systems to create a fully immersive three-dimensional environment.

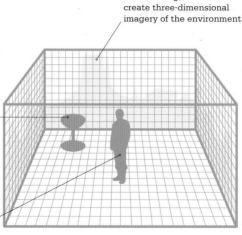

A replicator system creates physical props that have mass and can be manipulated by the user

The illusion of movement is created as the holographic environment shifts around a person while forcefield in the floor creates a treadmill effect for walking

Projectors located in the walls, ceiling, and floor create three-dimensional imagery of the environment

Holodeck malfunctions

One of the earliest recorded malfunctions of a holodeck by a Starfleet crew occurred on the *Enterprise*-D while it was on a diplomatic mission establishing contact with a species known as the Jarada. As Captain Picard was enjoying his favorite Dixon Hill detective holonovel with a few members of the senior staff, they became trapped in the simulation after a Jarada probe scanned the ship and triggered errant behavior in the program. The simulation took on a life of its own, with the safeties shutting down so that when a crew member was shot, he was critically wounded.

Computer, end program.
Traditional Deactivation Command

Picard was forced to continue to play out the dangerous scenario until members of the crew outside the simulation were able to free him in time for an all-important greeting with the impatient—and easily offended—Jaradans.

Several years later, the crew of Deep Space 9 experienced a malfunction in their transporter, which spread to one of the holosuites in Quark's Bar. The lives of several members of the senior staff were put in jeopardy when their sabotaged runabout exploded as they beamed out. With the crew's

The Doctor's mobile emitter

After "the Doctor" was activated and became the ship's full-time medic, the *U.S.S. Voyager*'s EMH (Emergency Medical Hologram) vastly expanded his range of functionality and personality. But initially he could only remain active within the confines of sickbay or have his program transferred to the ship's holodeck. Luckily, a brush with 29th-century technology in the 20th century gave him the mobility he desired.

When the *Voyager* crew found themselves on 1996 Earth, they encountered a computer magnate named Henry Starling who had appropriated and profited from technology he had taken from a crashed timeship. While he battled the *Voyager* crew, Starling managed to download the Doctor's program and take him hostage. Starling equipped the EMH with a stolen autonomous self-sustaining mobile holoemitter, technology unknown to the 24th century.

After he was rescued, the Doctor was able to retain the mobile emitter, leaving him "footloose and fancy free."

patterns stuck in the station's transporter buffer, their bodies were unintentionally diverted into the holosuite where they were merged with the characters in Dr. Julian Bashir's mid-20th century secret agent program.

Bashir and Elim Garak were forced to play out the scenario because they feared that shutting down the simulation would erase the crew from existence. At the same time, they had to protect the often exaggeratedly evil holosuite counterparts of their fellow officers, as any death in the simulation could cause the death of the real life versions. Eventually, Bashir realized he had to let the bad guy win to end the scenario safely. The crew managed to beam their trapped crew mates out of the simulation and into their rematerialized original forms.

The crew of the *Starship Voyager* were also forced to play out a holoscenario when trans-

dimensional photonic beings interacted with Tom Paris's Captain Proton space adventure. The photonic species believed the classic adventure serial—presented in black and white—to be real life and engaged in a war with the fictional characters who were led by the evil Dr. Chaotica. The *Voyager*

crew had to act out their holostory to bring about the end of the war, interacting with the photonic beings through the only means they would recognize. ■

See also: *U.S.S. Enterprise* NCC-1701-D, Jean-Luc Picard, The Doctor, Quark, *U.S.S. Voyager* NCC-74656

Double agents Garak and Bashir are compelled to play along in the secret agent holoworld program to save their friends trapped in its fictional setting.

SET PHASERS TO STUN

WEAPONS TECHNOLOGY

CAPTAIN'S LOG

NAME
Weapons technology

ARSENAL
Phasers, photon grenades, photon torpedoes, traditional bladed weapons

BRIEFING
Type 2 and 3 mid-24th-century Starfleet phasers have up to 16 settings:

1-3: Light to heavy stun
4,5: Thermal Effects
6-10: Disruption Effects
11-16: Explosive Effects

Handheld weapons that fired beams of energy in place of bullets were once the stuff of science fiction stories, but, by the 22nd century on Earth and even earlier on other planets, directed-energy weapons had become commonplace. This form of weapons technology has evolved to a point where a single weapon can deliver a beam with the capacity to stun or, as a last resort, kill an individual, with settings that offer several options in between. Each species of the known universe may approach the technology differently, but many of these directed-energy weapons share the same operating parameters. What follows is a brief overview of some of the more common weapons found in arsenals by the 24th century, although it is by no means a complete list.

Directed-energy weapons

The weapon of choice for Starfleet since a time predating the formation of the Federation has been the directed-energy weapon that came to be known as the phaser. An acronym for PHASed Energy Rectification, this powerful weapon can be used as a sidearm or a rifle. The same technology works on a much larger scale in Starfleet weapons systems with Starfleet vessels equipped with phaser banks that are capable of inflicting severe damage on enemy ships.

The foundation for energy weapons technology was established on *Enterprise* NX-01's first mission in 2151 when the crew was armed with newly invented phase pistols. This early form of technology had just two settings—stun and kill—but the phase pistol could also emit either an energy pulse or a sustained beam that was capable of cutting through solid rock. A previous energy weapon, the EM-33 pistol, was less accurate and had no stun setting.

There are two settings: stun and kill. It would be best not to confuse them.
Malcolm Reed

Personal defense Captain Kirk fires a Phaser Type-1 which is the standard basic sidearm for all 23rd-century Starfleet landing parties.

A century later, the phase pistol had evolved into the weapon most usually described as the phaser, which would continue to be in use by Starfleet officers for at least another hundred years.

The standard weapon is configured in three different designs. The Phaser Type-1 is a discreet phaser pistol, designed to fit into the palm of the hand. Although it is the least powerful of the phaser weapons, it has a range of settings from stun to kill.

The Phaser Type-2 is a slightly larger and more powerful handheld pistol-type weapon, which, in the 23rd century, incorporates a

smaller, removable hand phaser in its design. The 24th-century weapon is a self-contained version with a modified design. Phaser Type-3, the largest of the personal phased energy weapons, is based on a rifle.

Smart settings

Recent versions of the Type-2 and Type-3 weapons have up to 16 settings that dramatically extend their range of function: Light, medium, and heavy stun settings »

Two become one The 23rd-century Phaser Type-2 incorporates a removable Phaser Type-1 into a more substantial and powerful weapon.

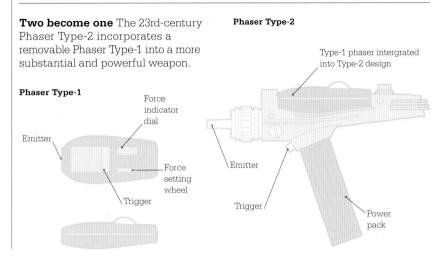

Phaser Type-1

Emitter

Force indicator dial

Force setting wheel

Trigger

Phaser Type-2

Type-1 phaser intergrated into Type-2 design

Emitter

Trigger

Power pack

Starship defenses Even in a possible future, Starfleet vessel *Enterprise*-D's state-of-the-art defenses include phaser arrays, torpedo launchers, and photon torpedoes.

cause unconsciousness for up to an hour. Thermal Effects settings cause neural damage and skin burns to Humans, and can penetrate simple, personal force fields and heat metal. A phaser set to Disruption Effects penetrates organic and structural materials and can kill humanoids. At the higher settings, most unprotected materials can be penetrated and vaporized. Set to Explosive Effects, a phaser vaporizes structural materials such as metal and rock with a rebound or absorption of energy. At the highest setting, a phaser can disintegrate 650 cubic meters of rock with one shot.

Just a little souvenir I picked up on Makus III. That was setting number one. Anyone want to see setting number two?
Guinan

Deadly disruptors
The disruptor is an alternate form of energy weapon popular with the Klingons, Romulans, and Breen. Like the phaser, disruptors come in pistol and rifle designs but generally only have stun and kill

settings—more violent species often have little use for subtlety. Disruptor weapons systems are often incorporated in their ships; the Klingons, for example, use a combination of disruptor arrays and canons as their primary weapons.

Although phasers can be set to cause explosions, a more accurate device is the photon grenade—a short-range, variable-yield weapon that emits an electromagnetic pulse. Like the phaser, a photon grenade adjusted to a lower setting can stun anyone nearby without damaging the surrounding area.

Photon torpedoes are powerful missiles that have become standard on Starfleet vessels. The casing of these self-propelled torpedoes houses a magnetic bottle containing a small amount of matter and antimatter that is combined upon impact, creating

Vulcan ceremonial weapons

Like Klingons, Vulcans still value the traditional hand weapons used in ancient customs and rites, and know how to use them. Although the species evolved into a particularly peaceful civilization, Vulcans commemorate these weapons in the colossal statues of their warrior ancestors.

The *lirpa* is a lethal weapon that is sharp on one side and blunt on the other. A metal staff connects a curved blade and a bludgeon, which can vary in size depending on use. A ceremonial *lirpa* has two ends that are somewhat oversized, whereas in actual combat a longer and more lightweight model is preferred.

The *ahn-woon* is a long leather strap weighted at the ends, which a skilled combatant can use as a whip or noose.

Modern Vulcans train in both hand weapons, particularly for use in the *kal-if-fee* mating ritual. Special commandos employ the *lirpa* when energy weapons are useless, such as in Vulcan's Forge, a vast desert canyon on their home planet, which has geo-magnetic instability.

---

the explosion. These missiles are fired from a starship's torpedo launcher at warp speed, making them the go-to weapon for a vessel traveling faster-than-light. It is a tradition on Starfleet ships that a crew man who dies in service is placed in a hollowed-out torpedo casing and launched into space.

Bladed weapons

Humans rarely use bladed weapons for actual combat, although fencing is still taught at Starfleet Academy as well as in holodeck simulations. Both Hikaru Sulu and Jean-Luc Picard have been trained with the weapon. However, few species in the 24th century continue to rely on bladed weapons the way Klingons do. This is no surprise as this ancient civilization honors its history in rituals and ceremonies that carry over to everyday life.

One of the most significant weapons in Klingon society is the *bat'leth*, or "Sword of Honor."

En garde In times of unsurpassed technological advancement, Starfleet crew still train with bladed weapons for combat and recreation.

At roughly a meter in length, this crescent-shaped blade includes two sets of points on its inside curve. Handholds are placed on the outer edge. The entire weapon is razor-sharp and can be used in combat, but its size makes it a cumbersome weapon. As such, it is largely saved for ceremonial purposes. Smaller handheld blades are more practical for the average Klingon, who in the 24th century still carries at least one bladed weapon at all times. The go-to hand weapon is the *d'k tahg*, a triple-bladed knife that can easily be holstered in a standard uniform. The less common *mek'leth*, a sword falling between the two previous blades in length, has ceremonial uses and is also a valuable part of a Klingon's personal arsenal. ■

See also: The Vulcans, Malcolm Reed, The Klingon Empire

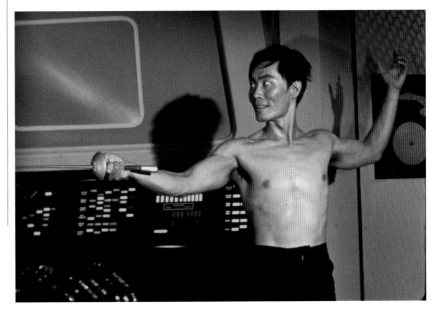

CAPTAIN TO BRIDGE
COMMUNICATORS

CAPTAIN'S LOG

NAME
Communicators

BRIEFING
For a time in the latter part of the 23rd century, Starfleet experimented with wrist communicators, but the technology was short-lived

Prior to the founding of the United Federation of Planets, personal communication devices had developed to function on subspace frequencies. This form of electromagnetic communication sent voice transmissions faster than the speed of light across interstellar distances via a subspace transceiver assembly.

Starfleet adopted the use of the aptly named "communicators" for its crews in the founding days of the organization, making these handheld devices standard issue on *Enterprise* NX-01.

The earliest forms of subspace communicators, used in the 22nd and 23rd centuries, were handheld devices with a flip-top antenna that doubled as a cover to protect the control mechanisms. This technology was standard issue for landing parties so the crew could maintain contact while in multiple locations on the planet, as well as connecting with the ship in orbit. On rare occasions, crew members could also use the communicator while on board a ship if the internal communications system was down, or if they needed to have unmonitored conversations because

Ship to shore The 22nd century communicator was one of the earliest Earth technologies to allow for personal subspace communication.

> 66
> Keep an open comlink.
> **Hoshi Sato**
> 99

the ship had been taken over by enemy forces.

Beyond voice contact with the ship, communicators also provided a coordinates lock that connected with the transporter system to track a crew member's precise location in the event of a beam out. In effect, the communicator became a homing transponder, which was especially useful in an emergency situation or if a landing party became incapacitated.

Talk to the badge
By the 24th century, the technology has become miniaturized to the point that it can fit into the insignia worn on Starfleet uniforms. The combadge—as it has become known—is a medallion made out

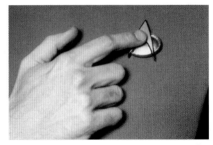

Pressing needs A gentle tap is all it takes to activate the 24th century communicator that has become a part of Starfleet's standard-issue uniform.

of a crystalline composite of silicon, beryllium, carbon-70, and gold. The convenience of a communication device worn on the left breast of a standard Starfleet uniform allows crews to use the combadge more easily when communicating while on the ship. The combadge links with the vessel's communication system, allowing crew members to speak directly with one another or with other parts of the ship, such as the bridge or the computer system. To activate the device, the user simply taps their forefinger on the insignia and speaks into it. Each combadge has a dermal sensor that allows it to respond to an individual user.

Like its predecessor, the combadge also serves as a tracking device, providing the coordinates of the person wearing it to a ship's computer. Additionally, combadges are programmed to activate automatically when the casing is destroyed, acting as a failsafe in case the wearer is seriously injured and requires rescue. The typical range of a combadge is about 500 kilometers, enough for most reasonable person-to-person communication while on a mission. A ship's communications system can boost the output of a combadge considerably, extending its range to 40,000 kilometers so a crew person can speak with the ship in orbit or other team members at a distance greater than 500 kilometers. ∎

See also: Universal translator

Kirk and his communicator When on off-ship missions, Captain Kirk relies on his communicator to relay his commands back to the crew.

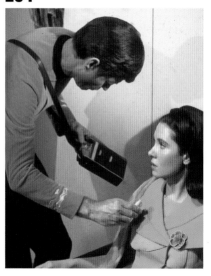

SUPER SCANNER
TRICORDERS

CAPTAIN'S LOG

NAME
Tricorders

FUNCTIONS
- **Data recording**
- **Large-scale and microscopic scanning**
- **Computer library**

BRIEFING
An essential tool on medical, scientific, and technological research-gathering missions

On the go The 23rd century tricorder—complete with shoulder strap—is the perfect accessory for any Starfleet officer.

Starfleet's mission to explore space is more than just a directive to visit unfamiliar planets. Officers are trained in a variety of scientific fields so they can learn all there is to know about a planet, species, or about space itself. One piece of advanced technology that has helped enormously in this quest for knowledge is the tricorder—a device created specifically for the research-gathering phase of an ongoing mission. Tricorders serve a variety of purposes, supporting operations on board ship or as part of a landing party or away team.

Originally a rather bulky piece of equipment, these versatile recorders of medical, scientific, and technological data have been miniaturized to fit into the palm of a hand. They are self-contained portable computing devices that employ a variety of sensors to gather all relevant information on a given subject. Although Starfleet tricorders can connect with a ship's computer to enhance their functionality, they are completely independent systems capable of their own data retrieval and analysis. A tricorder user in the field can learn almost as much from it as the ship's computer systems would reveal.

Data to go

Starfleet has produced specialized tricorders for medical, engineering, and other scientific purposes, and over the centuries, they have become standard issue. Crew members armed with the devices can scan everything from large swaths of a planet's surface to microscopic-level body scanning in a newly encountered species. A smaller handheld scanner that connects wirelessly to the tricorder can focus the sensors on a localized area. Tricorders can also be used to record the general experiences of the team. A tactile interface gives the user the ability to input information through touch as well as by voice. After crew members return to the ship, all data is collected and transferred to the ship's computer for a more thorough analysis of the mission.

How tricorders work

Like the communicator, tricorders rely on a subspace transceiver assembly for voice and data links to the ship and other devices. As such, the equipment has a similar range of 40,000 kilometers. By the mid-24th century, tricorders are capable of 6.91 kiloquads of data storage with 4.5 kiloquads of removable crystal chips containing the device's computer library. These chips allow for information to be swapped out, which frees up and expands the library function of the device. When the device is at risk of being destroyed or lost, the tricorder is able to perform an emergency upload to the ship's computer, transmitting its entire memory in 0.875 seconds.

The tricorder is a Starfleet essential but is also ubiquitous in the known universe as many species outside the Federation rely on devices of a similar concept to assist with their own exploration and study of the universe. ■

See also: Communicators

In the lab Dr. Crusher's medical tricorder is the go-to piece of diagnostic equipment in a 24th century starship's sickbay.

Away team, report.
Jean-Luc Picard

Maybe I'll start calling my tricorder 'Sally.'
Miles O'Brien

TRANSLATION MATRIX
UNIVERSAL TRANSLATOR

CAPTAIN'S LOG

NAME
Universal translator

FUNCTIONS
- **Translation matrix builds on exposure to new language**
- **Real-time translation**
- **Adapts to speaker's intentions**

BRIEFING
An indispensable aid to first contact with species

The universal translator is an indispensable piece of technology in a universe potentially filled with thousands of different species all with their unique collections of languages. The device is capable of providing a direct translation of different languages in real time, concurrent to the words being spoken. It is not perfect—due to the inherent challenges of the diverse range of languages across the known universe—but it is a piece of advanced technology that has proven invaluable to Starfleet personnel. It has been crucial in assisting them in their interactions with new species as well as with allies and enemies. Without it, the only option for explorers would be a lengthy period of study of a new language, starting from its roots.

How it works

The translator operates by analyzing conversation patterns and comparing brainwave frequencies to select comparable concepts from which two species conduct their conversations. For example, a simple glass of water might be referring to the glass, the water, the temperature, the clarity, or some other concept. The universal translator has to build its translation off the intention of the speaker rather than simply focus on the words being spoken.

Even with the continued advancements in its technology, the universal translator does not immediately begin translation when it is first exposed to new languages. The translation matrix requires a significant amount of exposure to the new language—preferably by recording two native speakers—before it can begin to build a foundation. The system

Body language The universal translator was of no use when Captain Janeway's stance caused offence to the Tak Tak, a Delta Quadrant species that use gestures as much as speech.

Speaking in stories

A universal translator's real-time capacity to accurately render words and syntax between languages does not necessarily yield a precise interpretation of meaning. In rare cases the psychological makeup of a species can make communication virtually impossible, regardless of the translation matrix in use.

Such is the case of the enigmatic "Children of Tama," or Tamarians, whose ego structure precludes a self-identity as most of us know it and also gives them highly abstract thought processes.

Their language consists entirely of metaphor because they speak using narrative imagery by referencing individuals and places in their mytho-historical stories. For instance, "Darmok and Jalad at Tanagra" means, more or less, "cooperation." "Temba, his arms wide" means "to give generously." "Shaka, when the walls fell" means "failure." "Sokath, his eyes uncovered" means "By Jove, I think you've got it!"

Consequently, Tamarians are incomprehensible to all but those with the patience and imagination to learn and understand their history.

will continue to expand on its matrix the longer it is exposed to a language, allowing it to grow in its value with extended use.

Technological evolution

In the earliest days of Starfleet, prior to the foundation of the Federation, universal translators were handheld devices that attached to a communicator. Because the technology was still in its infancy, it was important for a ship's crew to include trained exo-linguists who had studied different languages to assist with communication and help refine the device. The experiences of linguist Hoshi Sato during her time on *Enterprise* NX-01 were integral to the process of enhancing the precision of the translation matrix.

Over time the universal translator was improved, and the technology was miniaturized to the point where it could be worn

Early translator Captain Kirk's handheld universal translator was a ground-breaking device that continued to be refined and improved.

on the body, a useful refinement to coincide with the first meeting of the Coalition of Planets in 2155. This improved device was still somewhat bulky, but the technology continued to evolve so that by the 24th century the translator could be incorporated into the standard Starfleet combadge. Some species, like the Ferengi, have a smaller, more discreet version of the translator that can be placed in the ear.

In spite of the value placed on the universal translator, the study of languages remains a priority in Starfleet for times when the technology is compromised, or is unable to work with the intricacies of a particular language. ∎

See also: Hoshi Sato, Nyota Uhura, Communicators

HIDDEN DANGERS
CLOAKING DEVICES

CAPTAIN'S LOG

NAME
Cloaking devices

SPECIES WITH
CLOAKING TECHNOLOGY
- **Breen**
- **Klingons**
- **Kraylor**
- **Krenim**
- **Romulans**
- **Remans**
- **Suliban**
- **Voth**
- **Cardassian (on loan from Romulans)**
- **Federation (on loan from Romulans)**

I n the silent void of outer space, the ability to come up on one's enemy undetected can provide an important tactical advantage. By its very nature, Starfleet and the United Federation of Planets are opposed to the concept of sneaking around the universe, preferring to meet others openly and without hostility. The same is not necessarily true of species such as the Romulans and Klingons, who

both possess cloaking technology that allows them to hide their vessels from sensors—or even the naked eye—with an energy screen generator that effectively renders them invisible.

Romulans were the first notable galactic power to develop cloaking technology for their vessels. The Romulan Empire has consistently been an enemy to the Federation, so this has always been an issue, particularly as Starfleet is forbidden from working on developing cloaking technology as part of the Treaty of Algeron—a peace agreement between the Federation and the Romulans. In 2268, Starfleet became particularly concerned by advancements in

Cloaking technology isn't that easy to come by.
Quark

Cloak-and-dagger Captain James T. Kirk went undercover as a Romulan to gather intelligence on the species ultimate covert technology.

Romulan warship-cloaking ability. At the time, Captain Kirk and First Officer Spock of the *U.S.S. Enterprise* NCC-1701 were sent on a covert mission into Romulan space to retrieve a device for study.

Although the Romulans were highly protective of their cloaking technology, they did come to an agreement with the Klingon Empire to share technology in the mid-23rd century. The Klingon battle cruisers employed a similar design to their

Romulan counterparts and, now with the highly valuable cloaking technology, became a more notable threat to the Federation than ever before.

Balance of power

Cloaking devices give the Romulans and Klingons a significant advantage in combat situations, but in spite of its advancements, the technology does have its share of weaknesses. The power required to operate a cloaking device creates a considerable drain on ships' systems, rendering defensive shields inoperative and making it impossible to activate transporters or weapons systems.

In 2292 the Klingons developed a prototype bird-of-prey warship that was able to fire weapons while cloaked and the ship launched a devastating attack on the *U.S.S. Enterprise*-A. The Starfleet vessel took on serious damage before the crew determined that the Klingon ship was expending fuel in a manner that could be targeted with a modified torpedo. That torpedo forced the bird-of-prey out of cloak,

leaving it open to attack by the *Enterprise* and *Excelsior* starships. As the cloaking technology continued to improve over the decades, so did Starfleet's methods of detection.

In 2371, the Federation entered an agreement with the Romulan Star Empire to allow a single Starfleet vessel to use borrowed cloaking technology in their growing conflict with the Dominion. The *Starship Defiant* was chosen

Borrowed cloak The *U.S.S. Defiant*, a rare Federation warship, possessed even rarer cloaking technology, on loan from the Romulans.

to house the device under the arrangement that the cloak would only be used in the Gamma Quadrant, though that stipulation was later suspended. ∎

See also: The Klingon Empire, The Romulan Star Empire, The Earth-Romulan War

The *U.S.S. Pegasus*

Certain factions of Starfleet felt that concessions made by the Federation in the 2311 Treaty of Algeron to never develop cloaking technology was a serious tactical mistake. So they continued to secretly pursue that activity, with gruesome consequences.

In 2358 the *U.S.S. Pegasus*, under Captain Erik Pressman, was a testbed for new starship technologies—including weapons systems and experimental engines. That much was public knowledge. What was kept under wraps was that the *Pegasus* was also testing a "phasing cloak"—a

device which not only rendered a starship invisible, but could—theoretically—allow it to pass through matter.

The illegal tests engendered a crew mutiny, but then the technology went awry, causing an explosion. Consequently, the ship was sent drifting in a phased-cloak state toward an asteroid, where it rematerialized halfway, fused in solid rock.

The survivors did not reveal the illegal use of the cloak. The full story emerged 12 years later, and several high-ranking officials were court-martialed.

TECHNOLOGICAL DISTINCTIVENESS
BORG TECHNOLOGY

CAPTAIN'S LOG

NAME
Borg technology

FUNCTIONS
- **Nanoprobes**
- **Transwarp conduits and coils**

BRIEFING
The Borg's unsurpassed technological prowess both advances discovery and threatens the entire universe

The cybernetic drones of the Borg collective possess some of the most advanced technology in the known universe. By assimilating the combined technological and biological knowledge of all the distinctive species they encounter, the Borg absorb a wealth of information into their collective. This has led to

It's alive! A Borg autopsy on *U.S.S. Voyager* reveals that the advanced cybernetic body of a drone can be revived long after death.

some of the greatest discoveries in technological history, which Starfleet has, on occasion, been able to adapt for its own uses.

Nanoprobes
Borg nanoprobes are arguably the most destructive form of technology that has ever been encountered. A nanoprobe is a submicroscopic robot that is at the heart of the Borg assimilation process. Once nanoprobes are injected into the bloodstream of a victim, they attach to the blood cells and take over their function. The nanoprobes then spread through the infected being, forming a link to the collective as the body undergoes a physical change

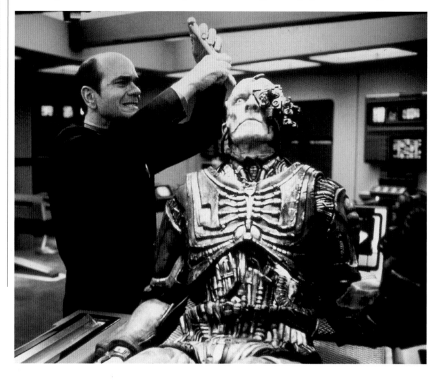

Unimatrix Zero

Deep in the subconscious of the Borg collective, there existed Unimatrix Zero: A virtual reality that one in a million drones could visit, gather with others, and live as individuals. It was their paradise. It was also a threat to the Borg Queen's control.

Unimatrix Zero started, some believe, as a random malfunction during the assimilation of a single drone with a certain recessive mutation. It spread to tens of thousands of others with the same mutation. Those drones could mentally retreat to that altered state during their regeneration cycles, but carried no memory of it afterwards.

Once the Queen discovered its existence, she went to great lengths to isolate the interlink frequency that enabled it. When the *U.S.S. Voyager* intervened, Unimatrix Zero ceased to exist, but its member drones retained their memories and united to form a resistance movement.

to include cybernetic parts. After assimilation, a fully mature drone has more than 3.5 million nanoprobes inside its body.

Nanoprobes also have some beneficial functions, and Starfleet has made great inroads using nanoprobes for purposes beyond assimilation. Many of these advancements are due to the work of the *U.S.S. Voyager* crew assisted by their Human crew member, Seven of Nine who was once assimilated by the Borg. In some instances, their work involved further weaponizing of the nanoprobes, but the *Voyager* crew also disovered a life-restoring

I've been analyzing the nanoprobes. They're efficient little assimilators. One can't help but admire the workmanship.
The Doctor

benefit. The fact that the Borg had successfully programmed nanoprobes to reverse the process of cellular necrosis spurred Seven of Nine to adapt the technique to revive crew mate Neelix after his death in a shuttle accident.

Transwarp network

The Borg have long possessed the ability to travel through artificially created transwarp conduits in a vast network consisting of thousands of corridors that allowed them to expand their reach in the Galaxy. These corridors cut through a realm of subspace known as transwarp space and have exit points in all four quadrants. By firing tachyon pulses of alternating frequencies, a Borg ship—known as a Borg cube—can open a conduit allowing the vessel to enter a matter stream that pulls the ship along at velocities more than 20 times higher than the maximum warp of a *Galaxy*-class starship such as the *Enterprise*-D. Transwarp coils allow the Borg to create new networks, expanding their reach in the universe.

The *Voyager*'s discovery of a transwarp hub in 2378 gave the

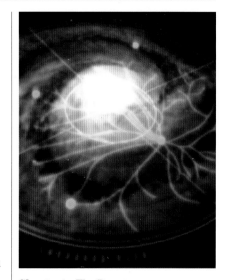

Shortcuts The Borg transwarp network is even more useful than the Bajoran wormhole for traveling across great distances in little time.

crew access to a network that allowed them to travel to the Alpha Quadrant, arriving a single light-year from Earth. As *Voyager* traveled through the corridor, the crew destroyed the interspatial manifolds, causing the hub to collapse behind them and severely disabling the Borg network. ∎
See also: Seven of Nine, The Borg Collective

NEW LIFE AND NEW CIVILIZAT

IONS

It is impossible to catalog all life in the known universe, but the task becomes infinitely more challenging when that life takes on other forms. A multitude of otherworldly beings exist in the universe, completely unrecognizable from typical humanoid bodies. Some are harmless creatures fulfilling nothing more than basic needs, while others are powerful beings playing god with little regard for the lesser species of the universe.

THESE ARE THE VOYAGES

WHERE NO ONE HAS GONE BEFORE

c.2050

Discovery of subspace sets stage for development of faster-than-light travel and communications.

c.2065

S.S. Valiant transits energy barrier at edge of the Galaxy, which imbues some Humans with psychokinetic powers.

2236

S.S. Columbia encounters illusion-creating inhabitants of planet Talos IV, later deemed too dangerous for further contact.

2268

First recorded interaction with parallel "mirror universe," home to cruel and totalitarian Terran Empire.

2063

Zefram Cochrane's first warp-speed flight on the Phoenix makes interstellar travel by Humans a reality.

2154

Enterprise NX-01 discovers spatial anomalies in Delphic Expanse are prelude to invasion by extradimensional "Sphere Builders."

2267

Ancient sentient time portal known as "The Guardian of Forever" discovered by U.S.S. Enterprise.

c.2270

Omega molecule, the most powerful substance known to exist, synthesized by Federation scientists, leading to disaster.

The Starfleet captain's oath refers to space as the final frontier. By the time that Starfleet was established on Earth in the 22nd century, Humans had already crossed many frontiers—in science, culture, and exploration. But the time and place which that phrase most brings to mind is the American Old West, where brave pioneers struck out into the great unknown, charting new territory and encountering new dangers on a regular basis. The comparison remains apt even in the late 24th century, when the membership of the United Federation of Planets numbers well over 150 worlds, yet great swathes of the Milky Way Galaxy are still to be explored.

As discussed in chapter 1, the perimeter of the Milky Way and its core are both ringed by powerful energy fields that make navigation close to impossible. But these are far from the only spatial anomalies that pose a challenge for travelers in space. Large, inhospitable areas with nicknames such as the Briar Patch and the Badlands can wreak havoc with ships' systems, while more localized rifts in the fabric of space and/or time have sent ships and their crews into the past, the future, and even other dimensions.

When a starship does overcome the perils of space travel to make first contact with an alien species, this too can present all manner of unknowns—from the best way to

establish peaceful relations with a humanoid species, to discovering whether a non-carbon based or non-corporeal phenomenon is even an actual living creature at all. Every life-form encountered by Starfleet

The final frontier has some boundaries that shouldn't be crossed.
Kathryn Janeway

U.S.S. Enterprise-A breaches "Great Barrier" at center of the Galaxy and encounters malevolent entity within.

2287

The Traveler transports *U.S.S. Enterprise*-D to Galaxy M-33, then to distant part of universe where thought and reality intertwine.

2364

Genetic information reveals that most humanoid species in the known universe share a common progenitor.

2369

"Red matter" developed as a means to create an artificial singularity, capable of containing a supernova.

2380

2293

U.S.S. Enterprise-B encounters "nexus," energy ribbon that leads to an alternative reality.

2369

First known stable wormhole discovered near Bajor, occupied by non-corporeal beings known as "Prophets."

2373

"Fluidic space," extradimensional realm discovered by Borg and explored by *U.S.S. Voyager.*

adds to the Federation's knowledge of the universe, but not all are met in peace. Some species act purely on instinct and kill to survive, while other, highly advanced beings look down on Humankind and their ilk, wielding immense powers without moral consideration.

Yet for all the challenges posed by life beyond the final frontier, there is no doubting the transformational effects of exposure to the Galaxy's unlimited wonders. In some cases, that transformation has even been literal—leading not to the discovery of a new species, but the creation of one. Contact with a race of machines endowed with artificial intelligence has caused individual

humanoids such as Captain Decker and Lieutenant Ilia of the *U.S.S. Enterprise* NCC-1701 to evolve into a whole new life-form, while encounters with species that seem to exist in a very different metaphysical plane have allowed Humans such as Starfleet cadet Wesley Crusher and Captain Sisko of Deep Space 9 to transcend linear existence and expand what it means to be a Human. Life in deep space has also led to debates that eventually gave positronic and photonic beings—androids and holograms—the same rights and privileges as organic life-forms.

Few, if any, of these discoveries and developments could have been foreseen or even imagined before

Humans first left Earth for the stars, and yet they only begin to describe the phenomena that Starfleet has so far encountered—and has still to encounter beyond the final frontier. ■

Man and machine Captain Willard Decker merged with the machine entity V'Ger to create a new life-form.

CAPTAIN'S LOG

Notable life-forms and cosmic phenomena discovered by Starfleet crews

ENTERPRISE NX-01
- Suliban
- Delphic Expanse

U.S.S. ENTERPRISE NCC-1701
- **M-113 creature**
- **Tholians**
- **Trelane**

U.S.S. ENTERPRISE NCC-1701-D
- **Armus**
- **Exocomps**
- **Farpoint life-form**
- **Moriarty program**
- **Nanites**
- **Nexus**

DEEP SPACE 9
- **Bajoran wormhole**

U.S.S. VOYAGER NCC-74656
- **Fluidic space**
- **Omega particle**

The Bajoran wormhole has become a valuable asset to the Federation, serving as a bridge to the Gamma Quadrant and the species that live there. But more than just a strategic and tactical location, the wormhole is a unique spatial anomaly opening up the universe to exploration and scientific study.

Wormholes are subspace tunnels that form throughout the universe. Usually, they are impossible to chart because their termination points are unstable, making their location unpredictable. This can endanger a vessel that encounters one. It is also possible to create an artificial wormhole when a ship's warp drive system is out of balance. A stable wormhole that can be charted and accessed in a controlled way is an unprecedented anomaly.

The wormhole that appeared in space near the planet Bajor was formed by verteron particles, which allow ships to pass through to the Gamma Quadrant using impulse power, as warp engines interfere with the process. In fact, it was warp energy that created a link to

> There's no such thing as 'the unknown,' only things temporarily hidden, temporarily not understood.
> **James Kirk**

the so-called "mirror universe" via the wormhole in 2370.

The people of Bajor consider the wormhole to be the fabled Celestial Temple—home to their Bajoran gods, the Prophets. Non-corporeal entities do indeed reside within its confines, and proved their allegiance to the people of Bajor by using their power over the wormhole to wipe out an invading fleet in the Dominion War.

Nanites, exocomps, and the meaning of life

In this remarkably rich, infinitely complex universe, not only does life find a way to spring into being under diverse circumstances, but so does consciousness. Sentience, or self-awareness, can be induced by genius cyberneticists such as Dr. Noonian Soong—creator of the androids B4, Lore, and Data—or it can arise through serendipitous happenstance.

This second option was the case when young Wesley Crusher accidentally created sentient life on board the *Enterprise*-D, simply by allowing a pair of microscopic robots called nanites to interact

outside their usual environment. The nanites began to replicate and quickly evolved into beings with language, curiosity, and a sense of purpose.

But what constitutes "life?" This question arose once more on the *Enterprise*-D when the artificially intelligent machines known as exocomps began to exhibit behaviors suggesting self-preservation and free will. The philosophical question was not conclusively answered, but the exocomps were deemed to deserve rights and protection within the Federation.

Next stop nexus El-Aurian scientist Dr. Tolan Soran went to deadly lengths to return to the timeless, wish-fulfilling realm known as the nexus.

Another spatial anomaly that has attained spiritual significance, this time among the El-Aurians, is the nexus. This non-linear temporal continuum is reached through an energy ribbon that passes through the Milky Way every 39 years. The nexus energy ribbon is a temporal flux phenomenon with the power to destroy starships in its path while, at the same time, absorbing individuals aboard those spaceships into its continuum.

The nexus is a euphoric realm in which time and space are meaningless, and reality is shaped by dreams and desires. When an individual has spent time in the embrace of the nexus, life outside it pales by comparison.

In some instances, anomalies amass in a particular area of space, making starship travel difficult. This was the case with the Delphic Expanse, which was home to the Xindi race during the 22nd century. The Expanse spanned approximately 2,000 light-years of space with a high number of volatile anomalies. Thermobaric clouds surrounded the Expanse, making entry to the region particularly difficult.

The Expanse was not a natural occurrence. The time-traveling entities the Makers (also known as the Sphere Builders) created the anomalies that fill the region. Races within the Expanse, including the Xindi, worshipped these beings as gods. The Makers took advantage of this and used their influence to convince the Xindi to attack Earth and start an interstellar war. By the end of the conflict, the *Enterprise* NX-01 crew had allied with some of the Xindi races and destroyed

their network of Sphere weapons. The resulting explosions destroyed the anomalies within the Expanse as well as the thermobaric cloud, causing the entire region to revert to normal space.

In 2373, the *U.S.S. Voyager* traveled to a continuum beyond the matter universe that was filled with organic fluid, but no stars, spatial anomalies, or planets. This region, known as fluidic space, was home to Species 8472, whose biogenetic technology made them a tempting target for the Borg. *Voyager* briefly teamed up with the Borg collective during its war with Species 8472, but Captain Kathryn Janeway was eventually able to broker a truce with Species 8472, leaving fluidic space to remain their sole, unchallenged territory.

Unique life-forms

Many of the Milky Way's civilized species share a common ancestry, »

> Save your compassion.
> It's revolting. You offer
> it like a prize, when
> in fact it's an insult.
> **Armus**

resulting in the familiar humanoid form of two arms and two legs on an upright, vertically symmetrical body. But not every intelligent life-form in the known universe falls within these parameters. The Founders, Species 8472, and the Xindi-Aquatics all possess traits very different from those of humanoids. But physical bodies represent only a fraction of the possibilities for life among the stars.

The Suliban were among the first species encountered by the crew of *Enterprise* NX-01. Though humanoid by birth, members of their society underwent artificial genetic alteration in order to carry out feats of strength, perception, and endurance that did not occur naturally in their species. One of the most notable was a shape-shifting ability that let them compress their bodies into a nearly two-dimensional form.

Two centuries later, the crew of the *Enterprise*-D encountered a life-form created when the inhabitants of an advanced world known as Vagra II found a way to remove their negative attributes as a means of erasing evil from their essence, and therefore from their society. The result was a malevolent life-form that resembled an oil slick, imbued with the worst qualities of an entire species. The being of viscous, black fluid was left behind when the Vagrans departed from their world, where it eventually became sentient and powerful, taking the name Armus.

When Armus caused the crash of an *Enterprise*-D shuttle, it used its malevolent powers to torture the crew, and then toyed with the away team that came to their aid. In the course of the ordeal, Armus killed Lieutenant Tasha Yar simply for its own amusement. When the rest of the personnel escaped the creature, the *Enterprise* posted a warning in orbit of the planet to protect others from the creature's powers.

Some life-forms have been exploited for their unique gifts. A prime example of this came during the first mission of the *Enterprise*-D, when the crew came to realize that a space station supposedly built by the Bandi was in fact a huge, shape-shifting creature forced to adopt the form and function of a planetary outpost. With the exploitation revealed, the *Enterprise* crew rendered aid to the normally spacefaring entity, enabling it to escape captivity and resume its natural form.

Some humanoid species are also equipped with abilities that far exceed, or differ greatly from, those of Humans themselves. One of the many exotic life-forms first recorded by the *Enterprise* during Captain James Kirk's famous five-year mission was the last surviving humanoid on the planet known as

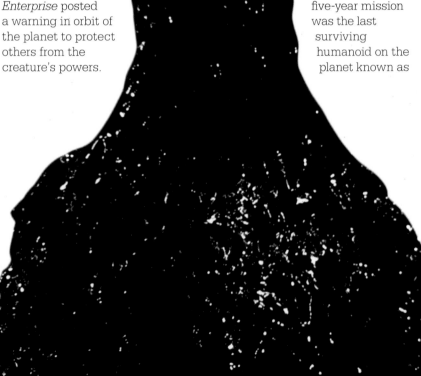

Evil incarnate Armus embodied the negativity of an entire species, and was left to fester on a world with no other inhabitants.

The Tholians

Of all the non-humanoid species to become spacefaring powers in the Alpha Quadrant, the Tholians are perhaps the most noteworthy. Physically, Tholians are similar to Earth's crab species, with six thin legs and two arms with elongated digits on both hands. Their torsos have sharply faceted, crystalline exoskeletons, and they can only survive in temperatures in excess of 200 degrees centigrade.

Behaviorally, the Tholians are more spiderlike. Their trademark tactic for dealing with an enemy vessel is to entrap it in a weblike energy field "spun" by two or more of their triangular ships. When the web is complete, the field contracts, destroying the vessel within.

To Human ears, the Tholian language sounds like screeches and chirps, but it is not beyond the interpretive capacity of the universal translator. Tholians are famous for being extremely xenophobic and territorial, but they can be diplomatic—up to a point. By the late 24th century, the Tholian Assembly engaged in ambassadorial relations with both the Romulan Star Empire and the Federation.

M-113. This being used psychic abilities, as well as hypnosis and illusion, to take on the appearance and manner of people who visited its world. With this camouflage, the creature was able to prey on other intelligent life-forms, feeding on all the salt from their bodies.

Kirk's crew also encountered a seemingly Human adult male on the planet Gothos who went by the name Trelane. However, he was in fact a youth from a powerful non-corporeal species who could take on Human form and reshape matter to create an Earthlike environment for his own entertainment. To the members of the *Enterprise* crew he abducted, he appeared infinitely powerful, but when his similarly skilled parents appeared, he was reduced to a sulky child.

New science
Federation worlds continue to expand the fields of science, particularly in the use of holographic technology that has brought about many benefits beyond entertainment in holodecks and holosuites.

One result of these developments has been the accidental creation of sentient photonic life, with the first known "living" hologram created on board the *Enterprise*-D. It was Lieutenant Commander Geordi La Forge who directed one of the ship's holodecks to create a truly challenging Sherlock Holmes story for Lieutenant Commander Data, resulting in a holographic Moriarty character sophisticated enough to be self-aware. *Voyager* later encountered a whole host of photonic life-forms in the Delta

It's life, Captain, but not life as we know it.
Spock

Quadrant, as well as encouraging the growth of its own holographic Doctor beyond the bounds of his original programming.

Perhaps one of the greatest—and most dangerous—scientific discoveries in the universe is the existence of the Omega molecule. Theoretically, a small amount of these highly unstable particles could power an entire planet, but the explosion of a single molecule could create subspace ruptures across several light-years, making space travel impossible throughout that region. After conducting its own catastrophic experiments, the Federation has banned all further research on the Omega molecule, with Starfleet bound by a secret Omega Directive that supersedes all other Starfleet General Orders. If a Starfleet captain discovers any evidence of the Omega molecule, they are under orders to destroy all research taking place and suppress any findings reached, in order to protect space from destruction. ■

See also: The Known Universe, Starfleet, *Enterprise* NX-01, Deep Space 9, The Xindi, Species 8472

THE TRIAL NEVER ENDS

THE Q CONTINUUM

CAPTAIN'S LOG

NAME
Q

SPECIES
Q

PARENTS
Q

OCCUPATION
Q

BRIEFING
Q had a history with Guinan, the El-Aurian bartender on board the *Enterprise*-D, whom he described as an "imp"

Of all the civilizations and species encountered by Starfleet, none compares to the Q Continuum. Claiming to have "always existed," the Q seem to be immortal, and all but omnipotent—with the ability to create and reshape matter, to generate entire fantasy worlds, and to effortlessly relocate themselves and others in time and space.

As a society, the Q Continuum operate within strict codes of conduct, but its methods and its morality are not always easy for other, less powerful species to comprehend. An eternity of existence has made the species arrogant, inflexible, and bored. Though they consider their level of evolution to represent the "ultimate

It's time to put an end to your little trek through the stars. Make room for other more worthy species.
Q

purity," their encounters with the species of the Federation led to discord within the Q Continuum, and even attempts to introduce an element of Humanity into it. In most of these dealings, it was one particular Q who represented the Continuum to Humanity and the Federation—and who proved to be a constant thorn in its side.

Humanity on trial
Starfleet's first experience of Q came during the first mission of the *U.S.S. Enterprise* NCC-1701-D in 2364. En route for Farpoint Station on the planet Deneb IV, the ship was brought to a standstill by an impenetrable barrier in space. Q materialized

Judge and jury For his first meeting with the *Enterprise*, Q assumed the role of a judge from the 21st-century "post-atomic horror."

on the bridge and gave the crew the option to return to Earth or be destroyed. Captain Jean-Luc Picard refused to comply, leading Q to transport him and three of his senior staff to a courtroom where Q was the judge and jury. When Q declared Humanity to be guilty of savagery, Picard proposed a test to prove him wrong. Q agreed, and Picard and his ship were allowed to proceed to Deneb IV.

On the planet, the crew ultimately learned that Farpoint Station was in fact a living being that had been enslaved and forced to take the form of a starbase. After assisting in its release, Q could not

deny that this showed a civilized sensibility, and let the *Enterprise* go on its way—but hinted that he would return again.

True to his word, Q plagued Picard over the next few years— returning on no fewer than seven occasions to test and tease the captain and his crew. On his first

Join the Q Among his many guises, Q mimicked the appearance of Lieutenant Commander Data when he encouraged William Riker to use the power of Q.

follow-up visit, he granted Q-like powers to Commander William Riker, in order to explore Human nature. When Riker rejected these new abilities, Q was summoned back to the Continuum. One year later, Q initiated Starfleet's first recorded contact with the Borg when he propelled the *Enterprise* 7,000 light-years across space into the path of a Borg cube.

As a result of these escapades and others, Q was stripped of his powers by the Q Continuum and turned into a mortal of his choice. He chose to become a Human on board the *Enterprise*, citing Picard as the closest thing that he had to a friend. Though Picard and his crew were unconvinced by Q's story, Picard granted him asylum from the countless beings in the universe that Q had »

Not from Nottingham Crusher, Worf, LaForge, Troi, and Riker were forced to play Merry Men to Picard's Robin Hood in Q's Sherwood Forest fantasy.

I refuse to believe that the afterlife is run by you. The universe is not so badly designed.
Jean-Luc Picard

tormented over the years. When one such species, the Calamarain, attacked the *Enterprise*, Q left the ship in a shuttlecraft in order to save the crew from his pursuers. This one selfless act was enough for the Q Continuum to restore Q's powers and welcome him back to the fold.

A debt of gratitude

Q's relationship with Picard and the *Enterprise* changed following his brush with mortality. On his next visit to the ship, Q professed a debt of gratitude to the captain and sought to teach him a lesson about love by casting him and Picard's former lover Vash in a Robin Hood fantasy, with the rest of the senior officers as Picard's Merry Men. Q himself took on the role of Sheriff of Nottingham. When the lifelike

experience was over, Q left once again—with Vash willingly going with him on a tour of the Galaxy. She later parted company with Q during his one recorded visit to the space station Deep Space 9.

The Continuum

Captain Janeway and Lieutenant Tuvok were the first Human and Vulcan to visit the Q Continuum. It was presented to them as manifestation they could comprehend, although the metaphorical imagery was difficult to decipher.

Q returned to the *Enterprise* on another altruistic mission in 2369, when Amanda Rogers, a seemingly Human woman, discovered that she was in fact a member of the Q Continuum. He helped her to come to terms with her growing powers, and eventually convinced her to take her place in the Continuum. Later that same year, he set about teaching Picard another valuable lesson, as the captain lay dying in the *Enterprise* sickbay. Given the chance by Q to change a defining

Time has become meaningless

The quiet roadhouse has never seen visitors before

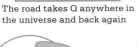

The road takes Q anywhere in the universe and back again

Everything old and new has already been discussed

Everyone is silent because there's nothing left to say

All the games have been played

moment in his own reckless past, Picard did so, and was returned to a future where he was not dying, but living a boring life without risk. After Picard acknowledged that his past choices were responsible for the man he was today, Q restored the timeline, and Picard's life was saved.

The following year, Q resumed the trial against Humanity, which he claimed had never stopped. He set Picard a paradoxical problem to solve, and caused him to journey between three periods in his own life in pursuit of a way to stop an anomaly in space from destroying Humanity entirely. When Picard reached the correct solution, Q was suitably impressed and promised to keep watching Humanity with interest, adding that the trial would never end. Though this Q was closer to the merciless being of old, he still admitted to giving Picard one or two helpful clues.

Inside the Continuum
Q made his first visit to the *U.S.S. Voyager* in 2372, when the crew released another member of the Continuum—who became known as Quinn—from his prison inside

Q, too Q's son, Junior, followed in his father's footsteps, creating interstellar mischief until his powers were revoked and his character tested on *Voyager*.

We were just getting to the good part!
Junior

a comet. Quinn had been placed there by the Continuum because he wished to die—which the rest of the Q would not permit—and upon his release, the familiar Q arrived to stop him. However, after hearing Quinn's arguments, Q made Quinn mortal, and even provided him with the hemlock to end his life.

As a result of Quinn's death, the Continuum was plunged into civil war. In an attempt to bring the two sides together, Q sought Janeway's help, proposing that she give birth to Q's child in order to bring a dose of Humanity to the Q Continuum. When Janeway refused, *Voyager*'s crew instead forced a ceasefire by traveling into the Continuum with help from a female Q and using the Continuum's own weapons against it. Q had his child with the female Q instead, and peace was restored to the Continuum.

Q's final visit to *Voyager* came when the Continuum relieved his troublemaking son of his powers and placed him in Janeway's care. In an echo of his father's behavior as a mortal, Junior—as he became known—acted selflessly when he was tested by Q, and father and son returned to the Continuum. ■

See also: *U.S.S. Enterprise NCC-1701-D*, Jean-Luc Picard, *U.S.S. Voyager NCC-74656*, Kathryn Janeway

J'accuse the Q

The Q who became known as Quinn rebelled against Q law by seeking to end his endless life. He argued that there was nothing left in the universe for him to see or do, and therefore his life was a cruel and boring burden to him. Quinn's fellow Q did not agree, however, and imprisoned him in a comet to stop his radical opinions from bringing chaos and dissent to the Continuum.

When the *U.S.S. Voyager* crew accidentally freed Quinn from his prison, the ship was drawn into the Q Continuum's dispute, and Captain Janeway convened a hearing to settle the matter. Quinn presented his case, and the Q known to the *U.S.S. Enterprise*-D the case against. Both agreed to abide by Janeway's verdict.

Q used his vast powers to present his case, calling upon witnesses including Sir Isaac Newton and Commander Will Riker. For his part, Quinn took Janeway into the Continuum to experience its stagnation.

Janeway found in favor of granting Quinn asylum as a mortal, but urged him to give finite life a chance. However, when Q made Quinn a mortal, he swiftly killed himself.

IN THE ARENA
THE GORN AND THE METRONS

CAPTAIN'S LOG

NAME
Cestus III

CLASSIFICATION
Planet

LOCATION
Beta Quadrant

POLITICAL AFFILIATION
**United Federation
of Planets (formerly
disputed)**

BRIEFING
**By the 2370s, Cestus III
was home to a thriving
Federation colony with
its own baseball league
featuring teams such as
the Pike City Pioneers
and the Cestus Comets**

In 2267, Captain Kirk and the crew of the *U.S.S. Enterprise* NCC-1701 made first contact with a pair of very different species following an attack on a Federation outpost on the planet Cestus III.

The Gorn
The Gorn are a reptilian species, slightly larger than Humans, with cold blood and scaly green skin. They boast greater than average strength and stamina, but little in the way of speed or agility. In the 23rd century, their spacecraft were considered a technological match for Starfleet vessels, with strong deflector shields and powerful disruptor weapons.

The Gorn were responsible for the attack on Cestus III, which they considered to be in their territory. After destroying the outpost, they faked a message from it to draw the *Enterprise* into a trap. When Kirk's ship responded, the Gorn attacked.

Gorn to be wild Captain James Kirk fights for his life in single combat with the captain of a Gorn ship.

Meet the Metrons A single Metron appeared to Captain James Kirk on the planet that served as their arena.

The Metrons

After exchanging fire with the Gorn on the surface of Cestus III and above, the *Enterprise* and its crew pursued the attacking ship as it moved off at warp 6. Both ships were brought to a complete stop, however, as they passed an uncharted solar system. With no power to the engines or weapons systems, the two craft were now at the mercy of the Metrons—an extremely advanced species with lifespans of well over a thousand years, and who appeared to Kirk in a humanoid form. The Metrons objected to conflict taking place in their territory, and assigned a planet where the captains of both ships could settle their feud—in a fight to the death. The winner and his ship would be permitted to go on their way, while the loser's vessel would be destroyed by the Metrons as a warning to others.

The battle

With the two captains abducted from their ships and deposited on the planet, Kirk had no choice but to fight. In single combat with the Gorn captain, he narrowly escaped death thanks to his greater speed, but his strength was no match for the powerful reptile. With no way to flee the planet, Kirk's only hope was ingenuity, and he set about constructing a makeshift weapon.

Kirk felled his opponent with gunpowder made from the planet's minerals and a cannon fashioned from a bamboo-like plant. Instead of following up with a death blow, however, Kirk chose not to kill the Gorn and appealed to the Metrons to end the contest. Surprised and impressed by this show of mercy, the Metrons allowed both captains and their vessels to go free. Faced with a Metron representative, Kirk expressed his hope that the Gorn and the Federation might come to a mutual understanding through dialogue. The Metron replied that maybe, in the far future, his people and Kirk's would do the same. ∎

See also: *U.S.S. Enterprise NCC-1701, James T. Kirk*

You are still half savage.
But there is hope.
Metron

Brewers and biters

Though first contact between the Federation and the Gorn did not occur until 2267, they were known to other Alpha Quadrant powers such as the Orion Syndicate more than a century beforehand. In 2154, the Orion privateer Harrad-Sar enjoyed a Gorn-brewed beverage called *meridor* with Captain Jonathan Archer and Lieutenant Malcolm Reed of the *Enterprise* NX-01. At the time, the Gorn Hegemony was already a power that spanned multiple planets, though the Orion would not be drawn to discuss them.

In the alternative timeline created by Nero's Temporal Incursion of 2233, the Gorn and the Federation had made first contact by 2259. In that reality, Dr. Leonard McCoy once delivered Gorn octuplets by Caesarian section—who proved to be biters from birth.

In the reality known as the "mirror universe" meanwhile, the Gorn were known to the Terran Empire and the Tholian Assembly by 2155—when a Gorn called Slar was killed by Archer's mirror counterpart, despite being faster and more agile than the Gorn fought by Captain Kirk in 2267.

LIFE OF ILLUSION
THE TALOSIANS

Wrong thinking is punishable. Right thinking will be as quickly rewarded. You will find it an effective combination.
Talosian Keeper

The people of Talos IV were all but wiped out in a war that devastated the surface of their planet millennia ago. The survivors retreated underground and became reliant on their highly developed mental capabilities to survive. They grew addicted to the lifelike illusions they were able to conjure, and lost the technological know-how to rebuild their society.

In 2236, a Federation ship, the *S.S. Columbia*, crashed on Talos IV with the loss of all but one of those on board—a Human woman called Vina. Having never seen a Human before, the Talosians repaired her injuries inexpertly, but were able to give her the illusion of a healthy body. Eighteen years later, Captain Christopher Pike and his crew on board the *U.S.S. Enterprise* NCC-1701 responded to a distress call from the *Columbia* that turned out to be another Talosian illusion. Pike was captured by the Talosians as part of a plan to repopulate the planet with his and Vina's offspring, but was freed when the Talosians came to realize Humanity's hatred of enforced captivity.

Following Pike's experience on Talos IV, Starfleet banned all travel there, to stop the Talosians from

No illusion Thousands of years after war ravaged Talos IV, plants clung on to life amid its rocky landscape.

duping other Federation species with their mental abilities. However, in 2267, Pike's erstwile science officer, Spock, defied the ban after the captain was permanently paralyzed in an accident. With the help of the Talosians, Spock took Pike back to Talos IV, where he could live an illusory but happy life, restored (within his mind) to the physical condition in which he had first visited the planet, and reunited with the beautiful Vina. ■
See also: *U.S.S. Enterprise* NCC-1701, Spock, Christopher Pike

THE ENERGY OF THOUGHT

THE TRAVELER

CAPTAIN'S LOG

NAME
Tau Alpha C

CLASSIFICATION
Planet

LOCATION
Tau Ceti system

BRIEFING
Inhabitants of Tau Alpha C, such as the Traveler, live on a different plane of existence from Humans

The being known as the Traveler had an advanced understanding of the relationship between space, time, and thought. He could phase in and out of the physical universe and shape reality using only his mind.

The Traveler came on board the *U.S.S. Enterprise* NCC-1701-D in 2364, acting as the assistant to a propulsion expert. In fact it was his own abilities that powered the warp drive experiments the pair carried out together—and which accidentally propelled the ship far beyond the Milky Way Galaxy. He explained that he meant the ship and its crew no harm, and merely wished to observe life-forms that he considered worthy of attention for the first time in their evolution. Though weakened by the mental exertion of sending the *Enterprise* so far beyond the known universe, he was eventually able to return it to its own galaxy. The Traveler left with a message for Captain Jean-Luc Picard that the young Wesley Crusher—son of the *Enterprise*'s Dr. Beverly Crusher—was destined for very great things.

In the years that followed, the Traveler watched Wesley's development and helped him when one of his experiments backfired and trapped his mother in an alternative reality. In 2370, he saw that Wesley had expanded his mind to a point where he could explore new planes of existence, and offered to be his guide on the journey. ■

See also: *U.S.S. Enterprise* NCC-1701-D, Wesley Crusher

You don't say The Traveler offered no introduction, saying only that his name was unpronounceable to Humans.

IN THEIR HANDS
THE PROPHETS

CAPTAIN'S LOG

NAME
Bajoran wormhole

CLASSIFICATION
Stable subspace corridor

LOCATION
Denorios Belt, Bajor system, Alpha Quadrant

BRIEFING
The wormhole is known as the Celestial Temple to the Bajorans, and the Eye of Destiny to the Klingons

The Prophets had been watching over the planet Bajor for at least 30,000 years before Starfleet commander Benjamin Sisko discovered their home—a stable wormhole close to the planet. Over that time, they had sent nine mysterious orbs to Bajor that could trigger deep and revealing visions, and which—as "Tears of the Prophets"—became the basis of the Bajoran religion.

When Sisko discovered the wormhole in 2369, it was hailed by the Bajorans as the "Celestial Temple," and Sisko as the Emissary of the Prophets—a leader whose coming had been long foretold. He later discovered that his birth had been orchestrated by the Prophets, and that he was destined to take his place alongside them.

The Prophets communicated with other life-forms through their visions, taking on the appearance of people known to the seer. In the physical world, they manifested as formless balls of energy, and could only communicate by possessing a corporeal life-form. Though they had no concept of linear time until it was explained to them by Sisko, they described themselves as "of Bajor" and took an interest in the affairs of that planet.

When war threatened Bajor, the Prophets intervened through Sisko to keep the planet out of the line of fire. They later wiped out an entire fleet of Jem'Hadar ships inside the wormhole rather then let Sisko die in battle with them. They also gave Sisko the ability to defeat the Pah-wraiths—enemies of the Prophets that threatened to destroy Bajor. ∎

See also: Deep Space 9, Benjamin Sisko, Kira Nerys, The Bajorans, Where No One Has Gone Before

Jake-o-vision The Prophets appeared to Sisko in the form of people from his life, such as his son, Jake, his late wife, Jennifer, and Captain Jean-Luc Picard.

THE FALLEN
PAH-WRAITHS

CAPTAIN'S LOG

NAME
Fire caves of Bajor

CLASSIFICATION
Geological formation

LOCATION
Bajor, Bajor system, Alpha Quadrant

BRIEFING
The beings known as the Pah-wraiths were imprisoned in the fire caves by the Prophets

Pah-wraiths and Prophets. All this talk of gods strikes me as nothing more than superstitious nonsense.
Damar

The Pah-wraiths and the Prophets were ancient adversaries who once shared a home inside the Bajoran wormhole. Over many thousands of years, single Pah-wraiths were trapped inside artifacts on Bajor, until the remaining Pah-wraiths were banished from the wormhole and imprisoned in the fire caves on Bajor. Their imprisonment was recorded in the Book of the Kosst Amojan, a Bajoran religious text that also detailed how they could be released, and this dangerous knowledge was closely guarded by the Bajorans for many centuries.

Like the Prophets, the Pah-wraiths could take physical form in visions, or by possessing other beings, but otherwise existed as flamelike balls of energy. In 2373, a single Pah-wraith escaped the fire caves and took over the body of Keiko O'Brien in an attempt to destroy the Prophets. A year later, a Prophet and a Pah-wraith were freed from an ancient artifact and did battle on Deep Space 9, with the Pah-wraith possessing Jake Sisko. On both occasions, the life-forms were forced to give up their host bodies after being exposed to chroniton particles.

Later in 2374, the Cardassian Gul Dukat released another Pah-wraith, which launched an attack on the wormhole, sealing its entrance. Dukat later took possession of the Book of the Kosst Amojan, and set out to release all the Pah-wraiths. On the verge of freedom, the Pah-wraiths revealed their plan to "burn the universe," but Benjamin Sisko sacrificed himself to seal them into the fire caves forever. ■
See also: Benjamin Sisko, Dukat, The Bajorans, The Prophets

Old flame When a Pah-wraith took control of Keiko O'Brien, her husband, Miles, was forced to do its bidding in order to keep her from harm.

THE CARETAKER
THE NACENE

CAPTAIN'S LOG

NAME
The Nacene

LIFESPAN
Over 1,000 years

BRIEFING
The Caretaker was also known as "Banjo Man," because his illusory Human form when communicating with the _Voyager_ was a man playing a banjo

The Nacene are extra-galactic life-forms that exist in non-corporeal form as sporocystian energy, but they can also manifest in humanoid form.

The Nacene are great travelers, but one of their galaxy-crossing adventures accidentally resulted in the planet Ocampa becoming uninhabitable. They left two of their kind behind to care for the Ocampa species. The pair became known as the Caretakers, and they began to oversee all of the Ocampa's needs. Living in a nearby array space station, they provided the species with sustenance and all-important water. However, their care was so complete that it began to inhibit the Ocampa's evolution.

In 2017 the female Caretaker, Suspiria, decided to take 2,000 Ocampa with her to a new home on her own array. Here she trained them to use their latent mental abilities so they could evolve beyond their physical forms and join her in Exosia, a place of pure thought and energy.

The search for protection
Around 300 years after Suspiria left, the remaining Caretaker realized he was dying. Fearing for the Ocampa, he sent an energy

> I can't believe that our Caretaker would forbid us to open our eyes and see the sky.
> **Kes**

Moral decision After the Caretaker dies, Janeway makes the difficult decision to destroy his array, rather than use it to return her crew to safety.

beam across the universe to attract a species to take over the Ocampa's care. In doing so, he captured more than 50 ships, including Federation vessels. Captain Janeway of the _Voyager_ showed the Caretaker how misguided his actions had been. He asked her to destroy his array after his death, protecting the Ocampa from the warrior species the Kazon. Janeway did so, but the Caretaker's former mate, Suspiria, later blamed the _Voyager_ crew for his death, attacking the ship in 2372. ∎

See also: _U.S.S. Voyager NCC-74656_, The Ocampa, Kes

ALL THAT YOU KNEW IS GONE

GUARDIAN OF FOREVER

CAPTAIN'S LOG

NAME
Guardian of Forever

CLASSIFICATION
Sentient time portal

SIZE
10 ft (3 m) diameter

BRIEFING
The Guardian was originally a conduit for a species that left its planet for a new age

The Guardian of Forever is neither a machine nor a being, but something between the two. It acts as a sentient time portal and was built by an ancient civilization over ten million years ago. The Guardian has the ability to speak and answer questions, and can pose questions to those it encounters. Its main function is to transport beings to other times and dimensions, but its true purpose is unclear.

Newspaper evidence Spock examines newspaper articles to work out how the two different timelines differ, and sees that in one, Hitler will win World War II.

In 2267 the crew of the *Enterprise* under Captain Kirk encountered the Guardian while studying time-distortion waves emitting from its planet. The distortion waves buffeted the ship, causing Dr. McCoy to accidentally inject himself with an overdose of a powerful drug. While experiencing delusions, McCoy beamed down to the planet and went through the portal, traveling back to Earth in the 1930s. Kirk and Spock then met the Guardian, who told them that McCoy had altered the timeline and as a result the *Enterprise* no longer existed. Kirk and Spock had no choice but to follow the doctor through the time portal.

The two men determined that McCoy had prevented the death of Edith Keeler, a social worker whose pacifistic message ultimately delayed America's entry into World War II. This gave the Nazis time to develop greater weapons and conquer the world. Kirk developed romantic feelings towards Keeler, but was forced to standby and watch as a car struck her down. The timeline was reset, allowing the future to play out as it should. ■

See also: Time Travel, James T. Kirk, Dr. Leonard "Bones" McCoy

TO LEARN ALL THERE IS TO KNOW
V'GER

CAPTAIN'S LOG

NAME
Voyager VI, then V'Ger

LAUNCHED
Late 20th century

ORIGIN
Earth

DEVELOPED BY
NASA

BRIEFING
A massive, sentient machine that returned to threaten Earth in 2271

In the late 20th century, Earth's National Aeronautics and Space Administration (NASA) launched the *Voyager VI* space probe, which was designed to record data and report back to the organization. The space probe disappeared when it was pulled into something that was believed to be a black hole. What NASA did not realize was that the probe had in fact emerged on the other side of the Galaxy, where it encountered a planet populated by living machines.

Voyager VI was primitive compared to the mechanical life-forms that found it, but they considered it a kindred soul and set about expanding its programming. The life-forms interpreted the probe's commands to collect data (to "learn all that is learnable") and to return to its creator as the reasons for its existence. They aided the probe in its goal by building a massive power field around it, which would help it return to Earth while continuing its quest for learning.

Around 300 years after its launch, *Voyager VI* returned to the Alpha Quadrant and plotted a course for Earth, having obtained so much knowledge that it had evolved to develop sentience. The probe was now so powerful that it could destroy everything in its path, including Earth. When the *U.S.S. Enterprise*, under the command of Admiral Kirk, intercepted it, they found something greater than the NASA machine that it once was. The mechanics at the heart of the construct now went by the name V'Ger, which was a derivation of its original name. In its search for the meaning of existence, V'Ger ultimately merged with *Enterprise* crew members Decker and Ilia to

create a new life-form that continued to explore the universe, while leaving Earth safely behind. ∎
See also: *U.S.S. Enterprise NCC-1701.*

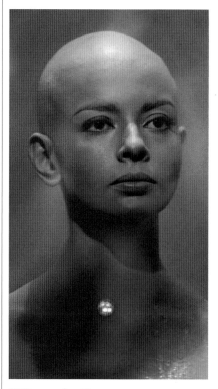

V'Ger probe *Enterprise* crew member and navigator Lieutenant Ilia was killed when the V'Ger probe stored her as digital memory for its own use.

THE DEVIL IN THE DARK

HORTA

NO KILL I
Horta

The Horta is a highly intelligent, silicon-based life-form with an amorphous shape. The species dwells underground on the planet Janus IV, a Federation mining colony. The Horta produces a strong corrosive acid that allows them to bore through solid rock—their source of sustenance. This acid is deadly to humanoids, as the Federation colony found out when some of their miners went missing.

When Captain Kirk and the crew of the *Starship Enterprise* first encountered the species, the female they met was the only known member of her species in existence. Once every 50,000 years the entire Horta race dies out except for a lone survivor, who is left to care for—and protect—the eggs of her species. These are stored in the Vault of Tomorrow, located in the Chamber of the Ages.

Horta eggs Miners mistook these eggs for useless silicon nodules and destroyed many of them.

The lone Horta was initially believed to be a mindless creature but was proved sentient when she left a simple message in English for the *Enterprise* crew. Eventually Spock was able to mind-meld with her and learn of her plight. The deaths of the miners were due to the Horta protecting her eggs, unaware that the miners intended no harm to her children. Spock was able to negotiate an agreement to share the planet and the Horta agreed to help the miners harvest the mineral-rich soil of Janus VI. ■

See also: *U.S.S. Enterprise NCC-1701*

FANTASTIC BEASTS
MUGATO, SEHLAT, AND TARG

Some of the most menacing threats in the universe come in the form of vicious beasts, some of which are considered quite normal on their own planet. While some societies fear these creatures for their horrific attributes, others keep them as pets.

Mugato
Mugato are carnivorous, apelike creatures native to the planet Neural. These powerful creatures have great physical strength and also carry a deadly venom in their fangs. Starfleet has no antivenom to counter this poison, but a local plant known as the *mahko* root forms the basis for a herbal remedy. Mugato are fiercely loyal to their mates—if one is killed, its mate will seek revenge on the killer.

Furry mugato These wild, ape-like beasts have a horn on their heads and spikes along their backs. Their fangs are short but highly venomous.

The sehlat Like many Vulcans, Spock had a pet sehlat as a child, which died after it was bitten by a lion-like desert predator known as "le-matya."

Sehlat
The sehlat is a fierce beast with long fangs, yet Vulcan children look upon them with the same affection Earth children feel for teddy bears (though they are always careful not to be late with dinner). Sehlats can be domesticated, but live naturally in the harsh desert of Vulcan's Forge. Wild sehlats will stalk humanoid prey who enter their territory.

Targ
The targ is a vicious animal that Klingon children keep as pets. Targ look like Terran boars, but have a row of spikes on their backs, a single horn on their heads and can be furry. Targ milk is an ingredient in some Klingon drinks, and their blood can be used to make the Klingon dish *gagh*. ▪
See also: Spock, Worf

A BUNCH OF HUNGRY LITTLE TRIBBLES

TRIBBLES

CAPTAIN'S LOG

SPECIES
Tribble

NATIVE PLANET
Unknown

DISTINGUISHING FEATURE
Asexual and born pregnant

BRIEFING
In the Kelvin Timeline, a deceased tribble helped Dr. McCoy realize that the eugenically altered blood of Khan Noonien Singh had regenerative properties

They're nice—they're soft, they're furry, and they make a pleasant sound.
Leonard McCoy

Tribbles may look cute and cuddly, but there are few non-intelligent creatures in the universe that can match their awesome potential for destruction. Under James Kirk, the crew of the *U.S.S. Enterprise* first became aware of the furry little creatures when interstellar trader Cyrano Jones gave one to Lieutenant Uhura in Deep Space Station K-7. Uhura brought the tribble back to the *Enterprise,* unaware that it might become an environmental menace.

Tribbles are a hermaphroditic species, born pregnant and capable of reproducing at a very fast rate. It is not unusual for a tribble to produce ten offspring in 12 hours and for those children to continue propagating the line just as rapidly. Such was the case during the *Enterprise* encounter in 2268, when tribbles threatened to overrun the ship and the K-7 space station. They decimated the stores of the highly valued quadrotriticale grains, but in doing so they revealed that Klingon had poisoned the stores, because many tribbles died after consuming it.

Engineer Scott beamed the surviving tribbles onto a Klingon ship, unwittingly launching one of the most devastating attacks in Klingon-Federation history. The tribbles became an ecological menace to Klingon society, and hundreds of Klingon warriors were charged with hunting them down before the pests destroyed Qo'noS.

Tribbles were then thought to be extinct until the Deep Space 9 crew took on a time travel mission to the past and returned with a tribble that quickly began to fill the space station with its offspring. ■
See also: Time Travel, James T. Kirk, Dr. Leonard "Bones" McCoy

Hungry tribble Tribbles are constantly reproducing, at a rate determined by how much food they consume.

GLOSSARY

antimatter
The principal fuel of starship warp engines, expended in controlled annihilation with ordinary matter to release the full potential of energy as per the equation $E=mc^2$.

assimilation
In Borg parlance, the process of acquiring technology or converting individuals into drones bound to the hive mind through injection of nanoprobes and replacement of body parts with cybernetic implants.

Augment
A genetically engineered individual with superior strength and/or intelligence, especially those associated with the 20th-century Eugenics Wars on Earth.

away team
Also known as a landing party, a squad of starship personnel assembled to conduct a mission off-ship, usually to a planetary surface or another spacecraft via a transporter or shuttlecraft.

Big Bang
The theoretical origin point of the known universe, approximately 13.8 billion years ago, whereby all matter, energy, space, and time expanded from a single point of infinite density.

bio-neural circuitry
Computer technology developed c. 2370 using synthetic neural cells to emulate the thinking patterns of living organisms, substantially improving the processing of complex data compared to conventional isolinear systems.

biotemporal
A term used to describe conditions or technologies impacting on living cells in ways that defy the normal flow of time, such as reversing the aging process, or exposure to chroniton particles.

bird-of-prey
A type of starship vessel which is visually reminiscent of large predatory birds, most commonly associated with warships from the Klingon empire and Romulan Star Empire.

Bussard collectors
Also referred to as "ramscoops," electromagnetic devices attached to a starship's warp nacelles used primarily to gather hydrogen for fuel, but modifiable for other interstellar gases and particles.

Changeling
Synonym for "shape-shifter." A term used by the Founders of the Dominion to describe their species, originally used as a pejorative against them by "solids."

chroniton
Subatomic particle that transmits temporal quanta, associated with time distortion phenomena including matter phasing, time travel, biotemporal flux, and spatial rifts.

Class-M planet
Classification of planet featuring environments best suited for humanoid life, such as rocky terrestrial worlds with oxygen-nitrogen atmospheres.

cosmological constant
Concept originally proposed by Albert Einstein placing a value on the density of energy in the vacuum of space, which is associated with the rate of expansion (or contraction) of the universe.

Dabo
Ferengi game of chance similar to roulette; shouts of "Dabo!" fill Quark's Bar when a player wins a spin of the wheel.

data stream
The transmission of information—usually one-way—between two sites, such as a transporter beam and the transfer of a holographic being to a distant location.

deflector
A directional force-beam generator used to "deflect" hazards such as debris, meteoroids, and microscopic particulates that could damage a starship at high velocities, also known as a deflector dish.

dilithium
Crystalline substance used in warp drive systems of starships to regulate matter/antimatter reactions in the warp core, found naturally on only a few planets.

disruptor
A type of directed-energy weapon used by Romulans, Klingons, Gorn, Breen, Cardassians, and other species.

doppelganger
Term describing an exact double or look-alike of a living individual, such as a clone, a look-alike android, a parallel universe counterpart, a "future self," or a shape-shifting impersonator.

elogium
The time of sexual maturation in Ocampa females, similar to puberty in Humans, occurring around the age of five years.

EMH
Acronym for "Emergency Medical Hologram," a holographic program used on most Federation starships by the late 24th century intended as a short-term supplement to medical personnel.

eugenics
Philosophies and practices aiming to improve the genetic quality of a species through selective breeding or genetic manipulation, including those on 20th century Earth which bred "supermen."

exobiologist
An individual who studies the biology of extraterrestrial life and the effects of alien surroundings on living organisms.

exolinguist
One who studies the languages of other species; also known as a xenolinguist.

extradimensional
Originating outside three-dimensional space and/or quantum reality of the known universe; examples include the Q, Species 8472, and the "Sphere Builders."

Federation Council
Governing body of the United Federation of Planets made up of representatives of the member worlds, based in San Francisco, United States of America, Earth.

first contact
Term describing an initial encounter between representatives of two species,

sometimes in the context of their first overt exposure to extraterrestrial life, resulting in notable sociological impact.

First Contact Day
Annual holiday celebrated by Humans on April 5, commemorating the first encounter between Humans and Vulcans subsequent to Zefram Cochrane's experimental warp flight in 2063.

gagh
Klingon delicacy made from serpent worms, usually served live, coming in at least 51 varieties including those which squirm, wiggle, and jump.

grand nagus
Supreme leader of the Ferengi Alliance and ultimate authority over all matters of commerce and economy, including the allocation of trade territories and other business opportunities.

Gre'thor
Klingon term for the afterlife realm where souls of the dishonored are condemned, equivalent to "Hell" or "Hades" in Human mythology. SEE: **Sto-Vo-kor**.

Great Link
Among the Founders of the Dominion, the intermingling of Changelings in their natural liquid form, a communal state of existence serving as the foundation of their society and their spirituality.

gul
Cardassian military rank roughly equivalent to a Starfleet captain, normally held by the commander of a vessel or installation; lower in rank than a legate, but higher than a glinn.

holodeck
Virtual reality system on 24th-century starships employing three-dimensional holographic projections and transporter-based replications of objects to simulate environments, characters, and narratives for use in training and recreation.

holosuite
Term used interchangeably with holodeck, but generally refers to facilities in locations other than starships, especially for commercial use such as those at Quark's Bar on Deep Space 9.

hull plating
External armor of a starship or shuttle

that minimizes damage from weapons fire and other hazards, especially when used in a polarized or ablative state.

hull polarization
Defensive technology used in starships, mainly in the 22nd century, that applies electromagnetic power to the metal hull making it more resistant to damage.

humanoid
Term describing a class of "Human-like" species with traits including intelligence, a bipedal form, generally mammalian, and originating on Class-M planets.

hypospray
Medical instrument for subcutaneous and intramuscular administration of medication using an extremely fine, high-pressure aerosuspension delivery system, eliminating the need for a needle to physically penetrate the skin.

IDIC
Acronym for "Infinite Diversity in Infinite Combinations," a Vulcan philosophy symbolized by an emblem consisting of a triangle that intersects the lower right portion of a circle.

impulse
Term referring to sublight velocity as it concerns starship propulsion; in contrast to warp drive, impulse drives use fusion reactions to generate thrust in space.

inertial dampers
Field manipulation system on starships that negates the extreme g-forces generated in rapid acceleration and deceleration of the vessel.

interlink frequency
Interactive neural signal transmitted across subspace throughout the Borg collective, connecting the minds of all drones via their interlink nodes.

interphasic rift
A puncture in the fabric of space resulting in an overlap of parallel dimensional planes, particularly referring to the artificially induced bridge to the "mirror" universe in Tholian territory.

inverse warp field
A type of subspace field generated by modified warp engines which can have the effect of "dropping anchor" at a point in space, or sealing a quantum fissure.

Jefferies tube
Service crawl-way on Federation starships providing crew with access to the ship's various systems.

kai
Title of the supreme religious leader of the Bajoran people, analogous to the Pope on Earth, elected to a life term from among, and by, the Vedek Assembly.

katra
Vulcan concept of the soul, or living spirit, which can be passed from one host to another, or to a "katric ark," through mind-melding techniques.

kiloquad
Unit of measure of data storage and transmission in Federation computer systems; larger units include megaquads, gigaquads, and teraquads.

latinum
Rare silver-colored liquid used as currency by the Ferengi Alliance and other worlds, typically in the form of ingots called "gold-pressed latinum."

LCARS
Acronym for "Library Computer Access and Retrieval System," the computer operating system and interface used on Federation starships, starbases, and space stations in the 24th century.

life-form
Any organism or entity which can be considered "alive," regardless of whether it conforms to current understandings of biology and physics.

light-year
Unit of length in astronomy equal to the distance that light travels in a vacuum in one Earth year, which is about 5.88 trillion miles or 9.46 trillion kilometers.

MACO
Acronym for "Military Assault Command Operations," a 22nd-century military organization on Earth which assisted *Enterprise* NX-01 on a joint mission to the Delphic Expanse.

metaphasic shielding
Technology that generates overlapping low-level subspace fields causing a ship to exist partially in subspace, allowing it to withstand the pressure, radiation, and energy of a star's corona.

mimetic simbiot
A type of clone created specifically to harvest tissue for the benefit of the genetic donor, with a short lifespan—just 15 days—yet still a sentient being.

mind-meld
Vulcan practice of telepathically linking minds to enable two individuals to share thoughts, memories, and consciousness; scientifically described as "synaptic pattern displacement."

molecular reversion field
A mysterious energy pattern in space that can destroy a ship's structure and disrupt certain aspects of an organism's transporter pattern, particularly genetic sequences related to growth.

nacelle
Outboard structure of a starship housing the subspace field generation coils of the vessel's warp drive engine, they are usually separated from the main body of the ship with pylons.

nanites
Microscopic mechanisms programmed to perform tasks within living cells such as intracellular surgery and DNA identification, (distinguished from "nanoprobes," the Borg term for nanites used in the assimilation process).

oo-mox
A Ferengi act of sexual foreplay that involves a gentle massaging of a Ferengi's ears (or "lobes"), considered one of their most erogenous zones.

parallel universe
A separate reality existing in an alternate space-time continuum with a different quantum signature, which on rare occasion can intersect the local universe via a quantum fissure or interphasic rift.

pattern buffer
Component of a transporter system that temporarily stores a subject's matter stream before rematerialization, allowing compensation for relative motion between the transporter and the target.

phage
A virus that infects bacteria by attaching a hollow protein tail to a cell wall and injecting DNA into the cell; also the incurable disease afflicting the Vidiians, killing thousands on a daily basis.

phaser
Acronym for PHASed Energy Rectification: a directed-energy weapon used in Starfleet either as a sidearm for individual personnel, or as ship-mounted arsenals often called phaser banks.

plasma conduit
Component of a starship's warp drive system which directs high energy electro-plasma from the warp core to the plasma injectors in the nacelle in order to power the warp coils.

Pon farr
A Vulcan time of mating, experienced every seven years when a neurochemical imbalance causes extreme emotional outbursts—and even death—if the mating instinct is not fulfilled.

positronic brain
Highly advanced computing device using the decay of positrons to form a neural network capable of artificial sentience, created by Dr. Noonian Soong for his androids Data and Lore.

praetor
Title of the leader of the Romulan Star Empire, who presides over the Romulan Senate and the Continuing Committee.

psychokinetic
Possessing the ability to move objects and manipulate physical surroundings using only thought and the power of the mind; also called telekinetic.

Qapla'
Klingon-language greeting that approximates to "success" or "good luck."

quantum signature
A unique resonance of matter at the quantum level that distinguishes a particular realm of reality from other parallel realities.

quantum slipstream
Advanced propulsion methodology developed by a Delta Quadrant species that uses a focused quantum field to break normal speed barriers, allowing a starship to exponentially exceed normal warp factors.

raktajino
Popular Klingon coffee-like beverage, served steamed or iced.

red matter
A substance, created or discovered in the late 24th century, capable of forming an artificial black hole with only a single drop when ignited.

refit
Process of overhauling a starship and re-outfitting it with upgraded equipment and technology, often to the degree of changing the structure of the vessel.

regeneration
In Borg parlance, the "sleep" mode for drones, taking place in an upright position connected to individually assigned alcoves; also used to describe the self-repair function of Borg vessels.

replicator
Device that uses transporter technology to reshape matter into new, preprogrammed forms such as food, drink, clothing, and machine parts.

runabout
A large variation on a shuttlecraft equipped for relatively short-range interstellar travel, including living quarters, replicators, a two-person transporter, and a detachable midsection module.

saucer section
The large circular or elliptical command section of many Federation starships, also known as the primary hull.

saurian
Term used to describe certain sentient species of a reptilian nature, particularly those with an evolutionary history similar to Earth dinosaurs.

secondary hull
The section of many Federation starships generally behind and below the primary hull which houses the warp drive, engineering and other support functions, and to which the nacelles are attached.

sentient
Term used synonymously with "self-aware," "intelligent," and "conscious," applied to beings who are considered evolved enough to be thinking entities deserving of rights, respect, and freedom.

shape-shifter
Generic term for any life-form with the ability to alter its form or appearance, often to mimic individuals, to hide,

or to experience a different existence. The Founders of the Dominion and the Traveler are among those who can shape-shift. SEE: **solids**.

shields
Energy fields surrounding a starship that protect it from damage by enemy attack or natural hazards; also referred to as deflectors, deflector shields, or screens.

shuttlecraft
Small, short-range vehicles intended primarily for transport from a starship to a planet's surface or within a solar system, usually possessing only impulse drive or limited warp capabilities.

shuttlepod
Smaller variation of the shuttlecraft carried aboard Federation starships, typically equipped for two crew members and limited to sublight travel across relatively short interplanetary distances.

singularity
Also called a "black hole," an object so dense that neither matter nor light can escape its gravity, created in nature by the collapse of a neutron star.

solids
Term used by some shape-shifting species, often in a pejorative sense, to describe species incapable of changing their form at will. SEE: **shape-shifter**.

spacedock
Also called drydock, a facility in orbit over a planet where a starship is constructed or can be docked for maintenance or refitting.

spatial scission
A divergence of subspace fields which can cause a region of space to "split" into two parallel planes, duplicating matter within it; the effect does not apply to antimatter.

sporocystian
Type of noncorporeal life-form believed to exist partially in the subspace domain, such as the extragalactic Nacene.

stardate
Timekeeping system used within Starfleet to provide a standard galactic temporal reference, compensating for relativistic time dilation, warp speed displacement, and other peculiarities of interstellar space travel.

Starfleet Command
Operating authority for the interstellar scientific, exploratory, and defensive agency of the United Federation of Planets, and the fleet of starships representing it. Command headquarters are located in San Francisco, United States of America, Earth.

starship
A manned spacecraft capable of viable interstellar travel through faster-than-light propulsion such as warp drive.

Sto-Vo-kor
Klingon mythological realm of the afterlife for the honored dead, equivalent to "Heaven" in Human mythology. SEE: **Gre'thor**.

subspace
Aspect of the space-time continuum outside the conventional three-dimensional framework of physics, can be utilized for faster-than-light communications and travel.

supernova
The explosion of a star at the end of its life from gravitational collapse, its brightness increases exponentially for a brief period, and then most of its mass is blown away.

temporal loop
Anomaly in the space-time continuum causing a localized fragment of time to repeat over and over, ad infinitum, sometimes with minor variations in successive iterations of the loop.

timeship
Spacecraft built to travel through time as well as space, especially those operated by Starfleet in the 29th century which navigated through time using artificially generated temporal rifts.

transporter
Technology that can instantaneously relocate persons or objects across space by converting matter to energy, beaming that energy to another location, then reassembling the subject.

transwarp
Term associated with velocities exceeding those allowed by normal warp theory, including a theoretical "infinite" speed, and a realm of subspace utilized by the Borg for artificial "conduits."

tricorder
Multipurpose handheld instrument used by Starfleet personnel for a variety of scientific, medical, and engineering applications; abbreviation of "tri-function recorder," referring to its functions of sensing, computing, and recording.

uridium
Unstable mineral used in Cardassian ship construction, generally in alloy form for their ships' sensor arrays.

vedek
High-ranking religious title on Bajor analogous to cardinal or archbishop in certain Earth religions, allowing membership in the powerful Vedek Assembly. SEE: **kai**.

warp
Term associated with faster-than-light travel using the manipulation of subspace to create an asymmetrical spatial distortion in order to propel a starship outside the restraints of conventional physics.

warp core
The main energy reactor powering the warp propulsion system of Federation starships through the intermix of matter and antimatter regulated with dilithium crystals and held in a magnetic containment field.

warp core breach
A failure of the magnetic seals and confinement fields of an antimatter storage system, leading to catastrophic destruction of a starship unless the warp core is ejected.

warp signature
A unique "fingerprint" of a warp-capable vessel created by neutrino emissions of its warp coils, making it identifiable both in terms of species origination, as well as individual ship.

wormhole
A distortion in space-time geometry creating a bridge between two separate, often distant, points in space and/or time, rarely stable or usable as a "shortcut" for starships or other vessels.

xenophobic
Exhibiting fear of, or prejudice against, other species and social groups, or anything deemed foreign or alien.

TV SERIES

The *Star Trek* television series' seasons and episodes are listed here with cast lists. For each season, writers' names are provided in full with a key to the abbreviations that are used in episode entries. Each episode has its original U.S. airdate.

Star Trek: **The Original Series**

Cast:

William Shatner as Captain James T. Kirk
Leonard Nimoy as Mr. Spock
DeForest Kelley as Dr. Leonard "Bones" McCoy
James Doohan as Montgomery Scott
Nichelle Nichols as Uhura
George Takei as Sulu
Walter Koenig as Pavel Chekov (seasons 2-3)
John Winston as Lt. Kyle
Majel Barrett as Christine Chapel

Season 1

Writers: George Clayton Johnson (**GCJ**); D.C. Fontana (**DCF**); Gene Roddenberry (**GR**); Samuel A. Peeples (**SAP**); John D.F. Black (**JDFB**); Richard Matheson (**RM**); Stephen Kandel (**SK**); Robert Bloch (**RBh**); Adrian Spies (**AS**); S. Bar-David (**SBD**); Jerry Sohl (**JS**); Barry Trivers (**BT**); Paul Schneider (**PS**); Theodore Sturgeon (**TS**); Oliver Crawford (**OC**); Gene L. Coon (**GLC**); Fredric Brown (**FB**); Don M. Mankiewicz (**DMM**); Steven W. Carabatsos (**SWC**); Boris Sobelman (**BS**); Carey Wilber (**CW**); Robert Hammer (**RH**); Nathan Butler (**NB**); Don Ingalls (**DI**); Harlan Ellison (**HE**)

Episodes:

1. The Man Trap; GCJ; Sep 8, 1966 **2. Charlie X;** DCF (teleplay), GR (story); Sep 15, 1966 **3. Where No Man Has Gone Before;** SAP; Sep 22, 1966 **4. The Naked Time;** JDFB; Sep 29, 1966 **5. The Enemy Within;** RM; Oct 6, 1966 **6. Mudd's Women;** SK (teleplay), GR (story); Oct 13, 1966 **7. What Are Little Girls Made Of?;** RBh; Oct 20, 1966 **8. Miri;** AS; Oct 27, 1966 **9. Dagger of the Mind;** SBD; Nov 3, 1966 **10. The Corbomite Maneuver;** JS; Nov 10, 1966 **11. The Menagerie, Part I;** GR; Nov 17, 1966 **12. The Menagerie, Part II;** GR; Nov 24, 1966 **13. The Conscience of the King;** BT; Dec 8, 1966 **14. Balance of Terror;** PS; Dec 15, 1966 **15. Shore Leave;** TS; Dec 29, 1966 **16. The Galileo Seven;** OC and SBD (teleplay), OC (story) Jan 5, 1967 **17. The Squire of Gothos;** PS; Jan 12, 1967 **18. Arena;** GLC (teleplay), GLC (story); Jan 19, 1967 **19. Tomorrow Is Yesterday;** DCF; Jan 26, 1967 **20. Court Martial;** DMM and SWC (teleplay), DMM (story); Feb 2, 1967 **21. The Return of the Archons;** BS (teleplay), GR (story); Feb 9, 1967 **22. Space Seed;** GLC and CW (teleplay), CW (story); Feb 16, 1967 **23. A Taste of Armageddon;** RH and GLC (teleplay), RH (story); Feb 23, 1967 **24. This Side of Paradise;** DCF (teleplay), NB and DCF (story); Mar 2, 1967 **25. The Devil in the Dark;** GLC; Mar 9, 1967 **26. Errand of Mercy;** GLC; Mar 23, 1967 **27. The Alternative Factor;** DI; Mar 30, 1967 **28. The City on the Edge of Forever;** HE; Apr 6, 1967 **29. Operation— Annihilate!;** SWC; Apr 13, 1967

Season 2

Writers: Theodore Sturgeon (**TS**); Gilbert Ralston (**GRn**); Gene Roddenberry (**GR**); John Meredyth Lucas (**JML**); Jerome Bixby (**JB**); Max Ehrlich (**ME**); Gene L. Coon (**GLC**); Norman Spinrad (**NSd**); Robert Bloch (**RBh**); Stephen Kandel (**SK**); D.C. Fontana (**DCF**); David P. Harmon (**DPH**); Art Wallace (**AW**); David Gerrold (**DG**); Margaret Armen (**MA**); Robert Sabaroff (**RS**); Jud Crucis (**JC**); John Kingsbridge (**JK**); Laurence N. Wolfe (**LNW**)

Episodes:

30. Amok Time; TS; Sep 15, 1967 **31. Who Mourns for Adonais?;** GRn; Sep 22, 1967 **32. The Changeling;** JML; Sep 29, 1967 **33. Mirror, Mirror;** JB; Oct 6, 1967 **34. The Apple;** ME and GLC (teleplay); ME (story); Oct 13, 1967 **35. The Doomsday Machine;** NSd; Oct 20, 1967 **36. Catspaw;** RBh; Oct 27, 1967 **37. I, Mudd;** SK; Nov 3, 1967 **38. Metamorphosis;** GLC; Nov 10, 1967 **39. Journey to Babel;** DCF; Nov 17, 1967 **40. Friday's Child;** DCF; Dec 1, 1967 **41. The Deadly Years;** DPH; Dec 8, 1967 **42. Obsession;** AW; Dec 15, 1967 **43. Wolf in the Fold;** RBh; Dec 22, 1967 **44. The Trouble with Tribbles;** DG; Dec 29, 1967 **45. The Gamesters of Triskelion;** MA; Jan 5, 1968 **46. A Piece of the Action;** DPH and GLC (teleplay); DPH (story); Jan 12, 1968 **47. The Immunity Syndrome;** RS; Jan 19, 1968 **48. A Private Little War;** GR (teleplay); JC (story); Feb 2, 1968 **49. Return to Tomorrow;** JK; Feb 9, 1968 **50. Patterns of Force;** JML; Feb 16, 1968 **51. By Any Other Name;** DCF and JB (teleplay); JB (story); Feb 23, 1968 **52. The Omega Glory;** GR; Mar 1, 1968 **53. The Ultimate Computer;** DCF (teleplay); LNW (story); Mar 8, 1968 **54. Bread and Circuses;** GR & GLC; Mar 15, 1968 **55. Assignment: Earth;** AW (teleplay); GR & AW (story); Mar 29, 1968

Season 3

Writers: Lee Cronin (**LC**); D.C. Fontana (**DCF**); Margaret Armen (**MA**); Edward J. Lakso (**EJL**); Jean Lisette Aroeste (**JLA**); Jerome Bixby (**JB**); Rik Vollaerts (**RV**); Judy Burns (**JBs**); Chet Richards (**CR**); Meyer Dolinsky (**MD**); Arthur Heinemann (**AH**); Joyce Muskat (**JM**); John Meredyth Lucas (**JML**); Lee Erwin (**LE**); Jerry Sohl (**JS**); Oliver Crawford (**OC**); George F. Slavin (**GFS**); Stanley Adams (**SA**); Michael Richards (**MR**); Jeremy Tarcher (**JT**); Shari Lewis (**SL**); David Gerrold (**DG**); Gene Roddenberry (**GR**); Arthur Singer (**ASr**)

Episodes:

56. Spock's Brain; LC; Sep 20, 1968 **57. The Enterprise Incident;** DCF; Sep 27, 1968 **58. The Paradise Syndrome;** MA; Oct 4, 1968 **59. And the Children Shall Lead;** EJL; Oct 11, 1968 **60. Is There in Truth No Beauty?;** JLA; Oct 18, 1968 **61. Spectre of the Gun;** LC, Oct 25, 1968 **62. Day of the Dove;** JB; Nov 1, 1968 **63. For the World Is Hollow and I Have Touched the Sky;** RV; Nov 8, 1968 **64. The Tholian Web;** JBs and CR; Nov 15, 1968 **65. Plato's Stepchildren;** MD; Nov 22, 1968 **66. Wink of an Eye;** AH (teleplay); LC (story); Nov 29, 1968 **67. The Empath;** JM; Dec 6, 1968 **68. Elaan of Troyius;** JML; Dec 20, 1968 **69. Whom Gods Destroy;** LE (teleplay); LE and JS (story); Jan 3, 1969 **70. Let That Be Your Last Battlefield;** OC (teleplay); LC (story); Jan 10, 1969 **71. The Mark of Gideon;** GFS and SA; Jan 17, 1969 **72. That Which Survives;** JML (teleplay); MR (story); Jan 24, 1969 **73. The Lights of Zetar;** JT and SL; Jan 31, 1969 **74. Requiem for Methuselah;** JB; Feb 14, 1969 **75. The Way to Eden;** AH (teleplay); MR and AH (story); Feb 21, 1969 **76. The Cloud Minders;** MA (teleplay); DG and OC (story); Feb 28, 1969 **77. The Savage Curtain;** AH and GR (teleplay); GR (story); Mar 7, 1969 **78. All Our Yesterdays;** JLA; Mar 14, 1969 **79. Turnabout Intruder;** ASr (teleplay); GR (story); Jun 3, 1969

Star Trek: The Animated Series

Cast:

William Shatner as Captain James T. Kirk
Leonard Nimoy as Mr. Spock
DeForest Kelley as Dr. Leonard "Bones" McCoy
James Doohan as Montgomery Scott and Arex
Nichelle Nichols as Uhura
George Takei as Sulu
Majel Barrett as Christine Chapel and M'Ress

Season 1

Writers: Samuel A. Peeples (**SAP**); D.C. Fontana (**DCF**); Marc Daniels (**MDs**); Margaret Armen (**MA**); David Gerrold (**DG**); James Schmerer (**JSr**); Walter Koenig (**WK**); Larry Brody (**LB**); Chuck Menville (**CM**); Len Janson (**LJ**); Stephen Kandel (**SK**); Paul Schneider (**PS**); Joyce Perry (**JP**); Margaret Armen (**MA**); Larry Niven (**LN**); David P. Harmon (**DPH**)

Episodes:

1. Beyond the Farthest Star; SAP; Sep 8, 1973 **2. Yesteryear;** DCF; Sep 15, 1973 **3. One of Our Planets Is Missing;** MDs; Sep 22, 1973 **4. The Lorelei Signal;** MA; Sep 29, 1973 **5. More Tribbles, More Troubles;** DG; Oct 6, 1973 **6. The Survivor;** JSr; Oct 13, 1973 **7. The Infinite Vulcan;** WK; Oct 20, 1973 **8. The Magicks of Megas-Tu;** LB; Oct 27, 1973 **9. Once Upon a Planet;** CM and LJ; Nov 3, 1973 **10. Mudd's Passion;** SK; Nov 10, 1973 **11. The Terratin Incident;** PS; Nov 17, 1973 **12. The Time Trap;** JP; Nov 24, 1973 **13. The Ambergris Element;** MA; Dec 1, 1973 **14. The Slaver Weapon;** LN; Dec 15, 1973 **15. The Eye of the Beholder;** DPH; Jan 5, 1974 **16. The Jihad;** SK; Jan 12, 1974

Season 2

Writers: Howard Weinstein (**HW**); David Gerrold (**DG**); Chuck Menville (**CM**); Dario Finelli (**DF**); Russell Bates (**RBs**); David Wise (**DW**); John Culver (**JCr**)

Episodes:
17. The Pirates of Orion; HW; Sep 7, 1974
18. Bem; DG; Sep 14, 1974 **19. The Practical Joker;** CM; Sep 21, 1974 **20. Albatross;** DF; Sep 28, 1974 **21. How Sharper Than a Serpent's Tooth;** RBs and DW; Oct 5, 1974 **22. The Counter-Clock Incident;** JCr; Oct 12, 1974

Star Trek: The Next Generation
Cast:
Patrick Stewart as Captain Jean-Luc Picard
Jonathan Frakes as Commander William Riker
LeVar Burton as Lt. Commander Geordi La Forge
Denise Crosby as Natasha Yar (season 1)
Michael Dorn as Lieutenant Worf
Gates McFadden as Dr. Beverly Crusher
(seasons 1, 3-7)
Marina Sirtis as Counselor Deanna Troi
Brent Spiner as Lt. Commander Data
Wil Wheaton as Wesley Crusher (seasons 1-4)
Diana Muldaur as Dr. Katherine Pulaski (season 2)

Season 1
Writers: D.C. Fontana (**DCF**); Gene Roddenberry (**GR**); John D.F. Black (**JDFB**); J. Michael Bingham (**JMB**); Katharyn Powers (**KP**); Michael Baron (**MB**); Herbert Wright (**HWt**); Richard Krzmeien (**RK**); Diane Duane (**DD**); Michael Reaves (**MRs**); Michael Halperin (**MH**) Worley Thorne; Ralph Willis (**RW**); Herbert J. Wright (**HWt**); Larry Forrester (**LF**); C.J. Holland (**CJH**); Gene Roddenberry (**GR**); Tracy Tormé (**TT**); Lan O'Kun (**LOK**); Robert Lewin (**RL**); Maurice Hurley (**MHy**); Patrick Barry (**PB**); Michael Michaelian (**MM**); Hannah Louise Shearer (**HLS**); Robert Sabaroff (**RS**); Karl Geurs (**KG**); Ralph Sanchez (**RSz**); Sandy Fries (**SF**); Richard Manning (**RMg**); Hans Beimler (**HB**); Joseph Stefano (**JSo**); Deborah Dean Davis (**DDD**); Deborah McIntyre (**DM**); Mona Clee (**MC**)

Episodes:
1/2. Encounter at Farpoint; DCF and GR; Sep 28, 1987 **3. The Naked Now;** JMB (teleplay); JDFB and JMB (story); Oct 5, 1987 **4. Code of Honor;** KP and MB; Oct 12, 1987 **5. The Last Outpost;** HWt (teleplay); RK (story) Oct 19, 1987 **6. Where No One Has Gone Before;** DD and MRs; Oct 26, 1987 **7. Lonely Among Us;** DCF (teleplay); MH (story); Nov 2, 1987 **8. Justice;** WT (teleplay); RW and WT (story); Nov 9, 1987 **9. The Battle;** HJW (story); Nov 16, 1987 **10. Hide and Q;** CJH and GR (teleplay); CJH (story); Nov 23, 1987 **11. Haven;** TT (teleplay); TT and LOK (story) Nov 30, 1987 **12. The Big Goodbye;** TT; Jan 11, 1988 **13. Datalore;** RL and GR (teleplay); RL and MHy (story); Jan 18, 1988 **14. Angel One;** PB; Jan 25, 1988 **15. 11001001;** MHy and RL; Feb 1, 1988 **16. Too Short a Season;** MM and DCF (teleplay); MM (story); Feb 8, 1988 **17. When the Bough Breaks;** HLS; Feb 15, 1988 **18. Home Soil;** RS (teleplay); KG & RSz and RS (story); Feb 22, 1988 **19. Coming of Age;** SF; Mar 14, 1988 **20. Heart of Glory;** MHy (teleplay); MHy and HWt & DCF (story); Mar 21, 1988 **21. The Arsenal of Freedom;** RMg and HB (teleplay); MHy and RL (story); Apr 11, 1988 **22. Symbiosis;** RL & RMg and HB (teleplay); RL (story) Apr 18, 1988 **23. Skin of Evil;** JS and HLS (teleplay); JS (story); Apr 25, 1988 **24. We'll Always Have Paris;** DDD and HLS; May 2, 1988 **25. Conspiracy;** TT (teleplay); RS (story) May 9, 1988 **26. The Neutral Zone;** MH (teleplay); DM & MC (story); May 16, 1988

Season 2
Writers: Jaron Summers (**JSs**); Jon Povill (**JPl**); Jack B. Sowards (**JBS**); Maurice Hurley (**MHy**); Brian Alan Lane (**BAL**); Burton Armus (**BA**); Les Menchen (**LM**); Lance Dickson (**LD**); David Landsberg (**DL**); Jacqueline Zambrano (**JZ**); Tracy Tormé (**TT**); Richard Manning (**RMg**); Hans Beimler (**HB**); John Mason (**JMn**); Mike Gray (**MG**); Wanda M. Haight (**WMH**); Gregory Amos (**GA**); Melinda M. Snodgrass (**MMS**); Scott Rubenstein (**SR**); Leonard Mlodinow (**LMw**) Steve Gerber (**SG**); Beth Woods (**BW**); Keith Mills (**KM**); Kurt Michael Bensmiller (**KMB**); David Assael (**DA**); Robert L. McCullough (**RLM**); Hannah Louise Shearer (**HLS**); Terry Devereaux (**TD**); Thomas H. Calder (**THC**); David Kemper (**DK**)

Episodes:
27. The Child; JSs & JPl and MHy; Nov 21, 1988 **28. Where Silence Has Lease;** JBS; Nov 28, 1988 **29. Elementary, Dear Data;** BAL; Dec 5, 1988 **30. The Outrageous Okona;** BA (teleplay); LM & LD & DL (story); Dec 12, 1988 **31. Loud as a Whisper;** JZ; Jan 9, 1989 **32. The Schizoid Man;** TT (teleplay); RM & HB (story); Jan 23, 1989 **33. Unnatural Selection;** JMn and MG; Jan 30, 1989 **34. A Matter of Honor;** BA (teleplay); WMH & GA and BA (story) Feb 6, 1989 **35. The Measure of a Man;** MMS; Feb 13, 1989 **36. The Dauphin;** SR & LMw; Feb 20, 1989 **37. Contagion;** SG & BW; Mar 20, 1989 **38. The Royale;** KM; Mar 27, 1989 **39. Time Squared;** MHy (teleplay); KMB (story); Apr 3, 1989 **40. The Icarus Factor;** DA and RLM (teleplay); DA (story); Apr 24, 1989 **41. Pen Pals;** MMS (teleplay); HLS (story); May 1, 1989; **42. Q Who;** MHy; May 8, 1989 **43. Samaritan Snare;** RLM; May 15, 1989 **44. Up the Long Ladder;** MMS; May 22, 1989 **45. Manhunt;** TD; Jun 19, 1989 **46. The Emissary;** RMg & HB (teleplay); RMg & HB and THC (story) Jun 26, 1989 **47. Peak Performance;** DK; Jul 10, 1989 **48. Shades of Gray;** MHy and RMg & HB (teleplay); MHy (story); Jul 17, 1989

Season 3
Writers: Michael Piller (**MP**); Michael Wagner (**MW**); Melinda M. Snodgrass (**MMS**); Richard Manning (**RMg**); Hans Beimler (**HB**); Ronald D. Moore (**RDM**); Ron Roman (**RR**); Richard Danus (**RD**); David Kemper (**DK**); Hannah Louise Shearer (**HLS**); Sam Rolfe (**SRe**); Robin Bernheim (**RB**); Ed Zuckerman (**EZ**); Ira Steven Behr (**ISB**); Trent Christopher Ganino (**TCG**); Eric A. Stillwell (**EAS**); René Echevarria (**RE**); W. Reed Moran (**WRM**); Drew Deighan (**DDn**); Dennis Putman Bailey (**DPB**); David Bischoff (**DB**); Sally Caves (**SC**); Shari Goodhartz (**SGz**); Peter S. Beagle (**PSB**); Fred Bronson (**FBn**); Susan Sackett (**SS**); Hilary J. Bader (**HJB**)

Episodes:
49. Evolution; MP (teleplay); MP & MW (story); Sep 25, 1989 **50. The Ensigns of Command;** MMS; Oct 2, 1989 **51. The Survivors;** MW Oct 9, 1989 **52. Who Watches the Watchers;** RMg & HB Oct 16, 1989 **53. The Bonding;** RDM; Oct 23, 1989 **54. Booby Trap;** RR and MW & RR (story) Oct 30, 1989 **55. The Enemy;** DK & MP; Nov 6, 1989 **56. The Price;** HLS; Nov 13, 1989 **57. The Vengeance Factor;** SRe; Nov 20, 1989 **58. The Defector;** RDM Jan 1, 1990

59. The Hunted; RB; Jan 8, 1990 **60. The High Ground;** MMS; Jan 29, 1990 **61. Déjà Q;** RD; Feb 5, 1990 **62. A Matter of Perspective;** EZ; Feb 12, 1990 **63. Yesterday's Enterprise;** ISB & RMg & HB & RDM (teleplay); TCG & EAS (story) Feb 19, 1990 **64. The Offspring;** RE; Mar 12, 1990 **65. Sins of the Father;** RDM & WRM (teleplay); DDn (story); Mar 19, 1990 **66. Allegiance;** RMg & HB; Mar 26, 1990 **67. Captain's Holiday;** ISB; Apr 2, 1990 **68. Tin Man;** DPB & DB; Apr 23, 1990 **69. Hollow Pursuits;** SC; Apr 30, 1990 **70. The Most Toys;** SG; May 7, 1990 **71. Sarek;** PSB (from an unpublished story by Marc Cushman & Jake Jacobs); May 14, 1990 **72. Ménage à Troi;** FBn & SS; May 28, 1990 **73. Transfigurations;** RE; Jun 4, 1990 **74. The Best of Both Worlds;** MP; Jun 18, 1990

Season 4
Writers: Michael Piller (**MP**); Ronald D. Moore (**RDM**); Rick Berman (**RBn**); John Whelpley (**JW**); Jeri Taylor (**JTr**); Ralph Phillips (**RP**); Lee Sheldon (**LS**); Joe Menosky (**JMy**); Thomas Perry (**TP**); Jo Perry (**JPy**); Brannon Braga (**BB**); Drew Deighan (**DDn**); J. Larry Carroll (**JLC**); David Bennett Carren (**DBC**); Kacey Arnold-Ince (**KAI**); Alan J. Adler (**AJA**); Vanessa Greene (**VG**); Harold Apter (**HA**); Stuart Charno (**StCo**); Sara Charno (**SaCo**); Cy Chermak (**CC**); Philip LaZebnik (**PLZ**); William Douglas Lansford (**WDL**); Bruce D. Arthurs (**BDA**); Dennis Russell Bailey (**DRB**); David Bischoff (**DB**); Marc Scott Zicree (**MSZ**); Maurice Hurley (**MHy**); Thomas Kartozian (**TK**); Pamela Douglas (**PD**); Shari Goodhartz (**SGz**); Timothy DeHaas (**TDH**); Ira Steven Behr (**ISB**) Randee Russell (**RRl**); Peter Allan Fields (**PAF**); Ted Roberts (**TR**); Michel Horvat (**RE**); Ken Schafer (**KS**); Timothy DeHaas (**TDH**)

Episodes:
75. The Best of Both Worlds: Part II; MP; Sep 24, 1990 **76. Family;** RDM; Oct 1, 1990 **77. Brothers;** RBn; Oct 8, 1990 **78. Suddenly Human;** JW & JTr (teleplay); RP (story); Oct 15, 1990 **79. Remember Me;** LS; Oct 22, 1990 **80. Legacy;** JMy; Oct 29, 1990 **81. Reunion;** TP & JPy & RDM and BB (teleplay); DDn & TP and JPy (story); Nov 5, 1990 **82. Future Imperfect;** JLC & DBC; Nov 12, 1990 **83. Final Mission;** KAI and JTr (teleplay); KAI (story); Nov 19, 1990 **84. The Loss;** HJB & AJA and VG (teleplay); HJB (story); Dec 31, 1990 **85. Data's Day;** HA and RDM (teleplay); HA (story); Jan 7, 1991 **86. The Wounded;** JTr (teleplay); StCo and SaCo and CC (story); Jan 28, 1991 **87. Devil's Due;** PLZ (teleplay); PLZ and WDL (story); Feb 4, 1991 **88. Clues;** BDA and JMy (teleplay); BDA (story); Feb 11, 1991 **89. First Contact;** DRB & DB and JMy & RDM and MP (teleplay); MSZ (story); Feb 18, 1991 **90. Galaxy's Child;** MHy (teleplay); TK (story); Mar 11, 1991 **91. Night Terrors;** PD and JTr (teleplay); SGz (story); Mar 18, 1991 **92. Identity Crisis;** BB (teleplay); TDH (story) Mar 25, 1991 **93. The Nth Degree;** JMy; Apr 1, 1991 **94. Qpid;** ISB (teleplay); RRl and ISB (story) Apr 22, 1991 **95. The Drumhead;** JTr; Apr 29, 1991 **96. Half a Life;** PAF (teleplay); TR and PAF (story); May 6, 1991 **97. The Host;** MHt; May 13, 1991 **98. The Mind's Eye;** RE (teleplay); KS and RE (story); May 27, 1991 **99. In Theory;** JMy and RDM; Jun 3, 1991 **100. Redemption I;** RDM Jun 17, 1991

Season 5

Writers:
Ronald D. Moore (**RDM**); Joe Menosky (**JMy**); Philip LaZebnik (**PLZ**); Michael Piller (**MP**); Rick Berman (**RBn**); Jeri Taylor (**JTr**); Lawrence V. Conley (**LVC**); Ron Jarvis (**RJ**); Philip A. Scorza (**PAS**); Brannon Braga (**BB**); Susan Sackett (**SS**); Fred Bronson (**FBn**); Grant Rosenberg (**GRg**); Sara Charno (**SaCo**); Stuart Charno (**StCo**); Hilary J. Bader (**HJB**); Pamela Gray (**PG**); Shari Goodhartz (**SGz**); T. Michael (**TM**); Adam Belanoff (**AB**); James Kahn (**JKn**); Barry Schkolnick (**BSk**); Paul Schiffer (**PSr**); René Balcer (**RBr**); Herbert J. Wright (**HJW**); Paul Ruben (**PR**); Maurice Hurley (**MHy**); Naren Shankar (**NS**); Peter Allan Fields (**PAF**); Gary Perconte (**GP**); Edithe Swensen (**ES**); René Echevarria (**RE**); Jean Louise Matthias (**JLM**); Ronald Wilkerson (**RWn**); Richard Fliegel (**RF**); Morgan Gendel (**MGl**)

Episodes:
101. Redemption II; RDM; Sep 23, 1991 **102. Darmok;** JMy (teleplay); PLZ and JMy (story); Sep 30, 1991 **103. Ensign Ro;** MP (teleplay); RBn & MP (story); Oct 7, 1991 **104. Silicon Avatar;** JTr (teleplay); LVC (story); Oct 14, 1991 **105. Disaster;** RDM (teleplay); RJ & PAS (story) Oct 21, 1991 **106. The Game;** BB (teleplay); SS & FBn and BB (story); Oct 28, 1991 **107. Unification I;** JTr (teleplay); RBn and MP (story); Nov 4, 1991 **108. Unification II;** MP (teleplay); RBn and MP (story) Nov 11, 1991 **109. A Matter of Time;** RBn Nov 18, 1991 **110. New Ground;** GRs (teleplay); SaCo and StCo (story); Jan 6, 1992 **111. Hero Worship;** JM (teleplay); HJB (story); Jan 27, 1992 **112. Violations;** PG and JTr (teleplay); SGz and TM and PG (story); Feb 3, 1992 **113. The Masterpiece Society;** AB and MP (teleplay); JK and AB (story); Feb 10, 1992 **114. Conundrum;** BSk (teleplay); PSr (story); Feb 17, 1992 **115. Power Play;** RBr and HJW & BB (teleplay); PR and MHy (story) Feb 24, 1992 **116. Ethics;** RDM (teleplay); SaCo & StCo (story); Mar 2, 1992 **117. The Outcast;** JTr Mar 16, 1992 **118. Cause and Effect;** BB; Mar 23, 1992 **119. The First Duty;** RDM & NS; Mar 30, 1992 **120. Cost of Living;** PAF; Apr 20, 1992 **121. The Perfect Mate;** GP and MP (teleplay); RE and GP (story); Apr 27, 1992 **122. Imaginary Friend;** ES and JTr (teleplay); JLM & RWn and RF (story); May 4, 1992 **123. I, Borg;** RE; May 11, 1992 **124. The Next Phase;** RDM; May 18, 1992 **125. The Inner Light;** MGl and PAF (teleplay); MGl (story); Jun 1, 1992 **126. Time's Arrow Part I;** JMy and MP (teleplay); JMy (story); Jun 15, 1992

Season 6

Writers: Jeri Taylor (**JTr**); Joe Menosky (**JMy**); Brannon Braga (**BB**); Frank Abatemarco (**FA**); Ronald D. Moore (**RDM**); Jean Louise Matthias (**JLM**); Ronald Wilkerson (**RWn**); René Echevarria (**RE**); Allison Hock (**AHk**); Ward Botsford (**WB**); Diana Dru Botsford (**DDB**); Michael Piller (**MP**); Robert Hewitt Wolfe (**RHW**); Naren Shankar (**NS**); L.J. Scott (**LJS**); Frank Abatemarco (**FA**); Morgan Gendel (**MGl**); James E. Brooks (**JEB**); Michael Medlock (**MMk**)

Episodes:
127. Time's Arrow, Part II; JTr (teleplay); JMy (story); Sep 21, 1992 **128. Realm of Fear;** BB; Sep 28, 1992 **129. Man of the People;** FA; Oct 5, 1992

130. Relics; RDM; Oct 12, 1992 **131. Schisms;** BB (teleplay); JLM & RWn (story); Oct 19, 1992 **132. True Q;** RE; Oct 26, 1992 **133. Rascals;** AHk (teleplay); WB & DDB and MP (story); Nov 2, 1992 **134. A Fistful of Datas;** RHW and BB (teleplay); RHW (story); Nov 9, 1992 **135. The Quality of Life;** NS (teleplay); LJS (story); Nov 16, 1992 **136. Chain of Command, Part I;** RDM (teleplay); FA (story); Dec 14, 1992 **137. Chain of Command, Part II;** FA; Dec 21, 1992 **138. Ship in a Bottle;** RE; Jan 25, 1993 **139. Aquiel;** BB & RDM (teleplay); JTr (story); Feb 1, 1993 **40. Face of the Enemy;** NS (teleplay); RE (story); Feb 8, 1993 **141. Tapestry;** RDM; Feb 15, 1993 **142. Birthright, Part I;** BB; Feb 22, 1993 **143. Birthright, Part II;** RE; Mar 1, 1993 **144. Starship Mine;** MGl; Mar 29, 1993 **145. Lessons;** RWn & JLM; Apr 5, 1993 **146. The Chase;** JMy (teleplay); RDM & JMy (story); Apr 26, 1993 **147. Frame of Mind;** BB; May 3, 1993 **148. Suspicions;** JMy and NS; May 10, 1993 **149. Rightful Heir;** RDM (teleplay); JEB (story) May 17, 1993 **150. Second Chances;** RE (teleplay); MMk (story) May 24, 1993 **151. Timescape;** BB; Jun 14, 1993 **152. Descent, Part I;** RDM (teleplay); JTr (story); Jun 21, 1993

Season 7

Writers: René Echevarria (**RE**); Jeanne Carrigan-Fauci (**JCF**); Lisa Rich (**LR**); Roger Eschbacher (**RER**); Jaq Greenspon (**JG**); Joe Menosky (**JMy**); Naren Shankar (**NS**); Christopher Hatton (**CH**); Ronald D. Moore (**RDM**); Brannon Braga (**BB**); Jeri Taylor (**JTy**); Hilary J. Bader (**HJB**); Nicholas Sagan (**NSn**); Dan Koeppel (**DKl**); Spike Steingasser (**SSr**); Jean Louise Matthias (**JLM**); Ronald Wilkerson (**RWn**); Shawn Piller (**SP**); Antonia Napoli (**AN**); Mark Kalbfeld (**MK**)

Episodes:
153. Descent, Part II; RE; Sept 20, 1993 **154. Liaisons;** JCF & LR (teleplay); RE & JG (story); Sep 27, 1993 **155. Interface;** JMy; Oct 4, 1993 **156. Gambit, Part I;** NS (teleplay); CH and NS (story); Oct 11, 1993 **157. Gambit, Part II;** RDM (teleplay); NS (story) Oct 18, 1993 **158. Phantasms;** BB; Oct 25, 1993 **159. Dark Page;** HJB; Nov 1, 1993 **160. Attached;** NSn; Nov 8, 1993 **161. Force of Nature;** NS; Nov 15, 1993 **162. Inheritance;** DKl and RE (teleplay); DKl (story) Nov 22, 1993 **163. Parallels;** BB; Nov 29, 1993 **164. The Pegasus;** RDM; Jan 10, 1994 **165. Homeward;** NS (teleplay); SSr (story) based on material by William N. Stape; Jan 17, 1994 **66. Sub Rosa;** BB (teleplay); JTy (story) based on material by Jeanna F. Gallo; Jan 31, 1994 **167. Lower Decks;** RE (teleplay); RWn and JLM (story) Feb 7, 1994 **168. Thine Own Self;** RDM (teleplay); CH (story); Feb 14, 1994 **169. Masks;** JMy; Feb 21, 1994 **170. Eye of the Beholder;** RE (teleplay); BB (story); Feb 28, 1994 **171. Genesis;** BB; Mar 21, 1994 **172. Journey's End;** RDM (teleplay); SP and AN (story) Mar 28, 1994 **173. Firstborn;** RE (teleplay); MK (story) Apr 25, 1994 **174. Bloodlines;** NSn; May 2, 1994 **175. Emergence;** JMy (teleplay); BB (story); May 9, 1994 **176. Preemptive Strike;** RE (teleplay); NS (story) May 16, 1994 **177/178. All Good Things...;** RDM & BB; May 23, 1994

Star Trek: Deep Space 9

Cast:
Avery Brooks as Commander/Captain Sisko
René Auberjonois as Odo
Nicole de Boer as Lieutenant Dax (season 7)
Michael Dorn as Lt. Commander Worf (seasons 4-7)
Terry Farrell as Lieutenant/Lt. Commander Dax (seasons 1-6)
Cirroc Lofton as Jake Sisko
Colm Meaney as Chief O'Brien
Armin Shimerman as Quark
Alexander Siddig as Doctor Bashir
Nana Visitor as Major Kira

Season 1

Writers: Michael Piller (**MP**); Rick Berman (**RBn**); Katharyn Powers (**KP**); Gerald Sanford (**GS**); Michael McGreevey (**MMG**); Naren Shankar (**NS**); Sally Caves (**SC**); Ira Steven Behr (**ISB**); Jill Sherman Donner (**JSD**); Robert Hewitt Wolfe (**RHW**); Hannah Louise Shearer (**HLS**); D.C. Fontana (**DCF**); Peter Allan Fields (**PAF**); Morgan Gendel (**MGl**); Frederick Rappaport (**FR**); Lisa Rich (**LR**); Jeanne Carrigan-Fauci (**JCF**); David Livingston (**DLn**); Sam Rolfe (**SRe**); Richard Danus (**RD**); Evan Carlos Somers (**ECS**); Hilary J. Bader (**HJB**); Kurt Michael Bensmiller (**KMB**); Nell McCue Crawford (**NMCC**) William L. Crawford (**WLC**); Don Carlos Dunaway (**DCD**); Jim Trombetta (**JTa**); Joe Menosky (**JMy**)

Episodes:
1/2. Emissary; MP (teleplay); RBn and MP (story) Jan 3, 1993 **3. Past Prologue;** KP; Jan 10, 1993 **4. A Man Alone;** MP (teleplay); GS & MP (story) Jan 17, 1993 **5. Babel;** MMG & NS (teleplay); SC & ISB (story); Jan 24, 1993 **6. Captive Pursuit;** JSD and MP (teleplay); JSD (story); Jan 31, 1993 **7. Q-Less;** RHW; (teleplay); HLS (story); Feb 7, 1993 **8. Dax;** DCF and PAF (teleplay); PAF (story); Feb 14, 1993 **9. The Passenger;** MGl & RHW and MP (teleplay); MGl (story); Feb 21, 1993 **10. Move Along Home;** FR and LR & JCF (teleplay); MP (story); Mar 14, 1993 **11. The Nagus;** ISB (teleplay); DL (story); Mar 21, 1993 **12. Vortex;** SRe; Apr 18, 1993 **13. Battle Lines;** RD and ECS (teleplay); HJB (story) Apr 25, 1993 **14. The Storyteller;** KMB and ISB (teleplay); KMB (story); May 2, 1993 **15. Progress;** PAF May 9, 1993 **16. If Wishes Were Horses;** NMCC & WLC and MP (teleplay); NMCC & WLC (story); May 16, 1993 **17. The Forsaken;** DCD and MP (teleplay); JTa (story); May 23, 1993; **18. Dramatis Personae;** JMy May 30, 1993 **19. Duet;** PAF (teleplay); LR & JCF (story) Jun 13, 1993 **20. In the Hands of the Prophets;** RHW; Jun 20, 1993

Season 2

Writers: Ira Steven Behr (**ISB**); Jeri Taylor (**JTr**); Peter Allan Fields (**PAF**); Michael Piller (**MP**); John Whelpley (**JW**); Robert Hewitt Wolfe (**RHW**); James Crocker (**JaCr**); Gene Wolande (**GW**); John Wright (**JWt**); Evan Carlos Somers (**ECS**); Steven Baum (**SB**); Hilary J. Bader (**HJB**); Mark Gehred-O'Connell (**MGOC**); Frederick Rappaport (**FR**); Gabe Essoe (**GE**); Kelley Miles (**KMs**); Joe Menosky (**JMy**); Jim Trombetta (**JTa**); Bill Dial (**BD**); Morgan Gendel (**MGl**); Paul Robert Coyle (**PRC**); Jeff King (**JKg**); Richard Manning (**RMg**); Hans Beimler (**HB**); Flip Kobler (**FK**); Cindy Marcus (**CMs**); Rick Berman (**RBn**); Gary Holland (**GH**)

Episodes:
21. The Homecoming; ISB (teleplay); JTr and ISB (story); Sep 26, 1993 **22. The Circle;** PAF; Oct 3, 1993 **23. The Siege;** MP; Oct 10, 1993 **24. Invasive Procedures;** JW and RHW (teleplay); JW (story) Oct 17, 1993 **25. Cardassians;** JaCr (teleplay); GW & JWt (story); Oct 24, 1993 **26. Melora;** ECS and SB and MP & JaCr (teleplay); ECS (story); Oct 31, 1993 **27. Rules of Acquisition;** ISB (teleplay); HJB (story); Nov 7, 1993 **28. Necessary Evil;** PAF; Nov 14, 1993 **29. Second Sight;** MGOC & ISB and RHW (teleplay); MGOC (story); Nov 21, 1993 **30. Sanctuary;** FR (teleplay); GE & KMs (story); Nov 28, 1993 **31. Rivals;** JMy (teleplay); JTa & MP (story) Jan 2, 1994 **32. The Alternate;** BD (teleplay); JTa and BD (story) Jan 9, 1994; **33. Armageddon Game;** MGl; Jan 30, 1994 **34. Whispers;** PRC; Feb 6, 1994 **35. Paradise;** JKy and RHW & HB (teleplay); JTa and JaCr (story); Feb 13, 1994 **36. Shadowplay;** RHW; Feb 20, 1994 **37. Playing God;** JTa and MP (teleplay); JTa (story); Feb 27, 1994 **38. Profit and Loss;** FK and CMs; Mar 20, 1994 **39. Blood Oath;** PAF (from an idea by Andrea Moore Alton); Mar 27, 1994 **40. The Maquis, Part I;** JaCr (teleplay); RBn and MP & JTr and JaCr (story); Apr 24, 1994 **41. The Maquis, Part II;** ISB (teleplay); RBn and MP & JTr and ISB (story); May 1, 1994 **42. The Wire;** RHW; May 8, 1994 **43. Crossover;** PAF and MP (teleplay); PAF (story); May 15, 1994 **44. The Collaborator;** GH & ISB and RHW (teleplay); GH (story) May 22, 1994 **45. Tribunal;** BD; Jun 5, 1994 **46. The Jem'Hadar;** ISB; Jun 12, 1994

Season 3

Writers: Ronald D. Moore (**RDM**); Ira Steven Behr (**ISB**); Robert Hewitt Wolfe (**RHW**); Tom Benko (**TB**); René Echevarria (**RE**); Christopher Teague (**CTe**); D. Thomas Maio (**DTM**); Steve Warnek (**SW**); Mike Krohn (**MKn**); Mark Gehred-O'Connell (**MGOC**); Hilary J. Bader (**HJB**); Evan Carlos Somers (**ECS**); Philip Lazebnik (**PLZ**); James Crocker (**JaCr**); Christian Ford (**CF**); Roger Soffer (**RSr**); David S. Cohen (**DSC**); Martin A. Winer (**MAW**); John Shirley (**JSy**); Ethan H. Calk (**EHC**); Joe Menosky (**JMy**); Robert Lederman (**RLn**); David R. Long (**DRL**); Gordon Dawson (**GD**)

Episodes:
47. The Search, Part I; RDM (teleplay); ISB and RHW (story); Sep 26, 1994 **48. The Search, Part II;** ISB (teleplay); ISB and RHW (story); Oct 3, 1994 **49. The House of Quark;** RDM (teleplay); TB (story) Oct 10, 1994 **50. Equilibrium;** RE (teleplay); CTe (story) Oct 17, 1994 **51. Second Skin;** RHW; Oct 24, 1994 **52. The Abandoned;** DTM and SW; Oct 31, 1994 **53. Civil Defense;** MKn; Nov 7, 1994 **54. Meridian;** MGOC (teleplay); HJB and ECS (story); Nov 14, 1994 **55. Defiant;** RDM; Nov 21, 1994 **56. Fascination;** PLZ (teleplay); ISB and JaCa (story); Nov 28, 1994 **57. Past Tense, Part I;** RHW (teleplay); ISB and RHW (story); Jan 2, 1995 **58. Past Tense, Part II;** ISB and RE (teleplay); ISB and RHW (story); Jan 9, 1995 **59. Life Support;** RDM (teleplay); CF and RSr (story) Jan 31, 1995 **60. Heart of Stone;** ISB and RHW; Feb 6, 1995 **61. Destiny;** DSC and MAW; Feb 13, 1995 **62. Prophet Motive;** ISB and RHW; Feb 20, 1995 **63. Visionary;** JSy (teleplay); EHC (story); Feb 27, 1995 **64. Distant Voices;** ISB and JMy (teleplay); Apr 10, 1995

65. Through the Looking Glass; ISB and RHW; Apr 17, 1995 **66. Improbable Cause;** RE (teleplay); RLn & DRL (story); Apr 24, 1995 **67. The Die is Cast;** RDM; May 1, 1995 **68. Explorers;** RE (teleplay); HJB (story); May 8, 1995 **69. Family Business;** ISB and RHW; May 15, 1995 **70. Shakaar;** GD May 22, 1995 **71. Facets;** RE; Jun 12, 1995 **72. The Adversary;** ISB and RHW; Jun 19, 1995

Season 4

Writers: Ira Steven Behr (**ISB**); Robert Hewitt Wolfe (**RHW**); Michael Taylor (**MT**); Lisa Klink (**LK**); Nicholas Corea (**NC**); Toni Marberry (**TMy**); Jack Treviño (**JTo**); Ronald D. Moore (**RDM**); René Echevarria (**RE**); David Mack (**DMk**); John J. Ordover (**JJO**); Hans Beimler (**HB**); Richard Danus (**RD**); Robert Gillan (**RG**); Tom Benko (**TB**); Barbara J. Lee (**BJL**); Jenifer A. Lee (**JAL**); Jane Espenson (**JE**); David Weddle (**DWe**); Bradley Thompson (**BTn**); Daniel Keys Moran (**DKM**); Lynn Barker (**LBr**); Majel Barrett-Roddenberry (**MBR**); Mark Gehred-O'Connell (**MGOC**); Naren Shankar (**NS**); Louis P. DeSantis (**LPDS**); Robert J. Bolivar (**RJB**); George A. Brozak (**GAB**)

Episodes:
73/74. The Way of the Warrior; ISB and RHW; Oct 2, 1995 **75. The Visitor;** MT; Oct 9, 1995 **76. Hippocratic Oath;** LK (teleplay); NC and LK (story) Oct 16, 1995 **77. Indiscretion;** NC (teleplay); TMy & JTo (story); Oct 23, 1995 **78. Rejoined;** RDM and RE; (teleplay); RE (story); Oct 30, 1995 **79. Starship Down;** DMk and JJO; Nov 6, 1995 **80. Little Green Men;** ISB & RHW (teleplay); TMy & JTo (story); Nov 13, 1995 **81. The Sword of Kahless;** HB (teleplay); RD (story) Nov 20, 1995 **82. Our Man Bashir;** RDM (teleplay); RG (story); Nov 27, 1995 **83. Homefront;** ISB and RHW; Jan 1, 1996 **84. Paradise Lost;** ISB and RHW (teleplay); RDM (story); Jan 8, 1996 **85. Crossfire;** RE; Jan 29, 1996 **86. Return to Grace;** HB (teleplay); TB (story); Feb 5, 1996 **87. Sons of Mogh;** RDM; Feb 12, 1996 **88. Bar Association;** RHW and ISB (teleplay); BJL & JAL (story) Feb 19, 1996 **89. Accession;** JE; Feb 26, 1996 **90. Rules of Engagement;** RDM (teleplay); DWe & BTn (story) Apr 8, 1996 **91. Hard Time;** RHW (teleplay); DKM and LB (story); Apr 15, 1996 **92. Shattered Mirror;** ISB and HB Apr 22, 1996 **93. The Muse;** RE (teleplay); RE and MBR (story); Apr 29, 1996 **94. For the Cause;** RDM (teleplay); MGOC (story); May 6, 1996 **95. To the Death;** ISB and RHW; May 13, 1996 **96. The Quickening;** NS May 20, 1996 **97. Body Parts;** HB (teleplay); LPDS & RJB (story); Jun 10, 1996 **98. Broken Link;** ISB and RHW (teleplay); GAB (story); Jun 17, 1996

Season 5

Writers: Ira Steven Behr (**ISB**); Robert Hewitt Wolfe (**RHW**); Hans Beimler (**HB**); Pam Wigginton (**PW**); Rick Cason (**RC**); Ronald D. Moore (**RDM**); René Echevarria (**RE**); Brice R. Parker (**BRP**); David Weddle (**DWe**); Bradley Thompson (**BTn**); David R. Long (**DRL**); Robert Lederman (**RLn**); Michael Taylor (**MT**); L.J. Strom (**LJSm**); Bryan Fuller (**BF**); Peter Allan Fields (**PAF**); Jimmy Diggs (**JD**); Edmund Newton (**EN**); Robbin L. Slocum (**RLS**); Gary Holland (**GH**); Ethan H. Calk (**EHC**); Truly Barr Clark (**TBC**); Scott J. Neal (**SJN**).

Episodes:
99. Apocalypse Rising; ISB and RHW; Sep 30, 1996 **100. The Ship;** HB (teleplay); PW & RC (story) Oct 7, 1996 **101. Looking for par'Mach in All the Wrong Places;** RDM; Oct 14, 1996 **102. ...Nor the Battle to the Strong;** RE (teleplay); BRP (story); Oct 21, 1996 **103. The Assignment;** DRL & RLn (teleplay); DRL & RLn (story); Oct 28, 1996 **104. Trials and Tribble-ations;** RDM & RE (teleplay); ISB and HB & RHW (story); Nov 4, 1996 **105. Let He Who Is Without Sin...;** RHW and ISB; Nov 11, 1996 **106. Things Past;** MT; Nov 18, 1996 **107. The Ascent;** ISB and RHW; Nov 25, 1996 **108. Rapture;** HB (teleplay); LJSm (story); Dec 30, 1996 **109. The Darkness and the Light;** RDM (teleplay); BF (story); Jan 6, 1997 **110. The Begotten;** RE; Jan 27, 1997 **111. For the Uniform;** PAF; Feb 3, 1997 **112. In Purgatory's Shadow;** RHW and ISB; Feb 10, 1997 **113. By Inferno's Light;** ISB and RHW; Feb 17, 1997 **114. Doctor Bashir, I Presume?;** RDM (teleplay); JD (story); Feb 24, 1997 **115. A Simple Investigation;** RE; Mar 31, 1997 **116. Business as Usual;** BTn and DWe; Apr 7, 1997 **117. Ties of Blood and Water;** RHW (teleplay); EN & RLS (story); Apr 14, 1997 **118. Ferengi Love Songs;** ISB and HB; Apr 21, 1997 **119. Soldiers of the Empire;** RDM; Apr 28, 1997 **120. Children of Time;** RE (teleplay); GH and EHC (story); May 5, 1997 **121. Blaze of Glory;** RHW and ISB; May 12, 1997 **122. Empok Nor;** HB (teleplay); BF (story); May 19, 1997 **123. In the Cards;** RDM (teleplay); TBC & SJN (story) Jun 9, 1997 **124. Call to Arms;** ISB and RHW; Jun 16, 1997

Season 6

Writers: Ira Steven Behr (**ISB**); Hans Beimler (**HB**); Ronald D. Moore (**RDM**); Bradley Thompson (**BTn**); David Weddle (**DWe**); René Echevarria (**RE**); Michael Taylor (**MT**); Pam Pietroforte (**PP**); Mark Gehred-O'Connell (**MGOC**); Marc Scott Zicree (**MSZ**); Philip Kim (**PK**); Joe Menosky (**JMy**); Harry M. Werksman (**HMW**); Gabrielle Stanton (**GSn**)

Episodes:
125. A Time to Stand; ISB & HB; Sep 29, 1997 **126. Rocks and Shoals;** RDM; Oct 6, 1997 **127. Sons and Daughters;** BTn & DWe; Oct 13, 1997 **128. Behind the Lines;** RE; Oct 20, 1997 **129. Favor the Bold;** ISB & HB; Oct 27, 1997 **130. Sacrifice of Angels;** ISB & HB; Nov 3, 1997 **131. You are Cordially Invited...;** RDM; Nov 10, 1997 **132. Resurrection;** MT; Nov 17, 1997 **133. Statistical Probabilities;** RE (teleplay); PP (story) Nov 24, 1997 **134. The Magnificent Ferengi;** ISB & HB; Jan 1, 1998 **135. Waltz;** RDM; Jan 8, 1998; **136. Who Mourns for Morn?;** MGOC; Feb 4, 1998 **137. Far Beyond the Stars;** ISB & HB (teleplay); MSZ (story); Feb 11, 1998 **138. One Little Ship;** DWe & BTn; Feb 18, 1998 **139. Honor Among Thieves;** RE (teleplay); PK (story) Feb 25, 1998 **140. Change of Heart;** RDM; Mar 4, 1998 **141. Wrongs Darker Than Death or Night;** ISB and HB; Apr 1, 1998 **142. Inquisition;** BTn & DWe; Apr 8, 1998 **143. In the Pale Moonlight;** MT (teleplay); PAF (story); Apr 15, 1998 **144. His Way;** ISB & HB; Apr 22, 1998 **145. The Reckoning;** DWe & BTn (teleplay); HMW & GSn (story); Apr 29, 1998 **146. Valiant;** RDM; May 6, 1998 **147. Profit and Lace;** ISB & HB; May 13, 1998 **148. Time's Orphan;** DWe & BTn (teleplay); JMy (story) May 20, 1998 **149. The Sound of Her Voice;** RDM (teleplay); PP (story); Jun 10, 1998 **150. Tears of the Prophets;** ISB & HB; Jun 17, 1998

Season 7

Writers: Ira Steven Behr (**ISB**); Hans Beimler (**HB**); René Echevarria (**RE**); Ronald D. Moore (**RDM**); David Weddle (**DWe**); Bradley Thompson (**BTn**); Philip Kim (**PK**); David Mack (**DMk**); John J. Ordover (**JJO**); Spike Steingasser (**SSr**); Peter Allan Fields (**PAF**)

Episodes:
151. Image in the Sand; ISB & HB; Sep 30, 1998 **152. Shadows and Symbols;** ISB & HB; Oct 7, 1998 **153. Afterimage;** RE; Oct 14, 1998 **154. Take Me Out to the Holosuite;** RDM; Oct 21, 1998 **155. Chrysalis;** RE; Oct 28, 1998 **156. Treachery, Faith, and the Great River;** DWe & BTn (teleplay); PK (story); Nov 4, 1998 **157. Once More Unto the Breach;** RDM; Nov 11, 1998 **158. The Siege of AR-558;** ISB & HB; Nov 18, 1998 **159. Covenant;** RE; Nov 25, 1998 **160. It's Only a Paper Moon;** RDM (teleplay); DMk & JJO (story); Dec 30, 1998 **161. Prodigal Daughter;** DWe & BTn; Jan 6, 1999 **162. The Emperor's New Cloak;** ISB & HB; Feb 3, 1999 **163. Field of Fire;** RHW; Feb 10, 1999 **164. Chimera;** RE; Feb 17, 1999 **165. Badda-Bing Badda-Bang;** ISB & HB; Feb 24, 1999 **166. Inter Arma Enim Silent Leges;** RDM; Mar 3, 1999 **167. Penumbra;** RE; Apr 7, 1999 **168. 'Til Death Do Us Part;** BTn & DWe; Apr 14, 1999 **169. Strange Bedfellows;** RDM; Apr 21, 1999 **170. The Changing Face of Evil;** ISB & HB; Apr 28, 1999 **171. When It Rains...;** RE (teleplay); RE & SSr (story); May 5, 1999 **172. Tacking Into the Wind;** RDM; May 12, 1999 **173. Extreme Measures;** DWe & BTn; May 19, 1999 **174. The Dogs of War;** RE & RDM (teleplay); PAF (story); May 26, 1999 **175/176. What You Leave Behind;** ISB & HB; Jun 2, 1999

Star Trek: Voyager

Cast:
Kate Mulgrew as Captain Kathryn Janeway
Robert Beltran as Chakotay
Roxann Dawson as B'Elanna Torres
Robert Duncan McNeill as Tom Paris
Jennifer Lien as Kes (season 1-3)
Ethan Phillips as Neelix
Robert Picardo as The Doctor
Tim Russ as Tuvok
Jeri Ryan as Seven of Nine (season 4-7)
Garrett Wang as Harry Kim

Season 1

Writers: Michael Piller (**MP**); Jeri Taylor (**JTr**); Rick Berman (**RBn**); Brannon Braga (**BB**); Jim Trombetta (**JTa**); David Kemper (**DK**); Skye Dent (**SD**); Timothy DeHaas (**TDH**) Tom Szollosi (**TSi**); Bill Dial (**BID**); Hilary J. Bader (**HJB**); Evan Carlos Somers (**ECS**); Michael Perricone (**MPe**); Greg Elliot (**GEt**); David R. George III (**DRG**); Eric A. Stillwell (**EAS**); Chris Abbott (**CA**); Paul Robert Coyle (**PRC**); Naren Shankar (**NS**); Joe Menosky (**JMy**); Kenneth Biller (**KB**); Jonathan Glassner (**JGr**); Jack Klein (**JaKn**); Karen Klein (**KK**); James Thornton (**JTn**); Scott Nimerfro (**SN**); Ronald Wilkerson (**RWn**); Jean Louise Matthias (**JLM**)

Episodes:
1/2. Caretaker; MP & JTr (teleplay); RBn & MP & JT (story) Jan 16, 1995 **3. Parallax;** BB (teleplay); JTa (story); Jan 23, 1995 **4. Time and Again;** DK and MP (teleplay); DK (story); Jan 30, 1995 **5. Phage;** SD and BB (teleplay); TDH (story); Feb 6, 1995

6. The Cloud; TSi and MP (teleplay); BB (story; Feb 13, 1995 **7. Eye of the Needle;** BD and JTr (teleplay); HJB (story); Feb 20, 1995 **8. Ex Post Facto;** ECS and MP (teleplay); ECS (story); Feb 27, 1995 **9. Emanations;** BB; Mar 13, 1995 **10. Prime Factors;** MPe & GEt (teleplay); DRG & EAS (story); Mar 20, 1995 **11. State of Flux;** CA (teleplay); PRC (story); Apr 10, 1995 **12. Heroes and Demons;** NS; Apr 24, 1995 **13. Cathexis;** BB (teleplay); BB & JMy (story); May 1, 1995 **14. Faces;** KB (teleplay); JGr and KB (story); May 8, 1995 **15. Jetrel;** JaKn & KK and KB (teleplay); JTn & SN (story); May 15, 1995 **16. Learning Curve;** RWn & JLM; May 22, 1995

Season 2

Writers: Jeri Taylor (**JTr**); Brannon Braga (**BB**); Kenneth Biller (**KB**); Jimmy Diggs (**JD**); Steve J. Kay (**SJK**); Arnold Rudnick (**AR**); Rich Hosek (**RHk**); Tom Szollosi (**TSi**); Larry Brody (**LB**); Michael Piller (**MP**); Anthony Williams (**AWs**); Joe Menosky (**JMy**); Lisa Klink (**LK**); Michael Jan Friedman (**MJF**); Kevin J. Ryan (**KJR**); Nicholas Corea (**NC**); Michael De Luca (**MDL**); Michael Sussman (**MS**); Gary Holland (**GH**); Shawn Piller (**SP**); Jeff Schnaufer (**JeSr**); Ed Bond (**EB**); Richard Gadas (**RGs**); Andrew Shepard Price (**ASP**); Mark Gaberman (**MGn**)

Episodes:
17. The 37's; JTr & BB; Aug 28, 1995 **18. Initiations;** KB; Sep 4, 1995 **19. Projections;** BB; Sep 11, 1995 **20. Elogium;** KB and JTr (teleplay); JD & SJK (story); Sep 18, 1995 **21. Non Sequitur;** BB; Sep 25, 1995 **22. Twisted;** KB (teleplay); AR & RHk (story); Oct 2, 1995 **23. Parturition;** TSi; Oct 9, 1995 **24. Persistence of Vision;** JTr, Oct 30, 1995 **25. Tattoo;** MP (teleplay); LB (story); Nov 6, 1995 **26. Cold Fire;** BB (teleplay); AWs (story); Nov 13, 1995 **27. Maneuvers;** KB; Nov 20, 1995 **28. Resistance;** LK (teleplay); MJF & KJR (story); Nov 27, 1995 **29. Prototype** NC; Jan 15, 1996 **30. Alliances;** JTr; Jan 22, 1996 **31. Threshold;** BB (teleplay); MDL (story); Jan 29, 1996 **32. Meld;** MP (teleplay); MS (story); Feb 5, 1996 **33. Dreadnought;** GH; Feb 12, 1996 **34. Death Wish;** MP (teleplay); SP (story); Feb 19, 1996 **35. Lifesigns;** KB; Feb 26, 1996 **36. Investigations;** JTr (teleplay); JeSr & EB (story); Mar 13, 1996 **37. Deadlock;** BB; Mar 18, 1996 **38. Innocence;** LK (teleplay); AW (story); Apr 8, 1996 **39. The Thaw;** JMy (teleplay); RGs (story); Apr 29, 1996 **40. Tuvix;** KB (teleplay); ASP & MGn (story); May 6, 1996 **41. Resolutions;** JTr; May 13, 1996 **42. Basics, Part I;** MP; May 20, 1996

Season 3

Writers: Michael Piller (**MP**); Brannon Braga (**BB**); Kenneth Biller (**KB**); Clayvon C. Harris (**CCH**); Michael Sussman (**MS**); Joe Menosky (**JMy**); George A. Brozak (**GAB**); Lisa Klink (**LK**); Geo Cameron (**GC**); Andrew Shepard Price (**ASP**); Mark Gaberman (**MGn**); Shawn Piller (**SP**); André Bormanis (**ABs**); Ronald Wilkerson (**RWn**); Jean Louise Matthias (**JLM**); Jeri Taylor (**JTr**); Jimmy Diggs (**JD**); Harry 'Doc' Kloor (**HDK**)

Episodes:
43. Basics, Part II; MP; Sep 4, 1996 **44. Flashback;** BB; Sep 11, 1996 **45. The Chute;** KB (teleplay); CCH (story); Sep 18, 1996 **46. The Swarm;** MS; Sep 25, 1996 **47. False Profits;** JMy (teleplay); GB (story); Oct 2, 1996 **48. Remember;** LK (teleplay); BB & JMy (story); Oct 9, 1996 **49. Sacred Ground;** LK

(teleplay); GC (story); Oct 30, 1996 **50. Future's End, Part I;** BB & JMy; Nov 6, 1996 **51. Future's End, Part II;** BB & JMy; Nov 13, 1996 **52. Warlord;** LK (teleplay); ASP & MGn (story); Nov 20, 1996 **53. The Q and the Grey;** KB (teleplay); SP (story); Nov 27, 1996 **54. Macrocosm;** BB; Dec 11, 1996 **55. Fair Trade;** ABs (teleplay); RWn & JLM (story); Jan 8, 1997 **56. Alter Ego;** JMg; Jan 15, 1997 **57. Coda;** JTr; Jan 29, 1997 **58. Blood Fever;** LK; Feb 5, 1997 **59. Unity;** KB Feb 12, 1997 **60. Darkling;** JMy (teleplay); BB and JMy (story); Feb 19, 1997 **61. Rise;** BB (teleplay); JD (story); Feb 26, 1997 **62. Favorite Son;** LK; Mar 19, 1997 **63. Before and After;** KB; Apr 9, 1997 **64. Real Life;** JTr (teleplay); HDK (story); Apr 23, 1997 **65. Distant Origin;** BB & JMy; Apr 30, 1997 **66. Displaced;** LK; May 7, 1997 **67. Worst Case Scenario;** KB; May 14, 1997 **68. Scorpion, Part I;** BB & JMy; May 21, 1997

Season 4

Writers: Brannon Braga (**BB**); Joe Menosky (**JMy**); Jeri Taylor (**JTr**); Kenneth Biller (**KB**); Lisa Klink (**LK**); Bryan Fuller (**BF**); Harry 'Doc' Kloor (**HDK**); Sherry Klein (**SKn**); Jimmy Diggs (**JD**); André Bormanis (**ABs**); Rick Williams (**RWs**); Andrew Shepard Price (**ASP**); Mark Gaberman (**MGn**); Robert J. Doherty (**RJD**); Steve J. Kay (**SJK**); Greg Elliot (**GEt**); Michael Perricone (**MPe**); Rick Berman (**RBn**)

Episodes:
69. Scorpion, Part II; BB & JMy; Sep 3, 1997 **70. The Gift;** JMy; Sep 10, 1997 **71. Day of Honor;** JT; Sep 17, 1997 **72. Nemesis;** KB; Sep 24, 1997 **73. Revulsion;** LK; Oct 1, 1997 **74. The Raven;** BF and HDK (teleplay); BF (story); Oct 8, 1997 **75. Scientific Method;** LK (teleplay); SKn & HDK (story); Oct 29, 1997 **76. Year of Hell, Part I;** BB & JMy; Nov 5, 1997 **77. Year of Hell, Part II;** BB & JMy; Nov 12, 1997 **78. Random Thoughts;** KB; Nov 19, 1997 **79. Concerning Flight;** JMy (teleplay); JTr (story); Nov 26, 1997 **80. Mortal Coil;** BF; Dec 17, 1997 **81. Waking Moments;** ABs; Jan 14, 1998 **82. Message in a Bottle;** LK (teleplay); RWs (story); Jan 21, 1998 **83. Hunters;** JTr Feb 11, 1998 **84. Prey;** BB; Feb 18, 1998 **85. Retrospect;** BF & LK (teleplay); ASP & MGn (story); Feb 25, 1998 **86/87. The Killing Game;** BB & JMy; Mar 4, 1998 **88. Vis à Vis;** RJD; Apr 8, 1998 **89. The Omega Directive;** LK (teleplay); JD & SJK (story); Apr 15, 1998 **90. Unforgettable;** GET and MPe; Apr 22, 1998 **91. Living Witness;** BF and BB & JMy (teleplay); BB (story); Apr 29, 1998 **92. Demon;** KB (teleplay); ABs (story); May 6, 1998 **93. One;** JTr; May 13, 1998 **94. Hope and Fear;** BB & JMy (teleplay); RBn & BB & JMy (story); May 20, 1998

Season 5

Writers: Brannon Braga (**BB**); Joe Menosky (**JMy**); Bryan Fuller (**BF**); Harry 'Doc' Kloor (**HDK**); Kenneth Biller (**KB**); Nick Sagan (**NSn**); Michael Taylor (**MT**); Jimmy Diggs (**JD**); Robert J. Doherty (**RJD**); Jeri Taylor (**JTr**); Kenneth Biller (**KB**); Scott Miller (**SM**); Rick Berman (**RBn**); Eileen Connors (**EC**); Bill Prady (**BP**)

Episodes:
95. Night; BB & JMy; Oct 14, 1998 **96. Drone;** BF and BB & JMy (teleplay); BF & HDK (story); Oct 21, 1998 **97. Extreme Risk;** KB; Oct 28, 1998 **98. In the Flesh;** NSn; Nov 4, 1998 **99. Once Upon a Time;** MT; Nov 11, 1998 **100. Timeless;** BB & JMy

(teleplay); RB & BB & JMy (story); Nov 18, 1998 **101. Infinite Regress;** RJD (teleplay); RJD & JD (story); Nov 25, 1998 **102. Nothing Human;** JTr; Dec 2, 1998 **103. Thirty Days;** KB (teleplay); SM (story); Dec 9, 1998 **104. Counterpoint;** MT; Dec 16, 1998 **105. Latent Image;** JMy (teleplay); EC and BB & JMy (story); Jan 20, 1999 **106. Bride of Chaotica!;** BF & MT (teleplay); BF (story) Jan 27, 1999 **107. Gravity;** NSn & BF (teleplay); JD and BF & NSn (story); Feb 3, 1999 **108. Bliss;** RJD (teleplay); BP (story) Feb 10, 1999 **109/110. Dark Frontier;** BB & JMy; Feb 17, 1999 **111. The Disease;** MT (teleplay); KB (story); Feb 24, 1999 **112. Course: Oblivion;** BF & NSn (teleplay); BF (story); Mar 3, 1999 **113. The Fight;** JMy (teleplay); MT (story); Mar 24, 1999 **114. Think Tank;** MT (teleplay); RBn & BB (story); Mar 31, 1999 **115. Juggernaut;** BF & NSn and KB (teleplay); BF (story); Apr 26, 1999 **116. Someone to Watch Over Me;** MT (teleplay); BB (story); Apr 28, 1999 **117. 11:59;** JMy (teleplay); BB & JMy (story); May 5, 1999 **118. Relativity;** BF & NSn & MT (teleplay); NSn (story); May 12, 1999 **119. Warhead;** MT & KB (teleplay); May 19, 1999 **120. Equinox, Part I;** BB & JMy (teleplay); RB & BB & JMy (story); May 26, 1999

Season 6

Writers: Brannon Braga (**BB**); Joe Menosky (**JMy**); Rick Berman (**RBn**); Ronald D. Moore (**RDM**); Bryan Fuller (**BF**); Bill Vallely (**BV**); Michael Taylor (**MT**); Juliann deLayne (**JdL**); André Bormanis (**ABs**); Mike Wollaeger (**MWr**); Jessica Scott (**JSt**); David Zabel (**DZ**); Robin Burger (**RoBr**); Raf Green (**RGn**); Kenneth Biller (**KB**); Robert J. Doherty (**RJD**); Gannon Kenney (**GKy**); Andrew Shepard Price (**ASP**); Mark Gaberman (**MGn**); Ronald Wilkerson (**RWn**); Paul Brown (**PBn**); Dianna Gitto (**DGo**); John Bruno (**JBo**); Robert Picardo (**RPo**); Michael Sussman (**MS**)

Episodes:

121. Equinox, Part II; BB & JMy (teleplay); RB & BB & JMy (story); Sep 22, 1999 **122. Survival Instinct;** RDM Sep 29, 1999 **123. Barge of the Dead;** BF (teleplay); RDM & BF (story); Oct 6, 1999 **124. Tinker, Tenor, Doctor, Spy;** JMy (teleplay); BV (story); Oct 13, 1999 **125. Alice;** BF & MT (teleplay); JdL (story); Oct 20, 1999 **126. Riddles;** RJD (teleplay); ABs (story); Nov 3, 1999 **127. Dragon's Teeth;** MT and BB & JMy (teleplay); MT (story) Nov 10, 1999 **128. One Small Step;** MWr & JSt and BF & MT (teleplay); MWr and JSt (story) Nov 17, 1999 **129. The Voyager Conspiracy;** JMy; Nov 24, 1999 **130. Pathfinder;** DZ and KB (teleplay); DZ (story); Dec 1, 1999 **131. Fair Haven;** RBr; Jan 12, 2000 **132. Blink of an Eye;** JMy (teleplay); MT (story); Jan 19, 2000 **133. Virtuoso;** RGn & KB (teleplay); RoBr (teleplay); BB (story); Jan 26, 2000 **134. Memorial;** RoBr (teleplay); BB (story); Feb 2, 2000 **135. Tsunkatse;** RJD (teleplay); GKy (story); Feb 9, 2000 **136. Collective;** MT (teleplay); ASP & MGn (story); Feb 16, 2000 **137. Spirit Folk;** BF; Feb 23, 2000 **138. Ashes to Ashes;** RJD (teleplay); RWn (story); Mar 1, 2000 **139. Child's Play;** RGn (teleplay); PBn (story); Mar 8, 2000 **140. Good Shepherd;** DGo & JMy (teleplay); DGo (story); Mar 15, 2000 **141. Live Fast and Prosper;** RoBr; Apr 19, 2000 **142. Muse;** JMy; Apr 26, 2000 **143. Fury;** BF & MT (teleplay); RBn & BB (story); May 3, 2000 **144. Life Line;** RJD, RGn and BB (teleplay); JBo & RPo (story) May 10, 2000 **145. The Haunting of Deck Twelve;** MS, KB and BF (teleplay); MS (story) May 17, 2000 **146. Unimatrix Zero, Part I;** BB & JMy (teleplay); MS (story); May 24, 2000

Season 7

Writers: Brannon Braga (**BB**); Joe Menosky (**JMy**); Mike Sussman (**MS**); Carleton Eastlake (**CE**), Robert J. Doherty (**RJD**); André Bormanis (**ABs**); Michael Taylor (**MT**); Mark Haskell Smith (**MHS**); Kenneth Biller (**KB**); James Kahn (**JKn**); Eric Morris (**EM**); Phyllis Strong (**PSg**); Robert Lederman (**RLn**); Dave Long (**DLg**); Bryan Fuller (**BF**); Raf Green (**RGn**); Jack Monaco (**JMo**); Larry Nemecek (**LNk**); J. Kelley Burke (**JKB**); Mark Gaberman (**MGn**); Rick Berman (**RBn**)

Episodes:

147. Unimatrix Zero, Part II; BB & JMy (teleplay); MS and BB & JMy (story); Oct 4, 2000 **148. Imperfection;** CE and RJD (teleplay); ABs (story); Oct 11, 2000 **149. Drive;** MT; Oct 18, 2000 **150. Repression;** MHS (teleplay); KB (story); Oct 25, 2000 **151. Critical Care;** JKn (teleplay); KB & RJD (story); Nov 1, 2000 **152. Inside Man;** RJD; Nov 8, 2000 **153. Body and Soul;** EM and PSg & MS (teleplay); MT (story); Nov 15, 2000 **154. Nightingale;** ABs (teleplay); RLn & DLg (story); Nov 22, 2000 **155/156. Flesh and Blood;** BF (teleplay, part 1); RGn & KB (teleplay, part 2); JMo and BF & RGn (story, part 1); BF & RGn (story, part 2); Nov 29, 2000 **157. Shattered;** MT (teleplay); MS & MT (story); Jan 17, 2001 **158. Lineage;** JKn; Jan 24, 2001 **159. Repentance;** RJD (teleplay); MS and RJD (story); Jan 31, 2001 **160. Prophecy;** MS & PSg (teleplay); LNk & JKB and RGn & KB (story); Feb 7, 2001 **161. The Void;** RGn & KB (story); Feb 14, 2001 **162. Workforce, Part I;** KB & BF; Feb 21, 2001 **163. Workforce, Part II;** KB & MT (teleplay); KB & BF (story); Feb 28, 2001 **164. Human Error;** BB & ABs (teleplay); ABs & KB (story); Mar 7, 2001 **165. Q2;** RJD (teleplay); KB (story); Apr 11, 2001 **166. Author, Author;** PS and MS (teleplay); BB (story); Apr 18, 2001 **167. Friendship One;** MT & BF; Apr 25, 2001 **168. Natural Law;** JKn (teleplay); KB & JKn (story); May 2, 2001 **169. Homestead;** RGn; May 9, 2001 **170. Renaissance Man;** PSg & MS (teleplay); ASP & MGn (story); May 16, 2001 **171/172. Endgame;** KB & RJD (teleplay); RBn & KB & BB (story); May 23, 2001

Star Trek: Enterprise

Cast:
Scott Bakula as Jonathan Archer
John Billingsley as Phlox
Jolene Blalock as T'Pol
Dominic Keating as Malcolm Reed
Anthony Montgomery as Travis Mayweather
Linda Park as Hoshi Sato
Connor Trinneer as Charles Tucker III

Season 1

Writers: Rick Berman (**RBn**); Brannon Braga (**BB**); Mike Sussman (**MS**); Phyllis Strong (**PSg**); Fred Dekker (**FD**); Maria Jaquemetton (**MJn**); Andre Jaquemetton (**AJn**); James Duff (**JDf**); Stephen Beck (**SBk**); Tim Finch (**TF**); André Bormanis (**ABs**); Chris Black (**CB**); Alan Cross (**ACs**)

Episodes:

1/2. Broken Bow; RBn & BB; Sep 26, 2001 **3. Fight or Flight;** RBn & BB; Oct 3, 2001 **4. Strange New World;** RBn & BB (teleplay); RBn & BB (story); Oct 10, 2001 **5. Unexpected;** RBn & BB; Oct 17, 2001 **6. Terra Nova;** RBn & BB; Oct 24, 2001 **7. The Andorian Incident;** FD (teleplay); RBn, BB & FD (story); Oct 31, 2001 **8. Breaking the Ice;** MJn & AJn; Nov 7, 2001 **9. Civilization;** PSg & MS; Nov 14, 2001 **10. Fortunate Son;** JDf; Nov 21, 2001 **11. Cold Front;** SBk & TF; Nov 28, 2001 **12. Silent Enemy;** ABs; Jan 16, 2002 **13. Dear Doctor;** MJn & AJn; Jan 23, 2002 **14. Sleeping Dogs;** FD; Jan 30, 2002 **15. Shadows of P'Jem;** MS & PSg (teleplay); RBn & BB (story); Feb 6, 2002 **16. Shuttlepod One;** RBn & BB Feb 13, 2002 **17. Fusion;** PSg & MS (teleplay); RBn & BB (story); Feb 27, 2002 **18. Rogue Planet;** CB (teleplay); RBn & BB & CB (story); Mar 20, 2002 **19. Acquisition;** MJn & AJn (teleplay); RBn & BB (story); Mar 27, 2002 **20. Oasis;** RBn, BB & SBk; Apr 3, 2002 **21. Detained;** MS & PSg (teleplay); RB & BB (story); Apr 24, 2002 **22. Vox Sola;** FD (teleplay); RBn, BB & FD (story); May 1, 2002 **23. Fallen Hero;** ACs (teleplay); RBn, BB & CB (story) May 8, 2002 **24. Desert Crossing;** ABs (teleplay) RBn & BB & ABs (story); May 8, 2002 **25. Two Days and Two Nights;** RBn & BB; May 15, 2002 **26. Shockwave, Part I;** RBn & BB; May 22, 2002

Season 2

Writers: Rick Berman (**RBn**); Brannon Braga (**BB**); Dan O'Shannon (**DOS**); Chris Black (**CB**); John Shiban (**JSn**); Mike Sussman (**MS**); Phyllis Strong (**PSg**); David Wilcox (**DWx**); André Bormanis (**ABs**); David A. Goodman (**DAG**); Allan Koeker (**AK**); Hans Tobeason (**HT**)

Episodes:

27. Shockwave, Part II; RBn & BB; Sep 18, 2002 **28. Carbon Creek;** CB (teleplay); RB & BB & DOS (story) Sep 25, 2002 **29. Minefield;** JSn; Oct 2, 2002 **30. Dead Stop;** MS & PSg; Oct 9, 2002 **31. A Night In Sickbay;** RBn & BB; Oct 16, 2002 **32. Marauders;** DWx (teleplay); RBn & BB (story) Oct 30, 2002 **33. The Seventh;** RBn & BB; Nov 6, 2002 **34. The Communicator;** ABs (teleplay); RBb & BB (story); Nov 13, 2002 **35. Singularity;** CB; Nov 20, 2002 **36. Vanishing Point;** RBn & BB; Nov 27, 2002 **37. Precious Cargo;** DAG (teleplay); RBn & BB (story) Dec 11, 2002 **38. The Catwalk;** MS & PSg; Dec 18, 2002 **39. Dawn;** JSn; Jan 8, 2003 **40. Stigma;** RBn & BB; Feb 5, 2003 **41. Cease Fire;** CB; Feb 12, 2003 **42. Future Tense;** MS & PSg; Feb 19, 2003 **43. Canamar;** AK; Feb 26, 2003 **44. The Crossing;** RBn & BB; Apr 2, 2003 **45. Judgment;** DAG; Apr 9, 2003 **46. Horizon;** ABs; Apr 16, 2003 **47. The Breach;** CB & JSn; Apr 23, 2003 **48. Cogenitor;** RBn & BB; Apr 30, 2003 **49. Regeneration;** MS & PSg; May 7, 2003 **50. First Flight;** JSn & CB; May 14, 2003 **51. Bounty;** HT and MS & PS (teleplay); RB & BB & MS (story); May 14, 2003 **52. The Expanse;** RBn & BB; May 21, 2003

Season 3

Writers: Rick Berman (**RBn**); Brannon Braga (**BB**); Mike Sussman (**MS**); André Bormanis (**ABs**); Brent V. Friedman (**BVF**); Chris Black (**CB**); Paul Brown (**PBn**); Jonathan Fernandez (**JFz**); Terry Matalas (**TMs**); Phyllis Strong (**PSg**); Manny Coto (**MCo**); David A. Goodman (**DAG**)

Episodes:

53. The Xindi; RBn & BB; Sep 10, 2003 **54. Anomaly;** MS; Sep 17, 2003 **55. Extinction;** ABs Sep 24, 2003 **56. Rajiin;** BVF & CB (teleplay); PBn & BVF Oct 1, 2003 **57. Impulse;** JFz (teleplay);

JFz & TMs (story) Oct 8, 2003 **58. Exile;** PSg; Oct 15, 2003 **59. The Shipment;** CB & BVF; Oct 29, 2003 **60. Twilight;** MS; Nov 5, 2003 **61. North Star;** DAG; Nov 12, 2003 **62. Similitude;** MCo; Nov 19, 2003 **63. Carpenter Street;** RBn & BB; Nov 26, 2003 **64. Chosen Realm;** MCo; Jan 14, 2004 **65. Proving Ground;** CB; Jan 21, 2004 **66. Stratagem;** MS (teleplay); TMs (story); Feb 4, 2004 **67. Harbinger;** RBn & BB; Feb 11, 2004 **68. Doctor's Orders;** CB; Feb 18, 2004 **69. Hatchery;** ABs & MS; Feb 25, 2004 **70. Azati Prime;** RBn, BB & MCo; Mar 3, 2004 **71. Damage;** PSg; Apr 21, 2004 **72. The Forgotten;** CB & DAG; Apr 28, 2004 **73. E²;** MS; May 5, 2004 **74. The Council;** MCo; May 12, 2004 **75. Countdown;** ABs & CB May 19, 2004 **76. Zero Hour;** RBn & BB; May 26, 2004

Season 4

Writers: Manny Coto (**MCo**); Mike Sussman (**MS**); Ken LaZebnik (**KLZ**); Alan Brennert (**ABt**); Judith Reeves-Stevens (**JRS**); Garfield Reeves-Stevens (**GRS**); André Bormanis (**ABs**); Michael Bryant (**MB**); Rick Berman (**RBn**); Brannon Braga (**BB**)

Episodes:
77. Storm Front, Part I; MCo; Oct 8, 2004
78. Storm Front, Part II; MCo; Oct 15, 2004
79. Home; MS; Oct 22, 2004 **80. Borderland;** KLZ; Oct 29, 2004 **81. Cold Station 12;** ABt; Nov 5, 2004
82. The Augments; MS; Nov 12, 2004 **83. The Forge;** JRS & GRS; Nov 19, 2004 **84. Awakening;** ABs; Nov 26, 2004 **85. Kir'Shara;** MS Dec 3, 2004
86. Daedalus; KLZ & MB; Jan 14, 2005
87. Observer Effect; JRS & GRS; Jan 21, 2005

88. Babel One; MS & ABs; Jan 28, 2005
89. United; JRS & GRS (teleplay); MCo (story); Feb 4, 2005 **90. The Aenar;** ABs (teleplay); MCo (story); Feb 11, 2005 **91. Affliction;** MS (teleplay); MCo (story); Feb 18, 2005 **92. Divergence;** JRS & GRS; Feb 25, 2005 **93. Bound;** MCo; Apr 15, 2005 **94. In a Mirror, Darkly, Part I;** MS; Apr 22, 2005 **95. In a Mirror, Darkly, Part II;** MS (teleplay); MCo (story); Apr 29, 2005 **96. Demons;** MCo; May 6, 2005 **97. Terra Prime;** MCo, JRS & GRS & ABs; May 13, 2005 **98. These Are the Voyages...;** RBn & BB; May 13, 2005.

MOVIE RELEASES

ORIGINAL SERIES

Star Trek: The Motion Picture
Directed by: Robert Wise
Written by: Harold Livingston (screenplay);
Alan Dean Foster (story)
Original U.S. release date: December 7, 1979
Cast:
William Shatner as Captain James T. Kirk
Leonard Nimoy as Mr. Spock
DeForest Kelley as Dr. Leonard "Bones" McCoy
James Doohan as Commander Montgomery Scott
George Takei as Lieutenant Commander Sulu
Walter Koenig as Lieutenant Pavel Chekov
Nichelle Nichols as Lieutenant Commander Uhura
Majel Barrett as Dr. Christine Chapel
Persis Khambatta as Lieutenant Ilia
Stephen Collins as Commander/Captain Willard Decker
Grace Lee Whitney as Ensign Janice Rand
Mark Lenard as Klingon Captain
David Gautreaux as Commander Branch
Jon Rashad Kamal as Lieutenant Commander Sonak
Marcy Lafferty as Chief DiFalco
Terrence O'Connor as Chief Ross
Michael Rougas as Lieutenant Cleary

Star Trek II: The Wrath of Khan
Directed by: Nicholas Meyer
Written by: Jack B. Sowards (screenplay);
Harve Bennett and Jack B. Sowards (story)
Original U.S. release date: June 4, 1982
Cast:
William Shatner as Admiral James T. Kirk
Leonard Nimoy as Captain Spock
DeForest Kelley as Dr. Leonard "Bones" McCoy
James Doohan as Commander Montgomery Scott
George Takei as Commander Sulu
Walter Koenig as Commander Pavel Chekov
Nichelle Nichols as Commander Uhura
Bibi Besch as Dr. Carol Marcus
Paul Winfield as Captain Clark Terrell
Merritt Butrick as Dr. David Marcus
Judson Scott as Joachim (uncredited)
John Winston as Commander Kyle

Ike Eisenmann as Midshipman First Class Peter Preston
John Vargas as Jedda
Kirstie Alley as Lieutenant Saavik
Ricardo Montalban as Khan Noonien Singh

Star Trek III: The Search For Spock
Directed by: Leonard Nimoy
Written by: Harve Bennett
Original U.S. release date: June 1, 1984
Cast:
William Shatner as Admiral James T. Kirk
Leonard Nimoy as Captain Spock
DeForest Kelley as Dr. Leonard "Bones" McCoy
James Doohan as Commander Montgomery Scott
George Takei as Commander Hikaru Sulu
Walter Koenig as Commander Pavel Chekov
Nichelle Nichols as Commander Uhura
Merritt Butrick as Dr. David Marcus
John Larroquette as Maltz
Mark Lenard as Sarek
Robin Curtis as Saavik
Christopher Lloyd as Commander Kruge

Star Trek IV: The Voyage Home
Directed by: Leonard Nimoy
Written by: Steve Meerson & Peter Krikes and Harve Bennett & Nicholas Meyer (screenplay); Leonard Nimoy & Harve Bennett (story)
Original U.S. release date: November 26, 1986
Cast:
William Shatner as Captain/Admiral James T. Kirk
Leonard Nimoy as Captain Spock
DeForest Kelley as Dr. Leonard "Bones" McCoy
James Doohan as Captain Montgomery Scott
George Takei as Commander Sulu
Walter Koenig as Commander Pavel Chekov
Nichelle Nichols as Commander Uhura
Mark Lenard as Sarek
Catherine Hicks as Dr. Gillian Taylor
Jane Wyatt as Amanda Grayson
Brock Peters as Admiral Cartwright
Robert Ellenstein as Federation President

John Schuck as Klingon Ambassador
Scott DeVenney as Bob Briggs
Majel Barrett as Dr. Christine Chapel
Robin Curtis as Lieutenant Saavik
Madge Sinclair as U.S.S. Saratoga Captain
Nick Ramus as Saratoga Helmsman

Star Trek V: The Final Frontier
Directed by: William Shatner
Written by: David Loughery (screenplay);
William Shatner & Harve Bennett &
David Loughery (story)
Original U.S. release date: June 9, 1989
Cast:
William Shatner as Captain James T. Kirk
Leonard Nimoy as Captain Spock
DeForest Kelley as Dr. Leonard "Bones" McCoy
James Doohan as Captain Montgomery Scott
Walter Koenig as Commander Pavel Chekov
Nichelle Nichols as Commander Uhura
George Takei as Commander Sulu
Lawrence Luckinbill as Sybok
David Warner as St. John Talbot
Charles Cooper as Korrd
Cynthia Gouw as Caithlin Dar
Todd Bryant as Captain Klaa
Spice Williams as Vixis
Melanie Shatner as Captain's Yeoman
Jonathon Simpson as Sarek
George Murdock as "God"
Bill Quinn as David McCoy

Star Trek VI: The Undiscovered Country
Directed by: Nicholas Meyer
Written by: Nicholas Meyer & Denny Martin Flinn (screenplay); Leonard Nimoy and Lawrence Konner & Mark Rosenthal (story)
Original U.S. release date: December 6, 1991
Cast:
William Shatner as Captain James T. Kirk
Leonard Nimoy as Captain Spock
DeForest Kelley as Dr. Leonard "Bones" McCoy

James Doohan as Captain Montgomery Scott
Walter Koenig as Commander Pavel Chekov
Nichelle Nichols as Commander Uhura
George Takei as Commander Sulu
Christopher Plummer as General Chang
Kim Cattral as Lieutenant Valeris
David Warner as Chancellor Gorkon
Rosanna DeSoto as Azetbur
Kurtwood Smith as Federation President
Brock Peters as Admiral Cartwright
Rene Auberjoinois as Colonel West
Leon Russom as "Bill" (Chief in Command)
Iman as Martia
Michael Dorn as Colonel Worf
John Schuck as Klingon Ambassador
Darryl Henriques as Romulan Ambassador Nanclus
Mark Lenard as Sarek
Grace Lee Whitney as Commander Janice Rand
Jeremy Roberts as Lieutenant Dimitri Valtane
Paul Rossilli as Brigadier Kerla
Robert Easton as Klingon Judge
William Morgan Sheppard as Rura Penthe Warden
Christian Slater as Excelsior Communications Officer

NEXT GENERATION
Star Trek Generations
Directed by: David Carson
Written by: Ronald D. Moore & Brannon Braga
(screenplay); Rick Berman & Ronald D. Moore
& Brannon Braga (story)
Original U.S. release date: November 18, 1994
Cast:
Patrick Stewart as Captain Jean-Luc Picard
Jonathan Frakes as Commander William T. Riker
Brent Spiner as Lieutenant Commander Data
LeVar Burton as Lieutenant Commander Geordi
La Forge
Michael Dorn as Lieutenant Commander Worf
Gates McFadden as Dr. Beverly Crusher
Marina Sirtis as Counselor Deanna Troi
Malcolm McDowell as Dr. Tolian Soran
James Doohan as Captain Montgomery Scott
Walter Koenig as Commander Pavel Chekov
Whoopi Goldberg as Guinan
Alan Ruck as Captain John Harriman
Jacqueline Kim as Ensign Demora Sulu
Jenette Goldstien as *Enterprise*-B Science Officer
Tim Russ as *Enterprise*-B Lieutenant
Barbara March as Lursa
Gwenyth Walsh as B'etor
Brian Thompson as Klingon Helmsman
Dendrie Taylor as Lieutenant Farrell
Patti Yasutake as Nurse Alyssa Ogawa
Kim Braden as Mrs. Jean-Luc Picard
Christopher James Miller as Rene Picard
William Shatner as Captain James T. Kirk

Star Trek: First Contact
Directed by: Jonathan Frakes
Written by: Brannon Braga & Ronald D. Moore
(screenplay); Rick Berman & Brannon Braga &
Ronald D. Moore (story)
Original U.S. release date: November 22, 1996
Cast:
Patrick Stewart as Captain Jean-Luc Picard
Jonathan Frakes as Commander William T. Riker
Brent Spiner as Lieutenant Commander Data
LeVar Burton as Lieutenant Commander
Geordi La Forge
Michael Dorn as Lieutenant Commander Worf
Gates McFadden as Dr. Beverly Crusher
Marina Sirtis as Counselor Deanna Troi

Alfre Woodard as Lily Sloane
James Cromwell as Zephram Cochrane
Alice Krige as The Borg Queen
Neal McDonough as Lieutenant Hawk
Michael Horton as Lieutenant Daniels
Dwight Shultz as Lieutenant Reginald Barclay
Patti Yasutake as Nurse Alyssa Ogawa
Robert Picardo as Emergency Medical Hologram
Don Stark as "Nicky the Nose"
Jack Shearer as Admiral Hayes
Hillary Hayes as Ruby
Eric Steinberg as Lieutenant Paul Porter
Marnie McPhail as Lieutenant Eiger
Cully Frederickson as Vulcan Captain

Star Trek: Insurrection
Directed by: Jonathan Frakes
Written by: Michael Piller (screenplay);
Rick Berman & Michael Piller (story)
Original U.S. release date: December 11, 1998
Cast:
Patrick Stewart as Captain Jean-Luc Picard
Jonathan Frakes as Commander William T. Riker
Brent Spiner as Lieutenant Commander Data
LeVar Burton as Lieutenant Commander
Geordi La Forge
Michael Dorn as Lieutenant Commander Worf
Gates McFadden as Dr. Beverly Crusher
Marina Sirtis as Counselor Deanna Troi
Donna Murphy as Anij
F. Murray Abraham as Ru'afo
Anthony Zerbe as Admiral Matthew Dougherty
Gregg Henry as Gallatin
Daniel Hugh Kelly as Sojef
Michael Welch as Artim
Mark Deakins as Tournel
Breon Gorman as Lieutenant Curtis
Stephanie Niznik as Lieutenant Kell Perim
Michael Horton as Lieutenant Daniels
Peggy Miley as Regent Cuzar

Star Trek Nemesis
Directed by: Stuart Baird
Written by: John Logan (screenplay);
John Logan & Rick Berman & Brent Spiner (story)
Original U.S. release date: December 13, 2002
Cast:
Patrick Stewart as Captain Jean-Luc Picard
Jonathan Frakes as Commander William T. Riker
Brent Spiner as Lieutenant Commander Data/B-4
LeVar Burton as Lieutenant Commander Geordi
La Forge
Michael Dorn as Lieutenant Commander Worf
Gates McFadden as Dr. Beverly Crusher
Marina Sirtis as Counselor Deanna Troi
Tom Hardy as Shinzon
Ron Perlman as The Viceroy
Dina Meyer as Commander Donatra
Jude Ciccolella as Commander Suran
Shannon Cochran as Senator Tal'aura
Michael Owen as Lieutenant Branson
Wil Wheaton as Wesley Crusher
Kate Mulgrew as Admiral Kathryn Janeway
Whoopi Goldberg as Guinan

ALTERNATE REALITY
Star Trek (2009)
Directed by: J. J. Abrams
Written by: Roberto Orci & Alex Kurtzman
Original U.S. release date: May 8, 2009
Cast:
Zachary Quinto as Young Spock
Leonard Nimoy as Spock
Anton Yelchin as Chekov
Zoe Saldana as Uhura
Chris Pine as Kirk
John Cho as Hikaru Sulu
Simon Pegg as Scotty
Eric Bana as Nero
Winona Ryder as Amanda Grayson
Bruce Greenwood as Christopher Pike
Jennifer Morrison as Winona Kirk
Ben Cross as Sarek
Clifton Collins Jr. as Ayel
Chris Hemsworth as George Kirk

Star Trek Into Darkness
Directed by: J.J. Abrams
Written by: Roberto Orci & Alex Kurtzman
& Damon Lindelof
Original U.S. release date: May 16, 2013
Cast:
Chris Pine as James T. Kirk
Zachary Quinto as Spock
Leonard Nimoy as Spock Prime
Zoe Saldana as Nyota Uhura
Karl Urban as Leonard McCoy
Anton Yelchin as Pavel Chekov
John Cho as Hikaru Sulu
Simon Pegg as Scotty
Bruce Greenwood as Christopher Pike
Benedict Cumberbatch as Khan Noonien Singh
Peter Weller as Alexander Marcus
Nazneen Contractor as Rima Harewood
Noel Clarke as Thomas Harewood
Amanda Foreman as Ensign Bracket
Jay Scully as Lieutenant Chapin

INDEX